Insiders' Guide® to Glacier National Park

Including the Flathead Valley and Waterton Lakes National Park

THIRD EDITION

By Susan Olin

Guilford, Connecticut

An imprint of The Globe Pequot Press

Insiders' Guide is a registered trademark of The Globe Pequot Press.

Cover photograph: Jack Hoehn, Index Stock
Back cover photographs: © 2003 www.clipart.com

Maps created by XNR Productions Inc. © The Globe Pequot Press

ISBN 0-7627-2680-6

Manufactured in the United States of America
Third Edition/Second Printing

Contents

Directory of Maps

Preface

Western Montana is an outdoor recreationist's summer dream and winter paradise. On warm sunny days the rivers are filled with the sounds of white-water rafters careening through deep river canyons where just hours before the quiet whip of the fly-fisher's line was the only sound to be heard. Hikers, trail riders, and mountain bikers seek solitude on nearby trails, where birding and wildlife watching abound. When the winds begin to chill and the leaves of the aspens take on a golden hue, the elk begin their poignant bugling, and hunters know the season is near. As soon as the sky, leaden with the color of winter, begins to drop soft ice crystals from above, skiers anticipate the first downhill run through fresh powder or a glide cross-country through a quiet forest.

Glacier National Park, with its knife-edged peaks and alpine fields filled with the splendid colors of summer wildflowers, is the reason many visitors first explore the northwest corner of Montana. A drive along Going-to-the-Sun Road introduces the inhabitants of cars, vans, and RVs to the many natural wonders the park offers and entices many to get out of the car for a closer look from trailside. For some the trip through the park is just the beginning of what will become a love affair with the entire region, and they simply have to find out more about Kalispell, the Flathead Valley, the Swan Valley, and the grand expanses on the park's eastern slopes.

One of the special things about Glacier is that it is not only a National Park, it is also part of an International Peace Park that extends into Alberta, Canada. A visit to the Alberta Visitor Centre in West Glacier, Montana, is a wonderful introduction to the offerings across the border, but a visit to the Prince of Wales Hotel by the shimmering Waterton Lake in the Canadian section of the Waterton-Glacier International Peace Park can only improve on your impressions.

To the south of Glacier, the Swan Valley and the Flathead Lake area are serious recreation destinations in themselves. They also provide a charming introduction to Kalispell and the towns that serve as gateways to Glacier National Park and are home to a wide variety of people who share a deep affection for the things that make the area such an incredible place to live and to visit. This area is renowned for its arts festivals, and a tour of any of the sometimes quirky but always interesting museums and well-known area attractions—such as the Stumptown Historical Society Museum in Whitefish and the House of Mystery near Columbia Falls—will add depth and insight to your western mountain adventures. A description of the wonders of this area would not be complete, however, without mentioning the major summer and winter playground—Big Mountain, one of Montana's premier ski resorts. At the foot of Flathead Lake is the Flathead Indian Reservation, home to the federated Salish/Kootenai tribes, and a visit to Polson or the other towns on the reservation serves as a great introduction to the history and culture of these Native peoples.

On the eastern side of the park, the Blackfeet Reservation contains a number of small towns that serve as jumping-off points for park explorations and offer great opportunities for long and highly enjoyable views of Montana's famed Big Sky Country. A trip to any of the region's museums and even visits to some of the local restaurants and motels will serve as a fascinating introduction to the Blackfeet culture and reservation life.

The rugged terrain of the slopes split by the Continental Divide belies the fragility of the ecosystems supported here. Not only have mining, logging, and industry had their effect on the pristine nature of the mountain setting, recreational use has affected it as well. Those who venture out in their hiking boots or on their skis must take responsibility for their actions and practice "no-trace" recreation if the attractions that draw us into this relatively wild place are to remain for future generations. After all, it is the beauty of the scenery and the solitude that keep us entranced.

If a visit to Glacier Country just isn't enough—and more and more people have found that it's not—then the real-estate and other relocation information located in this book will be just what you are looking for. From rustic log cabins in remote settings to elegant Victorian homes just blocks from downtown, this area offers something for all tastes. Helpful insights for retirees looking for a more northern exposure are also included, as is information about child care and education for the younger set.

The goal of this book is to provide newcomers and visitors alike with information about the very best and brightest offerings of a very special place full of special people and establishments. *Insiders' Guide to Glacier National Park* will help you explore all of the finest offerings of this delightful region with detailed information on restaurants, accommodations, and recreation. If you're staying for a week or a lifetime, the tips, facts, and insights gleaned from Montana insiders put all the information you need for your Glacier adventures within easy reach. We wish you luck on your wanderings and hope that you will come away with lists of your own favorites as well.

Acknowledgments

I would like to acknowledge and thank my coauthors of the previous editions of this book: Eileen Gallagher, Frank Miele, Jim Mann, Mary Pat Murphy, and Rima Nickell. Their hard work laid the foundations for the current edition; quite literally, it would not be here without them. Also important are the many neighbors we interviewed. For me, the enthusiasm of local people for their businesses and life in northwest Montana was truly exciting. In addition I would like to thank my father, David Olin, and my friends—especially Deirdre Shaw and Bill Hayden—for their support and help with the research for this book. Finally I would like to acknowledge Erin Turner of Falcon Press, who first contacted me for this project, and Mimi Egan and Paula Brisco at The Globe Pequot Press, who were wonderfully supportive as I worked on the current edition.

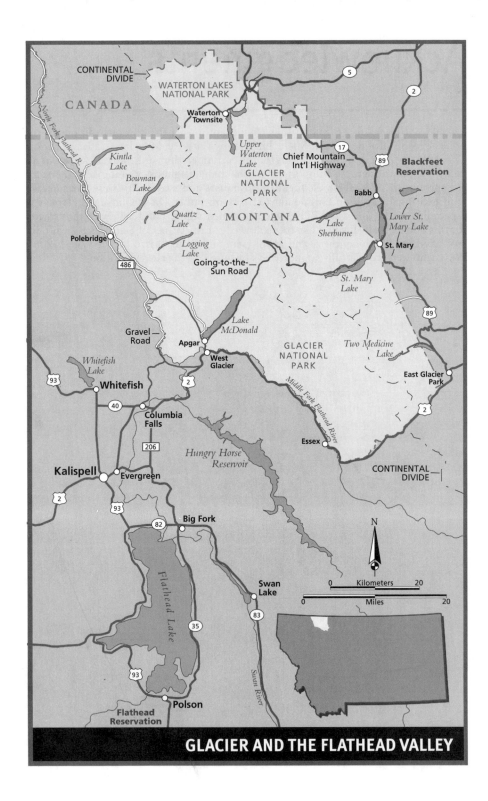

GLACIER AND THE FLATHEAD VALLEY

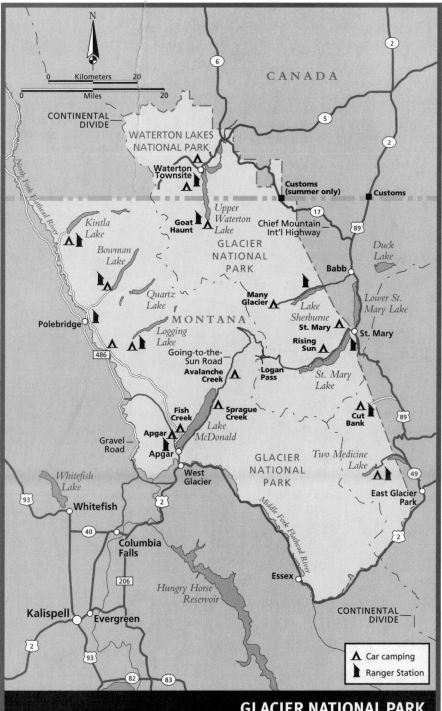

N

Kilometers 20

Miles 20

CANADA

CONTINENTAL DIVIDE

WATERTON LAKES NATIONAL PARK

Waterton Townsite

Customs (summer only)

Customs

Upper Waterton Lake

Goat Haunt

Chief Mountain Int'l Highway

Kintla Lake

Bowman Lake

GLACIER NATIONAL PARK

Babb

Duck Lake

Polebridge

Quartz Lake

MONTANA

Many Glacier

Lake Sherburne

Lower St. Mary Lake

St. Mary

St. Mary

Logging Lake

Going-to-the-Sun Road

Rising Sun

Avalanche Creek

Logan Pass

St. Mary Lake

Fish Creek

Sprague Creek

Cut Bank

Apgar

Lake McDonald

Apgar

Gravel Road

Two Medicine Lake

Whitefish Lake

West Glacier

GLACIER NATIONAL PARK

East Glacier Park

Whitefish

Columbia Falls

Middle Fork Flathead River

Essex

Kalispell

Evergreen

Hungry Horse Reservoir

CONTINENTAL DIVIDE

North Fork Flathead River

△ Car camping

▲ Ranger Station

GLACIER NATIONAL PARK

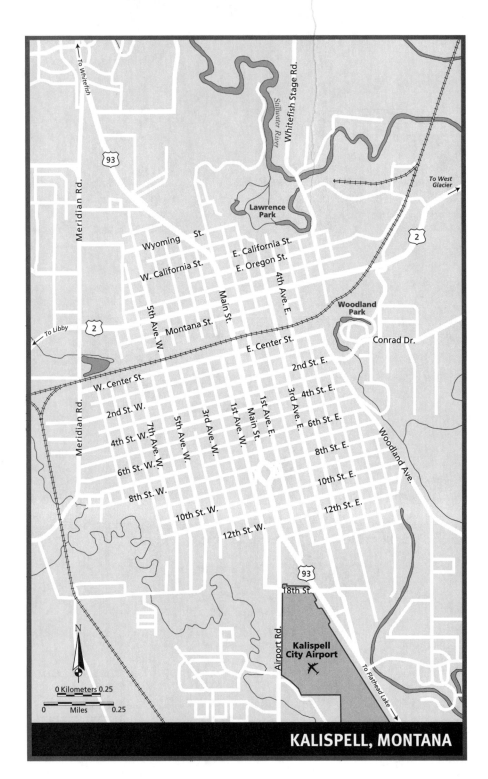

KALISPELL, MONTANA

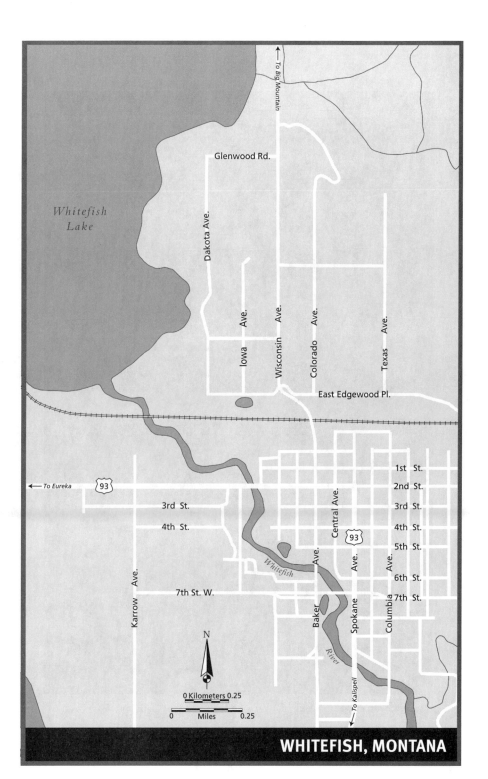

WHITEFISH, MONTANA

Glacier Country offers something for everyone. Photo: Perry Johnson, courtesy of Big Mountain Resort

How to Use This Book

From the fertile Swan and Flathead Valleys to the breathtaking, open expanses to the east of Glacier National Park, this guide to northwestern Montana's Glacier Country is designed to help you find what you're looking for and to introduce you to things you might never have imagined exist in this out-of-the-way place.

Of course it's probably because Glacier Country is somewhat out of the way that so many people choose to vacation or relocate here. The wildness of this place is a major part of its appeal to residents and visitors alike. You may be surprised to find out how easy it actually is to get here and how much the area has to offer in addition to great skiing, fishing, hiking, and other winter and summer recreation opportunities. Even if those things were what drew you here, you'll be amazed at what a hike through a Douglas-fir forest to an alpine lake can do for your appetite; you'll definitely need a hearty meal when you leave the woods, and you can indulge in one of the area's fine restaurants. And if carrying your tent and all of your gear to a backcountry campsite isn't exactly your idea of a way to spend a relaxing vacation, hints on great bed-and-breakfasts, cozy inns, downtown hotels, and even the more luxurious campgrounds (with running water and other amenities) may be more to your taste.

This book will help you get to Glacier and the Flathead Valley (see the Getting Here, Getting Around chapter) and help you make the most of your visit once you arrive. The Area Overview, History, Attractions, The Arts, Kidstuff, and Annual Events chapters are designed to give you some general information about Glacier and the Flathead Valley that will encourage and inform your visit—if the rumors of great outdoor recreation and spectacular scenery weren't enough. Each of these chapters and the Outdoor Recreation chapter give general information about what can be found throughout the region while providing details about the highlights and pointing you to additional sources of information about a variety of activities.

Once you've exhausted yourself with a full day of horseback riding, rock climbing, or rafting, you'll want something to eat and a place to rest. Later you may want to sample one of Montana's many new microbrews in an old-fashioned saloon setting. If souvenirs or some comfortable hiking boots are on your wish list, you may also want to visit the local hot spots for the latest in hand-carved grizzly bears or high-tech outdoor gear. In the market for antiques? There are dozens of venues for you to explore.

The sections of this book containing information about accommodations, nightlife, restaurants, and shopping are grouped by geography. If you're basing your adventures out of Bigfork, all of the best-and-brightest options for an overnight stay, a fine meal, a hearty ale, or sturdy cowboy boots in town or in the immediate area can be found within a few pages. Within each section are recommendations for a range of options from bed-and-breakfasts to RV parks and from kid-friendly hamburger joints to elegant dining rooms.

When your vacation comes to an end, and you just can't bear to leave all of Montana's wonders behind you, our handy relocation guide can give you information about real estate, health care, education and child care, and more. After you've settled into your dream cabin by the shore of Swan Lake, we're sure that you'll continue to use this book to inform all of your Glacier and Flathead Valley adventures.

Please let us know what you think about *Insiders' Guide to Glacier National Park*. The book will be updated regularly, and I want to hear from you about your own discoveries that you think should be included in the guide. Write to Insiders' Guides, c/o Globe Pequot Press, P.O. Box 480, Guilford, CT 06437-0480 or visit the Web site at www.insiders.com.

Area Overview

The Lay of the Land

Quirks, Foibles, and Other Important Information

Please Tread Lightly

In Glacier National Park and the Flathead Valley, the seasons are dramatic, wildlife is abundant, and nature is your constant companion. Rugged peaks rise majestically over pristine lakes, streams gurgle through the lovely valleys, and clear rivers carry fast-flowing fresh water. The forces of nature are a dynamic part of the landscape, which influences the dynamic nature of the residents who call it home.

Winter and summer, Glacier and the Flathead are marvelous places to visit, and residents will quickly tell you that living here has a vacation-like quality. But nature and its visible beauty isn't the only draw of the valley—the arts, annual festivals, and myriad attractions such as golf courses, museums, and excellent dining, lodging, and shopping draw visitors here and are supported by residents. From the smallest village to the area's largest towns, you'll never know what delightful surprises you'll find under the restaurant sign or behind the bed-and-breakfast door.

The Lay of the Land

Glacier National Park, carved out by ancient glaciers and dotted with those of more recent origin, is the center of one of the largest intact ecosystems in the United States. Its relative isolation from settlement has helped it retain its rich biological diversity, even though nearly two million visitors cross the park borders every year. The surrounding communities act as gateways to the park and its northern sister, Waterton Lakes National Park in Canada. Together the two parks are designated the Waterton-

Flathead National Forest. Photo: Nancy Hoyt Belcher, courtesy of Flathead Convention and Visitor Bureau

Glacier International Peace Park—so named in 1932 as the first such park in the world.

With the two parks at its center, it is natural to conclude that tourism is the mainstay of the surrounding communities. The knowledge that Flathead Lake, the largest natural freshwater lake west of the Mississippi River, is Glacier National Park's neighbor to the west will only strengthen that conclusion. Kalispell's population soars every summer to accommodate visitors, as do the populations of Bigfork and Columbia Falls on the north end of the lake and on the way into the park, Polson at the south end, and Whitefish—winter and summer with the Big Mountain Ski Area—is a vacationer's playground. The Swan Valley, located on Montana Highway 83, is a less-visited, equally beautiful vacation getaway. Tourism benefits the Blackfeet Indian Reservation, with its stunning views of the Rocky Mountain Front, and the Flathead Reservation, as well.

Don't be lulled into the belief that these communities exist only for tourism, however. These are vibrant, exciting towns with active arts communities, thriving businesses, and stunning settings. It's no wonder that more and more people make the Flathead Valley home every year. Festivals and events abound, from North American Indian Days in Browning to the myriad arts festivals held in communities from Whitefish to Polson. Families who have lived here for generations and newcomers fill the seats at these gatherings. This is a place where community still means something, neighbors share sugar, and everyone talks about how to keep deer out of the garden—though they'd willingly let the deer feed on their flower beds if the option was losing the wildlife and scenery that make up the wonder of the area.

Quirks, Foibles, and Other Important Information

As you wander through Glacier Country, the Flathead, and the Swan on your adventures, there are some things that you

should be aware may affect your journey, your recreation, and your safety. We cover a lot of these topics in Close-ups and Tips throughout the book, but there are still some good things to keep in mind as you hit the highway and head off to the park or out on the water.

1. This is a really large area—We don't call this Big Sky Country for nothing, and though residents in the area may think nothing of hopping in the car and driving a couple of hours to get to a particular restaurant or to find a trailhead, this book is arranged so that if you're in Whitefish, all of the restaurants, accommodations, and other amenities in the area are listed in the same section of the book. If you want to head off to a restaurant in Polson from Whitefish, figure out the mileage before you hit the road, and fill up on gas. Twenty-four-hour convenience stores exist out here, but you can't count on them being on every corner.

2. Our weather can change quickly—Even after a warm summer day, or while you're still out enjoying it, storm clouds can come up, showers will start, and temperatures will drop. Be sure if you're on the water or on the trail that you have appropriate gear to get you through a storm. Remember, too, that in winter the weather can be extremely cold; watch for signs of hypothermia when you're out recreating, and think about carrying emergency gear.

3. Heed road information—Going-to-the-Sun Road in Glacier National Park is generally closed from early to mid-October until early June because of snow, and other roads can become dangerous in winter weather. Exercise caution, and call the state highway information number, (800) 226-ROAD, for information on road conditions.

4. Make your reservations early—Though we expect visitors in the summer, the communities in this area and the facilities in the park are not unlimited in terms of the accommodations we can offer. Call early to reserve rooms and arrive early at campgrounds to guarantee a spot. Some campgrounds accept reservations as well,

Sources for Information on Glacier National Park:

Web site: www.nps.gov/glac/home.htm
Information phone: (406) 888–7800

Glacier National Park Visitor Centers:

Apgar: Located at the foot of Lake McDonald, 2 miles from the West Glacier entrance. Open 8:00 A.M. to 4:30 P.M. during shoulder season, 8:00 A.M. to 8:00 P.M. during peak season, weekends only during the winter. Weekdays during winter, please stop at the information desk at park headquarters.

Logan Pass: Opens with Going-to-the-Sun Road, usually mid-June. Peak season hours are 9:00 A.M. to 7:00 P.M. Usually closes for the season in late September.

St. Mary: Located at the foot of St. Mary Lake. Open 8:00 A.M. to 5:00 P.M. during shoulder season, 8:00 A.M. to 9:00 P.M. during peak season. Usually opens for Memorial Day and closes the third weekend in October.

Information is also available at Two Medicine, Polebridge, Many Glacier, and Goat Haunt Ranger Stations. Please check the *Waterton-Glacier Guide* for hours of service.

Entrance fees:

Single vehicle pass: $10. Valid for seven days.
Single person entry (foot, bicycle, motorcycle): $5.00. Valid for seven days.
Glacier National Park Pass: $20. Valid for one year from month of purchase.
National Parks Pass: $50. Valid for one year from month of purchase.

Please inquire about Golden Age and Golden Access passes. Golden Eagle passes are valid for park entry but are no longer sold by the park. Special fees are charged for commercial vehicles. These fees may be changed at any time.

Weather:

For historic weather averages, check Glacier National Park's Web site at www.nps.gov/glac/whatsnew/weather.htm. This page has links to current weather and forecasts, but scroll down a bit and you'll find a detailed table of average highs and lows as well as precipitation averages for the entire year. As you'll observe, June and November are the wettest months of the year; June often feels cooler than the average high listed of 71 degrees Fahrenheit. It won't be spring in the peaks for a while! But it can be beautiful at the lower elevations, including the whole Flathead Valley. July and August have average highs of 79 and 78, with average lows of 47 and 46 degrees Fahrenheit. Beautiful weather often lasts into September, but even then it's possible to start getting frost at night at high elevation. Indeed, if you're planning to camp or hike, be sure to bring warm clothes, because it can snow at any time of year (though the snow may not last long). These numbers reflect conditions in the park; the Flathead Valley can be considerably warmer in both summer and winter. Summer will see some days reaching into the 90s; sometimes in winter it rains rather than snows in the valley. Winter driving can be treacherous: "Black ice" sometimes forms on the roads when the temperature drops and rain freezes on the pavement.

Backcountry permits:

Backcountry permits are required for backpacking. There is a $4.00 per person per night charge. Permits are issued no more than 24 hours in advance and may be obtained at the Apgar Backcountry Permit Center, St. Mary Visitor Center, and Many Glacier, Polebridge, and Two Medicine Ranger Stations. Permit desk hours are somewhat limited: Be sure to check the current issue of the *Waterton-Glacier Guide* for details. A percentage of permits may also be reserved by mail in advance for a $20 fee. The entire backcountry camping guide is on-line at www.nps.gov/glac/pdf/bcguide_2002.pdf; please read about the reservation process carefully.

Distance from West Glacier to
Bigfork: 40 miles
Browning: 67 miles
Columbia Falls: 12 miles
East Glacier: 57 miles
Great Falls: 210 miles
Kalispell: 25 miles
Polebridge: 25 miles
St. Mary (via Going-to-the-Sun Road): 50 miles
Whitefish: 27 miles

While distances are useful, it's good to know that they don't always translate directly into time on the road. The 50 miles of Going-to-the-Sun Road between West Glacier and St. Mary take about 1½ hours to drive because the road is narrow and winding (and that's just drive time; you'll want to stop to admire the views). It's about 25 miles from West Glacier to Polebridge, but if you take the Outside North Fork Road, it'll take about 40 minutes; if you take the Inside North Fork Road, it could take more than two hours.

Some basic facts about Glacier National Park:
Established in 1910
Approx. one million acres
More than 1,100 species of plants
63 species of mammals
Annual visitation: approx. 1.8 million
Busiest months: July and August
Trails: 732 miles
Triple Divide Peak: Rivers drain to Hudson Bay, the Gulf of Mexico, and the Pacific
Highest peak: Mount Cleveland, 10,466 feet above sea level
Geology: Precambrian rocks are some of the oldest exposed rocks in North America
Glaciers: The park is named for the ice-age glaciers that scoured out these valleys, creating the dramatic landscape. Currently there are about 12 small glaciers that persist from the more recent "Little Ice Age."

Local Chambers of Commerce:
Bigfork: 8155 Montana Highway 35, P.O. Box 237, Bigfork, MT 59911; (406) 837–5888; www.bigfork.org

Browning: Cut Bank Area Chamber of Commerce, P.O. Box 1243, Cut Bank, MT 59427; (406) 873–4041; www.cutbankchamber.com

Columbia Falls: 233 13th Street East, P.O. Box 312, Columbia Falls, MT 59912; (406) 892–2072; www.columbiafallschamber.com

Kalispell: 15 Depot Park, Kalispell, MT 59901; (406) 758–2800; www.kalispellchamber.com

Polson: P.O. Box 667, Polson, MT 59860; (406) 883–5969; www.polsonchamber.com

West Shore (Somers, Lakeside): P.O. Box 177, Lakeside, MT 59922; (406) 844–3715; www.lakesidechamber.com

Whitefish: 500 Depot Street, P.O. Box 1120, Whitefish, MT 59937; (406) 862–3501; www.whitefishchamber.com

Fall in Glacier National Park. Photo: Carl Wells, courtesy of Flathead Convention and Visitor Bureau

and that reservation may save you hunting in the dark for a spot to pull into and set up the tent.

5. We do have bears and mountain lions—Though you will be lucky to see these wild creatures from a safe distance, please remember that they can be dangerous and follow the precautions outlined in this book's "Bear Aware" Close-up. We also have an abundance of other wild creatures—they are beautiful to view, but remember that you are the visitor in their habitat and treat them with respect. Respect for wildlife means giving them a wide berth. If your behavior changes the behavior of the animal you're watching, you're too close.

Please Tread Lightly

Throughout this guide, especially in the Outdoor Recreation chapter, we offer tips for being a responsible visitor to this somewhat fragile ecosystem. Let us take a moment here to emphasize that what makes this area special is its abundance of natural beauty, its biodiversity, and the people who care about both. The remoteness of Glacier National Park and the Flathead Valley and the cushion provided by the national forest on its west and south sides have helped sustain that diversity for the hundred years or more that settlement has been taking place in this area. Still, with two million visitors coming into the park every year, there is strain on our natural surrounding . . . it's unavoidable. Please keep your impact as minimal as possible so that our valleys and peaks will remain as they are for generations to come.

Getting Here,
Getting Around

By Air
By Car
By Bus
By Train

Montana is remote, it's large, and it's mountainous, three things that make getting here and getting around a challenge for visitors and locals alike, though it seems to get easier every day. It's not getting faster, though. Let's dispel that notion right off the bat. Yes, it is true that for nearly four years, Montana had no posted daytime speed limit. Instead, highways operated under the "Basic Rule," which stated that drivers had to drive in a reasonable and prudent manner based on road conditions and traffic. However, this author knows from experience that tickets were still distributed by our diligent and prudent highway patrol. We have since gone back to standard daytime speed limits with the support of our residents. This chapter should help you get here by plane, by car, by train, or by bus, and it will help you navigate the state once you're here. We still recommend a reasonable and prudent attitude to travel here—weather conditions, mountainous terrain, and long distances between services (like gas stations) should always be kept in mind.

By Air

Montana has three fairly large international airports—large compared to the tiny international airport at Glasgow in our state's far northeast corner—at Billings, Great Falls, and, lucky for the visitor to the Flathead Valley, Kalispell. If you fly into Billings or Great Falls, you'll have to make other arrangements to get to the Flathead by car or by bus. From Billings it's 463 miles to Kalispell and from Great Falls it's 229 miles. There are other regional airports at Bozeman, Butte, Helena, and Missoula.

Glacier Park International Airport
4170 Highway 2 East, Kalispell 59901
(406) 257-5994
Most people who fly in to visit the Flathead Valley will choose the Kalispell airport as their destination. It's serviced by Delta, Horizon, Northwest, and Big Sky. Car rentals are available at the airport, and some guest ranches will arrange to pick you up there.

Great Falls International Airport
2800 Terminal Drive, Great Falls 59404
(406) 727-3404

If you fly into Great Falls and rent a car to get to the Flathead Valley, be sure to visit the falls themselves to see what the members of the Lewis and Clark Expedition faced as they explored the Missouri River. The airport is serviced by Delta, Horizon, Big Sky, and Northwest.

Logan International Airport
1901 Terminal Circle, Billings 59105
(406) 657-8495
Billings is Montana's largest city, and it naturally has the largest airport. Car rentals are available at the airport, and you can fly in on Delta, Horizon, Northwest, Big Sky, or United/SkyWest. From there you may also be able to get a connecting flight to Kalispell.

Missoula International Airport
5225 Highway 10 West, Missoula 59808
(406) 728-4381
Flying to Missoula is also a good option for getting to the Flathead. It's closer than Great Falls, Billings, or Helena, the next-near option. Car rentals are available, and the airport is serviced by Delta, Horizon, United/SkyWest, and Northwest. While you're in Missoula and at the airport, you may be interested in stopping at the

Smokejumper's Training Center there to see how forest fires are fought.

By Car

Montana has 1,200 miles of interstate and 5,400 miles of primary highways, but remember this is Big Sky Country, and that just means they're long—not that it's complicated to find which one you need. There are three interstate highways: I-15 runs north and south, just to the east of Glacier National Park; I-90 runs northwest and southeast across the western two-thirds of the state, heading northwest toward Washington; and I-94 connects Billings with eastern Montana and North Dakota.

If you're coming in from the west, you'll take I-90, from the north or south, I-15, and from the east, I-90 or I-94. U.S. Highway 93 runs the length of the Flathead Valley from north to south, starting in Missoula at Interstate 90 and winding its way north and then west toward Washington. This will likely be your primary

Insiders' Tip

Consider flying into Spokane, Washington, or Calgary, Alberta, when visiting Glacier and the Flathead Valley. Airfare is sometimes less expensive, though you will probably have to rent a car.

travel corridor. Montana Highway 83 will take you through the Swan Valley—one of the most scenic drives in the state. U.S. Highway 2 will be your road into Glacier National Park and across the Blackfeet Reservation, and you can choose to explore Glacier from that road or from U.S. Highway 89 or Going-to-the-Sun Road. Highway 89 dips to the southeast to meet up with Interstate 15 at Great Falls.

Flights into the Kalispell airport can offer stunning views of the western mountains. Photo: gravityshots.com

The Whitefish Train Depot is a historic local landmark. Photo: Carl Wells, courtesy of Flathead Convention and Visitor Bureau

If you want to travel to Canada from Glacier and the Flathead, there are border crossings at Roosville (on U.S. 93, north of Eureka), open 24 hours a day; Chief Mountain (on Montana Highway 17, northeast of Glacier), open 7:00 A.M. to 10:00 P.M. from July 1 to August 31 and shorter hours in spring and fall only; and Piegan (16 miles north of Babb on Montana Highway 89), open 7:00 A.M. to 11:00 P.M.

Montana travel information is available by calling Travel Montana at (800) 847-4868 or (406) 444-2654. For information on road conditions statewide, call (800) 226-ROAD.

By Bus

Rimrock Trailways
(800) 255-7655, (406) 755-4011
Rimrock serves more than 60 Montana communities, including Whitefish, Great Falls, and Missoula. It also connects to points served by Greyhound Lines along I-90, including Missoula, Bozeman, and Billings.

Eagle Transit
(406) 758-5728
Eagle Transit is Kalispell's city bus. Call for schedules and route information.

By Train

Amtrak provides east and west passenger service across northern Montana, making stops in Libby, Whitefish, West Glacier, Essex, Browning, Cut Bank, Shelby, Havre, Malta, Glasgow, and Wolf Point. The terminuses are Chicago on the east and Portland and Seattle to the west. The railroad follows Montana's Hi-Line, as U.S. Highway 2 is known, and a trip on the Empire Builder is certainly a romantic way to see this part of the state. Most boardings and deboardings occur at Whitefish; call Amtrak at (800) 872-7245 for more information.

Bus Tours in Glacier National Park

Bus tours provide an opportunity to see Glacier while leaving the driving to someone else—and along winding, narrow Going-to-the-Sun Road, that can be a real advantage! Two different tour operators offer guided trips through Glacier National Park and the immediately surrounding area. Both make stops along the way for visitors to take photos, stretch their legs, and generally enjoy the scenery.

Glacier Park, Inc. (GPI) offers tours based out of their lodges, connecting the different areas of the park. Visitors traditionally have ridden in the historic red buses, built by the White Motor Company between 1936 and 1939. These vintage motor coaches have roll-back canvas tops that can be opened on sunny days for an open-air ride with views to the peaks above. Recently refurbished through a public-private partnership, the red buses are now gleaming like never before. They are certified as "new" 2002 vehicles, and they meet all current safety standards and run on efficient, low-emission propane/gas bi-fuel engines. But all their original charm remains, and drivers provide a narrative during the ride and answer questions for visitors just as always. The red bus schedule includes half-day and full-day tours to different parts of the park, including Logan Pass and Going-to-the-Sun Road, for prices ranging between $25 and $85. For more information, visit the Web site at www.glacierpark inc.com or contact GPI at (406) 756–2444. Reservations are required and should be made at least the day before you wish to tour; call the GPI transportation office at (406) 226–5666.

Sun Tours operates out of the east side, picking up visitors at Browning, East Glacier, and St. Mary. These guided tours of Going-to-the-Sun Road—Natos'i At'apoo—highlight Blackfeet history and culture, and all guides are Blackfeet. Sun Tours operates small modern buses with large windows and air-conditioning. Both private tours and tours of the Blackfeet Reservation can also be arranged. For more information, write Sun Tours, 29 Glacier Avenue, East Glacier Park, MT 59434, or phone (406) 226–9220 or (800) 786–9220.

The red buses, with their roll-back canvas roofs, offer their riders spectacular views of Glacier National Park. Photo: courtesy of VIAD Corporation

History

Just getting to the Flathead was enough to discourage many early-day settlers. Pioneers arrived on horseback or by horse and wagon, negotiating rough wagon trails that knifed through dense stands of virgin timber and up and down steep countryside. Fur trappers and traders preceded settlers in the early 1800s. But of course American Indians were the Flathead Valley's first inhabitants. Three main Indian tribes—the Kootenai; the Upper Pend d'Oreille, or the Kalispel Indians; and the Salish, known as the Flatheads—coexisted in the area. They hunted and fished in the area's many rivers and lakes and vied for territory with the warring Blackfeet Indians from the eastern side of the Rocky Mountains.

This country remains home today to the Confederated Salish and Kootenai tribes (Flathead, Pend d'Oreille, and Kootenai). The Treaty of 1855 sliced Flathead Lake into two halves, with the southern half designated reservation land. The Flathead Indian Reservation, which comprises 1.2 million acres, extends south to Ravalli. The Confederated Salish and Kootenai Tribal Complex is in Pablo. On the east side of Glacier National Park is the Blackfeet Indian Reservation.

Beginning about 1800 and continuing to 1820, traders and fur trappers sought adventure and wealth in the Flathead Valley, and their explorations would change the lives of the Native peoples forever. Canadian trappers and traders were some of the first to traverse the region, and Joseph Howse, one of the first white men to winter in the Flathead, was sent by the Hudson's Bay Company to establish the company's first fur-trading post in 1810–1811. This post at the north end of Flathead Lake was called Howse House (or Howse's House).

In the footsteps of the trappers followed the homesteaders, hungry for land and a new start. A heavy influx of homesteaders populated the region throughout the 1870s and 1880s; many were European immigrants who brought their agricultural heritage with them. Some claimed land on the shores of Flathead Lake, despite its being reservation land. By 1909 former reservation land around Flathead Lake cost about $1.25 to $3.00 per acre.

The arrival of the Northern Pacific Railroad at Missoula, Montana, in 1883 was one of the major contributors to the region's growth. By about 1887 (some accounts say the early 1890s) public transportation was available from Missoula via a spur line north to Ravalli, south of St. Ignatius. From Ravalli passengers and goods were loaded onto overland wagons or stages and transported to Polson on Flathead Lake's southern shore.

From Polson steamboats offered passenger service to the north end of the approximately 28-mile-long lake, connecting with Somers and Demersville, two early settlements. The first steamer to begin crisscrossing Flathead Lake was the *U.S. Grant,* and by 1916 at least 16 steamers regularly traversed the waters of the lake, the largest freshwater lake west of the Mississippi. Besides containing roomy freight decks with booms, many steamboats featured upper decks with private cabins for travelers and dining salons. The largest vessel, the *State of Montana,* was launched in 1889. It measured 150 feet long by 26 feet wide and was built for $25,000.

In the 1880s agriculture boomed in the rich, fertile Flathead Valley, and steamboats hauled grain crops and potatoes to market. The temperate climate around Flathead Lake enabled the successful cultivation of fruit orchards. Many tons of apples were produced and shipped to out-of-state markets. In the early 1900s the Bear Dance Ranch harvested 3,000 fruit trees and boasted more than 40 varieties of apples. Later sweet cherries were

12

introduced to the Flathead and became a major crop, which they remain today.

Steamboat transportation on Flathead Lake thrived from about 1885 to the 1920s, but in 1917, when the Northern Pacific Railroad built a branch line to Polson, the ease and speed of rail transportation hastened the end of the steamboat era. The Northern Pacific was not the only railroad to shape the history of the valley. It was empire builder James J. Hill's dream to build a railroad from St. Paul, Minnesota, to the West Coast. Some 6,000 men bent their backs surveying, grading, and pounding rails to the upper Flathead Valley to bring Hill's transcontinental railroad, the Great Northern Railway, west from the eastern Montana prairies through Marias Pass, which is located at the southern edge of Glacier National Park (elevation

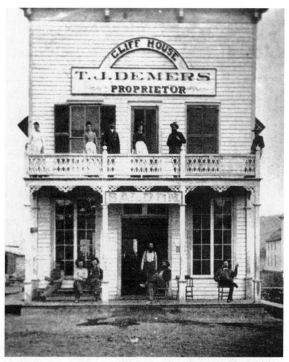

Demersville was once a center of activity in the Flathead Valley.
Photo: Thain White Collection

5,216 feet). Hill's idea was to fill his cars with passengers going west. He heavily advertised the agricultural opportunities of the Flathead Valley and offered cheap fares for homesteaders. The railway played a prominent role in giving homesteaders access to the hinterlands of northwestern Montana. By 1891 the train carried passengers to Columbia Falls and then to Kalispell. By the turn of the century, the Valley was home to more than 700 farms.

Two Early Towns Have Their Day

Preceding other towns springing up in the north Flathead Valley were the communities of Scribner and Selish. But historians consider Ashley, a somewhat later arrival, the valley's first real town. Established at the crossing of Indian trails near the Ashley Creek Bridge, it sat about 1 mile west of Kalispell's present-day business district, and some of Ashley's streets were incorporated into Kalispell when that city developed. The town was named for Joe Ashley, a trader who arrived in 1857, one of the valley's first settlers, but it would die shortly after Demersville and Kalispell blossomed overnight.

Demersville was located a few miles south of Kalispell on the Flathead River and was founded by merchant T. J. Demers. The location came to be considered the head of navigation on the Flathead River. Demers set up his general store first in a large tent, and later in a log structure. With his death in 1889, the store was sold and became the Missoula Mercantile Co. But Demersville boomed from 1888 to 1891 as steamboat traffic on Flathead Lake ferried the migration of settlers, their equipment, and supplies up the lake to Demersville and points north.

Demersville was a hell-bent town, with an abundance of saloons and gambling. Hope was that the Great Northern Railway would lay tracks to Demersville so that it would gain the double advantage of both rail and water transportation. But when the Great Northern Railway extended its main line to Kalispell instead, most of the town folded up and moved there.

Bigfork

The first wagon trails through this part of Montana followed the west shore of Flathead Lake. Thus the Bigfork area on the east shore was slower to be populated than its west shore neighbors. The town site perches on a bay where the Swan River spills into the northeast end of the nearly 200-square-mile Flathead Lake. The town was founded in 1902 when E. L. Sliter filed a town-site plat. (Some accounts say a year earlier.) He divided a portion of his 160-acre homestead into 11 blocks and about 95 lots. Sliter built the town's first hotel and general store and served as first postmaster. A 1903 photograph depicts Sliter's store, his hotel under construction, and three saloons. Some early businesses were the Bigfork Mercantile, the Flathead Commercial Company, and the E. J. O'Brien Hotel. The first restaurant built was Cheinies. A 1912 fire in Bigfork demolished many businesses. The Bigfork Light and Power Company constructed the first hydroelectric power plant at Bigfork in 1901. The plant, located on the mouth of the Swan River, harnessed energy derived from the turbulent waters and sent power and light to neighboring Kalispell. The University of Montana at one time operated its biological research station in Bigfork until the station was relocated to Yellow Bay in 1912.

Bigfork, with the surrounding area, has been known historically for production of exceptional fruit, because of the lakeshore's relatively mild climate. The first orchard is thought to have been planted by homesteader George Lakin in about 1885. City founder E. L. Sliter soon followed, clearing timber and brush and eventually accumulating more than 500 acres of farmland. When his orchards were in peak production, he had upwards of 5,000 apple, pear, plum, and cherry trees. The area is famous for its cherries; the in-

dustry as we know it today originated at nearby Wood's Bay in the 1890s.

Just where the town acquired the name Bigfork is unclear. Henry Elwood reported in his book *Kalispell, Montana and The Upper Flathead Valley* that local Indians told Sliter that the site was the "Big Fork" of the Flathead Valley's rivers, hence the name. Later the U.S. Postal Service shortened the name to one word.

Since this little town was founded, a century has passed, and Montana has again become a destination point. Appreciated as one of the last unspoiled spots to live, Montana enjoyed renewed popularity as a vacation and relocation spot in the late 1980s and continues to draw many out-of-state residents today. The economy remains strong, and Bigfork has thrived, although it remains unincorporated. A tourist town—the summer population swells to approximately 10,000—it is a draw in itself. Be sure to stop on your way to Glacier National Park. Bigfork is listed in *The Great Towns of America: A Guide to the 100 Best Getaways for a Vacation or a Lifetime,* by David Vokac.

It is home to the renowned Bigfork Summer Playhouse and performing arts center, fine-art galleries, gift shops, superb restaurants, and a world-class golf course. If you're traveling to Bigfork in mid- to late summer, don't miss sampling the region's sweet Flathead cherries.

Somers

The old company houses of this former lumber town on U.S. Highway 93 still are lived in, and time-worn dock pilings stretch out into Somers Bay; both are mute reminders that the quiet, historic community of Somers at one time enjoyed status as the second-largest town in the Flathead Valley. In the early decades of this century, Somers existed as a bustling shipping and logging hub and passenger port.

Built on the northwest end of Flathead Lake, Somers grew up almost overnight. The Great Northern Railway needed ties to continue its railway expansion, and the abundant lumber in the area was responsible for an economic boom.

Flathead Valley and
Glacier National Park Time Line

1810—Joseph Howse of the Hudson's Bay Co. spends the winter of 1810–1811 in Flathead Valley, establishing company's first local trading post—Howse House—at north end of Flathead Lake.

1857—Trader Joe Ashley first to settle in upper Flathead Valley on Ashley Creek. In 1883 community of Ashley founded, 1 mile west of present-day Kalispell.

1862—Major gold strikes in Montana bring prospectors swarming to the northern Rocky Mountains in search of mineral riches.

1885—First steamboat hauls freight and passengers up Flathead Lake, as the *Swan* sailboat is transformed into the *U.S. Grant* steamboat.

1887—Town of Demersville founded several miles south of Kalispell on Flathead River by Frenchtown merchant T. J. Demers.

1891—Great Northern Railway brings transcontinental rail service to the valley. Great Northern establishes Kalispell Townsite Co. and names Kalispell new railway division point. Kalispell becomes valley's leading town.

1893—Montana Legislature creates Flathead County from Missoula County.

1901—John O'Brien Lumber Company Mill built at Somers to manufacture ties for Great Northern railroad westward expansion. Somers becomes the second-largest town in the valley.

1902—Town site of Bigfork platted and filed by E. L. Sliter.

1902—Whitefish Townsite Co. established. Land surveyed and divided into lots.

1904—Main line of Great Northern moves from Kalispell to Whitefish for better routing by James J. Hill. Whitefish becomes new division point, which it remains today.

1905—Citizens vote to incorporate Whitefish.

1910—Glacier National Park created.

1910—Severe forest fires burn three million acres in Idaho and western Montana, including newly established Glacier Park.

1910—Flathead Indian Reservation opened for homesteading; Flathead Valley sees influx of pioneers.

1913—First of Glacier Park's Great Lodges built by the Great Northern Railway at East Glacier.

1927—Great Northern depot is built in Whitefish and becomes symbol of Whitefish.

1929—Half Moon Fire burns 100,000 acres, racing across Teakettle Mountain near Columbia Falls and into Glacier Park.

1929—First Great Northern passenger train, the famous Empire Builder, passes westbound through Whitefish.

1932—Waterton and Glacier Parks become world's first International Peace Park.

1933—Dedication ceremony atop Logan Pass kicks off official opening of Glacier Park's scenic Going-to-the-Sun Road.

1935—Big Mountain's Hellroaring Ski Club founded.

(Continued)

1937—First golf club organizes in Whitefish.

1939—Izaak Walton Inn at Essex on south fringe of Glacier Park is built to serve Great Northern locomotives and rail worker crews. Filled with railroad memorabilia, the inn today caters to cross-country skiers and tourists.

1947—Big Mountain ski area incorporates and is run by Winter Sports, Inc.

1950—A day's ski pass on Big Mountain costs $1.50.

1953—Hungry Horse Dam built. Structure is 564 feet high and is still the tenth-tallest dam in the United States.

1955—Anaconda Aluminum Plant built north of Columbia Falls. Plant operated for 45 years but shut down in January 2001.

1960—Whitefish Winter Carnival is formed. Remains a big part of today's Whitefish winter scene.

1964—Huge flood hits north Flathead Valley and floods Evergreen. Sections of highway and rail lines wash away at Marias Pass.

1967—In unrelated incidents grizzlies in Glacier Park kill two campers in same night, which becomes known as the Night of the Grizzlies.

1976—Glacier National Park designated a World Biosphere Reserve.

1988—Red Bench Fire burns 37,500 acres on west side of Glacier Park.

1990—Whitefish Stumptown Historical Society saves run-down railroad depot, restoring it much as it was when built in 1927.

1998—Blacktail Mountain Ski Area opens near Lakeside.

2001—Moose Fire burns more than 70,000 acres, mostly in Flathead National Forest and Glacier National Park.

2002—Ford Motor Company, in partnership with the National Park Service, refurbishes Glacier's famous fleet of historic red buses.

About 1900, James J. Hill, founder of the Great Northern Railway, contracted with John O'Brien of Stillwater, Minnesota, to build a sawmill capable of producing at least 600,000 railroad ties annually for 20 years. Additionally, 40 million board feet of lumber were contracted for each year. In turn the Great Northern was to build a 10-mile spur track from its main line through Kalispell to the O'Brien mill in Somers.

O'Brien purchased 350 acres of the Tom McGovern ranch and built the sawmill. The railroad recruited loggers from back home in Minnesota, offering them fare out to Montana for only $12.50. Besides Minnesota, other mill workers composing the labor force hailed from Sweden, Germany, Norway, and Italy. Somers was known for the friendliness of these hard-working, diverse ethnic groups.

Operations at the mill began in August 1901, and a boomtown was born. The boom lasted more than two decades until the 1920s when virgin timber resources became less plentiful. Logging was done in winter because it was easier to haul timber over snow. Logs were cut, loaded onto horse-drawn sleighs, and sledded to riverbanks or lakeshores, where they were stockpiled. In spring when the water was high, logs going to the Somers mill were driven down the Flathead, Whitefish, Stillwater, and Swan Rivers to enter the head of Flathead Lake, then towed by tugboat to a large pond in Somers Bay to be processed. The sawmill operated a planing mill for lumber, a sash and door division, and, for a time, a box factory. The Great Northern built the tie-treating plant and operated a power plant on the grounds to provide steam for all the operations.

Great Northern representative George O. Somers was in Somers during 1901 keeping track of the railroad's interests, the same year the town built a post office. Both the new post office and the new town needed a name, and the well-thought-of railroad official was chosen as the namesake.

The Great Northern acquired the sawmill from O'Brien in 1906 when he left Somers. Eventually the name was changed to the Somers Lumber Company. Operating a day and night shift every 24 hours, the mill could produce 225,000 board feet of lumber daily.

The company employed most of Somers' 500 inhabitants. The company provided their homes. According to Lou Bain and Frank Grubb in their book *Flathead Valley Yesteryear,* workers paid from $5.00 to $9.00 per month for rent. The lumber company furnished water and electricity. Workers were charged $1.00 per month for medical services from the company doctor.

In 1900 George Wilson constructed the first general store in Somers. The Flathead Commercial Company purchased it and did business there as the Normann and Smith Company. In 1933 Everit Sliter of Bigfork fame purchased the store interest of one of the original owners, and the store was named the People's Mercantile. Sliter became sole owner in 1937. Although not in the original location, the business still operates on Somers Road and today is a lumber and building supply center. The first hotel and eating house were under the roof of the McGovern ranch house in about 1900. The Somers Hotel and boardinghouse was constructed in 1901; also that year a company general store was opened by the Great Northern, and the post office was established.

Another historic Somers building is a popular restaurant today, which features fine dining. Tiebuckers Pub and Eatery is housed in the former office building of the Somers Lumber Company. Constructed in 1929, it shared space with the Great Northern, serving as its depot. The building has been put to many uses during the decades. According to the folks at Tiebuckers, it's been a makeshift school, a mini-mall, a cafe, and other businesses.

When growth was at its peak, the Great Northern offered not only freight service but also twice-daily passenger ser-

vice from Kalispell to Somers. Passenger traffic reached an all-time high about 1910 when the Flathead Indian Reservation, located at the southern end of Flathead Lake, was opened for homesteading. At that time passengers from either east or west were routed via the Great Northern to Somers, then ferried across Flathead Lake to Polson by steamboat, then carried south by the Northern Pacific Railroad—or vice versa. By the late 1920s traffic had dwindled considerably with the decline of the steamboat era, the advent of the automobile, and the availability of public bus transportation, causing the Great Northern to abandon its rail passenger service.

Similarly, as Somers was no longer a transportation hub, the old order was passing in the lumber business. Plentiful timber was no longer available, and in 1948 the Great Northern shut down the vast mill.

As in days gone by, residents of the town and surrounding valley enjoy unlimited recreational activities on Flathead Lake. You can enjoy sunbathing or boating at the public park and boat launch at Somers Bay. The *Far West* offers boat cruises, some with meals, as well as private charters.

Nearby Lakeside, south of Somers, also makes available to travelers a public dock and park. The first settlers of Lakeside consisted of a group of Methodist church congregationalists, who in 1896 attempted to set up an educational camp. The Reverend W. W. Van Orsdel, known as "Brother Van," helped purchase some 240 acres of lakeshore property at Lakeside, reported historian R. C. "Chuck" Robbin. The hopeful settlers called the camp "Chautauqua," namesake of the original Chautauqua site already established in New York state. Financial problems soon aborted the mission, and parts of the large tract were sold. John Stoner bought 25 acres and built a boardinghouse and opened Lakeside's first post office in 1901.

Lakeside nestles on the west lakeshore, where residents and visitors alike enjoy its spectacular lake and mountain panoramas. A growing village, Lakeside offers most services.

Columbia Falls

Columbia Falls, on U.S. Highway 2, reposes at the west entrance to Glacier National Park; travelers wind through Bad Rock Canyon to access the breathtaking and enchanting scenery of this renowned park. But like many Flathead Valley towns, Columbia Falls grew up around the Great Northern Railway. Railroad tycoon Jim Hill decided in 1889 to extend the line from the eastern plains of Montana to Puget Sound, Washington, without the benefit of government land grants. His major problem wasn't funding, however, but finding a feasible route over the Continental Divide through the Rocky Mountains. History records tales of other white men using the pass decades earlier. However, John F. Stevens, a Great Northern railroad surveyor sent by James Hill to locate a passable route, is generally credited with discovering Marias Pass. In 1891 the railroad line was completed through the pass to Columbia Falls, then on to Kalispell.

The townsite of Columbia Falls had already been established several years earlier, as settlers were drawn to the area's good farmland and generous supply of timber. In addition, coal discovered up the North Fork of the Flathead River was mined in limited quantities and barged downstream through Demersville and onto Flathead Lake, then transported by the Northern Pacific Railroad.

The group of pioneers who established the village named it Columbia or Columbus. The first townsite was located down on the flats next to the Flathead River, but early settlers decided their town stood a better chance up on dryer ground and closer to the coming rails. Much of the town had relocated to the present site before the railroad steamed into town.

Although it is not clear how residents named the town Columbia, speculation has it being named for nearby Columbia Mountain, a long, horizontal mountain situated at the mouth of Bad Rock Canyon, a mile or so to the east. When first postmaster Jim Kennedy applied for a town name in 1891, he was declined the

name Columbia, since a town in Montana was already called Columbus. It was believed that such a similar name would cause confusion. Mrs. Kennedy actually named the town by tacking "Falls" onto it, although no falls existed there then.

With the railroad coming, a group of enterprising Butte, Montana, businessmen looked ahead to profit. Organizing the Northern International Improvement Company and speculating that Columbia Falls would become the new division point for the railroad and land would be in high demand, they purchased the property from Mrs. Nellie LaFrombois, an Indian woman, for approximately $5,000 and platted it. Much of it was located in what would become the town's business district. Even railroad magnate Jim Hill thought the prices too steep, and he continued laying tracks to Kalispell, designating it the division point, instead. Kalispell citizens were sorely disappointed when Hill later moved the division point to Whitefish.

Moderate growth continued in Columbia Falls, the valley's oldest town. Beatrice Macomber reports in *Columbia Falls Yester-Years* that in 1891 the small community sported 18 saloons, a general store, men's store, barbershop, flour mill, sawmill and lumber company, and railroad depot. The year 1891 also marked the building of the town's first bank by James A. Talbott, a prominent businessman who could be called the father of Columbia Falls. He and G. E. Gaylord, both members of the Northern International Improvement Company, built the sophisticated 31-room Gaylord Hotel, which burned in 1929. Talbott donated land for the first Episcopal church and first school, erected in 1892. Here he built his family home, a lavish mansion with eight fireplaces and overlooking the Flathead River. Unfortunately it was ravaged by fire in 1941.

A coup for the town was Columbia Falls being chosen as the location for the "old soldier's home" in 1895, when Talbott's and the Northern International Improvement Company's offer to donate cash and equipment as well as acreage just outside Columbia Falls was accepted by the state board of review. Columbia Falls' bid was selected from among those of towns throughout the state. The governor approved the decision, and the two-story structure was built for the sum of $9,985. Columbia Falls citizens also donated $10,000 toward the project. By the end of 1908, the home provided care for 88 residents. The rules prohibited drinking and profanity, permitted smoking in rooms, and required a bath once a week. Residents were signaled to rise at reveille and had to be in their rooms when taps played each night.

In 1909 the citizens of Columbia Falls incorporated. The following year the modern amenities of electricity and telephone were installed in the town, and a sewer line was laid along Nucleus Avenue.

In its early years, the town's survival depended on the grain and lumber industries. Today lumber still plays an important role in the well-being of the economy, with Plum Creek operating a sawmill and couple of plants in town and Stoltze Lumber Company running a nearby mill. Construction of the Hungry Horse Dam near the little town of Hungry Horse gave a shot in the arm to the economy in the early 1950s, and some workers stayed and put down roots.

Another industry, vital to Columbia Falls economy since 1955, has been the Columbia Falls Aluminum Co. north of town. A processing plant employing hundreds of workers, it manufactured aluminum ingots.

But on January 26, 2001, for the first time in its history, the entire production plant shut down. With rising electricity costs, it became more lucrative for plant owners to sell the electricity they had contracted to purchase from the Bonneville Power Administration than it was to produce and sell aluminum ingots. Future reopening of the plant remains uncertain.

Whitefish

When trappers penetrated the unexplored forests of the north Flathead Valley as early as the 1850s, they shared the long alpine lake that settles at the base of the Whitefish Mountain Range with Native Americans who lived in the vicinity. Trappers and early settlers came to call this lake Whitefish Lake, named for the rich supply of whitefish that had long provided a staple diet for the Indians. When a permanent town was founded in the present location, it also was called Whitefish.

By 1883 the first settlers, John Morton and Charles Ramsey, had hewn homes out of the primitive countryside, near the mouth of the Whitefish River. Ramsey also constructed a rooming house for hunters and anglers who came for the abundance of fish and wildlife at the lake. By the end of the decade, lumbermen were lured to the valley for its dense timber stands. Loggers put Whitefish Lake to good use; nearby logs were cut and floated down the lake to the Whitefish River and then down the river to lumber mills in and around Kalispell. The first Whitefish sawmill was built by the Baker brothers, who played a prominent part in Whitefish's history. For a number of years, logging and farming were the main livelihoods in Whitefish.

The early site of Whitefish—at the foot of Whitefish Lake—was moved to its present location to be nearer the Great Northern railroad. The Whitefish Townsite Company was established in 1902 by a group of four individuals, and the land surveyed and platted. But it wasn't until the following year that articles of incorporation were filed for the company. The Whitefish Townsite Company hired loggers to cut the dense tree stands that spread over the townsite, and serious tree cutting began for the new railroad town. Although great progress was made, many stumps remained for a number of years after the trees were downed, earning the town the name "Stumptown." In 1905 townspeople voted to incorporate the village of Whitefish. The town council met for the first time, and the first census was gathered—the population of the boomtown was 950. Five years later citizens driving horse-drawn wagons down city streets still were forced to negotiate around tree stumps, so in 1910 the town council decided that prying out the offending stumps would be a good way for jail offenders to pay their debts. Thus, jailbirds

Going-to-the-Sun Road

Going-to-the-Sun Road cuts through the heart of Glacier National Park, providing most visitors with their best access to the subalpine and alpine regions of the park. The road winds up from the forests of the west side and the prairies of the east to top out at Logan Pass. Magnificent views are standard fare all the way along this winding mountain road. In itself an engineering feat, the road was completed in 1932 and opened to the public in 1933.

Many interesting episodes illustrate the difficulties of building the road. Considering the amount of blasting that had to be done, the steep angles at which the rock was worked, the state of technology, and the harsh environment, it is probably a testimony to safety that only three men died during its construction. But more than one man quit this job, even though it was during the Great Depression, when work was so hard to come by. One story tells of how, during the construction of the 408-foot-long east-side tunnel, workers had to shimmy down a hundred feet of rope over a cliff to get to the job site. Once there the work included removing the excavated rock from the tunnel by hand—it was impossible to get any power equipment down the steep slope. In another case, when preparing to blast one particularly large cliff just east of the Loop (the hairpin turn on the west side), workers wore wool socks over their boots to prevent sparks! In 1931 a Caterpillar tractor slipped off the road and rolled 200 feet down the mountainside. Its operator drove it back up with only minor damage.

The difficult environment continues to affect Going-to-the-Sun Road today. Opening the road over Logan Pass each spring is a major undertaking that begins in early April. Plows, a rotary plow, and a front-end loader begin their task of clearing the snow at low elevations, gradually working their way higher. The speed at which the road can be plowed depends on the depth of the winter's snowpack and spring weather conditions. Rain in the valleys can fall as snow up high, so that sometimes a stretch of road needs to be cleared more than once. Avalanches are inevitable in the springtime; avalanche watchers keep their eyes trained on the slopes above the road, looking for any sign of movement that could hazard the road crew and equipment. Fog can make it difficult to see above the road, making it impossible for avalanche watchers to assess safety and forcing plowing to end for the day. On occasion crews have had to plow their way home when an avalanche occurred behind them. As the plow crew works its way toward Logan Pass, the snow gets deeper and deeper. The last part of Going-to-the-Sun Road to be plowed is usually the Big Drift, which has measured as much as 80 feet deep when plowing began. The Big Drift must be surveyed each year so that the plows are sure they are plowing the road and not anything else! Going-to-the-Sun Road usually opens all the way over Logan Pass sometime between the last week of May and the third week of June. At that time the snowpack at Logan Pass Visitor Center is typically still about 12 feet deep. In the fall the road is closed down from Logan Pass in sections, beginning the third Monday in October unless weather has already closed it. Stretches of Going-to-the-Sun Road are plowed all winter along Lake McDonald and St. Mary Lake.

Maintaining the 70-year-old road is a challenge, too. Going-to-the-Sun Road is on the National Register of Historic Places, and preserving its historic character is one of the Park Service's goals. Over the last 15 years, reconstruction of the road has begun and will continue for sometime into the future. Although modern technology has advanced far beyond that which built the road, reconstruction is still in a very difficult environment with a short season. In addition, visitation to the park—and the number of vehicles that drive Going-to-the-Sun Road—has increased well beyond anything that could have been imagined in the 1930s. Thus rebuilding the road is no small problem—it has to occur during the peak season of the short alpine summer, when people visit, animals inhabit their mountain homes, and plants must bud, flower, and set seed. You may encounter delays due to construction during your drive over the pass—ask at the front gate as you enter; generally delays are short. Should you be stopped, why not take the opportunity to turn off your car's engine, enjoy the view, have a snack, and step outside for a moment?

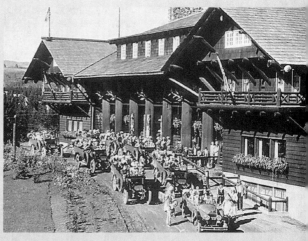

Cars flooded Going-to-the-Sun Road even in the early days of Glacier National Park. Photo: courtesy of VIAD Corporation

Logan Pass is the highlight of Going-to-the-Sun Road for many. It can be difficult to park here in the middle of the day; try arriving before 10:30 A.M. or visiting in the late afternoon—daylight is long in the northern summer. Or consider taking the park shuttle up and back from lower elevation—leave the driving to someone else and you'll enjoy the view that much more! Both GPI and Sun Tours offer bus trips that stop at Logan Pass. However you arrive, you'll admire the Garden Wall, the Hanging Gardens, and the view in 360 degrees on both sides of the Continental Divide. You might walk to Hidden Lake Overlook—look for ptarmigan nesting under the boardwalk and look for mountain goats—or perhaps strike off down the Highline for as far as takes your fancy. Or spend a few minutes with binoculars just scoping the slopes for mountain goats, bighorn sheep, or grizzly bears—all of which frequent Logan Pass.

Park statistics indicate that the average visit to Glacier National Park is about two hours—the time it takes to drive Going-to-the-Sun Road (see the loop tour description in the Attractions chapter). But after that, the average visit jumps to four days—once you get a taste of this place, you'll want to come back for more. Going-to-the-Sun Road is the just the beginning.

carried out a major effort toward town beautification.

The Great Northern Railway main line had come to the Flathead in 1891. In 1901 Great Northern announced that Whitefish would be the new division point on the main line because it offered more feasible routing. In 1903 a spur line was added that linked Columbia Falls with Whitefish, and James Hill pulled division headquarters out of Kalispell. The steel ribbon was rerouted in a more northerly route from Columbia Falls via Whitefish to Rexford, connecting to Libby and points west. Thus Hill eliminated the difficult current route, which crossed the Salish Mountains west of Kalispell. The "Columbia Falls Cutoff" was completed in 1904 from Rexford, Montana, to Whitefish.

Another reason Hill chose Whitefish as division headquarters was its proximity to Whitefish Lake. The lake provided a water supply for the railroad's steam-

Locals refer to the Flathead Valley as the Flathead, which derived its name from the Flathead Indians. No one knows for sure how the Flathead Indians came by their name, although several theories exist. A popular one is that when famous explorers Lewis and Clark came across the Indians near Hamilton, Montana, they saw some visiting Chinook Indians from the West Coast. The Chinooks flattened their children's temples with headboards on their papooses (cradles strapped to the back to carry babies). The explorers mistakenly called them all Flatheads. Another theory has it that other Salish Indians (a group of Northwest Indians whom the Flatheads belong to) had wedge-shaped heads, and the Flatheads didn't; they had flat heads.

Whitefish Lake and River also provided citizens with water. Frank Baker and a Mr. Rile hauled wagonloads laden with jostling barrels of water down bumpy city streets to provide residents a water supply; cost averaged 25 cents a barrel. The Baker brothers (there were five) reportedly owned much of the land adjoining the town. They gave liberally of their labor and money to help build a solid foundation for the fledgling town. Baker Avenue is named after them.

One of the town's first businesses was a tent saloon, with two entrepreneurs peddling whiskey to tree cutters clearing trees downtown on Central Avenue and Second Street. The town saw a building boom from 1903 through 1904. A mood of optimism prevailed. "By 1910, Whitefish had 1,479 people," Betty Schafer and Mable Engelter state in *Stump Town to Ski Town: The Story of Whitefish, Montana*, "a business district primarily along Central Avenue and Second Street, a water system, a light and power plant, telephones, some wooden sidewalks, and a couple of crosswalks, some graded streets, some filled gullies." The council was discussing sewers and parking. Civilization, indeed, had arrived.

A hundred years later many original downtown buildings remain in use, offering food, shopping, and services in this thriving resort town. The charm of yesterday is all around, and visitors are invited to take a historical downtown walking tour.

The heart of Whitefish has always been the Great Northern Railway. (Later it became the Burlington Northern Railroad.) The first official passenger train cruised by the train platform in October 1904 westbound to Seattle. The steam-powered train was on time, and the town's citizens were on hand to cheer. At the same time the city was formally proclaimed the railroad division point.

Beginning about 1913 passenger trains going through Whitefish followed the southern boundary of Glacier National Park during daylight hours so that summer travelers could enjoy the scenery while crossing the Continental Divide. The daytime schedule remains thus today,

powered equipment, and in winter crews of sawyers hauled out blocks of ice for Great Northern's icehouses. A natural means of refrigeration, the ice was used to cool fruit in the fruit express cars. Mechanical refrigeration later replaced the need for ice storage, and in the late 1970s the giant icehouses in Whitefish were demolished.

even after Amtrak took over passenger service in 1971. The famous Empire Builder passenger train rolled into Whitefish for the first time in 1929, and today it still carries both east- and westbound passengers past the park.

The first train depot built in 1906 was replaced in 1927 with a building described as English Tudor style. The multistory structure merged the half-timbered Tudor style with a Swiss-chalet look. The Swiss-chalet architectural vernacular was popular for the lodges being built at the time in Glacier National Park. By 1990 the aging depot needed refurbishing, and the Burlington Northern Railroad donated it to the Whitefish Stumptown Historical Society for restoration. (The Burlington Northern Railroad was formed in 1970 from the merging of the Great Northern Railway, the Northern Pacific Railroad, and numerous others.) The renovation of the treasured landmark returned its appearance and character to that of 1927, while adding modern amenities. Be sure to stop by the historical society museum located there—it's on the walking tour—to see the town's railroad history.

You'll see the "Rocky the Goat" logo, which the Great Northern chose for its trademark symbol in 1923. This author remembers as a child seeing "Rocky the Goat" emblazoned on Great Northern freight cars, a familiar sight for decades before the merger that created Burlington Northern ended Rocky's ride through the Flathead.

If the railroad was the heart of Whitefish, Big Mountain was—and is—its soul. Hiking and huckleberry picking have long been pleasurable pursuits on this huge mountain. Snow-encrusted trees called "snow ghosts" are a famous winter oddity found up on The Mountain. Skiers using homemade skis found a way to ski the mountain as early as 1935, without the benefit of a resort company to hack out and groom trails. The Hellroaring Ski Club had unofficially formed by 1935. A little more than a decade later—in 1947—two entrepreneurs from Great Falls and many interested Whitefish community members financed a fledgling resort operation called Winter Sports, Inc. Winter

Sports still owns and operates The Big Mountain Ski and Summer Resort.

Big Mountain is buried in 330-plus average inches of annual snowfall and offers a wide variety of terrain—some 3,000 skiable acres—for great downhill skiing. The resort, just a snowball's throw from Glacier National Park, continues to be a popular draw and a continued source of economic stability for the small resort-and-retirement community cradled in the valley below.

Kalispell

Kalispell may have been cut off of the Great Northern Railway's main line when the division point went north to Whitefish in 1904, but the town did not go bust, as had other early towns in the Flathead Valley that were bypassed by the railroad. Kalispell managed to remain the financial and commercial hub of the valley.

Back in 1891 when James Hill decided to relocate the division point from Columbia Falls to Kalispell, he sent Charles E. Conrad to find a site for Great Northern's facilities and the Kalispell Townsite Company. Conrad purchased part of a homestead on the west side of Kalispell. The land was surveyed, platted, and recorded under the name Hill chose: "Kalispel," derived from the Pend d'Oreille Indian language. Kalispell has at least two meanings: "camas" or "prairie above the lake."

Land speculators had also bought up nearby ranches and homesteads and divided them into lots in anticipation of the railroad coming. In spring 1891 when newly divided lots came on the market, an unheard of $100,000 worth of lots was snapped up overnight. Inside lots on Main Street measuring 25 feet were priced at $1,000, while corner lots cost as much as $1,250. The next month the first building was constructed.

Everyone eagerly anticipated the coming of the railroad, and December 31, 1891, was a red-letter day for the town. Historian Henry Elwood quoted a special edition of the *Kalispell Graphic* newspaper: "After eight months of waiting anxiety, the most devout and earnest wish of the people of Kalispell is consummated. The iron horse has at last snorted in the Garden of Eden of Montana. The locomotive pealed forth its welcome sound to the people of Kalispell." A silver spike was driven to hail the triumph amid a wildly cheering crowd, and the band played "Yankee Doodle." A parade, barbecue, and public ball were part of the festivities. The first passenger train steamed into Kalispell in summer 1892, complete with a dining car and sleeper, a colonist sleeper, a combination smoker and day coach, and a baggage car.

Kalispell enjoyed boom years from 1899 through 1901, with many residences and large brick buildings constructed.

Unfortunately the status of being Great Northern division headquarters didn't last more than about a dozen years. Jim Hill in 1904 relocated the division point north to Whitefish because of the difficult route west of Kalispell over the Salish Mountains. It was a sad day when the last train wailed a farewell salute to Kalispell. The railway kept the branch-line train connecting Kalispell with Columbia Falls, nicknamed the "Gallopin' Goose." But in 1950 the railroad discontinued that train, too, ending Kalispell's passenger train service.

Flathead County had been created out of Missoula County in 1893, and Kalispell had been voted county seat over Columbia Falls the following year. This helped to keep Kalispell stable when the railroad abandoned it. All county government business was conducted from Kalispell. By 1903 a permanent, three-story brick courthouse had been completed; it still is used today. (U.S. Highway 93 splits around it on South Main Street.) The town had a solid foundation—it had incorporated in 1892, and citizens had elected city officials. Water and electric light utilities were already created, as well as a post office and fire department. By 1904 a new city hall was operating, and progress had brought a library, hospital, and numerous churches.

On the commercial side Kalispell counted at least three national banks, stores representing almost every trade—from meat markets to furniture, and from hardware to photographers—and several posh hotels, including The West and the Grand Central. The fertile farmlands and lumber industry surrounding Kalispell also provided the town with a solid anchor.

The first buildings were mostly one-story structures built of wood. But building codes became stricter. "Because of fire codes, commercial-district buildings were later built of brick or other fireproof material," Katheryn McKay said in her book *Looking Back: A Pictorial History of the Flathead Valley, Montana.* "These brick buildings typically had corbeling or terra cotta decorations. Some earlier buildings had native rock pilasters, sills, and lintels. Cloth awnings shaded the shop windows, and most stores had recessed entries and glass block or leaded glass transoms." Several Kalispell-area brickyards furnished "common" brick, used locally.

Many of the historic downtown buildings are used today. Among the noteworthy is the old Kalispell Hotel on Main Street, now the Kalispell Grand Hotel, built in 1911 to serve upscale travelers. In the early days rooms cost $2.00 per night. After being closed, parts of the gracious landmark were remodeled, including the lobby, and it was reopened in 1991.

Just across the street stands the McIntosh Opera House, erected in the late 1890s. Its expansive upper floor served as stage for many kinds of entertainment—plays, recitals, music programs, dances, lodge meetings, wrestling matches, and other events. The presentation of "Uncle Tom's Cabin" drew one of the biggest-ever audiences—1,132 people. In 1905 when it was pressed into service as a gymnasium, you could watch basketball games on the top floor. Although the dancehall-cum-basketball-court lies vacant today, the main floor contains a busy western store, while an antiques mall sprawls in the basement.

Another prominent old building was the Kalispell Mercantile (KM Building). The mercantile originated in 1888 in Demersville as part of the Missoula Mercantile and was first operated from a tent. The fine department store was known for its quality, variety, customer service, and staff product knowledge, pointed out historians Lou Bain and Frank Grubb. In 1892 it was moved from Demersville to Kalispell, with its final location being First Avenue East and Second Street. Original store size was just 50 feet by 80 feet, but the store eventually grew to eight times that size. Known as northwest Montana's largest store, the Missoula Mercantile offered groceries, hardware and paint, appliances, china, farm tools, plumbing, sporting goods, mill supplies, and even firewood. Eventually the name was changed to the Kalispell Mercantile, and over the decades many Kalispell residents vied for a chance to work at the popular store. Modern competition forced the store to close its doors by 1980. Various businesses have occupied it since. Today the historic structure is being restored to its turn-of-the-twentieth-century character by owners Bill and Jana Goodman, who were named 1999 Business Man and Woman of the Year for their work by the Kalispell Chamber of Commerce. Original stained-glass windows were reinstalled as part of the exterior face-lift. Interior restoration that provides retail and business space is mostly completed. In 1999 a group of three local women formed the Kalispell Repertory Theater. It occupies the former ballroom and features a stage in the round. The theater runs four plays per season, including special Christmas programs. Several downtown restaurants advertise for a dinner/theater package. On the first-floor arcade, early black-and-white photos are a time line to the past. If you're in the mood for coffee, stop by Mel's Coffee Stand for a great cup of coffee and browse through Kalispell's early days.

Late in the 1990s two other treasured downtown buildings were renovated. The old Central School, opened in 1895, has been thoroughly overhauled, with pains taken to match original materials and to retain the building's integrity. The major renovation was made possible by $2.5 million in funds from the city of Kalispell and the leadership of the Northwest Montana Historical Society. From 1929 to 1969 the public school was the junior high. Then the Flathead Valley Community College took over the building. When the college moved to a new campus in 1990, Central School's doors closed. In 1999, heralding in a new century, the building reopened and is now known as the Northwest Montana Heritage, Education, and Cultural Center. Visitors are encouraged to stop by for a glimpse of the valley's history.

Nearby at 15 Depot Park, off Main Street, stands the original Great Northern Railway Depot. The Kalispell Chamber of Commerce, among other businesses, operates from the depot. Newly refurbished, respect for the depot's past was maintained during the remodel, while Montana-style casualness and comfort were incorporated.

These and other charming buildings are visible on the Main Street District walking tour. A second walking tour on the east side routes visitors by beautiful old residences, many built from 1900 to about 1920. Pick up a historical walking tour brochure at the chamber of commerce.

Not to be missed is the Conrad Mansion, built by Charles E. Conrad (see the Attractions chapter). James Hill had asked Conrad to take charge of the Great Northern's Kalispell Townsite Company, and Conrad is considered to be the founding father of Kalispell. A prominent businessman, Charles, with his brother William, established one of the town's first banks, the Conrad National Bank. Charles purchased 72 acres overlooking the east side of the valley and built the Conrad Mansion. Designed in the early Norman style, the mansion featured shingle cladding on the exterior. The unusual home contains 23 main rooms and 8 fireplaces. The opulent house belonged to the family until 1975, when it was gifted to the city. The house has been restored, and turn-of-the-twentieth-century antiques fill the rooms. Summer guided tours of the Conrad Mansion are available.

Today Kalispell remains the economic hub of the Flathead Valley. Tourism at nearby Glacier National Park continues to bring the town a steady, if modest, income. Lumber and agriculture are still major industries. In the mid-1990s out-of-state retirees "discovered" the valley; this continued influx has become a viable industry.

The Flathead experienced a building boom during the 1990s. The January/February 1999 issue of *Mountain Sports & Living* magazine rated Kalispell the number-one best mountain town in the country in which to live. The job market is not as glowing as the magazine reported, however. Montana ranks close to lowest in the nation for average wages per job, a ranking our governor and others are striving to change.

Although the job market is frustrating for many, most of us stay here for all of the reasons we hold dear—beautiful scenery, outdoor opportunities, close ties to family and friends, fresh air, and not too much noise or overcrowding. Yet. We are seeing growing pains, but living in the Flathead Valley remains a treasured lifestyle. And Glacier National Park is an enduring reason for visitors to come.

Glacier National Park

Here, serrated ridges and horn-shaped peaks reign over a jumble of turquoise lakes, waterfalls, cascades, river valleys, hanging gardens, and alpine meadows. Born of geologic and glacial violence, this random landscape couldn't be more perfect had it been designed and executed by Michelangelo. Like the ocean, its sheer scope has a way of putting humanity in its place.

—GEORGE BIRD GRINNELL,
Grinnell's Glacier: George Bird Grinnell and Glacier National Park

Rivers of ice carved the craggy pinnacles of the Rocky Mountains during a succession of ice ages occurring during the past two or three million years. About 10,000 years ago, during the last ice age, an enormous cap of ice several thousand feet thick and miles long covered Glacier National Park's high country. As it melted, it heaved down the canyons, sculpting new shapes and gouging out glacial lakes. The melted remains of the last ice age have long since shriveled up. Today's "new" glaciers formed sometime after the last ice age

ended. They are puny compared to the ice mantle that smothered the park eons ago. In fact they are shrinking—they are smaller than when they were mapped in the early 1900s. But Glacier Park remains an excellent natural setting in which to view the handiwork of glaciers.

Glacier Park was first home to Native Americans. The fierce Indian tribe of the northern plains who gained dominion over the others after the 1750s was the Blackfeet tribe. (The name Blackfeet came from an early group, who after walking through a burned-over prairie met another tribe, who called them Blackfeet, explained C. W. Buchholtz in his history of Glacier Park, *Man in Glacier*. The name also may have resulted from the black color of the soles of their moccasins.) The aggressive Piegan branch of the Blackfeet tribe protected its bison hunting grounds on the east side of the northern Rocky Mountains against other invading tribes, including the Kutenai, Flathead, and Kalispel Indians, who inhabited the west side. These Indians traversed Glacier's mountain passes to hunt for buffalo every year on the eastern plains. The feared Blackfeet retaliated by crossing the mountains and viciously raiding their camps, further establishing their supremacy.

It was mostly the Piegan who regularly used the trails of Glacier Park. Although extremely warlike, the Blackfeet were a very spiritual people. They, and members of other tribes, revered the mountains of Glacier and Waterton Parks, believing them home to the spirits. Many visited there to hold vision quests. In Glacier's northeast corner looms Chief Mountain, a symbol of the powerful medicine that Indians believe stirs in these mystical mountains.

Breaking the backbone of these crusaders of the plains was one unlikely factor—fashion. Plentiful in nearby mountain streams, the beaver attracted white trappers because it brought them top dollar for top hats. White traders and trappers established a permanent trading relationship with the Blackfeet by the 1780s, and the white man's foothold spelled the decline of the tribe. Captain Meriwether Lewis explored the headwa-

Blanketed in white, Glacier becomes a winter wonderland. Photo: Perry Johnson

ters of the Marias River on the return trip of the Lewis and Clark Expedition in 1806. His party viewed the front range of Glacier Park's mountains but for various reasons was unable to explore farther. The expedition stimulated additional interest in the Missouri region and Rocky Mountains, especially among the fur trade.

Finian MacDonald, a Scotsman, and two other traders were the first white men recorded to enter the lands encompassing present-day Glacier Park in 1810, Buchholtz said. Attacked by Blackfeet at Marias Pass, the party survived, but this episode convinced other fur traders to choose safer routes across the Rockies. By the 1850s more white men ventured into the area. Their purposes included government surveys to mark the international boundary between the United States and Canada, bringing Christianity to the Indians, and finding a transcontinental railroad route.

Major gold strikes in Montana in 1862 brought prospectors scouring Glacier's mountainsides in search of mineral wealth. Another rush to stake mining claims occurred soon after the Blackfeet sold the east side of the future park to the federal government. Gold, copper, quartz—even oil and coal—attracted those hoping for a lucky strike. Despite the initial promise, nothing was discovered in sufficient quantities, and soon after the turn of the twentieth century mining and drilling interest waned greatly.

The Blackfeet managed to dominate the area until the 1870s. By then the U.S. Army, episodes of smallpox, illegal whiskey proffered by whiskey traders, and the irrepressible surge of white men into their territory combined to break the power of the warring tribe. The decimation of great herds of bison, the tribe's main food source, brought quick starvation. (The shaggy beasts were annihilated by 1882.) Two proponents of the Blackfeet intervened in their welfare. James Willard Schultz, an American who lived among the Blackfeet, called their plight to the attention of George Bird Grinnell, prominent editor of *Forest and Stream* magazine. After Grinnell's visit to the reservation in 1885, his political influence helped increase government-subsidized food and supplies.

Anticipating a flood of American homesteaders and hoping to gain peace among local Indian tribes, Isaac Stevens, governor of the Territory of Washington (which included the Flathead Valley and Glacier Park), talked the Kootenai, Flathead, and Kalispel Indians of the park's west side into settling on a reservation on the southern half of Flathead Lake. Thus Glacier's west side became public lands.

In 1895 the Blackfeet sold the Ceded Strip—all of what is now Glacier Park east of the Continental Divide—to the federal government. The remaining Blackfeet land—the Blackfeet Reservation—borders the east boundary of the park. Names of Indian legends and chiefs were given to many landscape features in the park by Schultz and Grinnell.

Protection for a Pristine Wilderness

When George Bird Grinnell visited the starving Blackfeet, he was introduced to the St. Mary Lakes region. With James Schultz and an Indian as guides, he hunted and explored. Excited about the area, the editor of *Forest and Stream* magazine returned east and wrote a number of essays about his experiences. Grinnell returned many times. His articles extolled the exceptional scenery and wild-game hunting out West, which appealed to wealthy hunters, who further exploited the area.

Despite this use of the resource, Grinnell—and a handful of other proponents—came to believe that this special place should be protected. By 1891 a national conservation movement prompted the U.S. Congress to allow establishment of national forest "reserves" (later called national forests). Present-day Glacier Park was first protected as a forest reserve. But Grinnell's intent was to see the area established as a national park, and he lobbied to that end for 10 years. He was the most influential advocate in the founding of the park. Promoting his cause in a 1901 article in *Century* magazine, he bestowed the name "The Crown of the Continent" on the magnificent wilderness. His cause was furthered by the support of Great

Northern Railway officials, who saw tourism in the park as a way to promote use of their transcontinental train service.

By 1910 the period of heavy exploitation of the park's natural resources had pretty much ended. That year President Taft signed the bill to create Glacier National Park, and 1,600 square miles of wilderness were preserved. Today more than one million acres are protected within park boundaries. The first superintendent was Maj. William R. Logan. Waterton Lakes Forest Park, to the north of Glacier in Alberta, Canada, already had been established in 1895.

The act that created Glacier Park called for "preserving the park in a state of nature." But attempting to please everyone, the U.S. Congress also mandated that the park provide a "pleasure ground for the benefit and enjoyment of the people." Indeed, early-day emphasis was mostly on the value of recreational opportunities. The act also permitted mining, private land ownership, railroad routes, and harvesting dead and downed timber.

The Great Lodges

The Great Northern already carried passengers through the Glacier Park area before it was designated a park. To serve railroad travelers, the first private accommodations were built at the foot of Lake McDonald. The tourist cabins, built by Milo Apgar and Charlie Howe, were the beginnings of the village of Apgar. Escorted tours were available on the sparkling lake. This was the beginning of early-day tourism in the park.

In 1895 George Snyder built a two-story hotel at the present site of Lake McDonald Lodge. Later John and Olive Lewis acquired the property. (Legend has it John won it in a poker game.) The Lewises moved the first structure and commissioned a lodge to be built on the original site, which was to be in keeping with the style and grandeur of the other lodges being built in the park, only on a smaller scale. The Swiss-style architecture was similar to Great Northern's lodges, which were constructed of stone and log. Opened in 1914 as the only private hotel in the park, the Lewis Glacier Hotel operated for several decades before it was purchased by the National Park Service and became the present-day Lake McDonald Lodge.

Soon after the park was established, the Great Northern embarked on a flurry of building construction. Setting out to create a playground for the rich, Louis Hill, son of railroad tycoon James J. Hill, directed the building of several huge, rustic lodges within the park to attract tourists. A network of lodges and eight backcountry chalets were spaced a convenient day's horseback ride apart. (Horses and boats were the main method of seeing the park's splendors.)

The Great Northern began an enthusiastic advertising campaign with colorful railroad timetables depicting scenes of Glacier National Park. "See America First" became its slogan. First-class scenery required first-class accommodations Louis Hill believed, and the great lodges of the park provided every luxury. In this way the Great Northern became Glacier Park's first concessionaire. Concessions were managed and operated by a subsidiary of the Great Northern, the Glacier Park Hotel Company.

First of the extraordinary hotels, the Glacier Park Lodge, was erected in 1913. Almost immediately it proved inadequate to house the great number of visitors. (An annex soon doubled the original size.) Built at East Glacier, the lodge served as the eastern gateway to the park for arriving Great Northern passenger trains. It was modeled after the Forestry Building that was constructed for the 1905 Portland, Oregon, Lewis and Clark Exposition. Sixty trees were used in construction of the mammoth lodge, which the Great Northern hauled from Washington and Oregon—only one or two per flatcar, since each weighed about 15 tons. Measuring 36 to 42 inches in diameter, the bark-covered Douglas firs gave structural support in the lobby, while the cedars were incorporated into exterior verandas.

Equally as impressive was the Many Glacier Hotel. The park's largest chalet, it was a rustic showplace situated in breathtaking surroundings. It sat at the edge of a crystalline lake rimmed by chiseled peaks. Hill also built the Prince of Wales Hotel in Waterton (Canada).

Two of the park's original eight backcountry chalets remained in operation through 1992, and then they were closed by the National Park Service because of inadequate water and sewage disposal systems. Both Granite Park and Sperry chalets were restored and upgraded and are again open for visitor use. The ninth chalet is outside the park's west entrance at Belton. Belton Chalet has been renovated recently under private ownership. Today the main chalet, with a bar and restaurant, and the upper lodge with 25 rooms, are open May through October for guests. Two guest cabins (each with microwave and refrigerator) are open through the winter months.

The lodges and chalets enjoyed phenomenal popularity for several decades. When the automobile appeared on the scene, however, it precipitated long-term changes. Travel through this splendid wilderness was no longer the exclusive domain of the rich, but could be enjoyed by your everyday person. Motoring became a popular way to see Glacier Park. Use of the backcountry chalets, previously accessible only by horseback or foot, declined. In response to a growing need, the National Park Service opened public campgrounds. Business at the chalets and lodges dropped off. In addition, railroad traffic decreased. All this added up to capital losses for Great Northern. World War II would sharply curtail visitation to Glacier, and many of the park's facilities would be shut down. Most of the backcountry chalets deteriorated badly and never were reopened.

Going-to-the-Sun Road

A ribbon of road 52 miles long connecting the east and west sides of the park has for 70 years transported millions of adventurous travelers up Logan Pass over the Continental Divide—the backbone of the Rocky Mountains—and down the other

Guests enjoy an evening around the fire at Lake McDonald Lodge.
Photo: courtesy of VIAD Corporation

side. The road seems to be merely an eyebrow of a trail chiseled out of limestone, which hugs the mountainside. Building it was an engineering feat, rife with challenges. Steep climbs, snow avalanches, falling rock, and extremely steep dropoffs contributed to the grueling nature of its construction; two men were killed from falls, and one from falling rock.

In 1933 when Going-to-the-Sun Road opened, park visitation jumped a whopping 44 percent—mostly from automobile touring. Today an average of 1.8 million visitors travel through Glacier National Park annually. The picturesque, antiquated road needs to be reconstructed if it is to continue to accommodate the volume of traffic that floods it every summer. Park officials report that continuing summer roadwork will focus for the next several years on structural repairs to historic stone retaining walls and guard walls in the high-alpine area between the west and east tunnels. The road will not close, but you can expect 15-minute delays, officials caution, or for one trip across the entire road, a potential 30-minute delay. Rebuilding it won't change the road's original appearance or character.

The Park Today

In 1932 Glacier National Park and Waterton Lakes National Park, its Canadian neighbor, were named the world's first International Peace Park. Only a strip cut through dense timber designates the international boundary line, and managers from both parks maintain a strong working relationship and spirit of cooperation.

During the 1960s wilderness resource conservation gained renewed public awareness and favor. The Wilderness Act of 1964 provided for large natural areas of Glacier and other parks to be delineated "wilderness" and prohibited further development. Because of its unique natural and cultural qualities, Glacier Park was designated a World Biosphere Reserve in 1976. As always, park administrators continue to struggle with achieving a balance between protecting the resource and public use of it.

By the late 1990s the national Leave No Trace program gained strong momentum among many government agencies. Implemented in Glacier Park, the program promotes responsible outdoor-use ethics to the public to help us all preserve the pristine landscape of Glacier National Park.

Attractions

"Give a month at least to this precious reserve. The time will not be taken from the sum of your life. Instead of shortening, it will indefinitely lengthen it and make you truly immortal."

So wrote John Muir of Glacier National Park, which he also called "the most care-killing scenery" on the continent. Even if you can't take a month to explore Glacier Country, you'll find that each day offers countless opportunities to enjoy this magnificent place.

The lakes and mountains of western Montana dominate the lives of all who have ever lived in or traveled through this region. The lakes and rivers have been travel routes for Native American canoes and nineteenth-century steamboats; prehistoric trails have become paved roads for commerce and travelers; the mountains are ancient places of worship as well as a place of unparalleled backcountry recreation. For those of us living and traveling throughout Glacier Country today, the number of places to visit is huge—and it encompasses everything from theme parks to shops to historic buildings.

The "Attractions" represented here are chosen for one of a few reasons. Some offer a better view of the area—the gondola ride to the top of Big Mountain or Far West Cruises, for example. Others allow you to immerse yourself in the area's past, whether it's the history of the Plains Indians or a nineteenth-century logging town. Some "Attractions" are included because they are near and dear to the hearts of local residents—when you see the lines of folks in swimsuits waiting their turn at the top of the Big Sky Waterslide, you'll want to be there, too! The chapter closes with two driving loops that will take you through a good cross-section of Glacier Country—be sure to check out the book's recommmendations for each community along the way. Although the driving time for each of these routes is a matter of hours, each of them makes a great day trip. And, like John Muir, you may find that a few days is not enough.

Although the information here is as up-to-date and complete as possible, things may change. It's always good to call ahead to confirm prices and schedules.

So explore Glacier Country, and don't hesitate to turn off the road when something intriguing comes along!

Columbia Falls to Browning, U.S. Highway 2

Alberta Visitor Centre
West Glacier
(406) 888–5743

If Glacier Country is part of your grand tour of the Rockies, the Alberta Visitor Centre in West Glacier is a great place to start learning more about Wild Rose Country to the north. And even if West Glacier is as far as you're going, the Alberta Visitor Centre is worth a stop in its own right.

Immediately you'll be greeted by a life-size dinosaur model, reminding you that Alberta is the home of the Royal Tyrrell Museum, which houses the world's largest display of dinosaur skeletons. Photos so large you'll feel like you're walking into the mountains introduce you to two jewels of the Parks Canada system, Banff and Jasper. The Calgary Stampede—which some have called a "Mardi Gras of the North"—comes to life in displays and pictures, and you'll discover historic sites such as Head-Smashed-In Buffalo Jump or the Frank Slide. And for those who have always aspired to the Olympics, you can scream

Glacier Country offers many different ways and places to explore. Photo: Carl Purcell, courtesy of Flathead Convention and Visitor Bureau

down the (simulated) course on a real bob-sled from the 1988 Calgary Games—it doesn't take long but it's exhausting!

The copper-topped building houses a wealth of information about Alberta, its history, and its magnificent mountains. Although it is closed during the winter, in the summer its staff of friendly Albertans will answer questions for you. Even if you hadn't planned on going farther north, you might suddenly put Alberta on your itinerary!

Big Sky Waterpark and Mini-Golf
P.O. Box 2311, Columbia Falls 59912
(406) 892–5025
www.bigskywaterpark.com

Hot summer day in the Big Sky? For kids of all ages, there's no easier, more fun way to cool down than to spend the afternoon at the Big Sky Waterslide. You'll hardly be able to decide where to go next—the Big Splash River Ride, the Seven-Story Geronimo Speed Slide, the Roller Coaster Bullet Speed Slide, or the four Twister Waterslides. And Water Wars—a catapulting water-balloon game—will get your little brother going! For the very young or mellower crowd, minislides and a huge whirlpool may be just the ticket.

And, should you prefer to stay *dry*, the waterpark offers Miniature Greens Adventure Golf, a video arcade, beach volleyball, and a 1938 antique carousel that is quickly becoming a favorite. Bring your own picnic or pick up some snacks and drinks at the concession stand. Changing rooms have free lockers, and locks may be rented.

The Big Sky Waterpark is open from approximately Memorial Day to Labor Day, seven days a week. For full-day admission to the Waterslide, the adult fee (ages 11 and older) is $16.50; ages 3 to 10 pay $12.50; please inquire about nonrider admissions. Monthly passes are available for July and August. Group rates are available; please call to arrange group visits in advance. You'll find Big Sky Waterpark and Mini-Golf at the junction of U.S. Highway 2 and Montana Highway 206.

Big Sky Waterslide offers can't-miss family fun.
Photo: courtesy of Flathead Convention and Visitor Bureau

Hungry Horse Dam
Just south of U.S. Highway 2, Hungry Horse
(406) 387–3800

At 564 feet high and with a crest length of 2,115 feet across, the Hungry Horse Dam dwarfs every other structure in Glacier Country. Water cascades over the spillway to drop as much as 490 feet into the South Fork of the Flathead River. The capacity of the spillway is 50,000 cubic feet per second, and the reservoir has a total capacity of 3,468,000 acre-feet. The principal power benefit comes from the dam's storage of water from the spring runoff for later release when needed. On average this water generates 4.6 billion kilowatt-hours of power as it passes through a series of 19 downstream power plants. The numbers are as impressive as a visit to the dam.

Although tours that go into the dam have been discontinued since September 11, 2001, you can still get a good look at the dam—and appreciate its huge size—by stopping at the visitor center located overlooking the spillway. Displays and photos show the stages in building this fascinating structure, and they discuss the costs and benefits of damming a large river. The visitor center is open from 9:00 A.M. to 3:30 P.M. during the summer months.

Marias Pass Memorial Square
Crossed by Highway 2
12 miles west of East Glacier

At 5,216 feet above sea level, Marias Pass is the lowest pass through the Rocky Mountains in the United States. Nevertheless, it was one of the last to be discovered during westward expansion. Weather deterred some explorers, and the Blackfeet Indians, who controlled the region, would not lead exploring parties through an area they prevented other tribes from using as well. Explorer Meriwether Lewis of the Lewis and Clark Expedition came within 25 miles of the pass before a fateful encounter with the Blackfeet. Eventually the pass was named after the Marias River, which Lewis had named for his cousin Maria Wood.

At the pass Memorial Square commemorates the history of the immediate area. One statue is to John F. Stevens, chief surveying engineer for the Great Northern Railway, who located the pass in 1889. By 1892 the railroad was running trains over the pass.

The Theodore Roosevelt monument honors the president who made forest conservation a national policy and also marks the 25th anniversary of the U.S.D.A. Forest Service. Constructed in 1931, it is a 60-foot-tall obelisk sheathed in granite that was quarried near the state capital in Helena. Originally located in the center of the highway, it was moved to its present site in 1989.

William "Slippery Bill" Morrison, a trader and prospector who had squatters' rights to 160 acres of land at the Marias Pass summit, is also acknowledged. He donated a portion of his land for Memorial Square, and, according to his wishes, at his death in 1932 the balance of his property was also given to the federal government.

The Burlington Northern Stewardship Plaque, dedicated in 1991, recognizes the Burlington Northern Railroad's commitment to responsible stewardship of the environment. The railroad runs through important habitat for grizzly bears, mountain goats, elk, and other animals. This route has been an important transportation corridor since the arrival of the Great Northern Railway in 1892.

Marias Pass is a great spot to take a break on your way across the Continental Divide. You might enjoy your lunch with a view of Summit and Little Dog Mountains, the peaks that dominate Marias Pass from the north. The slopes below these peaks offer one of the best places to view the Lewis Overthrust Fault anywhere in Glacier National Park (see the Geology of Glacier National Park Close-up within this chapter). The rest area offers public outhouses as well as a seasonal Forest Service campground (see the Campgrounds section of the Glacier National Park chapter).

Three Bears Lake, a level, 15-minute trail walk north of the tracks, was dammed by the Great Northern Railway and its water used to refill steam engines. This earthen dam from the 1890s was broached recently to prevent its failure; now the little lake's water runs again to both sides of the Continental Divide, as it did before the arrival of the railroad.

Browning

Museum of the Plains Indian
P.O. Box 400, Browning 59417
(406) 338–2230

Native Americans have inhabited this region for thousands of years. The Museum of the Plains Indian takes a closer look at this history through the art, clothing, tools, and other possessions of the peoples that have known the high plains so well. Each of three galleries presents a different aspect of the Plains Indians' lives. The historic gallery reaches into the cultures of the past with exceptional displays, including traditional clothing, beadwork and quillwork, household utensils, and horse gear. These exhibits explore processes and skills required for daily life such as hunting, preparing skins for tanning, and creating clothing. A second gallery offers the 12-minute slide show "Winds of Change," narrated by Vincent Price and chronicling the way of life of the northern Plains Indians.

A third gallery features contemporary works of art by members of the northern plains tribes, including the Blackfeet. During the winter months, the works of four different artists are highlighted in individual shows. During the summer months, selected works from the preceding winter's shows are presented in a combined show; many of these works are available for purchase.

The Museum of the Plains Indian, located at the junction of U.S. 2 and U.S. 89, is open year-round. From June 1 to September 30, it is open seven days a week from 9:00 A.M. to 4:45 P.M. Admission is $4.00 for adults, $1.00 for ages 6 to 12, and free for children younger than age 6. For groups of 10 or more, admission is $1.00 per person. From October 1 to May 31, the museum is open Monday through Friday from 10:00 A.M. to 4:30 P.M., and admission is free. The museum gift shop has an excellent selection of books and Native crafts for sale.

Whitefish

Big Mountain Ski and Summer Resort
P.O. Box 1400, Whitefish 59937
(406) 862–1900
www.bigmtn.com

Rocky Mountain High? Probably the highest place around you can get without hiking is the top of Big Mountain, at almost exactly 7,000 feet above sea level. On a clear day you'll be able to see the Cabinet Mountains to the west, the Canadian Rockies off to the northeast, the peaks of Glacier National Park, and a magnificent view south to the Flathead Valley, including the Swan Range, the Mission Mountains, Blacktail Mountain, and Flathead and Whitefish Lakes. Summer or winter, it's magnificent.

The Glacier Chaser—Chair 1—offers access to the summit of Big Mountain both summer and winter. In the summer, gondola cars will lift you to the top in glass-enclosed comfort. The summer season typically runs from Memorial Day to late September, with the gondola operating from 10:00 A.M. to 6:30 P.M. during the shoulder season and from 10:00 A.M. to 9:00 P.M. during July and August. Round-trip price is $10.00 for adults and $8.00 for juniors and seniors; children younger than age 6 ride for free.

The Glacier Chaser chairlift and gondola allow full-mountain access for summer hiking and mountain biking. Photo: Perry Johnson

In the winter, sightseers may ride Chair 1 with a foot passenger ticket. They will be loaded on the open chairlift with skiers and snowboarders. The detachable quad lift slows at both top and bottom so that loading and unloading are not difficult. Sightseers are welcome to enjoy the winter view—as well as something hot to eat or drink—in the warmth of the Summit House. Chair 1 operates daily during ski season—Thanksgiving Day to early April (please call to confirm, as snow conditions may affect operation of the lift at early and late season)—from 9:30 A.M. to 4:20 P.M. Foot passenger tickets are $9.00 for one round-trip ride.

Great Northern Brewery
2 Central Avenue, Whitefish
(406) 863–1000
www.blackstarbeer.com

For those that know their beer . . . take an afternoon to visit Whitefish's Great Northern Brewery and Tasting Room. Built in 1994 by Minott Wessinger, the great-great-grandson of Oregon's Henry Weinhard, the brewery was located here to take advantage of the area's excellent water. The brewhouse is built in a gravity-flow arrangement and is mostly automated; for its size it is one of the most complexly designed operations in the country. A photo display describes the brewing process.

The Great Northern Brewery is currently producing six beers—Black Star Golden Lager, Black Star Black Lager, Black Star Amber Export, Wild Huckleberry Wheat Lager (a local favorite!), Wheatfish Hefeweizen, and Big Fog Amber Lager—as well as occasional seasonal brews such as Snow Ghost Special Edition Winter Lager. The Tasting Room—which boasts a spectacular view of Big Mountain as well as of the brewery—is open from noon to 6:00 P.M. Monday through Saturday in the summer, and from 3:00 to 7:00 P.M. Monday through Saturday in the winter. Souvenir items include a unique zip-on neoprene bottle case that not only keeps your beer cool, it floats, too.

Montana Coffee Traders
110 Central Avenue, Whitefish
(406) 862–7667
5810 Highway 93 South, Whitefish
(406) 862–7633, (800) 345–JAVA
www.coffeetraders.com

The story goes that, about 1981, RC Beall was having a cup of the world's worst coffee in an all-night railroad cafe. As he contemplated how to make a living in this little town, the taste of the weak, stale liquid bothered him. Suddenly he wondered if selling a good cup of coffee might translate into a business . . .

Just walking into Montana Coffee Traders will tell you why this once-small operation has flourished: The rich aromas of coffee permeate the establishment. A Whitefish institution, Montana Coffee Traders has grown to a major business. Most recently, Coffee Traders has opened a retail store right in downtown Whitefish. You can usually sample three or four brewed coffees; a sample of bistro or espresso coffees are also available for sale. Coffee paraphernalia—from press pots and grinders to filters and dishware—is abundant, and for those non-coffee-loving souls along for the ride, teas, baked goods, and various candies and treats are also thick. In short—indulge!

The original Coffee Traders building and its roasting facility are also open. This is a retail outlet, too, located just south of Whitefish on Highway 93—look for the covered wagon. Tours of the operation are also given. Please call in advance for groups wishing to tour the roasting facility.

Coffee Traders also operates a coffeehouse in Kalispell at 328 West Center Street; (406) 756-2326. Open from 7:00 A.M. to 5:30 P.M. Monday through Saturday, the coffeehouse serves delectable coffees and other drinks as well as baked delights. It also offers a breakfast menu from 7:00 to 10:30 A.M., and lunch from 11:00 A.M. to 3:00 P.M., with Sunday brunch from 9:00 A.M. to 2:00 P.M. With its warm, congenial atmosphere, it's a place locals go to run into each other.

Stumptown Historical Society Museum
Whitefish Railroad Depot, 500 Depot Street
Suite 101, Whitefish
(406) 862–0067
www.whitefishmt.com/stumphis

Even if you don't arrive in Whitefish by train, you'll want to make a point of visiting the historic depot. Like the train stations at West and East Glacier and the Izaak Walton Inn at Essex, it is built in the chalet style the Great Northern Railway developed for this area. Now owned by the Stumptown Historical Society, the building has been completely restored to its original 1927 appearance and is on the National Register of Historic Places. Be sure to check out the restored 1950s

Great Northern Railway Locomotive 181 on display outside the depot.

Inside you'll find the Stumptown Historical Society Museum, devoted to illuminating Whitefish's past. You'll see Native American beading; handmade quilts from the early-twentieth century; and photos and artifacts from the trapping, trading, and logging era that gave the region the name "Stumptown." Photos from the Great Northern Railway document its history—including wrecks and snowslides—and its tremendous influence. Train models, a telegrapher's desk, and dinner china with patterns exclusive to the Empire Builder service between Chicago and Seattle are a few of the objects that bring alive the railroad's impact on people across the northern plains. Posters as well as calendar art commissioned by the Great Northern—including Blackfeet portraits from the 1920s by the German painter Winold Reiss—offer a unique account of the past. Many other objects represent other aspects of local history as well.

Please call the Stumptown Historical Society Museum to confirm hours of operation, as times vary. Admission is free, but donations are greatly appreciated.

Whitefish City Beach
Whitefish Parks and Recreation
(406) 863-2470

Year-round this little jewel of a park is a real asset to the town of Whitefish. With its spectacular views north and west, it offers a quiet retreat for walkers and joggers in the fall, winter, and spring. In the summer it's a hopping hub of activity: two docks go in, the buoys go out, lifeguards arrive, and swimming happens everyday, all day.

Whitefish Parks and Recreation runs a small concession that sells snacks, drinks, and ice cream. Bathrooms are available. Several small pavilions are available to rent; please call in advance. City Beach also has a boat-launching ramp and boat dock.

Located at the southeast end of Whitefish Lake; take Baker Avenue north over the viaduct, turn left at the light on Edgewood, and follow signs to the lake.

Whitefish Ice Rink
Whitefish Parks and Recreation
P.O. Box 158, Whitefish 59937
(406) 863-2470

It is winter, it is cold, and you have been in the car all day . . . it is time to stretch a leg! Come out to the Whitefish Ice Rink and brush up on your triple axel—or, maybe, just enjoy cruising the Zamboni-groomed ice to your heart's content. Take a break to step inside and have a cup of hot chocolate at the snack bar . . . let your legs relax a moment, then back to the ice! The Whitefish Ice Rink is outdoors and lit at night . . . evening skating—perhaps under a light snowfall—is a special delight.

Located behind the Saddle Club in Mountain Trails City Park—5 blocks north of the train tracks on Wisconsin Avenue—the Whitefish Ice Rink operates from early November to mid-March. It offers open (public) skating sessions at specific hours morning, afternoon, or evening, every day of the week. The rink itself is open from 6:30 A.M. to 11:30 P.M., but hockey leagues and skating classes also use the ice, so be sure to check on the schedule. General admission is $4.00 for everyone age six and older; admission is $3.00 for the last sessions on Friday, Saturday, and Sunday. Children younger than age five skate free when accompanied by a paid admission. Skate rentals are $2.00 for all ages.

Tour the Conrad Mansion in Kalispell and journey into the past. Photo: courtesy of Flathead Convention and Visitor Bureau

Kalispell

Conrad Mansion
P.O. Box 1041, Kalispell 59903
(406) 755-2166
www.conradmansion.com

Step back in time—in the home of Charles and Alicia Conrad. Built in 1895 this Norman-style mansion reflects the wealth and elegance sometimes seen in the West in an era often known for its rough-and-tumble living. Charles Conrad, born and raised in Virginia, came west at the age of 18 and built a fortune in trade and freight on the Missouri River. Later he moved to the Flathead Valley and helped to found the city of Kalispell. His herd of buffalo sometimes pastured on what is known as Buffalo Hill in Kalispell today. He and his wife, Alicia, established a reputation for hospitality and generosity in the new town; from the Great Hall, with its massive stone fireplace and oak woodwork, servants escorted notable guests upstairs to bedrooms with marble lavatories, sleigh beds, and canopied four-posters. Alicia Conrad Campbell, the youngest Conrad child, donated the mansion to the city of Kalispell in 1975. Today all three floors, interior and exterior, have been restored to their original beauty. Inside you will see the Conrads' original furniture, clothing, and even toys; outside exquisite gardens surround the building. The Conrad Mansion offers a unique glimpse into the lives of privileged Montanans at the turn of the twentieth century.

The Conrad Mansion—located 6 blocks off Main Street on Fourth Street East—is open to the public from May 15 to October 15. Hours are 10:00 A.M. to 5:30 P.M. (May 15 through June 14); 9:00 A.M. to 8:00 P.M. (June 15 through September 15); and 10:00 A.M. to 5:30 P.M. (September 16 through October 15). Admission is $7.00 for adults, $6.00 for seniors, and $1.00 for children age 11 or younger. Call in advance for groups of 20 or more.

Hockaday Museum of Art
302 Second Avenue East, Kalispell
(406) 755-5268
www.hockadayartmuseum.org

The Hockaday Museum of Art, located in downtown Kalispell, provides an intimate setting for displays by both local and nationally recognized artists. The permanent collection features works of Montana artists such as Russell Chatham, Ace Powell, Gary Schildt, and Bob Scriver. Exhibits change on a regular basis and may include everything from the work of local watercolorists or photographers to historic doll collections to sculpture in a variety of materials. The building itself, originally constructed as a Carnegie Library, is now on the National Register of Historic Places.

The Hockaday Museum of Art is open Monday through Wednesday, Friday, and Saturday from 10:00 A.M. to 6:00 P.M.; Thursday from 10:00 A.M. to 8:00 P.M., and Sunday from noon to 4:00 P.M. Suggested donation is $5.00 for adults, $4.00 for seniors, and $1.00 for students age 12 and older; children younger than 12 are admitted free. Guided tours are available on request. The museum gift shop offers an array of fine works by Montana artists (see The Arts chapter for more information).

Lawrence Park
North end of Main Street, Kalispell
(406) 758-7718

Looking for some quiet time away from city busy-ness? Take a few moments to enjoy the out-of-doors here in town. While Lawrence Park also offers outdoor play equipment for children and pavilions to rent, it feels both a little more peaceful and "wilder" than Woodland Park (described below). Its paved path runs close to the Stillwater River and is sought out by walkers and joggers as well as bicyclists. Birders will enjoy getting out early in the day here to look for feathered friends. Because Kalispell Parks and Recreation runs all its public programs from Woodland Park, Lawrence Park is perhaps a more relaxed place for those seeking a quieter time outdoors.

Northwest Montana Heritage, Education, and Cultural Center
Central School Museum
Northwest Montana Historical Society
124 Second Avenue East, P.O. Box 2293
Kalispell 59903-2293
(406) 756–8381
www.digisys.net/museum

Built in 1894, Kalispell's Central School Museum is on the National Register of Historic Places and now houses the Northwest Montana Heritage, Education, and Cultural Center, opened in early 1999. It is a beautiful old building, newly renovated to high standards. Highlights of the Central School Museum include permanent and changing exhibits relating to the history of Central School itself; native nations of the area; the development of nonnative settlements; local industrial and technological development, including the histories of the logging, mining, and transportation industries in the area; Glacier National Park; and regional wildlands. The museum also has facilities for speakers, research, oral history, and genealogy, as well as public meeting rooms.

The Northwest Montana Historical Society operates the Central School Museum, which is open from Tuesday through Sunday. Please call for hours and admission fees.

Woodland Park
Second Street at Woodland Park Drive
Kalispell
(406) 758–7718

For a delightful afternoon in town, take some time to explore Woodland Park. In the summer you'll enjoy its formal gar-

dens and rose beds for their beauty and fragrance. Both a swimming pool and wading pool are open to the public for a small fee; please check with Kalispell Parks and Recreation for hours. To make a day of it—or for a bigger event—pavilions can also be rented in advance. When the lagoon freezes in the wintertime it is plowed and flooded for ice-skating, which is open to the public free of charge. Kalispell Parks and Recreation also offers day activities for children in the summer months; please call for a current schedule.

Somers

Far West Cruises
P.O. Box 248, Bigfork 59911
(406) 857–3203

It's hard to imagine anything more relaxing than an afternoon on the water—unless it's a dinner cruise on the water! The *Far West*, a 64-foot cruiser that carries up to 200 passengers, plies the waters of Flathead Lake daily. Its 1½-hour cruises show off the Flathead Valley and its surrounding peaks as only a view from the lake can. A full-service bar is open for all cruises; juices and sodas are also available. The boat has an enclosed lower deck and upper canopy deck for inclement weather.

Flathead Lake cruises begin in late May or early June; the season ends in late September or early October. The *Far West* tour leaves the dock every day at 1:00 P.M.; evening cruises depart at 7:00 P.M.

See Flathead Lake from the Far West.

Photo: courtesy of Flathead Lake Lodge

on Sunday, Monday, and Tuesday. Tickets are $11.00 for adults, $9.00 for seniors age 65 and older, and $7.00 for children ages 4 to 12. In addition to regularly scheduled cruises, be sure to ask about special trips such as brunch cruises, family picnic cruises, and dinner cruises. The *Far West* is also available for charter; please contact the office for details. Flathead Lake is the largest natural freshwater lake west of the Mississippi—30 miles long and 15 miles wide—and weather may occasionally cause cancellations for safety reasons. Reservations are encouraged; on some dates charters may preempt the cruise schedule. Please call ahead.

Please note that while the office is in Bigfork, *Far West* cruises leave from Somers Landing, 1 mile south of Somers on U.S. Highway 93 and 8 miles south of Kalispell. Just look for the big boat!

Dayton

Mission Mountain Winery
82420 U.S. Highway 93, Box 100
Dayton 59914
(406) 849-5524
www.missionmountainwinery.com

Connoisseurs may not immediately think of Montana when they think of wine, but the Mission Mountain Winery has produced quite a few award-winning wines recognized at both national and international competitions. Primarily Pinot Noir grapes are grown at the winery's Dayton location, but Mission Mountain also has vineyards in the Columbia Valley of Washington. Grapes grown there are crushed, transported as juice, and then fermented and bottled here in Montana. This family-run operation offers Johannisberg Riesling, Sundown (Riesling blended with Cabernet Sauvignon), Muscat Canelli, Chardonnay, Cabernet Sauvignon, Pinot Noir, and Pale Ruby Champagne.

The winery, located on the western shore of Flathead Lake, is open daily from 10:00 A.M. to 5:00 P.M. between May 1 and October 31. Stop by for a talk about the art and science of wine making as well as complimentary tasting, which includes special reserve wines available only at the winery. When the season is right visitors may also have a chance to watch harvesting of the grapes or bottling of the new wine. If you can't stop by, check the Internet Web site to view an updated wine list!

Polson

Polson-Flathead Historical Museum
P.O. Box 206, 708 Main Street, Polson 59860
(406) 883-3049
www.polsonflatheadmuseum.org

From buggies to boats, from the (Kerr) dam to documents, the Polson-Flathead Historical Museum depicts regional history with great variety and depth. Homesteaders, steamboaters, cattle ranchers, city developers, and Native Americans past and present all make their appearance—up to and including Calamity Jane, whose saddle is here. Polson's first building, a trading post, is restored and stocked as it was in the 1880s. Local histories described and illustrated here—of the Flathead Indian Reservation or the construction of the Kerr Dam, for example—provide insight into the broader history of the region and of the country at large. Local citizens, many of them descendants of early Montana pioneers, have made generous donations of family artifacts, documents, photographs, and even vehicles to enhance the museum's collection.

The Polson-Flathead Historical Museum is open between Memorial Day and Labor Day, from 9:00 A.M. to 5:00 P.M. Monday through Saturday, and 10:00 A.M. to 3:00 P.M. on Sunday.

Glacier National Park

Going-to-the-Sun Highway and U.S. Highway
2 Loop Driving Tour
Glacier National Park, West Glacier
(406) 888-7800

Going-to-the-Sun Road in Glacier National Park has been called one of the most beautiful drives in the country. This narrow, winding road leaves West Glacier, skirts Lake McDonald, and climbs from the forest floor up along mountain cliffs to summit at Logan Pass (6,646 feet above sea level), cross the Continental Divide, and descend again to St. Mary Lake and the windblown meadows of the east side. From St. Mary, turn south along U.S. Highway 89, which snakes along the edge of the eastern foothills and offers views to both the mountains and the prairie. At Kiowa Junction turn right on Montana Highway 49 to head toward East Glacier, by way of Looking Glass Pass and huge views of the Two Medicine Valley. In East Glacier you'll meet with U.S. Highway 2 for the last 60 miles back to West Glacier. In its first 12 miles, U.S. 2 rises gradually toward the Continental Divide at Marias Pass. At 5,216 feet above sea level, Marias is lower than Logan Pass, but Summit and Little Dog Mountains seem to tower over this wind-scoured, wild stretch of country. Once you begin the descent from Marias Pass, you'll be following first Bear Creek, then the Middle Fork of the Flathead River. These deep river valleys have a pristine lushness of their own. In no time at all you'll be back in West Glacier.

The total mileage for this remarkable tour is about 140 miles, and total driving time (in good weather in the summer and minus any delays due to construction) is only about 3½ hours. Nevertheless this is a good excursion to give a whole day to, because you'll want to stop again and again to take in views, watch animals, and learn more about the park. Picnic areas are located at several scenic points along the way if you wish to pack your own lunch. Restaurants and other facilities are of course located at various points along the route (see the chapter on Glacier National Park for more details).

To begin at the beginning: parts of Going-to-the-Sun Road can be driven year-long, but as winter comes, the higher portions are closed to traffic. The road typically reopens all the way over Logan Pass sometime in June—it has occasionally opened in May—everything depends on the snowpack and plowing conditions. The road will close to traffic over Logan Pass on the Monday after the third weekend in October, unless it has already been closed by weather. This means that driving the full loop tour is generally possible only

Insiders' Tip

You are in hypothermia country! Sometimes the combination of wind, moisture, and cold can cause hypothermia, even when temperatures are above freezing. Hypothermia is life threatening. The symptoms a victim exhibits are progressive shivering, slow reactions, stumbling and clumsiness, slurred speech, confusion, and loss of judgment. If hypothermia is untreated, coma and death may result within a few hours. Treatment should be immediate and decisive. Move the victim out of the weather to a sheltered spot; remove wet clothing and cover the victim; if necessary warm with another body. If the victim is conscious, administer small amounts of hot drinks. Many backcountry tragedies have occurred because hikers used poor judgment, induced by hypothermia. You can help prevent this condition by: dressing in layers to regulate your body temperature, wearing good rain and wind gear when appropriate, drinking lots of fluids, and minimizing prolonged exposure to wind and rain.

from sometime in June to sometime in early October. Please check with park visitor centers for conditions at the time of your visit. Snow has even been known to shut down Logan Pass (usually briefly) in July and August.

Length restrictions have been imposed for vehicles traveling over Logan Pass due to the narrowness of the road and increasing congestion. Vehicles exceeding 21 feet long may not drive over Logan Pass and are also prohibited from the stretch of Montana Highway 49 between Kiowa Junction and East Glacier (they can, alternately, take U.S. 89 from St. Mary all the way into Browning and pick up U.S. 2 there for the trip back to West Glacier). If your vehicle (or vehicle and attached trailer) exceeds 21 feet, please contact Glacier National Park for information on restrictions. Consider seeing Logan Pass with a Red Bus Tour or Sun Tour, or take the shuttle up.

Having taken care of all that—most people will be able to drive over Going-to-the-Sun Road in their own car or truck when they want to, which is usually in summer. So sit back, roll down the windows, and enjoy! You'll be offered the park newspaper—tailored to answer frequently asked questions—in exchange for a $10 entrance fee at the park gate. Apgar Visitor Center is just 2 miles ahead and a good spot to stop for information; you might ask for a brochure called "Points of Interest along Going-to-the-Sun Road." As you leave the Apgar area and head up Going-to-the-Sun Road, you'll be immediately treated to views of the peaks at the head of the McDonald Valley. Or perhaps you'll have a moody day, with fog lingering close to the lake and permitting you only occasional glimpses of what's ahead.

Everyone has a different idea about where you "just have to stop" along the road. It might be Lake McDonald Lodge, or Jackson Glacier Overlook, or an unnamed pullout along the shore of St. Mary Lake. Some like to pull off to read the roadside exhibits, which point out, describe, and explain prominent features. Others will incorporate short day hikes into their driving trip, perhaps the Trail of the Cedars, the Hidden Lake boardwalk, or the Sun Point Nature Trail. It's also possible to include one of the scenic boat cruises (see the Glacier Park Scenic Boat Tours entry) as part of your itinerary. Whatever you choose, you can't go wrong.

Logan Pass—the Continental Divide—is the high point of the trip, often figuratively as well as literally. Expansive views stretch north to Canada; tiny alpine wildflowers bloom in the ancient rocks; ptarmigan have been known to nest under the boardwalk; and bears are often enough seen in the meadows surrounding the visitor center. If stopping at Logan Pass is a high priority, consider arriving there before 10:00 A.M. or after 4:00 P.M.—you'll have an easier time parking and a less crowded subalpine experience! The Logan Pass Visitor Center's huge glass windows allow visitors to enjoy the view even when it's nippy outside. Park Service naturalists staff the visitor center and will happily answer questions—you might ask about "Alpine Talks" or short guided hikes. Glacier Natural History Association also offers sales of park-related books and other items. Keep in mind that between Lake McDonald Lodge and Rising Sun Motor Inn, no food or drink service is available. There is a phone at Avalanche, but then none until Rising Sun. Logan Pass Visitor Center has public washrooms and drinking fountains only.

You will no doubt discover your own favorite places along Going-to-the-Sun Road. As you leave the park at St. Mary, you enter the Blackfeet Reservation and will be within its borders almost until you reach Marias Pass on U.S. 2. You have several opportunities for side trips on the east side of the park: Many Glacier is about a 40-minute, 20-mile drive north of St. Mary; a winding dirt road leads into the Cut Bank Valley of the park, heading west from U.S. 89 some 12 miles south of St. Mary; or you might wish to explore the Two Medicine Valley, a 7-mile drive west from Highway 49. U.S. 89 and Montana Highway 49 are narrow, twisting roads that run along the foothills—take time to enjoy the scenery and drive carefully. You might choose to stay on U.S. 89 and drive out over the plains to Browning to visit the Museum of the Plains Indian, returning to U.S. 2 there.

Geology of Glacier National Park

Glacier National Park is a geologist's dream: Its rocks and formations vividly reveal the processes of formation. The park's geology could be the study of many years, but here's a four-stage thumbnail sketch to start:

Stage 1: Sedimentation. Glacier is mostly sedimentary rock, laid down approximately two billion years ago as silts and sands drifted to the bottom of the shallow ocean that then covered the area—the Great Belt Sea. Over time, these muds began to compress under their own accumulating weight. We see these rocks today in the brightly colored strata of the park: toward the bottom, the greenish-gray Apikuni mudstone or argillite; next, the reddish Grinnell mudstone (formed when the presence of more oxygen caused iron in the mudstone to oxidize; hence the red color); and finally the layers of harder limestone that make up most the peaks. Sometime later, magma from the earth's core expanded up through a weak layer in the sediments and spread out to form the black stripe seen running through some mountains: the diorite sill (also known as the Purcell sill). This intrusion of igneous rock is the hardest, most brittle rock in the park. In a few places it bubbled through the limestone layers and surfaced, still underwater, to form pillow basalts (such as are found at Granite Park).

Stage 2: Faulting and uplift. A mere 150 million years ago, major changes began again. Large plates under the earth's crust began to shift, with the North American plate and the oceanic plate just to its west starting to move toward each other. (Movement of plates is ongoing—consider the active San Andreas Fault in California, or the fact that the Himalayas are being pushed higher as the plate beneath the Indian subcontinent continues to ram into the Asian plate.) Eventually the pressure of the oceanic plate began to elevate the North American plate. Forces of compression became so great that a fold began to develop in the rock strata west of this area. Over tens of millions of years, pressure caused a huge slab of rock—at least 15,000 feet thick—to finally buckle, break, and slide as a unit some 50 to 100 miles to the east. These are the rocks of the Lewis Overthrust Fault that comprise Glacier National Park today. Evidence of faulting can be seen throughout the park in small ways—bent and angled rock strata—and on the big scale: at Marias Pass, for example, you can see where the rocks of the fault layer rode up and over the lower layers. And anywhere along the eastern front—where the mountains meet the plains—you'll be impressed with how suddenly the peaks stop and the prairie begins. That's the limit of how far the faulting process pushed this upper layer of rocks.

Stage 3: Glaciation. At this point we have a huge slab of layered rock shoved out onto the plains, marked only by some gentle, relatively shallow drainages. Enter the Ice Ages! About two million years ago, the most recent period of glaciation began. The whole planet became just a touch colder . . . more snow fell in the winter, less melted in the summer. In the northern climes, snow began to accumulate. As the snow grew deeper and deeper, its nature began to change: under the pressure of its own weight, crystals in the bottom of the snowpack began to deform and to turn into ice; further pressure then changed their molecular structure so that they became almost plastic. Where the ice had formed on a slope, gravity began to pull it downhill. The moving glaciers scoured away at the little valleys beneath them, over time turning them into the deep, U-shaped valleys we see today. Other glacial features include hanging valleys, aretes, horns, passes, and cirques. These glaciers—for which the park is named—all melted away a good 10,000 years ago.

Stage 4: The Little Ice Age, the present, and the future. The current glaciers in the park are the result of the Little Ice Age. Geologists argue about when it started, but it seems clear that these glaciers reached their greatest extent probably in the eighteenth century. They are now receding very quickly—this is the time to see them! Global climate change has been studied from data collected at these glaciers, and it is certainly an element in their disappearance. Blackfoot-Jackson, Grinnell, and Sperry are the largest of the glaciers today. Other factors affecting park geology today include the small but continual effects of wind and rain, freezing and thawing—all processes that tend to smooth out the rugged mountains. Slowly the peaks come down and the valleys are filled. Sometimes more sudden events dramatically change the landscape, such as avalanches and rock slides. In recent years an earthquake, centered on the Blackfeet Reservation, brought down a huge rock slide on Chief Mountain. Change is ongoing.

The Continental Divide also runs through Glacier National Park—the line separating watersheds flowing to the east from those flowing to the west. Look for Triple Divide Peak on your map—it's southwest of St. Mary at the end of the Cut Bank Creek drainage. This mountain marks the meeting of the Continental Divide with the Hudson Bay Divide, separating the park's waters into three: those which flow north and east to Hudson Bay and the Arctic Ocean; those flowing south and east into the Missouri, the Mississippi, and eventually the Caribbean; and those flowing west, out the Flathead and Columbia Rivers to the Pacific Ocean. The Continental Divide is also a significant weather maker: It stops the moisture from the Pacific with its wall of rock, so that more precipitation falls on the west side. The east side is drier and subject to the winds then rushing off the divide as they cool. The effects of these climatic differences are keenly visible in the park landscape—the west side supports lush forests, including a bit of true rain forest, while the east side is typified by open meadows and aspen groves.

Once you reach East Glacier, you'll be back on U.S. 2. This road is maintained year-round. As you head back west, though, you may find your vehicle battling the eastside winds! Train cars have been blown off the tracks in East Glacier—if the weather is like that, perhaps it's time to look for a hotel room! Most likely, though, you'll get a milder dose of what the Continental Divide regularly dishes up for the east side. Soon you'll top out at Marias Pass (see Marias Pass Memorial Square, above), and once you drop down to the west side those winds will likely vanish.

Between Marias Pass and West Glacier, you are following the path of the Middle Fork of the Flathead River. The Burlington Northern Railroad, successor to the Great Northern Railway that opened this area in the 1890s, shares this narrow corridor. Chances are you'll see more than one train wending its way up or down the pass. Extra "helper" engines are added to each train as it leaves Spokane, Washington, or Havre, Montana, to head into the mountains. As you drive through the Middle Fork, you'll notice snowsheds over the railroad tracks at certain places. These avalanche sheds slough huge amounts of snow off above the tracks so that trains can keep running in winter.

About 10 miles before West Glacier, you might keep your eyes out for Loneman Mountain, a double-topped mountain just across the river to the north. On its second summit sits Loneman Lookout, one of a network of fire lookouts once active in the park. These days most fire surveillance is done with small planes or helicopters, but these lookouts are still used when fire danger is high locally . . . and they make fascinating hike destinations.

The last few miles into West Glacier wind along a deep cut made by the Middle Fork of the Flathead River. The white water here draws kayakers and rafters . . .

look for their brightly colored clothing and boats. Often they "take out" at the West Glacier bridge—wet, but smiling!

With a little luck you'll be smiling too at the end of the day. And there's always more to come back and explore.

Glacier Park Scenic Boat Tours
Glacier Park Boat Company, P.O. Box 5262
Kalispell 59903
(406) 257-2426
www.montanaweb.com/gpboats

Cruise through the mountains on glacially carved lakes of blue-green . . . watch for wildlife on mountain slopes . . . see vistas that are not visible from roads . . . and learn more about Glacier National Park's history, geology, flora, and fauna. Glacier Park Boat Company invites you to cruise on Lake McDonald, St. Mary Lake, Two Medicine Lake, and Swiftcurrent and Josephine Lakes in the Many Glacier Valley. Each of the four locations offers several daily cruises that last from 45 minutes to 1½ hours. In conjunction with the boat ride, some cruises include National Park Service ranger-naturalist-guided walks to places such as Grinnell Glacier, St. Mary Falls, and Twin Falls. Boat trips can also be used as transportation to trails farther from the park roads. During peak season be sure to ask about sunset cruises on these spectacular mountain lakes.

Glacier Park Boat Company also offers small boat rentals. Please call to check on cost per hour and availability of canoes, kayaks, rowboats, or small motorboats at each location.

Adult fares for cruises run between $9.50 and $12.00, with children ages 4 through 12 riding for half price; children younger than age 4 ride free. Each location has its own schedule, opening in late May or early June and closing sometime after Labor Day. Glacier Park Boat Company has phone service during the summer months at Lake McDonald, (406) 888-5727; Many Glacier, (406) 732-4480; and St. Mary, (406) 732-4430. Don't miss the boat! Please allow yourself a good 10 minutes to park your car and walk to the boat dock.

Flathead Lake Scenic Drive

Flathead Lake is the largest natural freshwater lake west of the Mississippi, and peaks surround it—a combination that makes for scenery as striking as you'll find anywhere. Although the changes in landscape are not as dramatic as they are on the Going-to-the-Sun Road/U.S. Highway 2 loop, the ongoing change of perspective as you round the lake will continually surprise and please you. Sometimes the road runs close to the water's edge; sometimes it runs high through deep cuts made in the lakeshore bluffs. Parts of the valley are verdant and green, while others tend to be more open, windswept, and dry. The six units of Flathead Lake State Park—Wayfarers, Yellow Bay, Finley Point, Wild Horse Island, Big Arm, and West Shore (see the Outdoor Recreation chapter)—all offer opportunities to stop and do a little exploring. And various communities around Flathead Lake provide a wide range of services and points of interest.

The total distance around Flathead Lake is about 90 miles, and driving time (in good conditions in summer, minus time lost to any construction delays) is about 2½ hours. You'll probably want to plan on at least a half a day though, and why not more? Bring a camera—you'll want to make frequent stops to admire the views.

We could begin at any point, but let's begin in Bigfork since it's right on the water. Montana Highway 35 heads south toward Polson, rising and falling gently as it curves over the hills running down to the lake. Farther south the road will actually run right along Flathead Lake for some distance. You'll also drive through the famous cherry orchards and no doubt notice the many roadside stands along the way—if it's cherry season, it's time to stop!

As you enter Polson, Highway 35 joins U.S. Highway 93 at a T-intersection. Turning right will take you into the town itself; this might be a good opportunity to stretch a leg and take a break if you haven't already. The town offers a full range of services (see the Polson chapter) as well as the Polson-Flathead Historical Museum.

If you follow Seventh Avenue west out of town, signs will direct you to the Kerr Dam, about 8 miles below Polson. Completed in 1939, the Kerr Dam holds 1.1 million acre-feet of water at full pool; its construction converted Flathead Lake into a reservoir. Every year Kerr churns out more than one billion kilowatts of power. Montana Power Company pays rent to the confederated Salish-Kootenai tribes for use of the dam. In 1989, MPC dedicated a new vista overlook and recreation area here. The overlook provides a spectacular view of Kerr Dam, the Flathead River canyon, and MPC's power plant. The recreation area includes a boat launch, bathrooms, changing area, picnic tables, and drinking water.

Coming back to Polson, head north out of town on U.S. 93. Immediately after crossing over the Flathead River, you'll notice the high-and-dry hills southwest of Flathead Lake. As you climb the steep hill leaving town, this dry pocket will be left behind, but as you drive farther north look off to the west from time to time and you will see more open grassland. Variations in rainfall, slope, and soil can have marked effects on the landscape within very short distances.

Soon you'll see two fairly large islands in Flathead Lake—Wild Horse Island, which is part of Flathead Lake State Park, and Cromwell Island farther west, which is privately owned. Much romance surrounds Wild Horse Island, which is the home not only of a few wild horses but also bighorn sheep, deer, bald eagle, and the occasional black bear. One local legend says that Indians once used the island to hide their ponies from marauding tribes . . . but no one really knows if it's true. The horses that inhabit the island today are courtesy of the BLM's adopt-a-horse program. The bighorn sheep population is doing well, and some animals have occasionally been relocated to other places where sheep populations needed some bolstering.

Soon the road will sweep around Big Arm, treating driver and passengers to an eastward view of the islands and across the lake to the Mission Mountains. During the summer months the Mission Moun-

Insiders' Tip

Each season in the Northern Rockies has its own remarkable attributes. But summer and autumn offer the best times for hiking. By then heavy winter snowpack has finally melted, allowing access to the spectacular high country. Many locals prefer hiking during autumn. During this special time, crisp, clear days are common; aspen, birch, and larch display their golden hues; and the summer crowds are nowhere to be found.

tain Winery in Dayton opens a tasting room where visitors can sample select vintages. The vineyards are quite picturesque with their neat rows.

Continuing north on U.S. 93 toward Kalispell, the route passes through some huge road cuts in the bluffs along the western shore of Flathead Lake. Watch for the scenic pullout with its magnificent view—it's a good opportunity to stop for a few minutes and take photos. After you pass through the communities of Lakeside and Somers, look for the intersection of U.S. 93 with Montana Highway 82. Turn right—east toward Bigfork—here. This last stretch of road will take you through the open farmlands typical of the Flathead Valley. You'll pass once more over the Flathead River, this time flowing from the north into Flathead Lake. The slow-moving water in the river here creates excellent habitat for many birds, from migrating swans to bald eagles. You'll reach the junction with Montana Highway 35; a quick right turn and you'll be back to Bigfork in short order.

The Arts

The arts scene is remarkably healthy in the Flathead Valley. Let's face it, Kalispell, Montana, isn't on any-body's short list of art meccas, but it would be easy to spend several days (and several thousand dollars) just visiting the galleries in Kalispell, Bigfork, Whitefish, and Polson alone. At one time, of course, you would have expected to find only Western art in the studios and galleries around here, but that has changed re-markably quickly. Today many galleries in the area tend more toward the avant garde than the traditional, though you can easily find whatever you are looking for.

And that goes for theater, dance, and music, too.

The scenic grandeur that lures tourists to the Flathead Valley also lures permanent residents, and many of the recent settlers have brought with them a wide variety of tal-ents and interests that have fueled an artistic explosion over the past two decades. In-deed, given the valley's population base of fewer than 80,000, it is hard to conceive of the breadth of opportunities available here. But one look at the listings in this chapter will show that there is something for every interest, from foreign films to blues concerts to Western art.

In fact the Flathead Valley was ranked 52nd in the third edition of *The 100 Best Small Art Towns in America,* by John Villani (1998, John Muir Publications). Part of the reason for that is that most of the two million visitors a year to Glacier National Park pass through Kalispell and other Flathead communities and bring an influx of dollars into the local economy. During the summer months especially, that results in a healthy con-tribution to the arts through ticket purchases and actual art purchases.

Another part of the explanation is that Kalispell, Bigfork, and Whitefish have all de-veloped pride in their own artistic communities, so there is a hint of competition spurring each group to bigger and better things. An example of this can be found in the community-theater scene. The Whitefish Theatre Company (WTC) started in 1978, about the same time that the Flathead Valley Community College's drama department was closing its doors. The success of the WTC goaded Bigfork into tackling its own the-ater project, and the Bigfork Community Players were born. When Kalispell actors grew weary of the commute north or south to perform, the Flathead Valley Community The-ater was founded in the early 1990s, bringing the story full circle, as the new group is af-filiated with Flathead Valley Community College, which once again has a dynamic and energetic theater program.

And when the various towns of the Flathead are not trying to one-up each other, they are working together synergistically to create art that is greater than the sum of its di-verse parts, art that reflects the majesty of nature that is apparent everywhere here. An ex-ample is the Glacier Orchestra and Chorale, which draws members from across the Flathead Valley—from West Glacier to Polson—and sometimes beyond. Indeed, conduc-tor John Zoltek arrived from the Seattle area a few years ago and immediately sensed something special about the orchestra and the environs. "I have a very strong connection to nature," he said. "And so I am delighted to have this opportunity to work and live in the Flathead. Because of the beautiful land that surrounds the area, it is a prime location for beautiful music making."

There is plenty to do for the arts-minded. What follows is a listing of some of the best the valley has to offer in dance, music, art, and more. This summary is by no means complete, but includes a representative sampling from different communities and representing different styles. Do not expect to find every art gallery listed here. There are just too many of them, with a constantly changing lineup of exhibits, to be entirely inclusive. But it is easy to find additional galleries by stopping at any of those listed and asking where to go next. The Flathead Valley is tourist-friendly, and you won't have to look hard to find a helpful "native" who will point you in the right direction. This directory is just your starting point, not your final destination.

Museums and Art Centers

Bigfork Art & Cultural Center
525 Electric Avenue, Bigfork
(406) 837–6927

This community-run, nonprofit gallery exhibits artwork and crafts by local artists, with special showings in the summer. The gallery is open from April through December, with hours from 10:00 A.M. to 6:00 P.M. in the summer and slightly shorter in the spring and fall. In addition to the galleries, there is a year-round gift shop that features local artwork and various made-in-Montana crafts.

The Hockaday Museum of Art
Second Avenue East and Third Street
Kalispell
(406) 755–5268

This nonprofit gallery and museum is a longtime hub of the cultural scene in the Flathead. It could perhaps even be seen as

The Hockaday Museum of Art in Kalispell is a local treasure. Photo: courtesy of Hockaday Museum of Art

instrumental in developing a community spirit that has led to a range of artistic activities in the Flathead that go far beyond the Hockaday's offerings in the visual arts. Hugh Hockaday was an important figure in the area's arts community for more than 20 years, and when he died in 1968, the Flathead Valley Art Association, a group of artists who had just begun leasing the 1903 Carnegie Library building, decided to honor Hockaday by naming the new art center after him. A number of his art works are included in the permanent collection. Throughout the years, the Hockaday has brought a number of high-quality exhibits to the Flathead, including Deena des Rioux and her robotic portraiture; Tim Holmes, a sculptor who showed at the world-famous Hermitage in St. Petersburg, Russia; Russell Chatham, whose delicate watercolors depict the great wide-open spaces of Montana; Dale Chihuly, an internationally renowned glass sculptor; and Gary Schildt, a noted Western artist and member of the Blackfeet Tribe. Executive director Linda Engh-Grady oversees a program that also sponsors workshops with nationally known local artists such as Linda Tippets and Joe Abbrescia. There is a $5.00 admission charge, with discounts for students, seniors, and members. The Hockaday is open Monday through Wednesday, Friday, and Saturday from 10:00 A.M. to 6:00 P.M., Thursday from 10:00 A.M. to 8:00 P.M., and Sunday from noon to 4:00 P.M.

Museum of the Plains Indian
Junction of U.S. Highway 2 and
Montana Highway 89, Browning
(406) 338–2230

The museum offers a comprehensive collection of Blackfeet Indian tribal artifacts,

James Welch, Montana Author

As you travel through the Blackfeet Reservation, you drive through an area that has been inhabited for thousands of years. The Blackfeet Indians traversed the Old North Trail—which can still be traced in a few places where once thousands of dog-drawn travois made their way along the eastern front. Later the Blackfeet acquired horses and became known as the "raiders of the plains" for their fierce defense of their buffalo grounds. French trappers, Hudson's Bay Company traders, and Jesuit missionaries began to make their appearance as white civilization pushed westward. Smallpox and alcohol followed soon after, and eventually even the buffalo were lost. After such incredible changes, as well as those brought by the twentieth century, today the Blackfeet Nation numbers about 14,000 enrolled members, most of whom live on the Blackfeet Reservation.

James Welch is well-known for his novels about life among the Blackfeet and other northern plains tribes. Born in Montana of Blackfeet and Gros Ventre descent, he went to school on the Blackfeet and Fort Belknap Reservations. Later he studied writing and graduated from the University of Montana in Missoula, where he now lives. *Fools Crow* (1986), probably his best-known work, is set among the Blackfeet of the Two Medicine area in the 1870s, when white men are just beginning to influence the tribes significantly. It is probably the best reconstruction of precontact Blackfeet culture—or perhaps any precontact Indian world—ever written. Its protagonist, the young warrior Fools Crow, is born into the traditional world but will live to see it greatly changed.

Other works are set in contemporary times: two novels, *Winter in the Blood* (1974) and *The Death of Jim Loney* (1979), represent both hope and despair on the Highline—the high plains of Montana traversed by U.S. Highway 2. More recently, *The Indian Lawyer* (1991) spins the tale of a successful "Indian lawyer" in Helena, Montana, who decides to consider a bid for Congress. Welch's fiction speaks eloquently for those who find themselves still divided between two worlds.

Killing Custer: The Battle of the Little Bighorn and the Fate of the Plains Indians (1994) is a nonfiction account of that debacle that includes the Native American perspective. It originally grew out of work Welch did with director Paul Stekler for the PBS documentary "Last Stand at Little Bighorn," part of the American Experience series. As with his novels, here Welch provides a new depth to our knowledge of the past in his recapturing of Native American history. All these works are thoughtfully crafted pieces that will increase your appreciation for what was once buffalo country and the source of a very different way of life. Welch's latest titles are *Riding the Earthboy 40* (1998) and *The Heartsong of Charging Elk* (2000).

but it also has a collection of art by Native American artists and craftsmen, some of which is available for sale. The museum is open year-round; admission during the summer is $4.00 for adults and $1.00 for children ages 6 through 12. Please inquire about group rates. The museum is free during the winter season (October 1 through May 31).

The People's Center
53253 U.S. Highway 93, Pablo
(406) 883–5344

The cultural center focuses on the history of the Salish, Pend d'Oreille, and Kootenai Indian tribes, but also has exhibitions of Native American art. The facility includes a learning center, exhibit gallery, and gift shop, and interpretive, guided tours on the Flathead Reservation are offered.

Stumpton Art Studio
145 Central Avenue, Whitefish
(406) 862–9782
www.stumptonartstudio.org

Stumpton Art Studio is a grassroots, community-oriented, nonprofit visual arts center. It aims to provide a place where children and adults feel free and confident to express their inherent creative nature and learn about the world of art. In addition to workshops and lectures, there are exhibits by local artists and a variety of classes and camps offered year-round, including art treks up the Big Mountain in the summer. Painting, fiber arts, sketching, and sculpting all happen here—and don't forget to inquire about the Ceramics Annex.

Galleries

Abbrescia Fine Art and Pottery Studios
12 First Avenue West, Kalispell
(406) 755–6639
www.abbresciafineart.com

A gallery that carries the works of a Southwestern potter, a landscape oil painter, and a chain-saw artist, along with sculpture and historic etchings, might be considered somewhat eclectic, but in the case of the Abbrescia Studios, it's just a matter of keeping it in the family. Joe Abbrescia said the gallery opened in the early 1990s, when his family returned from an extended stay in Scottsdale, Arizona. "Essentially, this is our gallery, our studios and our showroom," he explained. "The gallery is mostly our own work. My wife, Sue Abbrescia, is a potter and sculptor. I'm a painter and sculptor, and our son, Tony, is a chain-saw wood carver. We have our studios in the back, and our showroom is in the front." Abbrescia's love of the genres also led the family to include a sampling of "early American illustrators such as Joseph Lynedecker and Howard Chandler Christy and etchings by Whistler, Zorn, and others," he said. Abbrescia, who is also an art restorer and appraiser, is renowned for his paintings of Glacier National Park and has done one-man shows in Venice, Boston, and elsewhere. His work, while very detailed, could almost be classified as impressionistic. Sue Abbrescia is noted nationally for her work making vessels, especially using a coil technique she adapted from traditional Southwestern methods.

Art Fusion
471 Electric Avenue, Bigfork
(406) 837–3526

Art Fusion features what owner Pamme Reed calls "eclectic contemporary art with the emphasis on fun." The gallery represents more than 60 Montana artists and has the most colorful display space anywhere in the art world. As you enter the gallery space, your attention will be drawn first to the floor, where a variety of brightly colored ceramics vie for your attention, then your eyes will turn to the walls, where playful art features both landscapes and portraits. Among the artists represented are Louise Lamontagne from St. Ignatius, who paints impressionistic landscapes; Rebecca Harrison of Kalispell, who is noted for her glassworks; Terry McGrath of East Glacier, whose richly colored photographs verge on the abstract; and Kirk Belding of Butte, who has a sampling of functional pottery with a bright and unusual trout motif. The gallery is open from 10:00 A.M. to 8:30 P.M. seven days a week, with somewhat shorter hours in the winter.

Artistic Touch
209 Central Avenue, Whitefish
(406) 862–4813

If you are looking for three-dimensional art, especially crafted items such as jewelry, metals, fiber, and ceramics, then by all means stop in and meet Mary Kay Huff, the owner-proprietor of Artistic Touch in Whitefish. She opened the shop in 1987 and displays her own work and that of a variety of other artists. "I look for things that are unusual, things you might not see in other places," she said. The emphasis is always on quality, with a large helping of local crafts and a smattering of fine art of regional distinction, especially metal sculpture. Mary Kay's adventurous spirit often brings a little something extra to the summerlong exhibits she puts up in the shop. "What we

Ken Bjorge at work in Bigfork. Photo: Buddy Mays, courtesy of Flathead Convention and Visitor Bureau

look for in shows is somebody whose work is interesting to begin with, and we ask them to do something they've always wanted to do for a show instead of just what they've been making money at." Examples of artists represented include potter Virginia Carter and Sarena Mann, who makes paper woman figures. Mary Kay herself specializes in silver- and gold-filled jewelry items. Artistic Touch is open from 10:00 A.M. to 5:00 P.M. Monday through Saturday and open on Sundays in the summer from 10:00 A.M. to 2:00 P.M.

Bjorge's Gallery
603 Electric Avenue, Bigfork
(406) 837-3839

When you ride down the hill into Bigfork Bay after turning off of Montana 35, one of the first structures that will catch your eye is Bjorge's Old Standard Gallery. Sculptor Ken Bjorge, along with his wife, Tammy, converted an old-time service station into a comfortable gallery and studio space. Then a few years ago, they built their home on top of the gallery, and the imposing three-story log structure is a perfect introduction to Bigfork's combination of artsiness and Western hospital-

ity. "This place is just magical—it really is—and there's room for even more artists in Bigfork," confides Bjorge, who gave up a career as a lawyer and law professor to move to Bigfork and start his midlife adventure as a wildlife and Old West sculptor. Bjorge's work is exhibited in various states of completion in the studio, and new work can be watched taking shape under the hand and knife of the sculptor. Bjorge does many commission pieces, and often monumental-size work, such as a pair of mountain lions, can be seen here before it is shipped to its final destination. The gallery, which is open from 10:00 A.M. to 8:00 P.M. seven days a week, also displays the paintings of Texan Oleg Stavrowsky and Montana artists Marnell Brown, Joe Ferrara, Jack Koonce, Linda Tippetts, and Brent Cotton.

Eric Thorsen Fine Art Gallery
547 Electric Avenue, Bigfork
(406) 837-4366

Oftentimes, it seems as though artists intentionally adopt an imposing or arrogant persona in order to keep themselves isolated from the demands of celebrity. Eric Thorsen is just the opposite—a painter who is so affable and charming it's a miracle he gets any work done at all in his studio and gallery when he'd rather obviously prefer to be chatting with the customers. "Our focus is on people coming in and seeing the process of creating sculpture," he said. Thorsen and his wife, Cyndy, opened the gallery in 1993, and it displays almost exclusively his own work, which has gained a worldwide reputation for excellence among wildlife-sculpture collectors. A public gallery is downstairs, and his studio is upstairs with several dozen works in progress scattered across a space that's perhaps 1,000 square feet. Every kind of wildlife imaginable is represented, whether it's bears, birds, or fish. In addition Thorsen is now exploring the artistic possibilities of the human form, and he is working on full-figure nudes as well as hands and heads. His naturalistic style is also gradually giving way to a more abstract work. Thorsen sells to collectors exclusively out of his gallery, sending the work worldwide. The gallery is open from 10:00 A.M. to 8:00 P.M. six days a week, with shorter hours on Sunday. During the winter the hours are also somewhat shorter.

The Gallery
6080 U.S. Highway 93 South, Whitefish
(406) 862–5569

One of the special pleasures of visiting a new place is trying to find the unlikely treasures, places that don't look like much from the outside but contain the pearl you've been looking for. The Gallery, south of Whitefish, is just such a place. On the outside it looks more like a carpenter's shop or a secondhand store. Just the unassuming name posted on a reader board above the entrance tells you that you have arrived at one of the Flathead's unique galleries. Owner Jessie Deats says that her motto is "to allow almost any local artist to display their art, at least one or two pictures." If you are hoping to make a discovery of an artist whose work is still affordable, this gallery is a perfect place to start. "We probably have 50 or 60 local artists, as well as prints from Bev Doolittle, Mark Ogle, and other better-known artists," says Deats. Among the local artists represented are John Atkin-

son of Whitefish, who does realistic Glacier Park landscapes; Gladys Pilch, who specializes in smaller scenics; and Taryl Bodily, who does futuristic work. You can also find chain-saw art, pottery, photography, and some sculpture. Most notable is the presence of oil painter Marvin Messing, whose surrealistic work is comparable to that of Salvador Dali. The only notable difference in their artistic accomplishments is that Dali painted at a time when surrealism was popular, but Messing says he paints from the heart, not to be popular. "He's a sweet old gentleman who studied at the Art Institute of Chicago, and we are the only gallery that carries his paintings," says Deats. "They are all original oils and often have religious themes." The Gallery is open 10:00 A.M. to 6:00 P.M. Tuesday through Saturday most of the year.

Glacier Gallery
1498 Montana Highway 35 East, Kalispell
(406) 752–4742
www.glaciergallery.com

One of the most extensive collections of Western art in Montana can be found right here in the Glacier Gallery. "We have paintings and bronzes from the early 1900s and the turn of the century," says manager Sandy Noble. The gallery is owned by Dr. Van Kirke Nelson, a noted art collector, and was opened in 1969. Today much of Nelson's extensive collection of Indian artifacts and Charles M. Russell memorabilia is on display periodically for their historical value. Old West paintings by such famed artists as Russell, Edgar S. Paxson, Frank Tenney Johnson, and Olaf Carl Seltzer are hung on the walls. There is also Southwestern art from Alfred Jacob Miller; an extensive collection of bronzes by Earle E. Heikka featuring pack trains and other Old West scenes; contemporary sculpture by Sherri Salari Sander, Tom Sander, and Frank Di Vita; and contemporary paintings by Charles Fritz, Gary Schildt, and Sheryl Bodily. In addition Glacier Gallery carries prints and a variety of hand-thrown pottery by four local potters. The gallery is open from 10:00 A.M. to 5:00 P.M. Monday through Saturday.

Linda Tippetts Fine Art
10 Somers Road, Somers
(406) 857–3110
www.tippettsart.com

Linda Tippetts is best known locally for winning $50,000 as the grand-prize winner in the 1992 Arts for the Parks contest for her painting "East Slope Tunnel on Going-to-the-Sun." That achievement certainly merits attention, but when you visit Tippetts' studio in Somers, you will discover that she has many more sides to her art. Yes she does mostly landscapes, but not always of Glacier Park. She is a "plein air" oil painter, which means she paints whatever she sees on her travels, and she travels plenty. You'll find work from Mexico, China, and Portugal in her studio, as well as scenes from across Montana. In addition she does nudes and figurals for a change of pace, although everything is very distinctively in her own broad-brushed, muscular impressionistic style. She built her studio and home in 1995, just off of U.S. 93 on an imposing hillside in Somers. She shows her paintings only by appointment to serious collectors. "The collector enjoys seeing the work in a home," Tippetts said. "It gives them a better feel for what they can do with the art in their own space."

Mark Ogle Studio
101 East Center, Kalispell
(406) 752–4217
www.markogle.com

Mark Ogle has established himself in recent years as one of the premier painters of America's national parks. He has won most of the top artistic awards in the Northwest and Canada, and he has frequently been among the top finishers in the National Parks Academy of the Arts annual painting competition. Glacier Park is his special love. "As the lower areas of the park see more visitors every year, it's refreshing to hike up where the air is thinner and the bears are free to romp around undisturbed," Ogle said. "We only see the tip of Glacier from the roads, and it's exciting to discover and paint some of the park's more remote regions. You find a different world up there, and it's a painter's paradise." He has also produced and sold oil paintings and prints of Yellowstone, Grand Teton, Yosemite, and Grand Canyon Parks, as well as parks in Alaska and elsewhere. His work is for sale exclusively in his own gallery, and even then it's hard for him to "keep in stock" since nearly 40 percent of his work is done on a commission basis. You can visit the studio and will frequently find Ogle at work on a new painting. He estimates he's painted more than 5,000 pieces, but he always has time to share his insights with visitors, and he's a noted raconteur with a love of not just art, but also the outdoors and the Western life.

Noice Studio and Gallery
127 Main Street, Kalispell
(406) 755–5321
www.noicestudioandgallery.com

Marshall Noice is typical of artists who are also gallery owners in the Flathead. He is accessible, voluble, and salable. You will find a wide selection of his work at his downtown Kalispell studio and gallery, ranging from naturalistic photography to abstract oil paintings. But more importantly, you will usually find him. That's one of the aspects of the Flathead art scene that is particularly rewarding for both the dedicated art collector and the curious tourist.

Noice has been photographing Glacier Park for more than 30 years, and that is perhaps what he is best known for. "My fine art photography is black and white," Noice notes. "That probably stems from the summer of 1977 when I was fortunate enough to spend the summer working with (pioneering landscape photographer) Ansel Adams in California. When I want color I want more of it than photography can give me, and that's why my paintings and pastels tend to be very bold. If I'm interested in a literal image, nothing does it better than a photograph, so painting in a literal fashion doesn't capture my imagination." The gallery also carries original work by about 20 or more Montana artists, including sculpture and paintings by such noted contemporary artists as Rudy Autio, Sheila Myles, Charlie Davis, Dave Shaner, and Michael Jones. There is also a sampling of Native American work.

The Northwest Ballet Company has long been headed up by Carol Jakes (center). Photo: Trevon Baker

"We get people who are used to seeing art in San Francisco and Seattle and then are surprised to see the same kind of work here," said Noice's wife and partner, Jackie.

Sandpiper Gallery
2 First Avenue East, Polson
(406) 883–5956

The Sandpiper is a fine-arts nonprofit corporation. The gallery features many wonderful displays, which rotate once or twice a month. Space has been devoted to well-known local artists such as watercolorists Barbara Mellblom and Karen Leigh as well as to school-age artists, photographers, potters, woodworkers, and more. The gallery is open Monday through Thursday from 11:00 A.M. to 4:00 P.M. and Friday and Saturday from 11:00 A.M. to 3:00 P.M.

Dance

Northwest Ballet Company
1411 First Avenue West, Kalispell
(406) 755–0760

The Northwest Ballet Co. is best known for their annual holiday presentation of "The Nutcracker" each Christmas season at the Bigfork Center for the Performing Arts. Carol Jakes, artistic director of the Northwest Ballet Company and the Northwest Ballet School in Kalispell, has choreographed and directed the show annually since the late 1970s in the Flathead Valley. The ballet company and school also perform other concerts during the year featuring classical ballet, ballroom dancing, and Broadway musical numbers. The ballet company is affiliated with the Dance Art Center run by Jakes.

Film

Whitefish Film Society
509 East Sixth Street, Whitefish
(406) 862–5994

The Whitefish Film Society is only a few years old but has already taken root as a beloved community institution. Under the directorship of Jill Zignego, the society has developed a mission "to bring alternative cinema to the Flathead Valley, especially foreign films and American independents," she said. Among titles that have been screened here are *The Full Monty*, *Mrs. Brown*, *Life is Beautiful (La Vita e Bella)*, and *Atanarjuat (The Fast Runner)*. Call for time and place of showing.

Music

Flathead Community Concerts Association
P.O. Box 75, West Glacier 59936
(406) 888–5033

When it was started several decades ago, the Flathead Community Concert series was pretty much the only top-name entertainment coming to the valley. Today there are many more options, but the Community Concert Series has continued to be popular because of the quality of the entertainment provided. A membership drive is held in April for the entire series, but sometimes individual concerts have some room left over. Write to the address above for season ticket information, or call ahead to see if any tickets will be available at the door for particular shows. Performers in the series have included the New York Theatre Ballet performing "The Nutcracker," the Aspen Wind Quintet, the Welsh Male Choir, and harpist Carol McLaughlin.

Flathead Valley Blues Society
P.O. Box 219, Somers 59932
(406) 857–3119

Steve Kelley, the founder and president of the Flathead Valley Blues Society, is better known 'round these parts as Big Daddy. And when Big Daddy plays, people listen. He's the leader of a band called Big Daddy and the Blue Notes and is frequently heard as opening act for major blues shows passing through the valley. Most of the major blues concerts these days are actually sponsored by the Blues Society, with as many as seven concerts a year bringing top names in Chicago blues and other blues genres to the valley. "There's a dual purpose to the Blues Society," Kelley said. "To perpetuate and support blues music, which is a true American art form, and also to provide alternative live music entertainment." Some of the top names to appear here include blues harp player Mark Hummel and Chicago blues giant Jimmy Rogers, as well as Andrew "Junior Boy" Jones, Larry Garner, and Coco Montoya.

Flathead Valley Jazz Society
Glacier Jazz Stampede
1705 East Second Street, Whitefish
(406) 862–3814

The Flathead Valley Jazz Society sponsors concerts and jazz parties throughout the year, bringing regional and local entertainment to the fore. But since 1994 the society has been best known for the Glacier Jazz Stampede, which has rapidly grown into one of the valley's most anticipated arts events each year. The Stampede, which is held in the early fall, is a traditional jazz festival, and something more. It draws some of the top names in the business, such as the Rhythm Rascals from Disney World in Orlando, Florida, Blue Street Jazz Band from Fresno, California, and the Uptown Lowdown Jazz Band from Seattle, Washington, along with local groups such as the Don Lawrence Orchestra. Already the largest event of its kind in western Montana, it counts on local participation as well as the hundreds of jazz fans who travel from festival to festival in search of their favorite music. In addition to Dixieland the festival always features ragtime music and has also included Latin jazz as well as the Big Band sound and modern jazz. The musicians perform on a rotating basis at four or five venues, usually including the Eagles Club and Elks Lodge.

Folkshop Music Series
221 U.S. Highway 93 South, Ronan
(406) 676–5333, (800) 984–FOLK

Folkshop Productions has been presenting concerts in the Mission Valley for more than 10 years, and it has gained a reputation for excellence as well as for doing good works. "We were looking for a way to raise money for disabled employment, and this is the best fund-raiser we have ever had," said Chas Cantlon, executive director of the Folkshops. Local businesses sponsor the concerts by covering the costs, so every ticket purchased goes directly toward the Folkshop mission of hiring the disabled. Among the many popular shows have been appearances by singer-songwriter Greg Brown, bluesman Spencer Bohren, folksinger Peter Ostroushko, and lots of bluegrass performers, such as Special Consensus and Vassar Clements. The Folkshop series has also sponsored modern-dance performances by the nationally renowned Ririe-Woodbury Dance Company as well as other repertory groups.

Glacier Orchestra and Chorale
P.O. Box 2491, Kalispell 59903
(406) 257–3241
www.glacierorchestrachorale.org

This group was one of 12 orchestras honored nationally by the American Society of Composers, Authors and Publishers for excellence in programming of contemporary music. John Zoltek took over as conductor a few years ago, and his dynamic mastery of difficult music has helped turn the orchestra into a showcase of fine talent. There are also frequent guest performers such as violin virtuoso Eugene Fodor or renowned composer and pianist (as well as Montana native) Philip Aaberg. The orchestra and chorale generally perform five concerts each season, starting in October, on through April. Each concert of the season is performed twice, on Saturday at Central School auditorium in Whitefish and on Sunday at Flathead High School auditorium in Kalispell. Get there early not just to guarantee a seat, but also because Zoltek leads most shows with a preview lecture 45 minutes before the concert. The holiday concerts in December are usually sellouts, so plan to buy tickets early. The orchestra is also the parent body of the Glacier Youth Orchestra & Glacier Children's Choir, which perform throughout the school year. Shauneen Garner conducts the Glacier Chorale and the children's choir.

Nordicfest
P.O. Box 791, Libby 59923
(406) 293–6430, (800) 785–6541

Every September the town of Libby in Lincoln County turns Scandinavian for the second weekend of the month. Nordicfest is a celebration of local and international culture. J. Neils came to the area from Wisconsin at the turn of the century to start a lumber mill. He brought with him many Scandinavian loggers and their families, and both logging and Nordic roots are remembered during the festival, which features a variety of musical and theatrical events as well as crafts and ethnic foods. A regular performer at the festival is the Don Lawrence Orchestra, the prominent Big Band based in Kalispell. Other performers over the years have been accordionist Myron Floren and other top names from *The Lawrence Welk Show*. There is also continuous free outdoor entertainment at the bandshell during the daytime.

Riverbend Concert Series
P.O. Box 237, Bigfork 59911
(406) 837–5888

If you'd like to enjoy a musical experience and still remain out-of-doors, you can't do better than the Riverbend Concert Series, which is held on Sunday evenings in Bigfork's Everit Sliter Memorial Park every summer from June through August. Musicians range from well-known local acts such as the Don Lawrence Orchestra to classical guitarist Stuart Weber. Tickets are available at the entrance. In case of rain, the concerts move to the Bigfork Elementary School gym.

Wooden Music
P.O. Box 630, Bigfork 59911
(406) 837–5795

Wooden Music got started in 1992 when Whitefish resident and finger-style guitarist Larry Pattis decided he couldn't live without seeing more of the acoustic music he loved. He scheduled appearances by Harvey Reid, Chuck Pyle, Greg Brown, and many others. The past several years, in the wake of Pattis's departure to Salt Lake City, however, Wooden Music has changed from a one-man show to a one-woman show and is now run by Susan Morrow of Bigfork. The concerts, held at various venues in the valley, remain of the highest caliber, featuring names such as Greg Brown, John Gorka, Cosy Sheridan, and the Drum Brothers.

Theater

Bigfork Community Players
P.O. Box 23, Bigfork 59911
(406) 837-1530

The Bigfork Community Players perform three or four plays every year from the late fall to the spring. In addition to enthusiastic casts, the plays boast of being produced in the Bigfork Center for the Performing Arts, where every one of the 450 or so seats is a good one. Plays performed include the female version of *The Odd Couple, On Golden Pond,* Woody Allen's *Play It Again Sam, Crimes of the Heart,* and Tennessee Williams' *Cat on a Hot Tin Roof.* A new addition to the offerings is the annual Montana Community Theater Festival, held in the spring each year, featuring as many companies as possible from around the state. The Players have also recently added a slate of children's theater workshops and productions such as *Once on This Island, Jr.* to their calendar.

Bigfork Summer Playhouse
P.O. Box 456, Bigfork 59911
(406) 837-4886
www.bigforksummerplayhouse.com

Every summer the Bigfork Center for the Performing Arts becomes the Bigfork Summer Playhouse as actors from across the United States come together to put on musicals and comedies. The Bigfork Summer Playhouse was begun in 1960 and has provided a training ground for hundreds of aspiring theatrical performers, technicians, and musicians. It has been under the direction of owners Don and Jude Thomson since 1971. The playhouse offers four musicals and a farce every summer, and more than 3,000 people from throughout the United States apply to join the company each year. Expect a variety of musicals and musical comedies such as *The Will Rogers Follies, Grease, Nunsense,* or *Greater Tuna.* Tickets are cheaper for performances before July 4 or if purchased at the beginning of the season. The box office opens about the middle of May. Starting then you can purchase tickets by telephone, mail, or in person. Discounts are available for groups. There are no performances on Sundays.

Flathead Valley Community Theater
777 Grandview Drive, Kalispell
(406) 756-3906

The community college has also gotten into the act the past few years—theatrically, that is. Joe Legate, the head of the theater department, has been instrumental in reshaping a theater program that was quite active in the 1970s but eventually went into hiatus. Legate arrived in Kalispell in 1992 from North Dakota, where he had spent several years teaching at Dickinson State University. He has also worked in theater programs at Clemson University, the University of Southern Mississippi, and the State University of New York. Though the theatrical program draws heavily from the students and faculty at the college, many of the shows use other members of the community as well. Look for a broad variety of shows, from pure farce to high drama. Recent offerings include *Strange Snow* and *Pump Boys and Dinettes* as well as student-directed plays.

The Port Polson Players
P.O. Box 1152, Polson 59860
(406) 883-4691

The Port Polson Players offer professional summer-stock theater in the recently renovated Clubhouse Theater in the Polson City Golf Course at Boettcher Park on Flathead Lake. The company was begun in 1976 by Larry and Pat Barsness, who also started the Virginia City Players, in

A scene from Little Shop of Horrors, *performed by the Whitefish Theatre Company.*

Photo: courtesy of Whitefish Theatre Company

Virginia City, Montana, in 1948. The Polson group was purchased by Neal and Karen Lewing in 1983 and they have run it successfully ever since, adding a year-round community-theater schedule to what started as just a summer-stock company. The larger-scale community-theater offerings are usually presented at the Polson High School auditorium. Among the titles presented have been *Fiddler on the Roof, Oklahoma, The Miracle Worker, The Glass Menagerie, Peach Pie Reunion, Tonight on Wild Horse Island,* and *Who Gets the Lake Place?* The Lewings also write a children's show every year, including adaptations such as *Sleeping Beauty* and original titles such as *Fortune's Fables.* The box office can be reached at (406) 883-9212 from June through September only.

Whitefish Theatre Company
1 Central Avenue, Whitefish
(406) 862-5371
www.whitefishtheatreco.org

This is the oldest continuing community theater group in the Flathead Valley, performing since the mid-1970s. The company prides itself on diverse productions including dramas, such as *All My Sons;* musicals, such as *The Music Man;* classics, such as *A Midsummer Night's Dream;* family shows, such as *A Christmas Carol;* and comedies, such as *Lost in Yonkers.* Now installed at the new I.A. O'Shaughnessy Cultural Arts Cen-

ter, the Whitefish Theatre Company also sponsors performances of modern dance and music from around the world.

Venues

Bigfork Center for the Performing Arts
526 Electric Avenue, Bigfork
(406) 837-4886

This 450-seat facility in Bigfork provides year-round entertainment. May through August, the Bigfork Summer Playhouse offers musical repertory theater, while at other times throughout the year, it is home to productions by the Bigfork Community Players, the Northwest Ballet, and many other groups. The playhouse is noted for its comfort and for the great view from any of the seats.

I.A. O'Shaughnessy Cultural Arts Center
1 Central Avenue, Whitefish
(406) 862-5371

The people of Whitefish are noted for giving generously to community projects, and during a several-year campaign, funds were raised to build a new center for the performing arts as well as a nearby library building. The I.A. O'Shaughnessy Cultural Arts Center includes a 300-seat theater facility, which had its grand opening on July 4, 1998. The Whitefish Theatre Company holds a long-term lease on the building and is now focusing its schedule on the thrust stage, which has seating on three sides, plus a balcony. Concerts, dance, and other theatrical presentations will also be booked into the facility year-round. The seating can also be pushed back to accommodate other presentations, such as the annual Halloween haunted-house fund-raiser.

Literary Arts

Authors of the Flathead
Flathead River Writers Conference
P.O. Box 7711, Kalispell 59904
(406) 881-4066

The Authors of the Flathead group has been meeting for more than 10 years and has just fewer than 100 members. The group conducts a craft-of-writing workshop or a speaker's meeting on most Monday nights. A recording at (406) 881-4066 has details on times, locations, and each week's topic, as well as other upcoming activities. Each year the group holds its annual Flathead River Writers Conference in early October at the Grouse Mountain Lodge in Whitefish. "The conference is getting an excellent reputation in writing circles from the Midwest to California and Canada," said conference spokesman Jake How.

The conference features a variety of writers, editors, and agents. Guests have included Jack Sowards, author of thousands of television episodes and movie screenplays, including *Star Trek II: The Wrath of Khan,* and Steve Chapple, a Livingston, Montana, author, who is noted for his book *Confessions of an Eco-Redneck* as well as countless magazine articles. The conference always includes editors or publishers who can help see new writers through the nuts and bolts of publishing. "The conference remains the most affordable of its kind in the northwest United States," said How. "The two days are crammed with speakers, panel discussions, and one-on-one workshops."

Yellow Bay Writers' Workshop
Yellow Bay Biological Research Station
311 Bio Station Lane (mile marker 17,
Montana Highway 35), Yellow Bay
(406) 254-2544

The annual Yellow Bay Writers' Workshop is held about the second week of August every year at the University of Montana's biological research station on Flathead Lake. It provides a thoughtful getaway at a scenic location in the company of other writers. The workshop faculty generally features four top writers, in addition to several special guests and readings. Previous faculty members have included humorist Ian Frazier, novelist Ron Hansen, naturalist Gary Nabhan, and Kalispell's own David Long, a noted novelist and short-story writer. Special guests include editors and agents talking about the business of writing. Nonpartic-

ipants of the workshops may still attend readings and lectures throughout the week for a nominal fee per session. For a schedule, send a stamped, self-addressed envelope to the Center for Continuing Education, The University of Montana, Missoula, MT 59812, or call the phone number listed. Participants in the workshop are selected after they submit a manuscript sample. Tuition and residency fees add up to more than $800.

Arts and Crafts

Arts in the Park
P.O. Box 83, Kalispell 59903
(406) 755-5268

Ever consider doing your Christmas shopping in July? You can get it all out of the way at the popular Arts in the Park festival held the last weekend in July at Kalispell's Depot Park (located at the intersection of U.S. 93 and Center Street). The festival is a fund-raiser for the Hockaday Museum of Art and has been held ever since the museum was founded in 1968. It calls itself the oldest and best juried art fair in Montana. At the very least it is a darn good time, regularly attracting as many as 10,000 people. More than 90 artists and artisans exhibit works every year in numerous media such as painting, sculpture, pastel, photography, glass, jewelry, pottery, ceramics, weaving, wood carving, leather, metal, and more. A few artists will also be on hand to demonstrate how they go about making their creations, and there are the usual generous helpings of musical entertainment and food that make these arts and crafts fairs so popular.

Bigfork Festival of the Arts
P.O. Box 237, Bigfork 59911
(406) 837-5888

The Bigfork Festival of the Arts, which is held the first weekend in August every year, features more than 70 artists, including some from as far away as Oregon, Washington, and California. Booths feature everything from paintings, prints, jewelry, stained glass, and pottery to

The Festival of the Arts in Bigfork attracts quite a crowd. Photo: Carl Wells, courtesy of Flathead Convention and Visitor Bureau

wooden toys, wearable art, and baskets. There are also a variety of food booths, including huckleberry milk shakes, German barbecue, and snow cones, as well as the usual hamburgers and hot dogs. Bigfork's main business street, Electric Avenue, is converted into a boardwalk for the festival, with opportunities for shopping both in the booths and in local shops, which sell everything from books to antiques to a wide variety of artworks. Musical performances throughout the day also provide entertainment, and there are activities for children at various locations.

Whitefish Arts Festival
P.O. Box 131, Whitefish 59937
(406) 862–5875

The Whitefish Arts Festival, which is held on the first weekend in July, has been held for about 20 years, and it never disappoints. The event is a feast both for the eyes and for the palate, featuring 80 artists from the Flathead Valley and beyond, as well as food vendors, local musicians and entertainers, and other fun. Up for sale will be every variety imaginable of paintings, woodcraft, pottery, original clothing, and other handicrafts. The festival is held on the Central School lawn in downtown Whitefish and is a fund-raiser for the Cross Currents Christian School, which can be reached at the number listed above. Admission is free.

Antiques

Postcard-perfect scenery, soul-satisfying outdoor recreational activities, and world-class golf greens all draw visitors to the Flathead Valley, but this corner of Montana yields another, perhaps unexpected, attraction. It is also known as the antiquing mecca of western Montana. From Bigfork and Somers on Flathead Lake north to Whitefish and on to Hungry Horse, you can find dozens of antiques malls and shops—at last count they numbered about 30, a fairly high number for a county with a population of just 73,000. Most antiques stores here keep the doors open year-round for those of us who search out the antiques experience no matter where we travel or what month of the year it is.

A logical way to antique the Flathead is to do a loop, beginning in Bigfork on Montana Highway 35, then crossing Montana Highway 82 (known locally as the Somers cut-off road). At its junction with U.S. Highway 93, turn south and proceed past Somers to visit one of the listings there. Then do a short backtrack up U.S. 93 and proceed north into Kalispell. (If you begin in Somers, reverse the process.)

Kalispell has the highest concentration of antiques stores. You'll want to plan extra time there to enjoy the pickings. Although space constraints limit this chapter to my top spots, be sure to visit other local antiques stores for more great "finds" as time allows. Many are interspersed along the way.

The listings here give a representative taste of what the Flathead Valley has to offer and include contact information, days of business, and a general overview of what you might find. It's a good idea to call ahead to make sure the business you want to visit is open, although the beautiful drive to any of these locations may be worth a trip in itself. Generally owners of the Flathead Valley's antiques stores are happy to open by

Hand-built furniture and home-decor items from recycled wood are sold at Old Town Antiques.
Photo: Eileen Gallagher

appointment if you are looking for something special and cannot visit during regular business hours. The top antiques stores are not rated numerically as to which are the best of the best, but are listed by location on the antiquing loop. I hope you enjoy your antiques tour!

Architectural Innovations
7975 Montana Highway 35, Bigfork
(406) 837-2328, (406) 837-2334
Telephone for e-mail address

Looking for a place to retire, Margrit Matter chose Bigfork after a vacation visit in 1991. Instead of basking in retirement, however, she finds herself thriving on running a busy antiques store and interior-design center in Bigfork, which she has called Architectural Innovations.

Established in summer 1998, the showroom contains Margrit's discerning Old World Antiques furniture line, composed of European antiques dating from the late 1700s through the early 1900s. Her store is a little out of the ordinary for this corner of the country. From her West Coast ties to the construction and remodeling industry, in which she worked before relocating here, she is able to bring in fine imported pieces.

Besides being originals, furniture selected for her store must still function properly and be in excellent condition, she says. Here you might find a pine piece from the former Czechoslovakia, an oak armoire from England or Belgium, or a carved bed of French walnut or cherry. You'll discover other quality pieces—hutches, wardrobes, dressers, settees, tables, desks, and accessories. Look also for salvaged architectural details and original European and American art. New to Architectural Innovations is a selection of beautiful European crystal from the former Czechoslovakia.

Margrit's home-design center houses several rooms featuring specialty items for your home. The electrical room highlights antique light fixtures and lamps; the plumbing room features an unusual variety of sinks—handpainted, granite, handblown glass, and copper. The kitchen showcases cabinets, sinks, faucets, knobs, and other hardware. In the tile room you will find a variety of floor tiles, from Mexican Saltillo to slate. Upstairs you can find

Insiders' Tip
Several of the antiques dealers in this area also maintain sites on the Internet. One such site belongs to a dealer at Timeless Treasures, who offers American dinnerware, glassware, and pottery at www.homegrown antiques.com.

wallpapers, fabrics, and carpet. Margrit's goal is for shoppers to find everything in-house. If a customer wants to mix new furniture with old, she offers new locally handcrafted pieces in a variety of woods.

The store is open seven days a week during summer. Off-season it is open Monday through Saturday and closed Sundays.

The Osprey Nest Antiques
6090 U.S. Highway 93 South, Somers
(406) 857-3714
Telephone for e-mail address

Look for a couple of osprey nests on tall platforms just off the highway approximately 2.8 miles north of Lakeside. They will signal your arrival at Osprey Nest Antiques. Here a huge red barn built in the late 1890s is settled comfortably on a low hill, sharing well-kept grounds with an old log cabin. Reminiscent of a New England country inn, the barn, with its wide porches and wicker furniture, beckons you to explore the more than 6,000 square feet of antiques housed within.

The ceiling, with its exposed wood rafters, log posts, and rough-paneled walls, gives the rambling building a cozy warmth. Charming displays filled with treasures from the past seem to trans-

Old drapery panels are recycled into colorful pillows at Old Town Antiques. Photo: Eileen Gallagher

port you into someone's home from days gone by.

Owner Karen Nagelhus, who established the business in 1988, has a good selection of oak, pine, and walnut furniture. You may find a harvest table or other country pine piece. Or you might come across Mission oak furniture, such as a 6-foot pine sawbuck table, circa 1840s.

The loft has the flavor of an old Adirondack cabin, complete with camp blankets, rugs, and early Adirondack accessory pieces. Karen's favorite is a gathering basket.

Expect to see glassware, kitchen utensils, stoneware, jewelry, tools, and Western memorabilia. You will run across a great selection of sterling-silver hollowware, lace and linens, and many primitive pieces. The library room has a fine collection of out-of-print books, as well as children's books.

Current favorites include the heaviest piece ever acquired by the shop: a 6-foot-by-6-foot oak icebox! Going outside her usual interests, Karen has recently acquired an original 1926 Josephine Baker poster; at the same time, a turn-of-the-twentieth-century Wooten rolltop desk is waiting here to find its future home.

While visiting you may see Karen creating her beaded bracelets, a newer item the store sells. Made from old trade beads from the early eighteenth and nineteenth century, glass beads, semiprecious stones, and sterling, these bracelets are one of a kind. Each signature piece is an attractive blend of color and texture. The response has been overwhelming, Karen says. Customers often buy the bracelets before she is finished making them.

The Osprey Nest was photographed by *Architectural Digest* magazine in 1991. *Architectural Digest* says, "The Osprey Nest is the best place in the valley for furniture."

The Osprey Nest is open year-round seven days a week.

Somers Antiques
210 Montana Highway 82, Kalispell
(406) 857–3234

At the intersection of U.S. Highway 93 and Montana Highway 82, look for the large signs advertising the Somers Antiques store. Go east of U.S. 93 on Mon-

tana 82. As you enter the yard, you pass by weathered furniture and bicycles. Miscellaneous old tables, chairs, cupboards, and iron headboards line the long porch. As you venture inside you are greeted by 6,000 square feet of antiques and collectibles displayed in a mercantile-type atmosphere. Crammed with items from a bygone era, this store will yield up everything from blanket chests to cupboards, pine tables to primitive wood benches, and ice-cream-parlor chairs to Coca-Cola soda-pop machines.

Owners Larry and Carol Ask, collectors themselves for about 25 years, offer several specialties at Somers Antiques. If you are looking for oak or pine, they provide a large selection of refinished furniture. The store is full of hundreds of old toys (some from Larry's personal collection), pedal cars, old bicycles, tools, and tins. Sporting paraphernalia, such as old fishing rods and golf clubs, mingles with other collectibles. You can find advertising signs, a piece of Western memorabilia, and lodge and cabin decor items. You might spot a handmade twig shelf, an old canoe converted into a bookshelf, or a reclining chair upholstered in cowhide.

"We usually have a good selection of old carpenter's tool chests," Larry says, "which work well for coffee tables."

Something you may not expect is a variety of Victorian-style lamps. Some of the floor lamps are old, while the table lamps are reproductions. Fringed and beaded shades, despite being new, impart a vintage look.

Somers Antiques is open year-round seven days a week in summer, from June to Labor Day. During winter the store opens at noon five or six days a week, but the schedule is flexible, so please call before you set out.

Southside Consignment Center and Antique Store
2699 U.S. Highway 93 South, Kalispell
(406) 756–8526

Fourteen antiques dealers and hundreds of consigners keep this 6,000-square-foot store south of Kalispell stocked with collectibles and antiques.

Owned by Donna Kouns, the rambling store offers a wide assortment of items. A stroll through here might turn up an old baker's table, a drop-leaf table, or a variety of hutches and dressers. You'll see lots of kitchen kettles, crockery, and old utensils. If you collect teacups, you may find a new favorite. Sterling-silver pieces, flatware, and rhinestone and antique jewelry add their sparkle to the mix. Old toys and books are interspersed among furniture and accessories. You might run across Western memorabilia, such as a branding iron or lariat.

Donna's favorite piece is a cast-iron wood cook stove with blue enamel, manufactured by Windsor.

At Southside Consignment goods can be viewed—and carted home with you—year-round Tuesday through Saturday. The store closes Sunday and Monday.

Timeless Treasures Antiques & Collectibles Mall
124 Main Street, Kalispell
(406) 752–4659

An attractive window display will charm you into visiting Timeless Treasures antiques store, easy to locate on Main Street (U.S. Highway 93). Old music from the 1950s, '60s, and '70s played on an old-fashioned record player greets you. Take a trip down music's memory lane with such greats as Frank Sinatra, Lena Horn, Billie Holiday, Johnny Mathis, and Simon and Garfunkel.

Diversity is the key to this 2,000-square-foot shop, says Linda Heim, who owns the business with husband Jim. The store is host for 31 dealers to showcase their wares. Many dealers focus on specialty items and either own their own antiques stores or have booths in other local antiques malls, as well.

A good collection of estate jewelry and costume jewelry, as well as hard-to-find books, are just some of the items you can expect to find at Timeless Treasures. Glassware, including Fenton and Depression glass and American-made pottery and dinnerware, is available here. Collectible cars and John Deere toys mingle with reproduction pedal cars. Old dolls and Victorian-style lamps with beaded and fringed shades add a touch of yesteryear.

Besides the specialty goods of the dealers, you are likely to find primitive kitchen items and furniture as well, Linda says. Or you might spot that rare Vaseline glass pickle jar with castor. Linda's favorite item is a beautiful black Victorian purse with a mauve bird-and-flower design.

A trip below to the downstairs might net you a medicine cabinet made from an old church window or a charming table with barley-twist legs.

Timeless Treasures is a pleasant stop and stays open year-round seven days a week.

Kalispell Antiques Market
48 Main Street, Kalispell
(406) 257–2800

Up the street on the corner of First and Main is a must-stop antiques mall at Opera House Square. Located in the historic opera-house building, the mall is downstairs, tucked under a spacious Western clothing store. The market sprawls across 10,000 square feet, making it the Flathead Valley's largest antiques mall, where 35 dealers display their merchandise. Proprietors are brother and sister Lee and JoAnn Eslick.

Since every square inch bursts with interesting items to look at, give yourself plenty of time to wend your way through three long rooms with aisles of booths.

The store features a wide selection of antiques and collectibles reference books, if you are looking for antiques guides.

Roseville pottery has long been a specialty at the Kalispell Antiques Market, with quite a bit of Fenton glassware also for sale. The market also boasts one of the best selections of vintage rhinestone jewelry in the valley. Look here for handmade primitive furniture and decorator items, which might include a pie safe with punched tin doors.

A large section of Western Americana books can be perused here. Depending on availability, you might run across books by noted Montana authors A. B. Guthrie, J. W. Schultz, and Frank Linderman. Or you might spot an old Hileman Glacier Park photo.

Western memorabilia and lodge decor items come in but go out quickly, since they remain ever popular in the Flathead, as do old hunting and fishing sporting goods.

Adding to the mix are original oak pieces, many from the late 1800s to early 1900s. Antique oak furniture might include a sideboard, buffet, dining table with chairs, or glass-fronted bookcase.

Other interesting collectibles range from old linens to vintage paper goods and an extensive collection of old and new Hummel figurines. JoAnn's favorite item in the store is an apartment-size oak ice box, manufactured by Garland.

She is seeing some current interest in the Art Deco look. "We have quite an increase in Art Deco collectibles," she says, "whether lighting or textiles."

The market welcomes visitors year-round seven days a week.

Angel Consignment
1420 Montana Highway 35, No. 103, Kalispell
(406) 752–1342

Go north to the intersection of Idaho (U.S. Highway 2) and Main (U.S. Highway 93) and take a right. Drive east just past the Snappy Sport Senter and take a right at the Square One shopping center.

At Angel Consignment owner Von Hines has filled her 2,700-square-foot space with old and not-so-old pieces. Von takes pride in the fact that she carries only solid-wood furniture, no pressed wood. Here the selection includes cherry, mahogany, oak, maple, walnut, cottonwood, and ash. She carries some solid-wood reproduction pieces, too. Spicing up the mix are a few rustic pieces, such as an old barnwood cabinet with mirror.

Greeting you as you shop from their birdcages are canaries and cockatiels. Von likes to have them around because they are great for "conversation and they keep the little kids busy," she says.

At Angel Consignment you might find an antique English gossip bench, or an antique oak spring rocker sporting its original springs and wheels. The store has a good selection of old library tables and secretaries. Or you might discover a 1920s Haywood Wakefield dining table with four chairs, a sheet music cabinet, or an old Hoosier cabinet with metal countertop and green glass knobs.

Most of the floor lamps are antiques. Von also carries some Roseville pottery. Artwork is either original oils or watercolors or good quality prints, she notes.

Von's favorite piece is an oak buffet from the 1910s or 1920s with ornately carved square feet. Its arched mirror reflects beveled glass, and the pulls are original. "Most of the old stuff all had the beveled glass," she points out.

Stop by and visit year-round Monday through Saturday, or Sunday afternoon.

Stageline Antiques
2510 Whitefish Stage Road, Kalispell
(406) 755–1044
www.stagelineantiques.com

Go back to U.S. Highway 93; turn north and drive out of Kalispell. After you cross West Reserve, continue driving north until you come to milepost 118. Turn east onto Tronstad Road. Drive to its intersection with Whitefish Stage Road, turn south, and go approximately ⅛ mile to Stageline Antiques on the west side of the road.

This pleasant country setting was made for a country store, and that's exactly what owners Bob and Chris Tolbert have created. For three decades they have amassed a collection of antiques guaranteed to thrill not only your child, but also the child in you. This is the oldest antiques store in the Flathead Valley.

Coca-Cola buffs will want to make this a must stop. Coca-Cola and other vintage signs crowd together on the exteriors of the garage and store. (The Tolberts collect Coca-Cola advertising themselves.) A good selection of gas pumps, restored by Bob, stand on the grounds as a reminder of the era of Mom and Pop stores.

Inside, expect to see tools of the trade from way back when—scales, bean counters, and old brass cash registers. An unusual piece is an old drugstore counter that says "Prescriptions." Another find is an 1880s to 1890s restored walnut watchmaker's cabinet.

When the Tolberts opened the store in 1968, they carried antique wood-burning kitchen cook stoves; you'll still find wood- and coal-burning stoves today, dating from the late 1800s through the 1920s.

Old toys and cars from the 1920s through the 1960s fill glass cases, including Bob's assortment of restored pedal toys. You might come across a rare 1926 Stutz pedal car.

Stageline Antiques would be a place to search for soda-fountain items and game-room collectibles, such as a 1957 Wurlitzer jukebox. If you want to take home a unique brass lighting fixture, Bob has restored a number of those.

A nostalgic highlight at Stageline Antiques is the hand-carved, 1890s wooden carousel horse.

The country store is open year-round six days a week, Monday through Saturday.

Cock-a-doodle-doo!
12 Lupfer Avenue, Whitefish
(406) 862-0776

If your whimsy is folk art, your penchant is for primitives, or your heart beats for American country, you should stop at Cock-a-doodle-doo! in Whitefish, just off Baker Avenue. What better symbol for Americana than a rooster crowing to one and all the delights of this treasure-cluttered antiques business located in a little red barn trimmed in white. Located in the alley behind owner Karen Heller's house, the shop was designed like an East Coast carriage house. The cheeky rooster on the shop's exterior proclaims the store is now open six days a week.

The scent of candles and potpourri greets you at this stop. In winter Karen keeps a pot of tea or coffee warming, which takes away the chill from diehard antiquers.

From shelves to floor, every square inch of this shop bursts with American country appeal. Country primitives, traditional handmade crafts, and reclaimed architectural pieces are what give this shop its distinction. Old cupboards and shelves with peeling paint hold decoys, crockery, and hand-pieced table runners. Look for crocheted rugs and old quilts, which add their homespun flavor. If you've been searching for a gateleg or drop-leaf table, you may find them here, with peeling paint or newly painted. Vintage 1930s and 1940s tablecloths may be spied rolled up and tucked in a crock or basket.

Karen is bringing in more new country accessories and giftware that blend well with her antiques. Some new items include Ohio-made crockery bowl sets and Amish door knobs. Also look for architecturally inspired accessories—all made from pieces of old houses. You might find a mirror to hang on your wall or other charming piece to take home.

Cock-a-doodle-doo! is open year-round Monday through Saturday. Check with Karen to see if more antiques are stored in her house. She might let you take a peek.

Karen is also responsible for the Big Sky Country Antique Fair—see the Insiders' Tip in this chapter.

A crowing rooster invites you in at Cock-a-doodle-doo! in Whitefish. Photo: Eileen Gallagher

Primrose Cove
14 Lupfer Avenue, Whitefish
(406) 863–2770

Primrose Cove is a newer shop that joins Cock-a-doodle-doo! and Old Town Antiques in the Railroad District of Whitefish. Specializing in English and European antiques, owner Tammy Stiff adds a new dimension to antiquing in the neighborhood. Be sure to stop by and check out her selection.

Old Town Antiques
13 O'Brien Avenue, Whitefish
(406) 863–9633

Right across the alley from Karen's shop is a tall, yellow house designed by owner Andrea Dunnigan to look like an old row house. Don't miss this antiques shop. Besides antiques you will find locally made reproduction furniture and home-decor items. Not only are the primitive reproductions made by local craftsmen, but they are also fashioned from old wood salvaged from the area. Barnwood from local homesteads has been given new life as wall cupboards and wood plate racks. Other pieces have been constructed using tongue-and-groove wood from the old Whitefish Masonic Temple when it was

remodeled. "All pieces have some history to them," Andrea says.

She designs the reproduction furniture and a local carpenter builds it—some on-site. She also has garage-sale finds refinished. A trip to Old Town Antiques might net you a cupboard with a salvaged window as a door. Other furniture to look for includes daybeds, reproduction cabinets, and harvest tables. If you fall in love with a table but it's not the size you need, she can have one built to fit your dining space. Some are constructed with salvaged wood, some with new wood. Tables can be painted to look old or done in a natural finish, whatever fits your style.

Upstairs, Andrea runs the textile part of her business, where she sews pillows and table linens from vintage drapery panels from the 1920s through the 1950s. The bright pillows and table runners are colorful accents when placed among her rustic wood furniture. Andrea also sews handmade pillows from natural linen.

Many of the store's items go to clientele furnishing second homes, Andrea says. An eclectic piece from Old Town Antiques will make a handsome addition to your cabin, cottage, or country home.

Old Town Antiques is open year-round Tuesdays through Saturdays.

Kidstuff

For a kid visiting the mountains in summer, what could be more fun than skipping rocks and splashing around in the cool water of lakes, creeks, and streams? How about a simulated bobsled ride, a trip in a gondola, or the ultimate in summer fun—traveling to a high mountain pass and making snowballs in July. In winter the snow is the thing. Skiing, snowboarding, sledding, ice-skating—and snowballs—will keep Mom and Dad out in the cold along with the kids. Hot chocolate might entice you to come inside long enough to get warm, and then you're out the door again.

Glacier National Park and the Flathead Valley both offer myriad activities for kids. Glacier isn't all that accessible in winter, and many "attractions" in the area close from late September until May or June, but summer brings the excitement of fast-moving water and the possibility of huckleberries. The Flathead is famous for its winter activities, making both seasons equally ideal for a visit to northwest Montana.

The following are our suggestions for some of the most kid-friendly activities in the area; let interest, ability, and stamina be your guide.

A Avalanche Lake Trail and Trail of the Cedars

On Going-to-the-Sun Road, about 5 miles east of Lake McDonald Lodge, is one of the best short family hikes in Glacier National Park. The trail leads from the Avalanche picnic area and campground about 2 miles on a gentle slope to a clear glacial lake. On a very hot day, you may be tempted to splash a bit in the water at the end of the trail, but remember that it is fed by meltwater from the glacier above and can be frigid. There is a wide shore at the lake, and there can be a crowd.

If the 2-mile hike seems a bit much for your group and you just want to stretch your legs, the 1-mile, wheelchair-accessible Trail of the Cedars is a good choice. It starts from the Avalanche picnic area and heads through a grove of trees with trunks 4 to 7 feet in diameter. An interpretive brochure is available to help you interpret the sights and sounds of the temperate rain forest around you.

B Big Mountain

In summer or winter Big Mountain is the place to be in the Flathead Valley. It doesn't have to be January for this ski area to be fun and exciting; some of the summer activities are really the most fun of all.

Hiking and mountain biking are available on the mountain for any age and all ability levels—you can either bring your own bikes or rent them there. Even hiking boots can be rented. Special programs for kids are available; call (406) 862-1900 for more information.

Two other kid-friendly activities are the gondola ride to the Summit House and the Environmental Education Center. The gondola—called the Glacier Chaser—makes the trip to the top, 2,000 feet of vertical gain, in about 10 minutes. A restaurant and picnic area are located at the Summit House—though you can feast on the views. The Environmental Education Center, run by the U.S.D.A. Forest Service, has interpretive displays on wildlife and habitats, complete with a children's activities corner.

Of course if these activities don't interest you, there's also horseback riding, wagon

Everyone will enjoy the view from Big Mountain's summit. Photo: Perry Johnson

rides, barbecues, telescope stargazing, a catch-and-release fishing pond, concerts, festivals, tennis, and golf.

Big Mountain is located on Big Mountain Road, just outside of Whitefish. To get there, take U.S. Highway 93 north through town and follow it when it turns west. Turn right onto Baker Avenue and follow it over the viaduct. It will turn into Wisconsin Avenue; follow it all the way to Big Mountain Road, which is marked with a flashing yellow light.

C Coram's Amazing Life-Size Maze

If wandering through the Super Maze at this popular Highway 2 attraction doesn't interest you, minigolf, go-carts, and squirting bumper boats might catch your fancy. You can't miss Amazing Fun Center—though you may miss the town of Coram if you don't look carefully—as you travel on Highway 2 to and from Glacier National Park and the Flathead Valley; you'll spot the giant wooden walls of the maze.

D Depot Park

Stop to gather local visitor information at the Kalispell Chamber of Commerce office (located in the historic railroad depot) while the kids stretch their legs in this grassy park. There is a shaded area with benches, perfect for a picnic—and if you're lucky you'll catch a performance at the gazebo.

The park is located at the corner of Center Street and U.S. Highway 93 (Main Street) in Kalispell.

E Even in the Rain!

Should you get a rainy day, Flathead County Library is open six days a week in Kalispell, Whitefish, and Columbia Falls, and five days a week in Bigfork. Each library has a kids' section specially designed for easy browsing by the younger set. "Story hours" happen on a regular basis, too; call ahead to see what's on. And the Whitefish library has a fireplace you may want to cozy up to as well! Phone numbers are: Kalispell, (406) 758-5820; Columbia Falls, (406) 892-5919; Whitefish, (406) 862-6657; and Bigfork, (406) 837-6976. For more information on the library system, check out the Web site, www.flathead countylibrary.org.

F Flathead Lake

Flathead Lake is the largest freshwater lake west of the Mississippi, and there are six state parks to enjoy along its shores. The fishing, picnicking, and swimming are great. Sailboats, motorboats, canoes, sailboards, and other watercraft are available to rent at several locations. Short cruises, evening cruises, and day trips are available from touring companies, as well. See the Kalispell and Polson chapters in this book for more information.

G Grizzly Bears

If you're lucky, you may see a grizzly bear while you're in Glacier National Park, but even if you don't, though, you'll know you're in bear country—everything from the Montana Grizzlies and Lady Griz sports teams to ministorage and dog schools are named for the bears! See how many "bears," of any kind, you can find in Montana.

Real grizzlies come in a large variety of sizes and colors. They can be blonde, brown, or nearly black. You can distinguish them from black bears by their distinctive faces (their noses turn up at the end of a rather dished-in profile) and by the large hump between their shoulders.

Make plenty of noise while you're hiking the trails, to warn the bears of your presence so that they can get out of your way. Talking loudly, clapping your hands, singing a song, or even yelling once in a while are good ways to make noise. Some people carry pepper spray in case of an encounter. See the Close-up on bear safety in this book for more information.

H Huckleberries

You'll notice huckleberry products—jams, jellies, pancake syrup, barbecue sauces, vinegars, and more—all over western Montana, but when you're in the Flathead Valley, you're near the self-proclaimed center of the huckleberry universe in the town of Hungry Horse. These small purple fruits are a true Montana delicacy, and it would be a shame to miss out on their juicy, messy goodness. At the Huckleberry Patch restaurant and gift shop on U.S. Highway 2 in Hungry Horse, you'll find all things huckleberry, including a very fine huckleberry pie.

The Outdoor Recreation chapter has more information about seeking out the purple fruits yourself, though the location of prized patches is a secret passed down from generation to generation in some families. U.S.D.A. Forest Service ranger stations in the area can give you a good idea of where to look if you're in the area at peak berry time—July and August. Be aware that bears are awfully fond of the berries, too. Make noise while you're picking and let the bears have the berries if they should happen upon you at their favorite patch.

Grizzly Bear DNA Project

Grizzly bears and Glacier National Park are inextricably linked in the minds of everyone who visits this place. Indeed, the power of the bear in the human mind is amply demonstrated throughout Montana: From sports teams to business names, the "grizzly" figures prominently in Montana life. And so it should: The wilderness area that stretches from Canada down through Glacier National Park and the adjoining Bob Marshall Wilderness is one of the last places in the lower 48 states where you have even a chance of seeing one of the great bears. Yellowstone also has grizzlies, but it's no longer clear that these two groups of bears are part of a continuous population.

The grizzly was listed in 1975 as an endangered species under the Threatened and Endangered Species Act. One element of getting the grizzly population on the road to recovery is finding out just exactly how many bears there are. This is tougher than it might sound: Until just recently, radio-collaring bears was really the only reliable way to identify individuals. Radio-collaring is very intrusive, very expensive, and very hard to apply to an entire population of animals, especially ones that frequent some of the least accessible parts of the country. But now scientists have developed DNA monitoring techniques that allow individual bears to be identified and tracked over long periods of time.

The Bear DNA Project is just that. Bear "sign" includes hair and scat, two sources of DNA that can be collected without direct contact with the animal. Over several summers, field stations were set up in Glacier with scent lures (no food rewards) to draw bears into an area where their fur would rub up against barbed wire. Known rub trees were set with barbed wire, also to collect hair. And many volunteers as well as project personnel documented their collection of scat from along Glacier's 700 miles of trails. Both the hair samples and the scat were then analyzed for their DNA content, producing an ID for the bear in question. In this way individual bears could be identified for the first time, giving researchers the first statistically sound estimate of the Glacier area's grizzly population. In addition DNA profiles can tell us more about the degree of genetic variation within these populations, the relatedness of individuals, and their sex—all information critical to intelligent bear management.

This is an ongoing study, and it may expand to include a much larger region in the near future. If you're interested, check out the Web site at www.nrmsc.usgs.gov/research/beardna.htm. Links will take you to a map of the study area, information on techniques, and photos (including some of bears). A link will also take you to the latest update, currently at www.nrmsc.usgs.gov/research/ bearDNA_update.htm. The Bear DNA Project is an exciting way to learn more about these bears without having to interfere with their normal, wild life.

Ice

To a certain extent, ice—really, really big and heavy ice—is what Glacier National Park is all about. Those peaks and valleys were formed by glaciers scouring the land and carving knifelike edges on the tops of mountains. In Glacier National Park you can play in the runoff from melting glaciers and you can actually walk out on glaciers yourself (given sufficient skill level and stamina in your group). One excellent place to see glaciers is the

Swiftcurrent Valley on the east side of the park. Step out on the boat dock behind Many Glacier Hotel to view Grinnell and Salamander Glaciers, or take a scenic boat cruise and get a closer look from Grinnell Lake.

J Jewel Basin

This hiking area in the Swan Mountains shines even in comparison to the recreation opportunities at Glacier National Park. There are more than 35 miles of hiking trails in the area, good for day hikes and short backpacking trips. This is a great place to introduce your kids to the backcountry experience.

The two best hikes for families are to Picnic Lakes and Birch Lake. Either are suitable for day hikes or short backpacks. The Picnic Lakes are 2.5 miles from the trailhead at Camp Misery on Forest Trail 8. Birch Lake is accessed from Forest Trail 717 and Forest Trail 7. A trail map is located at the parking area, and a forest ranger is frequently on hand to answer questions.

To get to Jewel Basin, take U.S. Highway 93 from Kalispell 7 miles south and turn east toward Bigfork on Montana Highway 82. Turn south at Montana Highway 35 and proceed to the flashing light, where you will turn east onto Montana Highway 83. At another flashing light, turn north onto Echo Lake Road. Signs will lead you to the Jewel Basin parking lot and trailheads.

K Kehoe's Agate Shop

On a rainy day or even when you've just had enough scenery and fresh air, this little shop in what used to be the town of Holt is a great place to visit with the kids. In addition to the colorful polished rocks called agates, this rustic shop—built in 1932—has a collection of petrified wood, minerals, gems, fossils, and thunder eggs collected from all over the world.

To get there from Bigfork, turn west from Grand Avenue onto Holt Drive at the flashing yellow light. Signs will lead you to the agate shop in 2.3 miles. The road ends at the shop, so you won't miss it.

L License-Plate Game

Montana's Big Skies and steep mountains mean lots of roads and lots of time spent in the car. Luckily, we get traffic from enough places to make the time-tested license-plate game fun for kids. See who can spot license plates from the most states and provinces. To make it more interesting, assign point values to the states based on their area or population ranking using your road atlas. The winner gets to decide what activity to try next.

M Mountain Goats

Though there are many places in Glacier Country where you might spot one of these agile creatures, one of your best options is 3 miles east of the town of Essex on U.S. Highway 2. There is a parking lot on the south side of the road, with a trail leading to an overlook at the end of the lot. On the steep cliffs above the Middle Fork of the Flathead River, you'll have a good chance of seeing billy goats, nannies, and kids, as well as elk and deer. The animals are attracted to the mineral deposits on the cliffs—most of their time here is spent in licking the rocks.

Nevada Barr's *Blood Lure*

Blood Lure . . . now there's an intriguing title! Nevada Barr, known for her mystery stories set in national parks, recently turned her attention to Glacier. Her story revolves around her park-ranger heroine, Anna Pigeon, who's been detailed to Glacier as a break from her usual road-patrol duties. Anna's headed out to collect samples for the Bear DNA project with the park biologist, Joan Rand, and a young volunteer, Rory van Slyke. But on their first night out in Glacier's backcountry, a bear comes 'round their campsite, and things start shaking . . . including Anna's tent. She emerges with one 3-inch shallow laceration, but Rory has disappeared . . . and the tracks of the griz are disappearing with the dew as it evaporates from the meadows of Fifty Mountain.

Nevada Barr used to work as a seasonal ranger for the National Park Service, and she does her homework for her fictional stories. She was along for the superintendent's hike in Glacier a few years ago, which indeed passed through Fifty Mountain (which is a huge meadow, so named because you can see 50 peaks from it). Her books are a fun read, and they have a certain authenticity to them that makes all the local park service people want to read what she's written when she's "done" their park. What will the plot be? Often it's loosely based on some real incidents. Who will turn up in the story? Occasionally real people crop up in her novels, more or less disguised: Kate Kendall, the director of the DNA project, is the only real person to be mentioned in *Blood Lure*, although other characters have features recognizable to locals. But perhaps what's best is Barr's ability to portray how the park service operates: what it's like to communicate with a radio where there aren't telephones; how long it may take for someone to hike into the scene of a backcountry crime; the local lingo for place names that aren't on the map. She stretches things a bit sometimes—be sure to get your information about the park *from the park*, not from fiction!—but she tells a good tale.

As a matter of fact, *Blood Lure* is good enough that, if you're feeling even a bit "bearanoid" before you head to Glacier, you might want to save this story for after your visit. Reading it by flashlight in your tent at Fifty Mountain might be a bit too scary . . . keep it instead for an evening at home next winter, curled up by the fire with something warm to drink!

N National Park Service

The National Park Service offers guided hikes and regularly scheduled interpretive talks throughout the park. You can see a schedule in the newspaper you receive at the entrance gate, or call (406) 888–7800 for more information on schedules and topics.

O Óhpskunakáxi

The Blackfeet name for the area around Many Glacier Hotel is *Óhpskunakáxi*, meaning "waterfalls," and this is one of the best places in the park to see the tumbling water up close. One of the best short hikes for families is to Apikuni Falls, a 0.7-mile hike with spectacular mountain views, colorful wildflowers, and the occasional Columbian

The trail to Grinnell Glacier attracts hikers of all ages. Photo: Susan Olin

ground squirrel to interest you along the way. The falls and the potential to see small, furry pikas (small mammals that look like short-eared rabbits) reward the steep but enjoyable journey.

To get to the hike, take Many Glacier Road 1 mile east of the hotel to the trailhead parking lot on the north side of the road near Apikuni Creek bridge.

P Polebridge Mercantile

If you have a four-wheel-drive vehicle, a visit to Polebridge—where you can see part of the west that is still wild—is one your kids will truly enjoy. The trip up the North Fork Road is a bumpy and dusty one, but the fresh-baked goods at the Polebridge Mercantile and the possibility of seeing bears, wolves, moose, elk, deer, mountain lions, and fields of wildflowers make it worthwhile.

Q Shhh . . . Quiet

Quiet hours in campgrounds mean that everyone gets a good night's sleep and is ready for the adventures of the next day. Particularly at the campgrounds in Glacier National Park and at the busy state parks around Flathead Lake, crowds mean noise. Observing quiet hours from 10:00 P.M. to 8:00 A.M. keeps everyone happy and refreshed for the next day's events.

R
Redrock Falls

This easy 1.8-mile hike in Glacier National Park is a great one for stretching the legs and for seeing waterfalls in the Many Glacier area. There are sedimentary red rocks along the way—you can also see a burn area from a major 1936 fire on your way to splashing in the lake or admiring the falls. Be aware that the icy pools at the bottom of the falls are not ideal for wading. The rocks are slippery and the water is very, very cold.

To get to the trailhead, go to the parking area across from the Swiftcurrent Camp store in the Many Glacier Valley. The hike starts at the parking area.

S
Skipping Rocks and Lake McDonald

Many an hour has been whiled away by children and adults skipping rocks, and the shores of Lake McDonald offer a great spot for this most serious of pursuits. Behind Lake McDonald Lodge is a boat dock—where you can rent boats and buy tickets for the guided lake tours—and beside the dock are some fine large rocks for sitting on, with the little skippers nearby. The time spent waiting for a table at the restaurant at the lodge will fly by.

T
Tyrannosaur at Alberta Visitor Centre

What could be more fun than visiting the *Tyrannosaurus rex* skeleton at the Alberta Visitor Centre? How about admiring its teeth and then going for a simulated bobsled ride?

It may be hard to tear your kids away from the exhibits at this visitor center, designed to introduce visitors to Canada's Waterton Lakes National Park. You don't have to cross the border to get there; the center is in West Glacier, just off Highway 2. See the Attractions chapter for more information.

U
Umbrella Weather?

Though outdoor recreation is the area's main attraction, there are, of course, times when inclement conditions drive even the hardiest adventurers inside. Two great options for

Insiders' Tip

Spending the Christmas holidays in the Flathead? You might want to know that Santa's sleigh flies over the valley each year, on some evening in December that no one can predict. Suddenly you'll look up and see a lighted sleigh moving through the sky. (You may hear that this has something to do with ALERT, the Kalispell Regional Medical Center rescue helicopter, but Santa has connections in many important places.) Children (as well as adults!) love it, and it's just one more reason to "be good" till Christmas!

Whitefish City Beach is a hot spot for kids in summer. Photo: Donnie Sexton

indoor family outings in Kalispell can be found at the Hockaday Center for the Arts and the Conrad Mansion. See The Arts and Attractions chapters, respectively, for more information.

V Vortex

The House of Mystery has to be the strangest attraction in Glacier Country, and we guarantee your kids will love it. Located on Highway 2 between Columbia Falls and Hungry Horse, you'll see the billboards before you actually locate the small house where everyone has stopped. Why is it a mystery? The folks who run it claim that the area around the house is in a gravitational vortex, causing the trees to grow sideways. The odd angles of the house may convince you . . . though whether it's the work of mysterious forces or optical illusion is something your kids will have fun trying to determine.

W Wild Horse Island

You may not see wild horses at this state park in Flathead Lake, but there are plenty of other attractions to entice you to rent a boat so you can set foot on shore or board the *Polson Princess* for a ride around the island. The island got its name from the Flathead and

Pend d'Oreille Indians, who used the island to protect their horses from raids by the Blackfeet. There are no facilities on the island, though the wildlife doesn't seem to mind. You may see the plentiful bighorn sheep, among others.

Xerophyllum tenax

The tall stalks with fluffy yellow heads that you keep seeing in campgrounds and throughout Glacier and the Flathead are called bear grass, but not because *Xerophyllum tenax* actually has anything to do with bears. Lewis and Clark—who skirted the eastern edge of this territory during their explorations of the Louisiana Purchase—named it bear grass because bears were often seen in its vicinity, and they assumed the bears ate it.

Now we know that the plant has more to do with elk, which eat the whole plant, and with mountain goats, which eat the parts untouched by winter's snow. Native Americans wove baskets and clothing from the plant.

The plants can grow to be 5 feet tall, and the fluffy head of flowers is generally about the size of a large fist. Be aware that the leaves, which lie in bunches close to the ground, are slippery . . . so watch your step.

A good "bear grass year" is a real treat. Photo: Susan Olin

Y Yellow, pink, red, and purple

Glacier National Park is full of wildflowers—and little ones are always tempted to pick them—encourage your kids to "take only pictures and leave only footprints." These wildflowers will please thousands of visitors if left in place.

Z Good Night's Sleep

Get your Z's at one of the campgrounds in the area or at a hotel or motel. Tomorrow is going to be a big day.

Annual Events

At our annual events—big and small, on sunny days and in the snow—you can expect residents to come out in full force and visitors to join in on the fun. Fiddling festivals, arts in the park, rodeos, powwows, and the ubiquitous huckleberry fill up our calendars of events and demand our attention. The following listings, organized by month, are just a sampling of some of the more time-tested events we hold in the shadows of our glorious mountains and on the shores of our lakes.

January

Winter in Montana is cold, snowy . . . and wonderful. So we tend to spend as much time outdoors as possible, and our annual events reflect that tendency. Winterfest in Seeley Lake is one of the most consistent offerings, but you can find cross-country ski races, downhill events, snowmobile runs, and winter games of all sorts nearly every weekend.

Winterfest
Seeley Lake
(406) 677–2880
www.seeleyswanpathfinder.com
Located at the south end of the Swan Valley, the community of Seeley Lake comes alive for their annual celebration of winter. Activities include ice-sculpture judging, dogsled rides, and snow softball, topped off by that mid-winter tradition—fireworks. The dates vary every year, so call the chamber of commerce at the number above or visit the Web site for information.

February

It's still cold out, so how about a nice evening torchlight parade and art walk? The folks in Whitefish cook up a special event every year in early February and have since 1960—the Whitefish Winter Carnival. Call (406) 862–3501 for more information about offerings in the community. For some reason, February also leads to thoughts of chocolates and other fine things to eat and drink. This is the month of wine and food festivals and chocolate fairs throughout the Flathead.

March

March may be spring some places in the world, but in the Flathead snow is still our main source of entertainment, not gardening. Be sure to check out local cross-country, telemark, and downhill ski races. This is also a good month to catch performances and concerts at local theaters. There's plenty to do, both indoors and out!

April

Well, in April the ski areas generally close and the snow recedes. Too bad. We'll have to venture elsewhere for our fun . . . how about a mystery weekend in Essex?

Murder Mystery
Izaak Walton Inn, Essex
(406) 888–5700
Call the Izaak Walton Inn early to get reservations for their Murder Mystery weekend. (There is also one held in October.) You'll arrive just in time for a crime, and then solve the murder before the weekend is out. Be sure to bring your cross-country skis; there may still be snow, and there are great trails out here on the southern tip of Glacier National Park.

World Cup Telemark Racing

Over the last 15 years, telemark skiing has seen a huge revival in the United States and Europe. Telemark skiers use "free-heel" equipment: their ski bindings connect only the toe, not the heel, of the ski boot to the ski. With this greater mobility—and instability—telemarkers are able to ski upslope as well as down, and so telemark has exploded as a way for winter enthusiasts to explore hilly backcountry terrain that would be inaccessible to either cross-country or alpine skiers. Crested Butte, Colorado, and Whitefish, here in Montana, have been the two American centers of telemark skiing. On the gentlest slopes of Big Mountain or Blacktail ski resorts, you'll see folks trying it out, starting to carve their turns with what at first seems like flimsy equipment. But people get addicted to telemarking—it's challenging and eventually becomes fluid and exciting, almost like a dance with the snow. Like all sports, telemark has its upper end, and telemark racing equals downhill racing for the gear, technique, and time its racers put into it. Locally Big Mountain sponsors a weekly race league, but in the last few years Big Mountain has also become a stop on the World Cup Telemark racing circuit. Check out the schedule of events: often World Cup telemark races occur in March. It's a great time to be in town, as "tele" racers come in from Sweden, Norway, Switzerland, Germany, Austria, and other countries to compete. You'll see them walking downtown in their racing colors as they visit local bars and restaurants . . . and you'll really want to see them up on the hill, demonstrating their unique sport. Telemark races include uphill sections and jumps as well as downhill gates, so it's an all-around ski competition that brings in unique winter excitement to the Flathead Valley.

Reid Sabin, World Cup Telemark Champion, enjoys Big Mountain's powder when he's not running gates.
Photo: Chuck Haney

May

Now it's starting to look like spring! You can celebrate the arrival of warm weather with a trip to the Cherry Blossom Festival at Bigfork, by hitting the water in a kayak race, or by heading to an early performance of the Montana Old-Time Fiddlers' Association.

Cherry Blossom Festival
Bigfork
(406) 837–5888
This area is famous for its cherry trees, and though the fruit usually gets all the press, this festival will surely make you think of the warm summer to come.

Whitewater Festival, Kayak Races and Parade
Bigfork
(406) 837–5888
The water will still be really cold—and really fast—so bring your wet suit and something warm for later. As much as we all love winter, sometimes we can't wait for spring to come, and the water festival brings it all the earlier.

Montana Old-Time Fiddlers' Association Jam
(406) 889–3539
This toe-tapping group of fiddlers of all ages performs at different venues throughout the Flathead over the summer months. Call for locations and dates.

June

Summer's festivals are just warming up in June, but there are plenty of offerings as the days get longer and warmer. Hit the water and the trail, but remember it's still early in the summer season and come prepared for all kinds of weather conditions. One of the most exciting events of the year—the opening of Going-to-the-Sun Road—usually takes place in June. It's a great time to see the park teeming with wildlife and showing its spring colors in banks of wildflowers.

July

Make sure your spring yard work is done, because with all of the offerings of the season you won't have much time on the weekends to do much more than mow. Starting in July and continuing through August, this is our busiest time of year.

Whitefish Annual Arts Festival
Whitefish
(406) 862–5875
Held on the lawn of Central School, this two-day event is filled with arts and crafts, food, and sidewalk sales. The whole community comes out for this event, and nearly everyone goes home with a locally made treasure. Sales benefit Cross Currents Christian School.

Arts in the Park
Kalispell
This juried art show held annually in Kalispell's lovely Depot Park is a benefit for the Hockaday Museum of Art in Kalispell. Fine arts and crafts, entertainment, and food are featured.

KERR Country Rodeo
Polson
www.northernrodeo.com
Bareback, saddle-bronc, and bull riding are all a part of rodeo action, and you'll find plenty of it here at the KERR Country Rodeo. The Northern Rodeo Association sanctions the event, so top performers are expected in all categories. Live country music is also a feature of the rodeo.

Montana Old-Time Fiddlers' Contest
Polson
(406) 323–1198
The Montana Old-Time Fiddlers meet all over the Flathead Valley to "jam" throughout the summer, but this is the main event. Held at the high school in Polson, several hundred fiddlers of all ages and skill levels gather for this foot-stomping gala. Admission is charged for the day and evening sessions.

There's nothing like a rodeo to bring out a crowd. Photo: Carl Wells, courtesy of Flathead Convention and Visitor Bureau

Standing Arrow Powwow
Elmo
(406) 849–5541
www.powwows.com

This is a great place to experience the culture of the Kootenai Indians, who share the Flathead Reservation with the Salish Indians. The event is held at the Kootenai headquarters in Elmo, on the west side of Flathead Lake. Dancing is the main event of the powwow.

Arlee Powwow
Arlee
(406) 745–4572
www.powwows.com

The one-hundredth anniversary of the Arlee Powwow was celebrated in 1998, and we hope it goes on for a hundred years more. The event is sponsored by the Confederated Salish and Kootenai tribes and takes place in Arlee, at the southern end of the Flathead Reservation. Dancing is the main feature of the powwow, and dancers wear traditional and nontraditional costumes. Native American crafts, clothing, and food items—such as the delicious fry bread—are sold at the powwow.

Lewis and Clark Festival
Cut Bank
(406) 873–4041

When you're on the Blackfeet Reservation, be sure to take some time to retrace the steps of two of the most famous and revered explorers in American history, Lewis and Clark. Cut Bank is near Two Medicine Fight Site—the location of Lewis's fatal meeting with the Blackfeet. This festival includes a parade, costume contest, and more. As the Lewis and Clark bicentennial approaches, events like this one are attracting bigger and bigger crowds. Camp Disappointment, the northernmost point of the transcontinental expedition, is 12 miles outside of Browning.

North American Indian Days
Browning
(406) 338–2230
www.powwows.com

This nationally recognized powwow is the highlight of the year on the Blackfeet Indian Reservation to the east of Glacier National Park. Dancers and visitors come from around the country to the capital of the reservation at Browning; a parade and a rodeo are also held during the weekend. The Museum of the Plains Indian is located in Browning and will provide good background for your powwow experience.

August

Northwest Montana Fair and Rodeo
Flathead County Fairgrounds

A highlight of summer in the Flathead Valley, the fair stretches over the last two weeks in August and offers everything from farm animals and 4-H projects to llamas and carnival rides. In between are horse races, pro-rodeo competitions, fireworks displays, and exhibits of anything you can imagine. Yes, there's even a demolition derby.

Huckleberry Days
Whitefish
(406) 862–3501

This annual ode to the tiny bright purple treasures we in Montana call huckleberries is filled with pie-eating contests, a huckleberry cook-off, and an arts and crafts fair. Be sure to go home with a purple tongue.

Bigfork Festival of the Arts
Bigfork
(406) 881–4636

After more than 20 years, this event continues to offer fun music, good food, and fine arts and crafts.

Sandpiper Outdoor Festival of the Arts
Polson
(406) 883–5956

Held on the courthouse lawn in Polson, this fine arts and crafts festival has been a Polson tradition for more than 30 years.

A highlight of the holiday season is Santa's Christmas Eve Torchlight Parade at Big Mountain. Photo: Kaua

September

Libby Nordicfest
Libby
(406) 293–6430

A short distance from the main corridor of activity in the Flathead Valley, this traditional Nordicfest is worth the trip down U.S. Highway 2 for food, dancing, woodcarving workshops, and the extremely popular quilt show. They do serve lutefisk if that's what you're craving.

Flathead Quilters Guild Show
   and Quilt Auction
Flathead County Fairgrounds
(406) 892–5864

This major quilt show has become a well-established Flathead County event. What a great chance to pick up a handmade piece of Montana history!

October

Glacier Jazz Stampede
Kalispell
(406) 862–3814

This jazz festival is one of the largest in Montana, bringing visitors from around the country to hear strains of traditional and Dixieland jazz over several days. Food, crafts, and sidewalk sales can also be found at festival venues.

November

In November we start gearing up for winter again, the ski areas open up, and we actually hope for snow. Kalispell is the first to offer a Christmas parade, and more will follow in the month to come.

December

The holiday season is upon us, and most communities offer lights and celebrations. Think snow at this time of the year; we want a white Christmas and a powder-filled New Year.

Night of Lights Parade
Columbia Falls
(406) 892–7529

Holiday Parade, Art Walk, & Tree Lighting
   Ceremony
Bigfork
(406) 837–5888

Santa's Christmas Eve Torchlight Parade
The Big Mountain, Whitefish
(406) 862–2900

Outdoor Recreation

This wondrous land in the Rocky Mountains—called by the Blackfeet backbone of the earth—this Jewel in the Crown of the Continent is a mecca for outdoor recreationists of all stripes. In this chapter you'll be guided to some of the best and brightest offerings of the region's recreational opportunities, and given some hints on keeping the area's pristine beauty intact for future visitors. Some precautions to take when recreating in the great outdoors are also included.

The Environment

With Glacier National Park at its core, Glacier Country is a giant mosaic created over three billion years by natural forces. Once a vast inland sea, the sediment and sea life deposited layers on the bottom that formed the limestone seen here today. Volcanic activity thrust up mountains to great heights; then the mountains suffered upheavals that slid the older layers over the younger ones.

This "block overthrust faulting" has created the steep rock faces on the east front and the somewhat more gentle slopes on the western side. The glaciers that retreated about 10,000 to 14,000 years ago sculpted the slopes more steeply, rounded other hills, and filled in low spots with glacial till.

Nature's work continued over many millennia with storms, floods, wind, and fire. The resulting landscape became home to the plants and animals that compose the regional ecosystem.

The variety of plant and animal communities reflects the broad ranges of climate, geology, topography, and soils. Elevations range from a low of 3,150 feet at the juncture of the North Fork and the Middle Fork of the Flathead River to 10,466 feet at the summit of Mount Cleveland. These elevation differences alone influence different life zones. From the temperate rain forest of the Lake McDonald Valley one can go to conditions like the Arctic tundra simply by climbing to Logan Pass at 6,000 feet. The variations in moisture, wind, sun, and shade at each elevation multiply the local microclimates.

The area we are looking at comprises three million acres of nearly unbroken wilderness. It is bounded by Waterton Lakes National Park on the north, Montana Highway 83 on the west, 89 on the east, and 200 on the south. It encompasses Glacier National Park and the Great Bear, Bob Marshall, and Scapegoat Wilderness Areas in the Flathead and Lewis and Clark National Forests. A million acres are in Glacier National Park, 2.36 million acres in the Flathead National Forest, and the remainder in state and private ownership. The Swan Range runs uncut by a road for 100 miles.

Within this wild circle still remains one of the largest intact temperate ecosystems in the world. Virtually all populations of plants and animals—carnivores and herbivores, predators and prey, and the plants that sustain them—remain

The Moose Fire of 2001

On August 14, 2001, a lightning strike began a fire near the Whitefish Divide, in the Flathead National Forest west of Glacier National Park. Although the fire ran almost entirely through unpopulated forest areas, and only a few buildings were lost, it was a huge natural event that preoccupied residents and visitors to the Flathead and Glacier National Park. To give some idea of the kind of resources that are involved in fire fighting, here are some statistics from the Moose Fire: approximately 71,000 acres burned, of which 36,000 were in Flathead National Forest, 27,600 in Glacier National Park, 6,500 in state lands, and 900 in private land. Fighting the fire included cutting 96 miles of fire line, dropping 3,800,000 gallons of water, and dropping 364,480 gallons of fire retardant. This required 280 people (including 5 fire crews), 3 helicopters, 6 engines, 1 water tender, 2 excavators, 2 skidders, and a backhoe. Cooperating agencies included the National Park Service, the U.S.D.A. Forest Service, the U.S. Fish and Wildlife Service, the Bureau of Land Management, the Bureau of Indian Affairs, the Canadian Ministry of Forestry, numerous state agencies, rural volunteer fire departments, and several private companies. The suppression cost at 88-percent containment was $19,265,000.

Immediate impacts on the area included a lot of smoke. While the smoke probably drove some visitors away, it also brought in others interested in watching a major fire burn. Large parts of the Flathead National Forest and Glacier National Park were temporarily closed during the fire, but in summer 2002, public interest in the burn was so high that the Forest Service and National Park Service offered jointly led public tours through the area as a means of promoting public education about wildfire.

If you have a chance, take a drive up the Inside or Outside North Fork Roads and view the changes brought about by the Moose Fire. You'll notice the abundance of wildflowers springing up from the ash. Previous experience with the Red Bench Fire in 1988 suggests that certain birds that depend on insects will increase, deer will increase, and soon a tiny new lodgepole forest will begin to spring up under the blackened one. A whole new round of life has begun in the wake of the fire.

almost as they were before Euro-American explorers and trappers first ventured here 250 years ago. In Glacier and Waterton Lakes National Parks alone live more than 1,000 kinds of plants, 25 major tree species, 264 bird species, nearly 60 kinds of mammals, and 17 species of fish.

The larger predators include grizzly and black bears, mountain lions or cougar, gray wolves, coyote, fox and lynx, badger, marten, and mink. Larger prey animals include moose, elk, white-tailed and mule deer, mountain goats, and bighorn sheep. These are accompanied by their smaller neighbors such as beaver, snowshoe hare, pine squirrels, deer mice, and meadow voles. Even the nearly exterminated bison that once roamed the plains by the thousands are represented by a penned herd in Waterton Lakes National Park. The Flathead River system is one of the few areas in the country that still support self-sustaining, genetically pure populations of native westslope cutthroat and bull trout.

The Continental Divide—The Great Divide—the north to south mountainous spine bisecting the region, exerts a major influence on weather, capturing rainfall from warm, moisture-laden air masses moving in from the coastal states on the western side of the mountains. The mountains also restrict the westward flow of cold, continental Arctic air masses from east of the Rockies. The eastern slopes are dry, hot, and windy, and beyond them lies the vast upland prairie that once supported the great bison herds. In the high country weather can be extremely changeable, and both sunshine and snow are possible any time of the year.

Water has been and continues to be another powerful force shaping the landscape and influencing habitat. The Flathead River's three forks drain Glacier National Park, thousands of acres of the Flathead National Forest, and part of British Columbia. The U.S. Congress includes 219 miles of these waters as part of the National Wild and Scenic Rivers System. Sometimes heavy spring rains, a deep mountain snowpack, and warm temperatures that hasten snowmelt combine to swell one or more of the forks and the main river beyond their banks. The riverbed constantly changes as the waters eat away the bank at some places and deposit soil and debris at others. The Stillwater, Whitefish, and Swan Rivers wind their way through forests, agricultural fields, and urban areas. The St. Mary River heads north carrying Glacier's waters to Hudson Bay. Numerous swift mountain creeks carve through their rocky channels to forest and meadow below.

Disturbances to the land, both natural and human-caused, influence plant and animal communities. This landscape has evolved with fire as a constant force for change and renewal. Frequent low-intensity surface fires kill the small trees and shrubs and leave the more fire-resistant trees largely intact. Many tree and plant species, especially the pines—ponderosa, lodgepole, western white, and whitebark—and western larch depend on fire to perpetuate their life cycles. Lodgepole pine, which maintains its seed in fire-resistant cones for several years, is often abundant on sites where whole stands have been destroyed. Some seeds remain dormant in the soil for decades and sprout after a moderate fire. Aspen, huckleberry, fireweed, and grasses quickly move in to regenerate the vegetation. Grizzly bears and elk feed on many of these "pioneer species." Native Americans commonly burned prairies and pine-forest understory plants to improve grazing for deer, elk, and bison.

Introduction of nonnative species, most notably fish and noxious weeds, has also disrupted natural habitats. Native fish have suffered from habitat loss, food competition, and disease from the presence of these "exotics." Noxious weeds, introduced largely by Euro-American settlers in crop or pasture seeds over the past two centuries, are so aggressive they have infested millions of acres, choking out native plants and destroying fish, wildlife, and livestock habitat. Spotted knapweed, leafy spurge, and Saint-John's-wort are among more than a dozen noxious weeds targeted by weed-control programs of all Montana counties. Landowners are responsible for eradicating weeds from their property.

Plant and Animal Communities

With abundance of streams, rivers, lakes, and wetlands in the broad Flathead Valley, the riparian plants and animals form one of the area's major habitats. In valley bottoms at about 3,000 feet in elevation, black cottonwood, willow, alder, and red-osier dogwood dominate the tree and shrub species growing along the waters, often mixed with a smattering of conifers and trembling aspen. Biologists estimate 82 species of wildlife may depend on these riparian marshes and forests, including enormous numbers of migratory birds, eagles, and osprey. Spotted sandpipers bob along shorelines; red-winged and yellow-headed blackbirds share the cattail marshes and sloughs with muskrat, beaver, and raccoons. River otters, weasels, and mink can also be found here. Even the rare northern-bog lemming has been spotted in Lake McDonald's marshes. White-tailed deer find good browse in the grasses, sedges, and shrubs. The haunting cry of the common loon, long gone in many states, still adds its magical notes to nature's symphonies on large and small lakes across Glacier Country. The colorful harlequin duck may be seen on the rushing cold, mountain streams in and around Glacier National Park during its breeding period.

From 3,000 to 4,000 feet, trembling aspen, paper birch, and black cottonwood continue to dominate valley bottoms, especially in riparian areas, often encircling grassy fields and forming a transition to the higher coniferous forests. Their yellow and gold autumn foliage stands out against the green of conifers. Also found here are serviceberry, chokecherry, mountain maple, red-osier dogwood, and alder. Wild geranium, arnica, and Oregon grape grace the forest floor. This is habitat for white-tailed deer, moose, and wolves. Montana's State Bird, the western meadowlark, shares the open areas with LeConte's sparrow and the savannah sparrow. The low- to mid-elevation (3,000 to 4,000 feet west of the divide; 4,000 to 5,000 to the east) dry montane forest is typified by Douglas fir, ponderosa pine, lodgepole pine, and limber pine with understory species such as ninebark and mountain maple. These forests often have open crowns with a grassy understory that provides winter habitat for mule deer, elk, and bighorn sheep. In stands of old growth, predators like the goshawk hunt.

The wetter mid-montane forest reflects the Pacific maritime weather influence in the lush growth of trees, shrubs, ferns, mosses, and wildflowers. Western red cedar and western hemlock are common, along with Douglas fir, western larch, and spruce. The understory is typically luxuriant with many ferns, wildflowers, shrubs, and mosses. This habitat is typical of the McDonald Creek drainage ranging from 3,100 to 4,000 feet. In the old-growth forests live western tanagers, Swainson's and varied thrushes, Townsend's warblers, Hammond's flycatchers, and brown creepers. Sharp-shinned and Cooper's hawks prey on birds and small mammals. The snowshoe hare is common, and the lynx that preys primarily on this hare is reported to be returning. A magnificent stand of old-growth western red cedar can be seen at Avalanche campground and the shoreline of McDonald Lake's upper end. The 1910 fire destroyed a much larger population of this species.

In the subalpine forest (above 5,000 feet) spruce and subalpine fir dominate along with whitebark pine in higher elevations. Douglas fir is common on south-facing slopes. Near the upper limits trees thin out and mingle with treeless communities, creating parklands with spectacular displays of wildflowers, mosses, and lichens against a backdrop of breathtaking scenery. East of the divide subalpine fir and lodgepole pine dominate. Mule deer, pine marten, and black bears inhabit these forests.

In the highest elevations the plants and animals of the alpine community have adapted to the long, cold winters and cool, short growing seasons. Only a few trees and shrubs can survive, such as arctic willow, dwarf birch, and fir, hugging the ground and stunted by the searing winds and frigid temperatures. Mosses and lichens cling to bare rock; alpine bogs resemble a miniature landscape for a kingdom of little people. Alpine meadows astound the eye for a few July and August weeks with wildflowers of every color including heather, gentian, bear grass, and glacier lily. The rare dwarf alpine poppy is unique to this area in both Glacier and Waterton Lakes National Parks. Grizzly bears dig for glacier lily and spring beauty bulbs. Ptarmigan, pika, hoary marmot, wolverine, and mountain goat call this home. Bighorn sheep graze in high meadows and golden eagles nest on the cliffs. Logan Pass, the Hidden Lake Trail, and the Highline Trail provide the easiest access to this habitat.

Remnants of the native grasslands that once covered the Great Plains now occur mainly in broad, arid, low-elevation basins. Bluebunch wheatgrass, fescues, and needlegrasses dominate these areas. Although primarily found on the park's east side, they move quickly into areas soon after a forest fire, as at Polebridge where the Red Bench Fire burned the forest in 1988. Wildflowers thrive in these grasslands, the blossoming peaking in May and June in the lower elevations. Common species are yarrow, fleabane, potentilla, spirea, locoweed, and lupine. Wild geranium is a major food item for elk and white-tailed deer. This is also the habitat for badger, coyote, savannah sparrow and chipping sparrows, northern harrier, and prairie falcon. East of the divide Two Dog Flat provides a splendid grassland wildflower display peaking in June, with pasqueflower, lupine, Indian paintbrush, gaillardia, asters, and shooting stars in abundance. Exotic weed species have infested many of these prairies, especially east of the divide where forage grasses have been extensively planted for livestock grazing. Sagebrush, symbol of the romantic Western movie set, also grows in this environment and is common east of the divide, and found in a few spots west of the divide at Round Prairie and other areas along the Inside North Fork Road.

Glacier Country heavily depends on its wealth of natural treasures to support its economic activities, including farming, ranching, timber harvesting, tourism, and outdoor recreation. Between 1969 and 1992, employment and personal income grew substantially because of these wildlands' attractions. People are striving to maintain their freedoms and frontier lifestyles while also preserving the area's wildness, purity, clean air, water, and unlittered landscapes. Farmers and ranchers struggle to maintain their family operations as cities and towns expand outward to engulf them. Park visitors and area business people debate road access and development within the park. Families and businesses dependent on timber cutting in the national forests as well as wilderness

Insiders' Tip

Backcountry campers in Glacier Country should carefully select gear to minimize bulk and weight but maximize safety and comfort. Your comfort level will be greatly enhanced if you take clothing that keeps you warm and dry and that can be layered. Wear clothing next to the skin that wicks away moisture and dries quickly. Bring a portable camp chair to relax in comfort. An empty stuff sack can easily be converted into a pillow by stuffing it with extra clothing. Consider wearing gaiters to keep rocks, brush, and snow out of your boots. Sometimes a mosquito net is a welcome commodity in the backcountry.

An angler enjoys a day of fly-fishing in Montana's pristine waters. Photo: courtesy of Montana's Finest Resorts

advocates and forest recreationists apply diverse pressures to the Forest Service on such issues as road access and timber-harvest methods and quantities. Despite these ongoing conflicts about how best to manage these lands and resources, local governments and private groups are working to achieve a balance between preservation and development. The Flathead Basin Commission, created by the Montana State Legislature in 1983 to monitor and protect Flathead Lake's water quality, has been working with Canadian, U.S., and state and local agencies to collect data and develop methods for guarding the waters in this important watershed. Volunteers monitor pollution levels on 30 lakes that flow into the basin. Landowners and managers are encouraged to use best management practices to reduce runoff into streams and rivers feeding the lake. Flat-

head County has initiated a water-quality task force, which will be able to institute measures to protect the large, and so far unpolluted, aquifer underlying the Flathead Valley.

Private groups such as the Flathead Land Trust, the Nature Conservancy, and Montana Land Reliance work with private landowners to protect agricultural and wildlands from development and provide additional habitat for plants and animals. Organizations such as the Flathead Audubon Society, the Montana Native Plant Society, and the Glacier Institute conduct field trips, classes, and meetings to educate the public about plants, birds, and their habitats. The Flathead National Forest and Glacier National Park and Montana Department of Fish, Wildlife and Parks all have public adult- and school-educational programs. Through a variety of public meetings, forums, and workshops and active involvement in development and conservation issues, Citizens for a Better Flathead promotes "Smart Growth," so that population growth and development occur in such a way they do not unduly diminish the area's resources and values.

This chapter will suggest an array of possibilities for experiencing this immensely varied, fascinating country—from simply walking a few paces from your vehicle to see a stunning vista or look more closely at a wildflower to taking an all-day hike, a raft trip, or a ski tour into a wilderness setting. It will guide you to a few of the most special places and recommend other information sources to suit your needs and desires.

Nature Viewing

Fascinating plants and animals are everywhere in Glacier Country and are yours to view with only a little travel and effort. The many habitats are described in the environment section and give you a general idea of where they are likely to occur. Nature observation is particularly exciting here not only because of the uncommon creatures, but also because so many are concentrated in a small geographic area. With the naked eye an observant person can see many of them. With binoculars or a spotting scope, the opportunities magnify wonderfully.

You'll probably want to see mountain goats, elk, bald eagles, and grizzly bears—from a distance, of course. The many creeks, rivers, lakes, and wetlands provide prime habitat for migratory waterfowl and songbirds, osprey and beaver, river otter and mink. Wildflower lovers will revel in the variety of species from the spectacular displays of color in alpine settings along Going-to-the-Sun Road to the roadside plants everywhere in autumn. In this section we list a few specific places you'd be most likely to see the starring attractions such as mountain goats or bighorn sheep. These areas include wildlife refuges and production areas and places to see wildflowers.

Wildlife-Watching Tips

You can make wildlife watching fun for yourself and safe for the animals you watch by observing a few basic behaviors. You'll enjoy the animals the most when you observe them undisturbed in their activities. Wear subdued, natural colors. Be unobtrusive, move slowly and quietly, and hide behind boulders or vegetation. Learn as much about the wildlife as possible before trying to observe them, such as where and when they are found. Most animals are usually most active and visible while feeding in early morning and late evening. Don't look directly into an animal's eye; that could frighten it away. Keep your distance; use binoculars or a spotting scope. If you're taking pictures, use a 400-millimeter lens. Don't feed the animals. An excellent pamphlet called *A Guide to Ultimate Wildlife Watching* expands on these points and can be obtained from the Forest Service or Montana Fish, Wildlife and Parks (addresses listed below). Also look for the highway signs with the brown and white binoculars logo and the words WILDLIFE VIEWING AREA, with an arrow pointing to the site.

Grizzly Bears

These large bruins roam open woods and meadows foraging their diet of grasses, roots, berries, insects, and occasionally young elk or deer. They also feed on carrion at kill sites of mountain lions and other carnivores. In spring they are commonly seen grazing on the newly emerging vegetation at the edges of avalanche chutes along Going-to-the-Sun Road and in lower meadows in the St. Mary and Two Medicine Valleys. In July and August look for them in the alpine meadows and at Logan Pass digging the bulbs of glacier lilies and spring beauties. They oftentimes frequent the park's west side along the North Fork. They are as fond of huckleberries as people are, and in summer and early fall you should expect to see them raking the berries into their mouths in order to fatten up before going to ground for the winter. Bears are unpredictable and may attack without warning. Always observe the "bear country" precautions described in the Be "Bear Aware" Close-up in the Columbia Falls and the U.S. Highway 2 Corridor chapter.

Rocky Mountain Bighorn Sheep

These large ungulates with the massive horns prefer high rolling valleys and high rocky slopes and cliffs on the park's eastern side where the winds keep them snow-free in winter. They graze on grasses, shrubs, and forbs and during harsh winters can be viewed in the lower valleys. Although sometimes seen on Going-to-the-Sun Road, especially at Logan Pass and along the Highline Trail in early summer, the best places to view them are on the east side, especially in the Many Glacier Valley. Be sure to look up as you hike the trails to Iceberg Lake, Ptarmigan Tunnel, or Grinnell Glacier. In the fall listen for the crashing of the males' horns during the mating season. A small herd of bighorns can usually be seen on a visit to Wild Horse Island.

Mountain Goats

One of the most easily observed mammals in the park, these daredevil cliff jumpers favor precipitous slopes where they can evade predators. In the winter they seek south-facing slopes where they can forage shrubs, grasses, sedges, lichens, and forbs. Logan Pass is almost a sure bet for seeing goats, and they become traffic stoppers on Going-to-the-Sun Road, where their white coats are easily spotted on the cliffs above the road. Hikers often encounter them at Gunsight Pass. Goat Lick, along Highway 2 near Essex, is another popular place. Goats hang out just across the Flathead River and are sometimes visible from the parking area or from the Goat Lick, a short trail walk from the road.

Elk or Wapiti

If you visit Glacier Country in autumn you might be lucky enough to hear the bugling of the male elk as they herd their harems and challenge other males during the breeding season. These larger cousins of the deer prefer coniferous forests interspersed with openings such as logged or burned areas and open grasslands bordered by shrubs and trees. They spend summers in high-elevation mountain meadows and are difficult to see. In winter, spring, and fall they may be seen in the St. Mary Flats area near the park visitor center, at Two Dog Flats and the Many Glacier Valley, and the southeast corner of the park near East Glacier. On the west side sightings have been reported in a wintering area along U.S. 2 east of Belton Hills, in the North Fork Valley, and in the grasslands along the Quarter Circle Bridge Road near Apgar. Check with a ranger about current sightings.

Gray Wolves

Wolves have made a comeback in Glacier Country after being virtually wiped out in the early twentieth century. Park biologists believe two packs have established themselves in the park and at least two more in the national forest. Most sightings have been reported in the North Fork Valley and it's possible to find their large paw prints in sand along the river and along the Inside North Fork Road at Hidden Meadow where they prey on small rodents. They shy away from people so consider yourself lucky if you actually get to see one. Do listen for them at night on the park's west side or in the Whitefish Range. There's nothing quite so thrilling as the wolves' evening chorus on a moonlit night in the Montana wilderness.

Pacific Harlequin Duck

For just a few weeks in mid-April until May, we can watch the entertaining courtship of these small dark-gray and white ducks on the frigid mountain streams in and near Glacier Park. They return from their winter home on the Pacific coast to the same streams where they hatched, to mate and raise another brood. Their antics as they maneuver the rapids in the waters of McDonald Creek express their clownlike plumage. This is a rare opportunity and one that attracts many locals year after year. They are also seen in the Big Creek drainage.

> # Insiders' Tip
>
> The most mysterious animal of all at Glacier National Park is a brown mountain goat . . . well, it has horns like a goat, but it's brown with a whitish rump patch. . . . It's true: You'll never see this animal in a guidebook: it's the *female* bighorn sheep. While most mammal guides include a picture of the bighorn ram—with its highly recoznizable, curling horns—they usually neglect the ewe, which looks very much the same but grows a set of short spiky horns instead (which in fact look like the horns of a goat). In the spring and summer, the females with their young live separately from the bachelor bands of males, who thus are not around to provide a clue to what this exotic animal might be. . . .

Bald Eagles

Even if you live where they are common, the sight of our national symbol always gives pause to the viewer. Its large size and bright white head against its dark body make it easy to spot. You may even locate a nest. Look for the birds near water, particularly along the North Fork of the Flathead River and major lakes, including Lake McDonald, Two Medicine, and St. Mary Lakes in Glacier National Park.

Wildlife Management Areas (WMA)

Montana has set aside areas across the state to provide winter range for deer and elk and breeding areas for waterfowl and upland game. Besides helping maintain healthy populations of these animals, these WMAs are great places to view a variety of wildlife and plants. Some are closed during wintering and breeding seasons. Many wetlands are closed during the spring nesting season. Signs at parking areas and trailheads specify the closure dates.

Waterfowl Production Facilities— Somers Bay

The north shore of Flathead Lake is a duck and goose paradise and pretty close to heaven for the other species that dwell or pass through there. Starting at the fishing access on Somers Bay, where waterbirds can be seen almost anytime of year, there is a nearly continuous strip of meadows and marshes that extends east almost to Bigfork. It's a great place to see redwinged and yellow-headed blackbirds, flickers, geese, ducks, and other waterfowl and the occasional deer. There are trails and small, informal parking areas. You can stroll in varied habitats or take a picnic and sit with the sun in your face and a breeze from the lake in your hair. This area is closed during the breeding season between March 1 and July 1.

Smith Lake Waterfowl Production Area

Located 7 miles west of Kalispell south of U.S. Highway 2, this 1,040-acre area encloses a lake and extensive marshes. It is a good area for viewing shorebirds, including phalaropes, yellowlegs, and waterfowl such as mallards, widgeons, pintails, and gadwalls. Also seen are Canada geese, grebes, gulls, tundra swans, and American bitterns that nest there. In the spring and fall, look for sandhill cranes in the western grassy meadows, or bluebirds nesting in boxes along the approach road. This is closed from March 1 to July 1.

Wild Horse Island

Bighorn sheep, mule deer, coyotes, bald eagles, ospreys, and the remnant of a wild horse herd live on this island. The mature forests of Douglas fir and ponderosa pine and flower-covered uplands also support goshawks, coyotes, marmots, mink, and numerous songbirds. Hiking trails lead to good viewing places.

Creston National Fish Hatchery

At this 74-acre hatchery located along a beautiful spring creek, you can see up to a million rainbow and cutthroat trout and learn how they reproduce in captivity. The facility raises and produces eggs for propagation in stocked streams and lakes. Birding for fish-eating birds is also excellent—osprey, great blue herons, kingfisher, and magpies. Canada geese nest near the picnic area and the young can be seen in the summer. The hatchery is open daily from 7:30 A.M. to 4:00 P.M.

Swan River National Wildlife Refuge

This 1,568-acre refuge is best seen by canoe, but a walk along Bog Road (generally impassible to vehicles) can yield sightings of some of its 171 bird species, including bald eagles, great blue herons, Canada geese, wood ducks, and yellowlegs. Keep an eye out for a glimpse of some of the large mammals found there seasonally, including elk, deer, moose, and grizzly and black bears. The refuge lies at the southern end of Swan Lake. It is closed from March 1 to July 1. Signs on the highway alert you to the entrance road.

Wildflower Viewing

"There is no color known to man that is not reproduced from its most vivid hues to the most delicate tints by the plants and rocks of Glacier Park," writes George Ostrom in his book, *Glacier's Secrets.* He adds, "If I were a painter, I'd go bananas ten times a day running into this kind of arrangement of flowers, lichens, and colored rocks." He expresses so well the thrilling sensation of coming upon the plants in Glacier Country. People simply don't believe how stunningly beautiful they are until they behold them with their own eyes. Be prepared for spectacular summer displays in the alpine meadows, but don't overlook the cheering brightness of the first buttercups in early spring or the last of the Indian paintbrush in fall. Because wildflowers are generally limited to a short blooming period, refer to the following list for suggestions as to when you are most likely to see certain plants and particular locations where they are known to grow.

May

Some of spring's first wildflowers appear this month in Wayfarer's and Lone Pine State Parks and on the Columbia Mountain trail near Columbia Falls. Among them are buttercups, glacier lilies, bluebells, and wild crocus.

June

Violets, pyrola, foamflower, and queen's cup bead lily come into bloom in the cedar-hemlock forests around Lake Mc-Donald. Wildflowers of the prairies and foothills begin to peak in June—look for pink shooting star and "lakes" of blue camas on the park's east side. The more colorful members of the fescue-wheatgrass grassland such as yarrow, purple fleabane, Saint-John's-wort, cinquefoil, spirea, lupine, and wild geranium put on bold displays at many locations, notably at lower elevations along Going-to-the-Sun Road, in the Polebridge area, and at Two Dog Flats on Going-to-the-Sun Road southwest of St. Mary.

July and August

The Danny On Trail on the Big Mountain, Jewel Basin, and Logan Pass are prime areas for viewing the spectacular but brief displays of alpine wildflowers. At elevations between 6,000 and 7,000 feet, blooms of every color include those of heather, gentian, Indian paintbrush, bear grass, and glacier lily. At Logan Pass you may find the rare dwarf alpine poppy. Stop at the Flathead National Forest Big Mountain Education Center for infor-mation and nature programs on the mountain.

August and Early September

Roadsides everywhere bloom in autumn. The backroads such as the North Fork Road, Camas Road, Hungry Horse Reservoir roads, and open areas along national forest roads treat you to the last of the season's Indian paintbrush, goldenrod, and asters and the beginning of the reds and golds of fall's trees and shrubs.

Huckleberry Picking

The area's exalted huckleberry is either more or less than you expect. For some people from wild blueberry country, such as Maine, northern Michigan, and Minnesota, the huckleberry is overrated. For others, the huck's wild tartness is far superior to the sweetness of its eastern cousin. For those who have never tasted either, the huckleberry is an unsurpassed blue-black globe of flavor and aroma worth the effort to pick or price to buy.

The berries provided sustenance in lean times for travelers, including the Lewis and Clark exploration team in 1805, and both Native American and white residents during the Depression, when whole families moved to the harvest sites and camped out, picking and preserving the berries. The huckleberry holds both culinary and ceremonial significance for the Salish and Kootenai peoples, who dried the berries for use in stews and pemmican.

The huckleberry industry, which has grown in recent years, produces a hundred different products, including preserves, pies, syrups, candies, and cosmetics, and most visitors take their huckleberries the easy way from the local purveyors, but if you want to try your hand at picking them yourself, here are some tips:

The best picking is usually found in areas opened up by forest fires or timber cutting, or along old roads. You can tell where the berries are prolific by where a lot of cars are parked. Try forest trails and abandoned logging roads when accessible spots get picked over.

The huckleberry shrub prefers north-facing slopes between 3,500 to 7,000 feet elevation, in moist, acid soils typical of coniferous forests. It grows from a foot to 6 feet tall and has short elliptical leaves. The white or pinkish bell-shaped flowers mature into small blue or black berries. They usually begin ripening from mid-July to mid-August, depending on the elevation, and they can be found on the highest slopes as late as October.

A battle of the berries may be in the making as humans take more and more of the harvest and grizzly bears are left with scarcely enough to fatten up for winter hibernation. In 1998 a lean huckleberry year, diminished even more by determined pickers, drove grizzlies in unusual numbers into residential areas in search of food and thus caused the termination of several grizzly bears.

You can buy a map of huckleberry areas at forest service district ranger offices, campgrounds, and the forest supervisor's office in Kalispell.

On the Trail—Hiking

Good, old-fashioned walking and bicycling are two of the most economical and simplest ways to explore this vast area with its infinite variety of environments and hundreds of miles of trails. Truly there is a trail for all hikers and bikers who want to leave their vehicles and steep themselves in this unsurpassed natural environment.

This section and the next will introduce you to a few of the best, easy-to-reach hiking and biking opportunities in Glacier Country and lists resources that can provide equipment, guidance, and information.

Hiking opportunities span trails of every description suitable for every type of walker, stroller, backpacker, and even the visitor in a wheelchair. The trails described here range from less than a mile to several miles, which can be accomplished in no more than a long day, even for slower sojourners. For short, short hikes in urban

Alpine wildflowers and breathtaking views greet visitors at Hidden Lake Overlook.

Photo: Carl Wells, courtesy of Flathead Convention and Visitor Bureau areas, check the individual city park descriptions. For longer day hikes and overnight and longer backpacks, consult *Hiking Glacier and Waterton Lakes National Parks* and *Wild Montana* (see the For More Information chapter). If you decide after you get here to do some backpacking, you can find rentals and maps to assure a satisfying backcountry experience. Check the resource list at the end of this chapter.

Safety and Comfort

Good, sturdy shoes or hiking boots and proper clothing are a must for enjoyable, safe hiking. Even in midsummer when the hot, dry days resemble Arizona weather, in the mountains the weather can change quickly to penetrating cold, wind, rain, and even snow. When hiking or biking, always carry headwear, mittens, and bodywear that is warm and wind and water repellent. In the mountains, hypothermia is possible even in the summer. Also carry more water than you think you'll drink. Keeping hydrated is critical to maintaining stamina and avoiding heatstroke in summer and hypothermia in winter. A small backpack or fanny pack stocked with a first-aid kit, water, and high-energy snacks such as nuts, fresh or dried fruit, and granola bars is indispensable for any but a few minutes' walk from your vehicle. Be sure to pack out all food wrappers, as well as fruit peels and cores, because even though biodegradable, they attract animals—including bears—to the trailsides. Observe signs or rangers' warnings of bear activity and take appropriate precautions. (See the Be "Bear Aware" Close-up in the Columbia Falls and the U.S. Highway 2 Corridor chapter.)

Although you can drive to many of the higher-altitude trailheads, don't forget that at several thousand feet above sea level, oxygen is less available and people with breathing or heart problems should be cautious.

Hiking Opportunities

National Forest Trails

The hundreds of miles of trail are mapped and described in a packet available from the forest supervisor's office in Kalispell and the district rangers' offices.

The Big Mountain

Big Mountain Village, Whitefish

Big Mountain's summit provides an array of hiking possibilities, with some of the most exquisite scenery in Glacier Country. Because the summit is snow-free only a few months, it's a treat to see the displays of alpine wildflowers and open meadows during July and August. Hiking season at lower elevations begins in June, but on the summit it begins after July 1 and lasts into September. The lift stops operation in early October and begins again when the ski season opens at Thanksgiving.

The Danny On Memorial National Recreation Trail is one of the most popular hiking trails for people seeking premier views, easy accessibility, and sections of varied length and difficulty. It was named in memory of a Forest Service silviculturist and nature photographer known for his beautiful pictures of the area, who died in a skiing accident on Big Mountain. It is actually six different hikes totaling 5.6 miles. The more ambitious hikers ascend it from the trailhead right above the Chalet in The Village, a distance of 3.8 miles taking about two hours. Others ride the gondola up to the Summit House and hike down. Two of the connecting trails are the East Rim Trail, which is a half-mile loop path along the summit, and the 3.8-mile Flower Point Hike back to the lift. Trail maps are available at the chair lift and the Summit House and Chalet at the Big Mountain Village.

Lone Pine State Park

Just 10 minutes southwest of downtown Kalispell, this Montana state park offers panoramic views from its trails of Kalispell, much of the Flathead Valley, and into Glacier Park. The 0.75-mile Overlook Trail begins near the visitor center. It's a wheelchair-accessible, self-guided interpretive trail leading to the Flathead Valley Overlook. The park also has 2.5 miles of multiuse trails for hiking, biking, and horseback riding with benches along the way for resting and meditation. From

Visitors and locals find some of the area's best nature viewing and hiking on the Big Mountain.

Kalispell go west on U.S. Highway 2 to Meridian Road, then south on Meridian to Foy's Lake Road. Proceed for 4 miles and turn left at the park sign.

Jewel Basin

This highly popular hiker-only area is noted for its beautiful scenery that features alpine lakes, mountain streams, meadows, rocky peaks, dense conifer woods, and wildflower displays. There are trails for nearly every age and ability. Many hikers aim for the high peaks that dominate the 15,340-acre area, but open country on the lower slopes affords views for the more casual walker or those with children. Mountain bikes and horses are excluded from the area. Jewel Basin is being loved to death and forest service managers trying to protect the resource have introduced new regulations this year to help reduce visitor impacts: Dogs must be leashed and groups hiking the area are limited to no more than 12 people. If you seek solitude, check with the rangers' office to see where there might be fewer people hiking that day. Located at the north end of the Swan Mountain Range between Kalispell and Hungry Horse Reservoir, the parking lot accessing the trails is reached by taking Echo Lake Road from Montana State Highway 83 and following the signs to Jewel Basin.

Glacier National Park

Most high-elevation trails in Glacier Park are only hikeable in midsummer after the snows have melted and into early fall, so be prepared to take an alternate route if ice and snow are still a factor.

Apgar Lookout Trail

West Side This short but moderately difficult trail ends at Apgar Lookout at 5,236 feet and rewards you with views of Lake McDonald and the full length of the Livingston Range. It begins on a primitive road, then leads over switchbacks across the foothills, giving glimpses of Great Northern Mountain, the Flathead Range, and Swan Range. To reach the trailhead, turn just inside the park's west entrance at the sign for the Glacier Institute Field Camp. Follow it to the T, turn right, and go a short distance to a V-intersection and take the left fork at the sign for Quarter-Circle Bridge. Go about a mile beyond the bridge and look for trailhead signs.

Avalanche Lake

West Side This lovely and not-too-difficult 2-mile trek begins in giant old-growth cedars on the wheelchair-accessible Trail-of-the-Cedars boardwalk, continues on a moderately steep trail along Avalanche Gorge through well-timbered hillsides, and emerges at the alpine lake nestled in a cirque among the peaks. For a first hike in Glacier Park, this is an especially satisfying one to take with a ranger-naturalist, and these interpretive walks are scheduled regularly throughout the season. See the park newspaper for times and just show up at the scheduled time at the Avalanche parking lot.

Hidden Lake and Hidden Lake Overlook Trails

West Side The 3-mile (6-mile round-trip) hike from the Logan Pass Visitor Center to Hidden Lake conveys you quickly into Glacier's high country on a moderately easy trail. It climbs to Hidden Lake Pass, where Mt. Reynolds and Bearhat Mountain dominate the skyline and Hidden Lake lies below. The trail to the overlook then drops nearly 700 feet to the north shore of the lake. Or you can go only the mile and a half to the Hidden Lake Overlook (3 miles round-trip on the boardwalk) and observe the intriguing tiny alpine wildflowers along the way. Whatever you choose this is a rare opportunity to experience an alpine ecosystem's plants and animals while savoring views of other Glacier high country. Interpretive information is available at the visitor center.

Highline Trail

West Side Little climbing and dazzling scenery await you here because you start at the top. The Highline Trail runs nearly 20 miles along the Continental Divide from Logan Pass into the Waterton Valley in Canada. It connects to several other trails going deep into the backcountry.

Forests and Fire Nature Trail

If you hiked the Huckleberry Nature Trail before the summer of 2001, your drive to the trailhead will be the same, but the hike will be completely different! The former Huckleberry Nature Trail weaved through a forest mosaic as it explored the processes of fire and regrowth following the 1967 Huckleberry Mountain Fire. However, now another layer has recently been added to the exploration of this area: The Moose Fire reburned this area in 2001. The Park Service has now renamed this the Forests and Fire Nature Trail and is coming out with a new trail brochure that will be ready for the summer of 2003. This will be a great spot to learn how plant and animal communities respond to fire.

St. Mary Falls, Virginia Falls, and Baring Falls Trails

East Side With trailhead parking areas along Going-to-the-Sun Road, the area offers interconnecting trails you can choose from to make a short hike to a single falls or hike them all. These hikes make a pleasant way to stretch your legs and view St. Mary Lake, its impressive surrounding mountains, and the creeks, gorges, and waterfalls there. From the St. Mary Falls pullout, you can hike the 1.2 miles to the falls and then go the additional .7 mile to Virginia Falls. The Baring Falls trailhead is located on Going-to-the-Sun Road about .3 mile west of Baring Creek. The St. Mary Falls Trail pullout is on the south side of the road about 6.5 miles east of Logan Pass and a mile west of Sunrift Gorge.

Ptarmigan Tunnel

East Side Some of the best park scenery is yours on this popular east-side trail. Allow a full day for this sometimes steep 4-mile hike that begins at Swiftcurrent and follows one of the best-engineered trails in the park, which includes a tunnel blasted through the mountain. Go through it and catch a view of the remote Belly River drainage. Hikers often spot grizzlies along this trail.

The trail begins across Going-to-the-Sun Road from Logan Pass Visitor Center at 6,646 feet in elevation and runs mostly level for the first 3 miles to Haystack Butte, making it suitable for a short out-and-back trip for seniors and young children. From Haystack Butte, the trail continues 4 more miles along the divide to Granite Park Chalet, and then drops 2,300 feet over 4 miles to the Loop parking lot on Going-to-the-Sun Road. Veteran hikers caution that this long downhill is hard on the knees. It's a nice all-day hike if you can shuttle with another car or have someone pick you up at the bottom.

Hiking Equipment Rental

Rocky Mountain Outfitters
135 Main Street, Kalispell
(406) 752-2446

This shop specializes in equipment, clothing, and information for the hiker and backpacker. They rent packs, climbing shoes, and other items. They have a good selection of books and maps and will help you plan a trip and know the best places to go for people of all sorts of abilities.

On the Trail—Biking

Flathead County is striving to become a biker-friendly area, but it has a long way to go to be a real biker's mecca. The county and its communities have been working to create a network of bike trails and bike routes that are envisioned to connect all the major populated areas within the decade. In populated areas a few short paved or hardened bike paths serve mostly the nearest residents. For vacationers who have brought or rented bikes and want a short jaunt in town, Woodland and Lawrence Parks in Kalispell have pedestrian-bike paths. There are also trail segments in Whitefish as well as in Columbia Falls.

The new historical trail in Somers is especially attractive for families with young children. This 1.5-mile paved hike-bike path provides a friendly place to meet local strollers and bikers, young and old. You can't miss the trailhead in Somers, with its large overhead sign announcing the Great Northern Historic Trail. Park along the road and enter the trailhead next to Tiebucker's Pub and Eatery (see

Scenic views await mountain bikers of all skill levels. Photo: Perry Johnson

Biking in the National Forest

The miles and miles of national-forest roads provide some of the best biking in Glacier Country because they can convey you into some of the most scenic and uncrowded areas of these wildlands. Bikes are allowed on all trails and roads, except in designated wilderness areas.

Tally Lake Ranger District

The Tally Lake District, north of Whitefish, has a network of easily accessible trails and roads suitable for individuals and families. Beginning mid-May to mid-June (depending on the year), bikers can spend the day biking, picnicking, and observing the wildlife and birds attracted by Tally Lake, reportedly the deepest lake in Montana. The district and Glacier Cyclery employees have mapped 10 good rides ranging from beginner to advanced difficulty levels. Mostly loops, they traverse a combination of singletracks and logging roads around the 4,800 feet altitude with little vehicle traffic. A local biker recommends the Reid Divide Trail as a "premier ride." It follows the ridge about 10 miles on a surface of mostly soft-packed forest duff before dropping down to the lake. Bikers have spotted varied wildlife, including moose, black bear, and porcupines. By late September snow has usually begun on the higher trails. The map is available at the district office and Glacier Cyclery (see listing in the Bike Rentals section of this chapter for further infomation).

The Big Mountain

Ride the gondola up to the top, then cruise down the trails on your bike. More than 20 miles of singletracks lead riders to stunning views of the Canadian Rockies, Glacier National Park, and the Flathead Valley. Summit Trail runs on an 8-mile singletrack between the top and the village. Another 12 miles of trails begin at the base of Chair 2. Twenty miles of trails lower down the mountain wind through forests and meadows accessed from the outpost. No trail fees are charged, but

the Kalispell chapter). You get panoramic views across the Flathead Valley to the Whitefish and Swan Mountain Ranges. The varied habitat along the open meadows, conifer-covered cliff-sides, and watery slough make it a great place for songbirds, waterfowl, small mammals, and wildflowers. This new trail is well-used by local families who stroll, jog, bike, in-line skate, or otherwise, with nonmotorized locomotion, which is the only kind allowed.

Mountain biking makes great sense in this great outdoor expanse, and that's the kind of cycling that's most popular. The following lists a few of the more accessible and popular bikers' destinations.

Enjoy the area's scenic bike trails. Photo: Steve Bly, courtesy of Flathead Convention and Visitor Bureau

there is an additional fee for bikes on the gondola. Rentals complete with helmets, water bottles, and trail maps are available at the hike-bike shop, conveniently located in the village.

Strawberry Lake Trail

The 10 bike trails at the north end of Jewel Basin have been mapped. The map can be obtained from the Forest Service. The trails are routed on a combination of Forest Service roads and unmaintained trails with a beginner's loop, and experienced bikers say the main 20-mile loop will challenge even the strongest cyclists. It's perfect for those seeking a challenging route amidst the beauty.

Glacier National Park

Bicycling in Glacier National Park can be fun, but roads are narrow and winding with little or no shoulder and congested during the main visitor season. From June 15 through Labor Day, bicycling is prohibited from 11:00 A.M. to 4:00 P.M. daily on Going-to-the-Sun Road from Apgar to Sprague Creek Campground and from Logan Creek to Logan Pass. There are no restrictions east of Logan Pass or on bikers traveling west. It generally takes about 45 minutes from Sprague Creek to Logan Creek and three hours from Logan Creek to Logan Pass.

Bicycles may be used only on established roads and designated routes. Bike travel is prohibited on all Glacier hiking trails except for the paved Apgar hike-bike path. Waterton permits biking on roads and has four hiking trails that bikers may travel.

Bike Rentals

Glacier Cyclery
336 East Second Street, Whitefish
(406) 862–6446

Here you can rent mountain bikes, touring bikes, and kids' bikes by the half day, full day, and week. The $25 mountain bike daily rate includes a helmet and a water bottle you can take with you. These

Insiders' Tip

For a springtime bicycling treat available only to those who are on the spot, check out the plowing report for Going-to-the-Sun Road in Glacier National Park. There's a couple of weeks each spring—usually late April or early May—when stretches of the road on the west side have been plowed, but the roadbed itself is still too damp to bear the weight of automobile traffic. During this period when the pavement is drying out, the park opens the road to hikers and bicyclists. It's a wonderful treat: You can drive as far as the road is open to cars— usually to Lake McDonald Lodge or Avalanche Creek— and then unload your bike and start riding! With just hikers and bicyclists on the road, there's a sort of holiday feel as the pace is mellow; people stop, get out their binoculars to scan for wildlife, and chat with friends and neighbors. How far you can go depends on the plowing operation, but sometimes you can bike as far as the Loop (which makes for a great downhill run back—be sure to wear your helmet). Please remember the road is "officially" a trail at this time and not open to dogs. And dress warmly! It's usually a good 5 to 10 degrees colder up here than in the Flathead Valley.

folks worked with the Tally Lake Ranger District to develop a map of the best trails on the district, so they will steer you to the best local cycling areas on roads or trails. They also rent panniers, trailers, and car racks.

Wheaton's
214 First Avenue West, Kalispell
(406) 257–5808
Wheaton's is a long-established, full-service bike shop that offers sales, service, and rentals. They rent mountain bikes, with sizes for both kids and adults, for $20 per day (including helmet). Regular store hours are Monday through Saturday from 9:00 A.M. to 6:00 P.M. and Sunday from noon to 4:00 P.M.

Horseback Riding

If a horseback trek in Glacier Country is indispensable to your experience here, stables are handily located in and near Glacier National Park. Outfitters offer different trips from one hour in duration to all day at a range of costs from $18 per hour to $125 per day. The season for horse riding in the park is short because of the wet or snowy trail conditions.

Mule Shoe Outfitters
P.O. Box 322, West Glacier
(406) 888–5010, winter (928) 684–2328
Mule Shoe runs guided trips into the park's backcountry during the summer months from two stables in the park. The stable located across Going-to-the-Sun Road from McDonald Lodge begins trips in late May; call (406) 888–5121. The Many Glacier stable opens in early June; for information, call (406) 732–4203.

Rawhide Trail Rides
12000 Highway 2 East, West Glacier
(406) 387–5999
Located close to Glacier Park, this outfitter provides guided horse treks into the surrounding Flathead National Forest lands. They open mid-May and operate to mid-October, depending on the season's weather. They also offer backcountry

Trail riding is a popular Glacier Country activity.
Photo: courtesy of Flathead Lake Lodge

overnight trips and saddle-paddle trips in conjunction with a rafting outfitter. They are easy to locate behind the covered wagons at Rawhide Trading Post.

On the Water

A river runs through it; and creeks, sloughs, lakes, and wetlands are abundant. In Glacier Country, wherever you look water defines the landscape. Trying to imagine it without alpine lakes mirroring the mountains, creeks rushing to the Flathead River, and Flathead Lake's azure expanse is like trying to imagine the Arctic without icebergs or the Sahara Desert without sand. These waters give passage to treasured places difficult to reach by land. They bring exhilaration and excitement where they boldly rush through rapids or peace and tranquility where they quietly pool. There's a water adventure awaiting all seekers.

More and more opportunities become possible as local businesses seek to provide the best and most up-to-date equipment for the increasing number of recreationists attracted to these waters. Area kayaking and sailing events draw participants and spectators from near and far.

If you brought your canoe, kayak, rowboat, or sailboat, you're set to hit the water. If you didn't, rentals are available and affordable. If you've never been on the water, now is the time to get your feet wet with one of the established and reliable guide services, whose staffs want to give you nothing but a wonderful experience on their home waters.

Keeping Our Waters Wild and Wonderful

With more and more people discovering Glacier Country as a place to live and vacation, growing numbers of people are on the waters. The local, state, and federal agencies charged with managing the resources for the benefit of ecosystems and the residents who live and play there need the cooperation of visitors to assure they remain enjoyable for generations to come. The primary agencies dealing with water recreation in the area are the Flathead National Forest, Glacier National Park, and Montana Fish, Wildlife and Parks (FWP). They have lots of handy resource materials regarding regulations, maps and guides, and other materials to help make your water play safe and enjoyable. They are listed at the end of this section.

Warnings and Regulations

Glacier Country's streams and rivers vary greatly in their water conditions. High water from spring runoff usually begins in May and peaks in June on most river stretches. Always check with the agency in charge and scout the area as much as possible yourself. Whether you bring your own vessel or rent one, seek advice from local dealers, who usually get the latest scuttlebutt from local river runners about current conditions.

Glacier Country's changeable weather is particularly significant for lake boaters. High winds can descend quickly on Flathead Lake and small craft are advised to stay close enough to shore to return safely.

Personal flotation devices (life jackets) must be worn on flat-water trips as well as white-water adventures.

If you are floating in the fall, check on hunting seasons and take precautions in national forest and Montana state lands when going ashore and walking away from the water course. Trespassing on private land can sometimes be a problem. Public-access areas are usually well-defined, but many shorelines are a mix of public and private ownerships, which are not always well-marked.

It is a little-known fact that, despite legitimate concerns about bears and bear safety, the number-one killer in Glacier National Park is not bears but drowning. Two water fatalities occurred in the summer of 2002, both when visitors stepped too close to the edge of rushing water and fell in. In one case it took more than a week to recover the young man's body, which was trapped below a waterfall. In other years boaters have been taken by surprise in the spring by shifts in the rivers over the winter. High spring runoff has taken its toll, and sometimes death has followed from hypothermia rather than immersion itself. Be careful—learn the local conditions, go with experienced people, dress appropriately, and use the right gear. If you don't come home, you can't go out again.

Powerboats

Montana boating regulations require all motorboats and personal watercraft (PWC) such as Jet Skis to be registered and numbered, including out-of-state boats used here more than 90 consecutive days. These regulations also apply to sailboats 12 or more feet long.

Recent regulations include more stringent wake restrictions for northwestern Montana. With a few exceptions all watercraft must maintain no-wake speeds within 200 feet of the shoreline of all lakes. All watercraft must maintain no-wake speeds on lakes 35 acres or less.

Children age 12 years or younger must be accompanied by someone at least 18 years old to operate a motorboat or PWC of more than 10 horsepower. Youths age

13 to 14 must have a Montana motorboat operator's safety certificate or be accompanied by someone who is at least age 18. Persons renting motorboats or PWCs more than 10 horsepower must be at least age 18. There are strict regulations regarding boat operation, including wake restrictions, launching and mooring, harassment of wildlife, waste discharge, noise limitations, and others. Personal flotation devices (PFDs), such as life jackets, and other safety devices, such as fire extinguishers, are required in most circumstances. You can pick up a copy of the regulations at Montana Fish, Wildlife and Parks. We recommend another helpful brochure available from the same offices: *Ethics, Etiquette and the River Recreationist.*

If you decide to go on a guided trip or commercial boat cruise, the U.S. Coast Guard advises that prospective riders are responsible for their own safety and should check out the operators of boat rides and cruises and follow these guidelines. Before leaving the dock talk to the operator about the driver or guide's qualifications and try to ascertain that the person in charge of your watercraft is not impaired by drugs or alcohol. Do they know first-aid and CPR? A smart skipper will take time to give passengers a review of safety equipment and rules of conduct. Check out the equipment for individual personal life jackets, radio, fire extinguisher, and navigation lights and how to use them. If you had to, could you start, stop, and steer the boat, or turn on navigation lights? Also find out the trip plan, the route, and the return times.

Paddling Montana, by Hank and Carol Fischer, *Three Forks of the Flathead River Floating Guide,* published by the Glacier Natural History Association, and a Flathead National Forest map should be especially useful for planning your water recreation in Glacier Country. The map, besides showing river and lake access on Forest Service lands, gives a wealth of information on all public lands, including lists of lakes, camping and other recreation areas with keys to services and opportunities at each. It's well worth its $6.00 cost. With these in hand your dream

> ## Insiders' Tip
>
> Glacier National Park is not dog friendly. Because of the presence of bears and mountain lions, dogs must be on a leash at all times in developed areas and along roads. Dogs are not permitted on trails at all. The major reason for this is that bears chase dogs . . . and dogs run back to their owners. Dogs also may not be left unattended in cars. Kennels are available in the Flathead Valley if you plan to backpack or do extended day hiking in the park.

water vacation will be a matter of a little research and decision making. To get you started we offer a few suggestions.

Glacier National Park

Glacier National Park's lakes provide some of the best quiet and scenic paddling in the area and allow intimate exploration of shorelines seldom reached on foot. Even on the lakes where tour boats cruise, an unhurried day of gliding these crystal lakes can be nothing but pleasure.

The park doesn't charge fees for boating but does have regulations, a set of which can be obtained at headquarters or visitor centers. Canoes, kayaks, and sailboats are permitted on all park waters except upper McDonald Creek between Mineral Creek and Lake McDonald. These areas are closed to all types of boating and floating to protect the harlequin duck. Personal watercraft such as Jet Skis are currently prohibited on all park waters. Privately owned, motorized boats are prohibited except on Lake McDonald, and St. Mary, Two Medicine, and Bowman Lakes, the latter being limited to 10 horsepower or less. Wearable personal flotation devices must be on board for each passenger and children must wear theirs while aboard. The park imposes both permanent and temporary shoreline closures in a few areas, usually to protect breeding wildlife. Always check with a ranger to be sure what's in force during your stay.

Canoes, rowboats, and low-power motorboats can be rented at Two Medicine, Many Glacier, and at Apgar and Lake McDonald Lodge on Lake McDonald. For those who seek a really quiet, pristine canoeing spot and don't mind traveling a long, primitive road to get there, we recommend Kintla Lake on the park's west side. It's a perfect jewel surrounded by heavily forested mountains, with no motorboats allowed and only a small primitive campground. But don't tell anyone else about it.

Area Lakes and Rivers

The larger and many of the smaller lakes have one or more easily reached boat-access sites. Flathead Lake State Park has them at each of its five units. Whitefish Lake State Park has a ramp on the southwest shore. Swan Lake's public access is located at the recreation area just north of the town of Swan Lake. Popular Forest Service access sites include Tally Lake northwest of Whitefish, Ashley Lake west of Kalispell, and numerous locations on Hungry Horse Reservoir reached from East Reservoir Road (turn off U.S. 2 at Martin City) and West Reservoir Road leaving U.S. 2 at the Hungry Horse Ranger Station. Motorized boats are permitted on these lakes, but check with Fish, Wildlife and Parks to see if waterfowl-nesting-season restrictions are in force in some areas.

Flathead Lake Marine Trail

Flathead Lake Marine Trail is designed specifically for kayaks, canoes, and small sailboats, with a network of access points and stopover areas. It would be useful for planning a day or multiday outing around the lake, with stops at islands in the middle of the lake. It's a perfect opportunity to spot the famed Flathead Lake Monster. Campers pay overnight and vehicle-parking fees at Flathead Lake State Park. Between October and April, parks provide no drinking water. Pack-in, pack-out rules apply, and no pets are allowed at Wild Horse Island. Diamond-shaped signs mark landing areas. A trail map and guide is available from Fish, Wildlife and Parks.

The Flathead River

The Flathead River has a split personality. Each of its three branches, the North Fork, Middle Fork, and South Fork, offer distinct environments and adventures. Some or all of these forks are included in the National Wild and Scenic Rivers, a total of 219 miles. The Middle Fork, where *The River Wild* was filmed, is suitable only for skilled rafters and kayakers or those with guides. The South Fork, which lies mostly in the Bob Marshall Wilderness, is only accessible on foot or horseback except for one section in the central part at Cedar Flats River Access. This fork has classes II and III waters with one gorge that is rated class V to VI, and must be portaged—definitely only for the experienced. The North Fork arises in Canada and forms the western boundary of Glacier National Park. It has several public access points from both Inside and Outside North Fork Roads. It flows clear and cold through conifer-covered mountains and is suitable mostly for intermediate and expert floaters. During spring runoff, which begins in May and can last into July, fast currents and logjams offer thrills and challenges. The best conditions are usually from mid-July to mid-August. The section between Polebridge and Big Creek is suitable for beginners only during low water and fair weather, and floaters should be watchful of riffles, logjams, and narrow channels.

For the first-time or short-time visitor, the Flathead's best offering is its main stem below the South Fork's junction just above Columbia Falls. After spring runoff it flows leisurely on the remainder of its

Flathead Lake is big enough to delight every sailor. Photo: Carl Wells, courtesy of Flathead Convention and Visitor Bureau

journey to Flathead Lake through a braided channel among sloughs that provide habitat for waterfowl, raptors, and beaver. It makes a good half- or full-day outing in good weather. Public access ramps are at Kokanee Bend, Pressentine Bar, and Old Steel Bridge.

Swan River

The Swan River careens northward 40 miles to Swan Lake from its three Mission Mountain headwater lakes, then gradually slows as it continues another 10 miles to its delta in Flathead Lake at Bigfork. The channel is heavily forested and bordered by abundant wildlife habitat. The upper Swan is narrow and even in its wider lower portions, logjams make it technically demanding and sometimes treacherous, especially in high water. If the Swan's beauty makes you yearn to put in your canoe, two stretches are worth exploring. In low water, 2 to 3 miles above Swan Lake the river slows and meanders at a pace suitable for beginners. Put in at the county bridge just above the Swan River National Wildlife Refuge, where waterfowl, shorebirds, deer, muskrat, and other wildlife are often spotted. The Swan also attracts many streamside anglers, so you may see more people than you expect, but it's still a quiet experience. Local floaters favor the 7-mile trip beginning at the bridge east of Ferndale, which is easy enough for beginners during low water in August and September. Leave the final mile, "Wild Mile," to daredevil kayakers.

Swimming

Opportunities for water play are abundant in Glacier Country, whether it's swimming, wading, building sand castles on a river sandbar, or collecting pretty, colored stones along the lakeshores. It's generally an informal affair and often the kids play along the riverbank while Mom and Dad fish. Many of the numerous public-access areas on lakes and rivers are free of charge and all you need is a bathing suit and advisedly protective footwear, as few areas have sandy beaches. All units of Flathead Lake State Park charge a day-use fee

that includes the use of shorelines, some of which have swimming areas roped off. For the most part you can swim anywhere on public lands and should take care you don't trespass on private land. The water is gloriously clean and clear nearly everywhere.

Popular swimming areas include Flathead Lake, Whitefish Lake City Beach, Foys Lake, Whitefish Lake State Park, Lake McDonald, and Hungry Horse Reservoir. Woodland Park in Kalispell has a swimming pool, including a wading pool. Call (406) 758-7812 for hours and season. Columbia Falls also has a municipal pool. To inquire about swimming there, call Columbia Falls City Pool, (406) 892-3500.

Sea-Kayaking Guides and Rentals

Glacier Sea Kayaking!
390 Tally Lake Road, Whitefish
(406) 862–9010

Oceangoing fiberglass sea kayaks are stable crafts that anyone in moderately fit condition can operate with guidance for an enjoyable adventure around the shores of Flathead Lake. Glacier Sea Kayaking! offers classes in a supportive learning environment through Flathead Valley Community College. Group sizes are small with a high guide-to-student ratio. Call for equipment reservations and rates, as well as to schedule individual or group instruction. In addition to paddling classes, Glacier Sea Kayaking! offers a variety of other topics, such as navigation and gourmet outdoor cookery.

Glacier Sea Kayaking! also specializes in multiday trips, with destinations that include Yellowstone Lake, the San Juan Islands off Seattle, Washington, and the Missouri River. This last trip is becoming especially popular as the Lewis and Clark bicentennial approaches: Consider booking your boat now to float down what Lewis and Clark struggled up 200 years ago! The float is generally four to five days long and includes a chance to hike and climb in the White Cliffs area. Glacier Sea Kayaking! is also known for its gourmet meals, prepared for your floating pleasure.

Glacier Sea Kayaking! offers Necky, Northwest, and now two British-made kayak brands, Nigel Dennis and Valley Canoes (yes, a canoe is a kayak in Britain) for sale. Kayaks are available for rent but you must take a 1½-hour safety lesson prior to rental.

Silver Moon Kayak Company
1215 North Somers Road, Kalispell
(406) 752–3794
www.silvermoonkayak.com

Sea kayaking is clearly booming in the Flathead Valley, and it's easy to see why. It offers a quiet, low-impact way to explore lakes and big rivers, and many boats have the capacity to support extended trips as well as day excursions. More and more of the boats around the Flathead are coming from Silver Moon Kayak Company, owned and operated by Susan Conrad and Bob Danford. Like other operations, they offer a variety of boats for sale and rent, including Eddyline, Boreal, and Walden brands; half- and full-day guided trips; moonlight tours (of course!); and instructional classes taught by ACA-certified instructors. Classes range from recreational paddling, all-women's classes ("BIBS"—Babes in Boats), to all-out eskimo rolling, and class sizes are deliberately kept small to promote personal attention. Silver Moon also maintains a fully stocked kayak shop. No need to order, go home, and wait for your paddle gear to arrive; it's here, right now!

Whitefish Sea Kayaking
321 Columbia Avenue, Whitefish
(406) 862–3513

Whitefish Sea Kayaking focuses on making kayaking in the immediate area—Whitefish Lake, Whitefish River, and Flathead Lake—convenient and affordable. Owner Mark Roy carries Seaward and Current Designs boats, which are available for sale or rent. They rent for $20

Sea kayaking is booming in the area as a quiet but exciting way to explore lakes and large rivers.

Photo: Silver Moon Kayak Company

per half day or $30 for a full day, and the company will drop off and pick up the boats for free in the Whitefish area. Whitefish Sea Kayaking also offers regular tours of Whitefish Lake, Whitefish River, and Flathead Lake, at a rate of $55 for a half-day (three hours) or $75 for a full-day tour (six hours). Boaters bring their own snacks or lunches. Moonlight and custom tours are also available, as are lessons in rescue or advanced paddling skills. Please call for rates; there is a two-person minimum.

Canoe and Kayak Rentals

Rocky Mountain Outfitters (RMO)
135 Main Street, Kalispell
(406) 752–2446
RMO rents "demo" white-water boats to those considering making a purchase.

Ski Mountain Sports
200 Wisconsin Avenue, Whitefish
(406) 862–7541
Ski Mountain Sports rents Wenonah canoes for $35 a day, including life jackets and paddles. For an additional $10, they will drop off and pick up your group from either end of the Whitefish Canoe Trail.

Rafting Guides and Rentals

These folks love the rivers and want you to love them, too. They also are passionate about keeping these waterways and the plants and animals living there healthy and happy for generations to come. They are all established companies with experienced guides. Their prices for half- and full-day raft and kayak trips are within a few dollars of each other, with similar equipment and services provided. Charges for half-day raft trips run about $40 for adults, $30 for children. Full-day trips cost about $73 for adults, $48 for children. Some or all gear is provided at this cost. These trips also have a scenic option that has little or no white water. The companies also offer hike-raft, hike-horseback, extended wilderness trips, fishing excursions, fly ins, and other enticing combination packages, each distinctive to the

company offering them. If you're single or a couple, expect to share a raft with strangers, from four to six others. The main tours feature some measure of white water, depending on the month and melting snowpacks feeding the rivers. Scenic cruises provide relaxing jaunts on quieter stretches. Most companies require a four-person minimum for them, but nothing seems hard and fast with these folks. They want to give you the best deal they can. They are delighted to tell you about their menus of river trips. Check out their Web pages for more detailed information.

Glacier Raft Company
6 Going-to-the-Sun Road (next to the Alberta Visitor Centre), West Glacier
(406) 888–5454, (800) 235–6781
www.glacierraftco.com
Established in 1976, Glacier Raft Company is the oldest continuously operating raft company in Montana. It also gained prominence as host and technical adviser for production of the Hollywood movie *The River Wild.* Glacier Raft runs multiday, full-day, and half-day trips on both the North and Middle Forks as well as the main stem of the Flathead River. Eight riders on a raft is the norm, with a minimum of four. Full-day trips include a barbecue lunch. They also rent inflatable kayaks for self-guided trips on the calmer stretches and provide shuttles.

Great Northern Whitewater Raft and Resort
U.S. Highway 2, West Glacier
(406) 387–5340, (800) 735–7897
www.gnwhitewater.com
Great Northern's office is easy to spot 1 mile west of the Glacier Park entrance, by the red caboose on the hill. Now more than 25 years in business, Great Northern takes you down the Middle Fork of the Flathead River. They usually operate from mid-May into early October. In high water during spring, they use larger rafts holding 10 to 12 people. Late-season trips or when water levels are lower use six-person rafts. Morning trips come with a complimentary breakfast. They rent inflatable kayaks for self-guided trips on the Middle Fork only. With Swiss-style chalet rental, raft trips, and fishing excursions, Great

Glacier Country visitors find thrills and spectacular scenery rafting the Flathead River's Middle Fork.
Photo: Carl Wells, courtesy of Flathead Convention and Visitor Bureau

Northern can be your nonstop vacation center.

Montana Raft Company and Glacier Wilderness Guides, Inc.
Box 330, West Glacier 59936
(406) 387–5555, (800) 521–7238
www.glacierguides.com

Begun in 1983, Montana Raft Company and Glacier Wilderness Guides is the only company permitted to guide hikers in Glacier National Park. Its guides are knowledgeable about the area's natural history. During its season, from May 15 to September 30, it guides white-water trips on the Middle and North Forks of the Flathead River. It runs smaller rafts with six to eight people maximum, but a four-person minimum for the scenic float. All its trips are guided and fees include all necessary equipment. All-day tours feature a deli lunch. It is located 1.5 miles west of

the west entrance to Glacier. Glacier Wilderness Guides offers 3-, 6-, and 10-day backpacking trips.

Wild River Adventures
11900 U.S. Highway 2 East, P.O. Box 272
West Glacier 59936
(406) 387–9453, (800) 700–7056
www.riverwild.com

Wild River Adventures is entering its 20th year of guiding white-water rafting trips on the Middle and North Forks of the Flathead. The company also rents inflatable kayaks and rafts. Raft rentals cost $150 per day and they may require that you have a guide, depending on your experience and river levels. Prices include a full wet-suit package with everything else needed. Its season runs from May 15 to September 15. They are located 1 mile west of the west Glacier National Park entrance.

In the Snow—Skiing and Other Winter Sports

Winter in Glacier Country revolves around snow—how much, what kind, and how best to get out in it. Snow transforms the land into a winter wonderland and offers a menu of exciting outdoor adventures for young and old, timid and adventurous. Deep snow and frozen waterways make accessible places in the park, national forests, and lakes that are either difficult or impossible to reach at other times of the year. The possibilities range from a high mountain snowmobile tour to skiing in the silence of Glacier National Park's valley forests. For many insiders, winter is the best season and the reason they moved here.

Skiing, both alpine and Nordic, becomes the central preoccupation in many people's lives and in the area's economic life. The same folks you see biking and hiking in summer head for the slopes after work and on weekends. Snowboarding has skyrocketed in popularity. One of the things that makes the area so desirable is that the outdoor opportunities are so many and so close to the cities and towns. In fact you can cross-country ski in town in Kalispell, and just a couple of minutes outside Whitefish.

As in other seasons, winter weather differs, often drastically, on either side of the Continental Divide. On the west side winters are generally cloudy, cool, and wet. Only occasionally does the mercury dip below zero, as the cloud cover and moderating influences of Lake McDonald in Glacier National Park and Flathead Lake keep temperatures in the teens and twenties. Areas east of the Divide tend to be much colder, less snowy, and more windy. Driving can be tricky as the high winds pile the snow into deep drifts on the roadways and you can experience whiteouts with near-zero visibility.

Locals will generalize about the weather, then tell you there really is no typical winter. The winter of 1996–1997 deposited 12 feet of snow in the Flathead Valley, and cross-country ski courses stayed open into April. Snow was sparse the following year, disappointing all skiers, snowmobilers, and ski resorts. In 1998–1999 the ski resorts reveled in frequent powder showers, and cross-country skiing continued well into March even at the lowest elevations.

Snow in the valley bottoms can be deep or disappointing. But even when there's little snow down below, you can almost always find plenty in the mountains above 5,000 feet. The mountains receive about 80 percent of their precipitation as snow. While those clouds are hanging over the mountaintops blotting out the sun, they are dropping snow on the peaks, amassing a snowpack that usually lasts well into summer. As late as June, I've seen bikers with skis or snowshoes strapped to their backs heading up Going-to-the-Sun Road (before it opens to vehicles), where they will stash their bikes and take off into the remaining high-country snow.

With thousands of miles of forest roads and trails, backcountry snowmobiling ranks high on the list of winter activities. For the less ambitious or adventurous there are rinks for ice-skating, in-town hills for sledding and tubing, and even mushers who will take you for a dogsled ride.

Winter Safety Tips

Don't let winter's soft, snowy beauty dull your awareness of its hazards. Lack of awareness and planning can be fatal. Whether you are snowshoeing, skiing, snowmobiling, or hiking, when you're away from towns in Glacier Country, you are "out there" and you are on your own.

If you are venturing into the backcountry, travel with a partner, let someone know where you are going and when you expect to return, be sure you're in shape for the level of exertion you plan, check the weather and road conditions, and carry emergency-survival equipment and supplies.

The risk of hypothermia and frostbite hovers just beyond your mitts and parka, even when it doesn't seem that cold. It is the primary killer of outdoor enthusiasts.

Emergency Gear

Glacier National Park and the surrounding wildlands provide unbounded recreational opportunities for the outdoor enthusiast. However, hidden amid the scenic grandeur of the area are risks and hazards that can be deadly. Precipitous terrain, swift and cold water, wild animals, and ever-changing weather are all factors that contribute to the wildness of the area.

It is important that you engage in outdoor activities that are compatible with the skill and physical capabilities of everyone in your group. Always evaluate your group and assess the hazards before leaving on your trip. Avoid traveling solo and advise family or friends of your route.

Responsible backcountry travelers are always prepared for the unexpected. Specific equipment that you bring should be governed by the type of outing that you engage in, but consider taking the following as standard emergency gear:

- ☐ Map and Compass. A topographic map of your area, as well as a compass.

- ☐ First-Aid Kit. Being able to treat injuries and illness in the field can make a big difference in the well-being of someone in your party. Emergency medical services may not be readily available.

- ☐ Emergency Signaling Device. Be prepared to signal both aerial and ground search-and-rescue personnel. Helpful items include a whistle, a signal mirror, and an emergency signal that sends up smoke.

- ☐ Fire Starter. Your survival could depend on your ability to make a fire. Consider taking a candle and cigarette lighter. Fine steel wool or rubber bands make good fire "kindling."

- ☐ Adequate Food and Water. Calorie intake and hydration (enough water) are essential to your comfort and safety. Boil, filter, or treat backcountry water to avoid giardiasis. Carry extra high-energy snacks.

- ☐ Reliable Wind and Rain Gear. This is hypothermia country. A sturdy rain and wind parka and pants are a must to enable you to stay warm and dry.

- ☐ Bivouac Bag or Space Blanket. Be prepared for an unplanned night in the mountains. These items can help provide some protection from the elements. Carry a piece of insulated pad to provide insulation between your body and the ground.

- ☐ Layered Clothing. Dressing in layers of clothing allows you greater opportunity to regulate your temperature.

High technology has surfaced in the wilderness in the form of satellite phones. Many look at these devices as an intrusion into the "wilderness experience," while others consider the "dial-a-rescue" potential. Unregulated, these phones remain a personal choice. However, keep in mind that they could lead to a false sense of security—they can't take the place of common sense and appropriate skill.

With hypothermia, a person's inner core is chilled, resulting in slowing of mental and physical responses. Be alert to common symptoms—drowsiness and confusion. Once hypothermia has set in, external sources of warmth are necessary to restore the victim to normal. To stave off hypothermia drink plenty of liquids, stay dry, wear layers of warm clothing, and snack frequently.

Frostbite can also mar your trip if you don't wear warm clothing and avoid exposing skin in freezing or windy conditions in which windchill becomes a factor. Be alert for whitening tissue and numbness in cheeks, noses, fingers, or toes, which are especially prone to frostbite.

Avalanches

Avalanches can occur at any time during the winter. Snowmobilers are at greatest risk because their powerful machines can carry them into the highest and most-avalanche-prone reaches. They outnumber other Montana snow recreationists in avalanche deaths each year.

An understanding of avalanche conditions is the snowmobiler's and skier's best defense, but if caught in an avalanche a survival kit can save a life.

Experts advise the following:

· Avoid mountainous terrain after heavy snowfall or prolonged high winds.
· Avoid crossing steep slopes and steep-sided canyons.
· Keep to the windblown side of ridges.
· Learn avalanche danger signals.
· Carry and know how to use transceivers, probe poles, and shovels.

If caught in an avalanche:

· Remain calm so that you can remember what to do.
· Get away from your snowmobile. Try to stay on the surface and "swim" toward the side of the avalanche.
· As you stop, try to paw an airspace around your face. If you are a survivor, mark the place you last saw the victim, look for him or her downhill from there, and probe the area. Unless help is close, stay with the victim and keep searching.

A half hour is all the time you usually have to save your companion's life.

For information about avalanche conditions, contact Glacier Country Avalanche Center at (406) 257-8402 or (800) 526-5329 (Montana only) or visit www.glacier avalanche.org. The For More Information chapter lists some helpful books on avalanche safety, as well.

Downhill Skiing

Big Mountain Ski and Summer Resort
Big Mountain Road, Whitefish
(406) 862-1900, (800) 858-5439
www.bigmtn.com

The Big Mountain attracts winter sports enthusiasts from all over the United States and Canada. It is among North America's largest ski and summer resorts, with more than 3,000 acres of skiable terrain and a view from the 7,000-foot summit. Snowfalls annually shower the peak with about 300 inches of the white stuff. *Ski Magazine* readers consistently rank the Big Mountain No. 1 in Montana and among the nation's top 20.

Especially renowned for its powder, the half-century-plus-year-old resort offers a fine experience for every level of skier. Besides following the 81 marked trails, skiers can enjoy the freedom of open bowl and tree skiing. An atmosphere of celebration usually permeates the village area as skiers, snowboarders, tubers, and sightseers buy their tickets, debark busses, and circulate between the lifts and slopes and the restaurants, pubs, and shops. Just 5 miles from downtown Whitefish, "the village" attracts not only skiers, but also locals and visitors.

A variety of lifts, from a gondola and high-speed quad lifts to a platter and T-bar, will get you to your desired height and location on the mountain, whether you are a novice or schuss boomer.

The 2002–2003 daily rates were $47 for adults, $34 for ages 7 to 18, and $39 for seniors age 62 and older. Children age six and younger ski free. The more adventurous can hitch a 12-person Snowcat ride to a summit ridge, then descend on skis through powder-covered glades. Make reservations for a four-hour session with the Ski School. In a group of 3 or more people, the cost is $60 per person; for 2 people, it's $90 per person; for an individual, it's $180.

Lighted slopes extend your skiing day Wednesdays through Saturdays, December through March from 4:30 to 9:00 P.M. for $14. The Big Mountain Ski School has many programs and rental equipment is available for alpine and Nordic skiing and snowshoeing. There is also a day-care center. The Big Mountain's ski season runs from Thanksgiving until the second week of April. The Shuttle Network of Whitefish runs the "Snow Bus" to the Big Mountain Village from locations throughout Whitefish free of charge.

Blacktail Mountain Ski Area
P.O. Box 1090, Lakeside 59922
(406) 844–0999
www.blacktailmountain.com

"Uncrowded, affordable and friendly" describe the features skiers find in Glacier Country's newest downhill ski area. The spectacular views and top-notch slopes on the summit of Blacktail Mountain make the 14-mile drive through national forest from Lakeside well worth the effort. As you reach the top on a wide, well-maintained Forest Service road, vistas greet you across Flathead Lake and the Flathead Valley to the Swan and Mission Mountain Ranges. The road heads west from U.S. Highway 93 leaving just south of Lakeside. It takes 30 to 45 minutes to drive from Kalispell to the summit and lodge.

Blacktail first opened in early December 1998 after a flurry of construction to complete the 200-acre development on 1,000 acres of national forest lands. It straddles the mountain's 6,676-foot summit, which receives average yearly snowfalls of 250 inches. In a reverse of most alpine situations, skiers descend from the "base" lodge and pick up the lifts at the lower terminal some 1,440 feet below. The 24 groomed runs cover 13 miles of trails with a full range of challenges for every level of skier.

Blacktail attracts many people who seek affordable alpine skiing in a relaxed setting with all the necessary amenities. There's reasonably priced day care for the

Waist-deep powder and snowghosts—a skier's dream. Photo: gravityshots.com

children, who can also take skiing or snowboard lessons from qualified instructors. You can also savor the views and the food at one of the two restaurants, or have a hot drink in the lounge *after* you've conquered the slopes.

During Blacktail's season, from mid-November to April 1, it is open Wednesdays through Sundays and holidays 9:30 A.M. to 4:30 P.M. It offers two double chair lifts, one triple lift, and one beginner's platter. Daily ski-rental package prices are $15 for adults, $12 for children, and $22 for snowboards and gear. Full-day passes in 2002–2003 cost $27 for adults, $18 for students and juniors (ages 8 to 18). Children age 7 and younger and seniors age 70 and older ski free. Season and family passes are also available.

Cross-Country Skiing and Snowshoeing

The Big Mountain Nordic Center
The Outpost Ski Shop, Big Mountain Road
Whitefish
(406) 862–1900, (800) 858–5439
www.bigmtn.com

Take to the wide trails hovering around the 5,000-foot level that let the beginner enjoy the easy ones and the advanced skier take the challenge of steep runs, all winding through conifer woods. These trails are some of the first in the area to receive snow.

The Outpost and Nordic Center, with its large parking area and activity area, are reached by the Big Mountain Road. Park your car and walk to the trailhead, which leaves just below the Outpost building.

Groomers sweep and set tracks daily on the 9 miles of trails with both classic and skating lanes. The 1.5-mile Weasel Trail is lighted for night skiing Wednesday through Sunday.

The ski shop sells the $5.00 daily cross-country passes, rents skis and boots, and arranges lessons and tours. They also rent snowshoes and teach you how to use them. Snowshoe lanes and trails run around the cross-country area. The season extends from about Thanksgiving until early to mid-April.

Glacier Nordic Center and Outback Ski Shack
1200 Highway 93, Whitefish
(406) 862–9498 (November 1 through
March 31)
kalispell.bigsky.net/outback

Located at the Whitefish Lake Golf Club, the Outback Ski Shack offers conveniently accessible, affordable skiing just west of Whitefish. Nearly 7.5 miles of gently sloping trails wind around the golf course, with views of Whitefish Lake and the Whitefish Range. It's a perfect course for beginners and intermediates, but the racers in town also train there because it's easy to get to for a noontime run. The Glacier Nordic Club sponsors the center and has the trails groomed daily for ski skating and track skiing. Nearly 2 miles of trail are lighted nightly, making for a pleasant after-dinner family activity. Glacier Nordic Ski School offers instruction programs including classes for kids, seniors, skate skiing, and classic skiing. The club asks a $5.00 donation, which, along with club memberships, covers the cost of grooming and equipment. No dogs or snowshoes are permitted.

Outback Ski Shack rents ski equipment packages for half and full days (24 hours). Costs are $10 for a half day and $14 for a full day for adults; children's prices are $8 and $10, respectively. Skiers with small children can rent a pulk (child-towing sled) for $5.00 per hour or $20.00 per day.

Glacier Ski School offers daily lessons at 1:00 P.M. in touring, skate skiing, and classic group. Please inquire for rates.

The center trails are generally open from mid-December through mid-March. For more information contact the Glacier Nordic Club, P.O. Box 433, Whitefish, MT 59937.

Buffalo Hill Golf Club
1176 North Main Street (P.O. Box 1116)
Kalispell 59903
(406) 756–4545

Located a stone's throw from downtown Kalispell, the club opens its 27-hole golf course to cross-country skiers when snow conditions permit, usually from December 1 to March 1. Beginners and intermediate skiers will enjoy a relaxed tour on the gentle slopes, along the Stillwater with views of the mountains. Trails are not groomed, but skiers soon have tracks leading to the best slopes and scenery. This is a perfect choice when you have only a short time to get your blood racing. Warm your toes and tummies with food and beverages at the cozy clubhouse. It's open from 9:00 A.M. to 5:00 P.M., Mondays through Fridays throughout the year.

Izaak Walton Inn
U.S. Highway 2, at Milepost 180, Essex
(406) 888–5700
www.izaakwaltoninn.com

Thirty kilometers of scenic backcountry trails await you at this historic location on U.S. Highway 2 between West Glacier and Marias Pass near the Continental Divide.

Snow Country magazine named the Izaak Walton one of the top-10 cross-country ski resorts in the Rockies.

The inn was built in 1939 to house winter snow removal crews working on the Great Northern Railway tracks. Railroad workers still stay there and the track complex behind the building evokes the excitement and romance of a long-distance train ride through the west. Helper engines still push trains over the pass from the rail yard. Some vacationers, both local and continental, arrive by Amtrak train for their ski holiday. A new bridge across the railroad tracks now offers convenient, safe passage to ski areas.

Railroad buffs will enjoy the yard activity and memorabilia such as signal lanterns, historic posters, and dining-car menus carrying out the inn's decor. Eighteen and a half miles of groomed and tracked trails appeal to beginner and advanced skiers on scenic slopes ranging from 3,000 to 4,500 feet in altitude. Lights on the Starlight Trail permit nightly skiing until 11:00 P.M.

The high elevations, with earlier and heavier snows than most other areas, yield a longer season, from late November to mid-April. You often have the trails to yourself. This area is perfect for snowshoeing, and trekkers can take several trails that are marked specifically for them. Around every bend in the trail lies a postcard view of distant snow-covered mountains or an intimate scene of a snow-banked mountain creek. A real favorite with advanced skiers is the half-mile loop along the Flathead River.

You can rent skis, snowshoes, and ski sleds here. They also offer ski lessons and guided trips into both Glacier Park and the Bob Marshall Wilderness. A $10 daily pass admits you to all trails.

Snowboarding's popularity is still growing, and not just with the younger set. Photo: Jeff Curtes, courtesy of Big Mountain Resort

Glacier Wilderness Resort
U.S. Highway 2, at Milepost 163, Nyack Flats
(406) 888–5664
www.glacierwildernessresort.com

Located 10 miles east of West Glacier, this year-round resort nestled in the conifer forests grooms 12 miles of national forest trails leading right from their door, and they don't charge for the access. Beginner and intermediate skiers will enjoy these trails coursing about the 3,500-foot elevation. For the more adventurous skiers, ungroomed trails lead into the higher elevations and more challenging touring. For early season skiing, call ahead for snow conditions, as first snow dates vary from mid-October to mid-December.

Swan Valley Nordic Ski Club
P.O. Box 5082, 71284 Montana Highway 83
Swan Lake 59911
(406) 886–2080
laughinghorselodge.com

The newest Nordic ski association in the area, the Swan Valley Nordic Club makes its headquarters at the Laughing Horse Lodge in Swan Lake. Sixty kilometers of trails, some groomed, in the nearby national forests await cross-country skiers and ski lockers are available. For a ski vacation, you can sleep in one of their log cabins, dine in their rustic dining room, and warm up by the wood stove in the common room. See the accommodations section of the Swan Valley chapter for more information.

Flathead National Forest Trails

The immenseness of the area and the vast network of Flathead National Forest roads beckon the backcounty skier to endless pleasure. Most of the roads remain unplowed and are used by both skiers and snowmobilers. The Tally Lake, Swan Lake, and Hungry Horse districts offer groomed trails where snowmobiles are prohibited. Forest Service maps identify the roads suitable for skiing. Maps are available from the supervisor's office in Kalispell or the district offices. For general recreation information call (406) 758-5204.

Round Meadows, Tally Lake Ranger District

Off the beaten track in the Flathead National Forest, 15 miles northwest of Whitefish, Round Meadows has nearly 7 miles of intermittently groomed trails open between mid-December and mid-March. Mostly beginner and intermediate slopes wind through woods and meadows. Snowmobiles and dogs are prohibited. Logging may restrict or close some trails. For information call the district ranger in Whitefish, (406) 863-5400.

Blacktail Mountain, Swan Lake Ranger District

Twenty-five miles of groomed or packed forest trails lead you along scenic ridges and slopes with panoramic views of Flathead and Mary Ronan Lakes and the Mission and Swan Mountains. Trailheads and parking area for the lower and upper runs are about 6 and 8 miles from Lakeside on Blacktail Mountain Road. At about 5,500 feet, this area offers 7 miles of easier and 18 miles of more difficult trails.

Flathead County Recreation Department grooms the trails regularly. For a ski condition report, call (406) 758-5800. For area information call the Swan Lake Ranger District, (406) 837-7500.

Jewel Basin, Hungry Horse Ranger District

This is a spectacular and popular backcountry use area, with 15,349 acres of high mountains with 35 miles of trails, some suitable for backcountry skiing. Take Echo Lake Road from Montana Highway 83 northeast of Bigfork and follow the signs to Jewel Basin. For information call the Hungry Horse Ranger District at (406) 387-3800.

Essex area

Several miles of touring trials lie along the Middle Fork of the Flathead River across from the Izaak Walton Inn. The inn grooms the trails intermittently and has Forest Service trail maps.

Glacier National Park Winter Activities

Winter simply magnifies Glacier Park's special magic. The snow-covered roads become pathways into silence and into the heart of scenic areas away from crowds and cars. The season finds increasing numbers of skiers and snowshoers making the park their haven, with new residents exploring their new home ground and conferencegoers taking a day to recreate. Vacationers have discovered it as a way to unwind from the high speed and activity levels of the Big Mountain. The park prohibits snowmobiles anywhere within its boundaries. Check at park headquarters, (406) 888-7800, for snow conditions. A cross-country skiing brochure with map and descriptions is available at the Apgar Visitor Center, which is open winter weekends from 9:00 A.M. to 4:00 P.M., (406) 888-7939.

Upper Lake McDonald

Going-to-the-Sun Road is kept plowed to McDonald Lodge, where it is barricaded. From there skiers and snowshoers take two popular routes: the 11-mile round-trip through the cedar-hemlock forest along McDonald Creek to Avalanche Picnic Area or the 5-mile loop from the barricade to the footbridge across the creek and back downstream to Lake McDonald Ranger Station Road.

Apgar–West Glacier

Several routes lead from two parking areas here: at the horse barn reached by taking the first left off Going-to-the-Sun Road after the entrance station and at the barricade on Camas Road just beyond the McDonald Creek Bridge. The trails range from 2 to 3 miles round-trip to nearly 12 miles. The park brochure describes them in detail.

Polebridge

From the Polebridge Ranger Station parking area, four popular routes follow either relatively level unplowed gravel roads into broad open meadows or lead to the hilly and sometimes icy 12-mile round-trip to Bowman Lake. Several of these are especially suitable for families with small children. To reach the ranger station, take the North Fork Road leading from Columbia Falls toward the Canadian border, but check on road conditions, especially after heavy snows.

St. Mary

From the special parking area near the Hudson Bay District Office (just south of the town of St. Mary) several routes, including short loops, lead into level areas and rolling hills with views of St. Mary Lake and the Red Eagle Valley. Some are specially designated and marked.

Two Medicine Valley

Two Medicine Road, which remains unplowed, is used as a ski trail with several destinations, long and short, easy and strenuous, through this highly scenic valley. Start at the end of the plowed road, usually 4 miles north of East Glacier near the junction of Highway 49.

Wagner's Duck Lake Lodge
P.O. Box 218, Duck Lake Road, Babb 59411
(406) 338–5770

East of Glacier, tourist activities come to a near-dead stop during the winter. The visitor is greeted by boarded-up inns, restaurants, and shops. In Babb, on the Blackfeet Indian Reservation, Wagner's offers year-round accommodations—including rooms, meals, and information about winter recreation in the area. If you're happy with unpretentious, down-home comfort, Wagner's will suit you. It's located only 2 miles from world-famous Duck Lake, renowned for its enormous rainbow trout. Ice fishing is popular and it's a short driving time to Glacier National Park's cross-country ski areas. Wagner's also rents an ice sailboat. With these activities and 350 acres of lands to explore by snowmobile, Wagner's makes a good winter headquarters east of the Divide.

Glacier Park Ski Tours
728 Kalispell Avenue, Whitefish
(406) 862–2790; (800) 646–6043, PIN 3724

How'd you like to spend a day in Glacier's winter backcountry with a guide who'll safely escort you to prime locations and interpret the wondrous landscape you encounter? Put yourself in the hands of experienced guides who are skilled in winter mountaineering, avalanche safety, and first aid. Owner Rusty Wells brings more than 20 years of guiding experience to the business and says people really appreciate being able to go out with a guide who knows the natural history, the trails and how long it takes to travel them, and how to get to the best spots for scenery, wildlife, or terrific skiing. He has trips for just about every interest and ability: day tours, backcountry tours with overnights in an igloo, and evening tours on full-moon nights. Day tours, including a meal, cost $200 for 1 to 3 people, $250 for 4 people; each additional person is $30. Please inquire for multiday and full-moon trip rates.

Snowmobiling

This is truly a snowmobiler's paradise with more than 200 miles of groomed snowmobile trails and nearly 2,000 miles of USDA Forest Service roads that can lead you into great hill climbing, powder play, and spectacular ridgetop views of Glacier National Park, the Flathead Valley, and the Canadian Rockies. Snowmobile organizations are instrumental in keeping the trails maintained in cooperation with the Forest Service and groomed during the long season in the high country. They educate other riders about safety, outdoor survival, and avalanche awareness to keep the sport enjoyable for all. One of the area's most popular trails is the groomed Skyland–Two Medicine Snowmobile Trail that meanders along the Continental Divide, back and forth between the Flathead and Glacier Counties. Well-marked trailheads and parking areas border U.S. Highway 2 at the pass. Maps are available from the Cutbank Snowgoers or the Lewis and Clark National Forest, see below.

Cutbank Snowgoers
Box 301, Cut Bank 59427
Lewis and Clark National Forest
1101 15th Street North, Box 869, Great Falls
(406) 791–7700

The Cutbank Snowgoers grooms trails east of the Continental Divide and the trails on Marias Pass that traverse both the Flathead and the Lewis and Clark National Forests.

Flathead Snowmobile Association
P.O. Box 5041, Kalispell 59903

The Snowmobile Grooming Coalition, composed of area businessmen, supports the association financially through donations and fund-raisers.

J & L RV Rentals
1805 Highway 2 West, Columbia Falls
(406) 892–7666
www.jandlrvrentals.com

You're not a skier but ache for a snowy mountaintop adventure? A guided snowmobile excursion is a good bet for an unforgettable experience in the Whitefish Range high country. J & L RV Rentals of Columbia Falls operates a snowmobile guide service under a special-use permit with the forest and runs tours in conjunction with the Big Mountain and on their own. Guides are trained in avalanche awareness, CPR, and first-responder training.

At the Big Mountain, two three-hour guided tours leave daily from the Summit lift area, at 9:00 A.M. and 1:00 P.M. The charge, including a lift ticket, is $125 for a single rider, $145 for two, and no charge for a rider younger than 12 years old. Full-day trips begin at $225. A boots, gloves, and suit package rents for $25. Helmets and transceivers are mandatory and are issued at the trailhead at no charge. All trips are guided, but they provide plenty of free playtime (supervised) for fun. More details can be found at www.bigmtn.com—click on "winter" and then click on "snowmobiling." Call for reservations at (406) 862–2900.

J & L also offers rental equipment and guide service at its shop in Columbia Falls. Guides are optional, but first-timers are strongly encouraged to engage a guide. Rentals of machines and gear-clothing packages come with orientation about the equipment and directions to the area's snowmobile routes. Helmets and transceivers are mandatory. J & L will deliver the machines to the main local trailhead at Canyon Creek Road, about 5 miles north of Columbia Falls on the North Fork Road. This trail system accesses the Whitefish Range trails from the opposite side of the Big Mountain and leads into a wonderland of high-country tracks running north to Red Meadow within 15 miles of Canada. Half-day rates begin at $100, full days at $150. They also rent trailers. Owner John Altenburg says people should feel free to call the shop for trail or other information. About a third of the people who come into the shop are just seeking information, and that's fine with him because he just wants to see people out there having fun.

Other Winter Sports/ Activities

Dogsled Rides

Dog Sled Adventures
P.O. Box 34, Olney 59927
(406) 881–BARK

Located 20 miles north of Whitefish on U.S. Highway 93, exactly 2 miles north of Olney, on the east side of the road, a half mile past mile marker 147.

With a Montanan the 1999 Iditarod Race winner, dog sledding seems an appropriate way to spend a day in Glacier Country. Dog Sled Adventures takes you on a 1½-hour trip along a 12-mile loop through the Stillwater State Forest with a team of fast and friendly Alaskan huskies and other breeds. Afterwards they pamper you with hot chocolate and cookies by the fire and exchanging of tall "tails." Wear warm clothes, including hat and mittens, and bring sunglasses. If it's very cold you will be encased in a warm cocoon of down and elk skins. After the trip you can pet the dogs. Reservations are advised. The cost is $60 for adults and $30 for children.

Ice-Skating

Frozen lakes and ponds abound in Glacier Country, but you won't see many ice-skaters on them, because snow is usually too plentiful to keep them shoveled, with the possible exception of the Blackfeet Indian Reservation, where winds tend to keep lake surfaces clear. Skaters can take advantage of two public rinks. Woodland Park's rink has a warming hut and offers rentals and lessons during December and January for children and adults. See the Kalispell section of the Attractions chapter for more information on Woodland Park.

Mountain Trails Ice Skating Center
725½ Wisconsin Avenue, Whitefish
(406) 863–2477

The rink is just outside Whitefish on the way to the Big Mountain. Whitefish Parks and Recreation runs the facility, which is open for public skating on a variable daily schedule. It is also open Friday and Saturday nights from 6:00 to 11:30 P.M. and Sunday afternoons from 2:00 to 7:00 P.M. It offers rentals, skate sharpening, and instruction.

Sledding and Tubing

Some people enjoy sledding and tubing when conditions are right. It can provide inexpensive, convenient family fun when only a few hours are available. The Big Mountain has set aside a tubing area and families can slide on popular hills in Kalispell, Whitefish, and Columbia Falls. Municipal recreation departments can guide you to sliding hills and places where you can rent equipment.

Hunting and Fishing

Hunting

The long-standing tradition of hunting wild game to fill the winter larder still burns strongly in Glacier Country as elsewhere in Montana. The homesteading way of life counted the harvest of meat and fish from the woods and rivers as a vital means of supplementing field crops or cash from timber. The abundance of fur-bearing mammals brought the first non-Native people to the mountains, and northwestern Montana is still one of the few places in the country where trappers can still trap wolverines, pine marten, and some other species. Bird hunters find upland game birds here, especially ring-necked pheasant, Hungarian partridge, and several species of grouse. Ducks and geese are abundant, with Canada geese so common that some hunters are calling them "flying carp."

Realistically, however, Glacier Country hunting is limited compared to other areas of the state. This is because well over half of the land is either in Glacier National Park, where no hunting at all is allowed, or on the Blackfeet and Flathead Indian Reservations, where only limited game-bird hunting is open to the public. National forest lands in Glacier Country are largely roadless wilderness areas and require backpacking or horseback to reach the game. The remaining, more accessible national forest acres, state forests, state recreation lands, and private lands do provide hunters with opportunities for whitetail, mule deer and game-bird hunting. Hunters seeking a challenge can take home an elk if they are willing to stalk in steep terrain. Moose, bighorn sheep, and mountain goat hunting permits are granted through drawings. Out-of-state hunters tend to be few, perhaps because of the cost and difficulty in obtaining big-game permits which, except for black bear and mountain lion, are awarded to non-residents only through drawings.

For those who want to include hunting in their Glacier Country visit, a guided trip with one of the licensed outfitters provides a good option. A list of outfitters is available from the Montana Outfitters and Guides Association, listed at the end of this chapter.

Licenses and permits are obtained from the Montana Department of Fish, Wildlife and Parks (FWP) offices or from license agents. People using Montana State Trust lands for hunting, fishing, or simply walking must also have a state recreational-use license, also available at FWP and Montana Department of Natural Resources and Conservation. Regulations and dates of seasons change from year to year so it's wise to get a copy of the most current ones from FWP or the Flathead and Blackfeet Indian Reservations.

Fishing

Although not generally acclaimed as a "fishing destination," Glacier Country satisfies many anglers, both local and visiting, with food and diversion in scenic splendor that more than compensates for any deficiencies. A rich variety of lakes, rivers, and streams attracts a dedicated bunch of local anglers on a regular basis, rain or shine, cold or wind. Trophy lake trout, or Mackinaw, still thrill their catchers and send them home with either something to display on their walls or some great eating with friends and family. Fly fishers and catch-and-release enthusiasts will find some exciting fishing.

Montana's Fishing Access Sites program provides recreational opportunities for residents and visitors. These sites have parking areas, usually either vault or flush toilets, and are well marked with the brown and white, hook-and-fish logo on road signs leading from the main highways.

Fishing license requirements for Montana residents are as follows: younger than age 12, no license is required; youths ages 12 through 14 need only a conservation license; people ages 15 through 61 must purchase both a conservation and fishing license; and those age 62 and older need only the conservation license. The conservation license costs $4.00; the fishing license, $17.00. Nonresidents younger than 15 need no license if they are with a licensed adult, but the combined catch limit is the same as for a single fisher. Anglers over 15 years old must buy a conservation license and a fishing license. The two-day nonresident fee for both is $22. Full-season licenses are $60. No license is required for fishing in Glacier National Park. Call (406) 888-7800 for information about fishing there. Resource agencies of the Flathead and Blackfeet Indian Reservations require permits to fish on the reservations.

Streams and rivers open for fishing the third Saturday in May and close November 30. Lakes and reservations are open year-round, with a few exceptions.

Catch and Release

In northwestern Montana anglers may not deliberately fish for bull trout except on Swan Lake, where the limit is one; bull trout are a federally listed threatened species. Pictures and descriptions of this species are available at FWP and fishing shops. Some other species are restricted to catch and release on local streams and lakes. Check the current fishing regulations for such restrictions.

If you practice catch-and-release fishing, improve your techniques to reduce stress on fish. Use hook-removal tools and if you must handle the fish, use soft, wet gloves, or at least wet your hands.

· Use barbless hooks for fast and easy hook removal.
· Artificial lures and flies cause far less mortality than bait.
· Play the fish as rapidly as possible, not to its total exhaustion.
· Don't squeeze the fish or put your fingers in its gills when removing the hook. If deeply hooked, cut the line as close to the mouth as possible; don't yank the hook out.
· Release the fish only after its equilibrium is maintained. If necessary, gently hold the fish upright facing upstream and move it slowly back and forth.

In order to prevent both the introduction of non-native fish into new areas and the spread of disease, it is illegal to move live fish and aquatic insects, or to use live bait or to dump bait buckets.

Fishing the Lakes

Mountain lakes generally are icebound until mid-June or early July. Trails to some may not be cleared until midsummer or later. Inquire about conditions at the agency in charge of the public lands where

Fly-fishing the Middle Fork of the Flathead River adjacent to Glacier National Park.
Photo: Montana's Finest Resorts

the lakes are located or at local fishing-supply shops. Be prepared for biting insects and unpredictable weather. In Glacier National Park, Lake McDonald and St. Mary Lake are more renowned for their beauty than for their fish. The best fishing lakes are said to be on the east side, but on either side the very best fishing is in the less-accessible lakes that require a 4- to 10-mile or better hike. We've listed a few of those accessible by vehicle or a short, easy hike.

Avalanche Lake, Glacier National Park

In a lovely alpine setting surrounded by mountain peaks, Avalanche Lake is an easy 2-mile hike from Avalanche Creek Campground on Going-to-the-Sun Road.

Cutthroat trout is the main species here and 8- to 10-inch fish are in good supply mainly in June and July.

Bowman Lake, Glacier National Park

The best time to catch the resident lake trout, kokanee, and cutthroat in Bowman Lake is right after spring breakup and in the fall. The boat access ramp lies just beyond the campground. The campground is about 7 miles from the Polebridge Ranger Station on a poor dirt road.

Church Slough

About 6 miles southeast of Kalispell, Church Slough, a large oxbow lake, lies along Lower Valley Road. It is popular with local anglers for it yields largemouth bass, northern pike, and yellow perch. A boat helps the catch.

Echo Lake

Echo Lake is known for its largemouth bass, northern pike, and yellow perch. Sunfish are also caught here. You can launch your boat at the state ramp at Echo Lake Marina. Parking and shore access are poor. The best fishing is in the spring and fall.

Flathead Lake

Flathead Lake seldom freezes over so year-round fishing does take place, attracting anglers seeking its renowned trophy lake trout as well as whitefish and yellow perch. Somers Bay, Woods Bay, and state park units have boat launches. There is a small fee at the state parks for day use or camping. Parking areas are set aside for boat trailers. Somers and Wayfarers State Parks are wheelchair-accessible.

Hidden Lake, Glacier National Park

Set in a beautiful alpine cirque, Hidden Lake is a scenic fishing site for Yellowstone cutthroat. A moderately strenuous 3-mile hike from Logan Pass will offer spectacular scenery, and you're likely to see mountain goats on the way. The lakeshore is accessible for easy bank fishing. Bring polarized glasses to see fish through the bright reflections on the water.

Josephine Lake, Glacier National Park

June and July are the best months to catch the brook trout and kokanee in this small lake just a 1.5-mile walk from Many Glacier Hotel. If you have a light canoe or inflatable kayak, take it.

Kintla Lake, Glacier National Park

Continue on about 12 miles beyond the Bowman Lake turnoff on the Inside North Fork Road and you come to one of the prettiest lakes in the park, with reasonably good fishing as well. Boat fishing is best, but shore fishing is also satisfying away from the road and campground. It has cutthroat, lake trout, and some kokanee.

Swan Lake

Swan Lake attracts many boat anglers who use the launch ramp at the state recreation area just north of the town of Swan Lake. There is little shore access. From May through October kokanee, rainbow trout, westslope cutthroat, and northern pike can be taken. This is the only place it is legal to take bull trout; the limit is one.

Swiftcurrent Lake, Glacier National Park

You could practically throw a line into this lake from your room at the Many Glacier Hotel. But for best results do your angling in June or July from a boat and try to bag some brook trout reputed to run about 10 inches.

Tally Lake

On the Tally Lake Ranger District northwest of Whitefish, Tally—the state's deepest lake—is nearly 500 feet deep. The fishing is not the best, but it's a perfect spot for a family outing when some members want to fish and others want to bike, hike, or just picnic. There's a boat launch at the campground. Try your luck at the cutthroat, rainbow, kokanee, and northern pike.

Two Medicine Lakes, Glacier National Park

The beauty of these lakes—lower, main, and upper—makes it a joy to fish with a

Swan Lake attracts anglers with its quiet, scenic setting. Photo: Ann Purcell, courtesy of Flathead Convention and Visitor Bureau

fairly good chance of catching rainbow and brook trout. Most run under 15 inches. Best fishing is in June and July.

Creeks and Rivers

The Flathead River system offers a wide variety of fishing opportunities. The other rivers have either poor fishing or poor access. The Stillwater and the Whitefish are slow and bordered by pastures and urban development, but there are a few places where people fish successfully for northern pike and rainbow trout in the spring. On the Swan River the inexperienced boater or angler will have the safest, most satisfying experience with a guide. Brush and logs make it difficult and sometimes dangerous to navigate or wade, and private land ownership closes off a lot of the shore access.

Anglers seeking a more serious fishing experience in Glacier Country are advised to hire a guide or consult the extensive array of books about Montana fishing that give detailed descriptions of the waters, fish, lures or bait, and techniques needed for best results.

Flathead River

The Flathead River system is vast and much of it, especially the Middle Fork and South Fork, lies deep in the wilderness, and that's where the most interesting fishing occurs, according to the experts. The North Fork, which is road-accessible along much of its way, has bull trout, westslope cutthroat trout, and mountain whitefish. The four-hour float from Big Creek to Glacier Rim is a popular float among locals. The main Flathead channel below Columbia Falls offers reasonably good populations of westslope cutthroat, mountain whitefish, and rainbow trout from Columbia Falls to Kalispell, especially between Pressentine and the Old Steel Bridge.

Fishing Charters

Flathead Lake charter fishing doesn't usually start up until early May when the lake is full. During the winter months and on into April, water levels are so low the larger boats cannot get to the water. The Flathead Lake charters use downriggers to catch the Mackinaw lake trout that is the main species now caught, and their large size makes them the preferred species with most anglers. The outfitters do not generally sell licenses, so to avoid delays call ahead and arrange to buy your license elsewhere the day before.

A Able Fishing Charters and Tours
Marina Cay, Bigfork
(406) 257–5214

Located in the motel-restaurant complex at the intersection of Grand Drive and Montana Highway 35, A Able has been running charters for 18 years. Owners Shorty George and Jeannie Goggins use both large and small covered boats with bathroom facilities for their fishing charters on Flathead Lake. They take all comers, including children, and have had guests in their eighties. No experience is necessary to catch fish. On morning charters fish are guaranteed: no fish, no pay. Charter costs include all equipment and a snack or meal depending on trip length. Half-day (five hours) small-boat trips for one or two people are $230, for three or four, $270.

The full day (nine hours) costs $330 for one or two, $385 for three or four. The larger boats are $25 more.

Bagley Guide Service Fishing Charters
Woods Bay Marina, Bigfork
(406) 837–3618

Owner Dusty Bagley brings years of Flathead Lake fishing experience, top-of-the-line boats, and state-of-the-art equipment to his charter fishing cruises. He guarantees you will catch lake trout that usually range from 5 to 15 pounds. He offers half-day and full-day cruises for up to five people. Toilet facilities are provided on some boats. Bagley's charters operate out of Woods Bay Marina, located about 4 miles south of Bigfork. Call for current prices.

Glacier Anglers
U.S. Highway 2, West Glacier
glacierraftco.com

A branch of Glacier Raft Company, this full-service fly shop and outdoor store is located ½-mile west of West Glacier. The shop features fishing and outdoor gear, rentals, and gifts. Inquire about their half-day, full-day, and multiday guided fishing trips. Glacier Raft Company also rents nine fully furnished deluxe cabins overlooking the mountains of Glacier National Park. Call for current trip rates.

Lakestream Fly Fishing Shop
334 Central Avenue, Whitefish
(406) 862–1298

Lakestream's most popular trips are their drift-boat floats down the Flathead River. They also guide anglers down the Swan River and on private lakes. They can take you where you are most likely to find cutthroat, rainbow, and lake trout, pike, bass, and whitefish by boat or as a walk-wade trip. Their jet boats get you through the meanders on the lower Flathead. Waders, rods, reels, and other equipment are included in the trip price unless unusual gear is requested. Their experienced guides have the patience of Job and can assist you with either spinner or fly-fishing. Their main goal is to show you a good day whether you catch fish or not. Lakestream offers group and private fly-fishing classes at Big Mountain and other locations.

The Northern Rockies Outfitter
7680 Highway 2 East, Columbia Falls
(406) 892–1188
www.northernrockiesoutfit.com

Owner Richard Birdsell offers guests a variety of fishing opportunities based on his years of experience guiding and instructing fly-fishing. Trips include Flathead River drift-boat floats for native cutthroat and rainbow trout, mountain-lake fishing and hike-in mountain-stream fishing. Lake trips go mainly to the Badger–Two Medicine area on Glacier Park's east side for wade-walk or float-tube fishing. Half-day river floats trips cost $225 for two people, full-day, $325. Call for current prices of other trips.

Golf

Glacier Country golf courses don't have to toot their own horns. Lots of others are doing it for them. In September 2000, *Golf Digest* named the Flathead Valley among the top-50 best golf venues in the world. *Golf Digest* had earlier described Flathead golf as having "terrific courses, excellent weather, welcoming locals, unparalleled natural beauty and prices that seem too good to be true."

You will find a course suited to your golfing goal whether it's to enjoy a few relaxing hours in the unsurpassed scenery with friends and family or to test your mettle on a tough 9 or 18 with other scratch players. The mild valley weather often means you can golf an extended season. It's not unusual to see players on the course in mid-December or mid-March. All the courses listed are open to the public. Consistent with a popular retirement area, several clubs are affiliated with a golf community. Some of the golf clubs and area hotels have teamed up to provide package deals for accommodations and course admission.

Yardages mentioned are for the men's white tee. Greens fees and cart rentals are quoted for 18 holes on 18-hole courses. Rates are for guaranteed advance, regular season. Two- or three-day advances cost a few dollars less. Cart rates are per person. All courses prohibit pets and metal spikes.

Flathead Valley Golf Association provides a central reservation service at (800) 392-9795.

Buffalo Hill Golf Club
1176 North Main Street, P.O. Box 1116
Kalispell 55903
(406) 756-4530, (800) 342-6319
www.golfmt.com

Buffalo Hill Golf Club ranks consistently on *Golf Digest*'s list of top courses and places to play. The 27-hole, target-oriented course keeps golfers returning to play in one of the most picturesque, natural settings anywhere. Along with the spectacular views of the Swan and Whitefish Mountains and plays along the Stillwater River, golfers often see moose and other wildlife. The buffalo herd of the original owner is no longer there, but the name evokes its history. The original, stand-alone Cameron Nine is a 3,200-yard, regulation, par-36 course. The 6,284-yard,

par-72 Championship 18, designed by Robert Muir Graves in the classic 1930s style, retains its push-up and multilevel greens and offers challenges you can increase from the back tees. This course has the highest slope rating in the Flathead Valley. The rustic log clubhouse encloses the pro shop and full-service lounge and restaurant. Call for current greens and cart fees.

Eagle Bend Golf Club
279 Eagle Bend Drive (P.O. Box 1257)
Bigfork 55911
(406) 837-7310, (800) 255-5641
www.golfmt.com

Golf Digest has rated this 27-hole resort course the No. 1 golf course in Montana and among the top 50 in the nation. Flowing in and around trophy homes and condominiums, the original 18 holes enclose the natural features of rocky cliffs and mammoth outcroppings, stands of Douglas firs and cattail marshes with landscaping in a skillful blending of human and natural developments. Views of Glacier's peaks and the Salish Mountains east of Flathead Lake provide a 360-degree scenic feast. The 6,189, par-72 course attracts high handicappers and scratch golfers who seek a variety of challenges. The newest nine, designed by Jack Nicklaus, provides a stand-alone course running along the lake and ponds. The pro shop, restaurant, and Hap's Bar share the large clubhouse near the entrance. Main season (June 2 through September 16) greens fee is $57. Off-season fee, $34.

Glacier Park Lodge Golf Course
East Glacier Park

History and scenery combine to make this nine-hole golf course a unique experience. It was built in the late 1920s by railroad magnate James J. Hill alongside the resort hotel that tied in with his goal of bringing eastern tourists to Glacier Country on the railroad he was constructing from Minnesota to the Pacific Coast. The course resembles others of that era designed by its New York golf-course architect. The par-36 course runs 3,300 yards with some unexpected tight and blind shots. Sitting east of the Continental Divide, Glacier

The Flathead Valley is becoming known for its beautiful golf courses. Photo: courtesy of Marina Cay Resort

Park Lodge experiences the vagaries of eastern-slope weather, including stiff winds, but displays magnificent views from its fairways lined with lodgepole pine and quaking aspen. The season runs from mid-May to mid-October.

Glacier View Golf Club
River Bend Drive, West Glacier
(406) 888–5471

Situated next to Glacier National Park, Glacier View Golf Course has earned its reputation as a friendly, family-oriented course. The 4,856-yard, par-68 course is characterized by open fairways and small greens. To create more challenges, they have gone to a three-tee system and roughed up the rough with water and sand. It's an ideal golf course for golfers looking for a way to combine Glacier Park touring with 9 or 18 holes on the links in the same day.

Meadow Lake Golf Resort
100 St. Andrews Drive, Columbia Falls
(406) 892–2111
www.meadowlakegolf.com

Although mainly known for the premier natural setting and scenic beauty of its location just minutes from Glacier National Park, Meadow Lake is no pushover according to local golfers. Its narrow, tree-lined

fairways and water hazards have created a difficulty that helped get the par-72 course rated as a "Top 500 U.S. Public Golf Course" by *Golf Digest* and a "must play" course by *Golf Magazine*. The 18-hole, mid-season greens fee is $48, cart fee is $14.

Northern Pines Golf Club
3230 U.S. Highway 93 North, Kalispell
(406) 751–1950, (800) 255–5641
www.golfmt.com

This 18-hole course combines traditional Montana-style courses and classic Scottish links with its tree-lined fairways and natural water hazards of the Stillwater River and a 20-acre lake. *Golf Digest* rated it the No. 2 golf course in Montana in 1999. The lack of trees on the opening nine reveals its recent conversion from a 250-acre potato field. The 6,180-yard, par-72 course is characterized by deep rough and lots of fairway mounding against a backdrop of the Whitefish and Swan Mountain ranges. Visit their deli snack bar and pro shop. Greens fee is $47, cart rental, $14.

Polson Country Club
111 Bayview Drive, Polson
(406) 883–8230

This vintage golf course situated on Flathead Lake's southern shore features spectacular views of the lake and the Swan and Mission Mountain ranges. The original nine holes, opened in 1936, are short with tight, conifer-lined fairways and small greens. The newer front nine plays 300 yards longer in a more open setting. This nine along with a new one being developed will tie in with each other and the original nine, with its historic log clubhouse, will stand alone. The existing 18 holes measure 6,089 yards with a par of 72. The greens fee is $28, cart rental, $22.

Village Greens Golf Club
500 Palmer Drive, Kalispell
(406) 752–4666
www.montanagolf.com

Affordability and superb greens-keeping attract many golfers to this course in suburban Kalispell known for its fine bent-grass greens. Both nines on the 5,907-yard, par-70 course have an abundance of water, plenty of fairway mounding, ponds, and white sand. Try the new 6,401-yard championship tee. Check out its all-grass driving range and full-service pro shop and deli. Its all-season greens fee is $29; cart fee is $22 per cart.

Whitefish Lake Golf Club
Highway 93 North, Whitefish
(406) 862–4000

Montana's only 36-hole golf complex is also one of its older ones. *Golf Digest* ranked the course among Montana's top five in 1996. With views of Whitefish Lake and the Whitefish Range, including Big Mountain, this tight, tree-lined course emphasizes accuracy over distance.

Whitefish Lake's establishment was a product of politicking during the 1930s for the New Deal's Works Progress Administration. WPA would fund a landing strip and the citizens of Whitefish, who wanted a golf course, were willing to put up matching money. Pilots and golfers ended up sharing the green strips serving as both fairway and runway and the conflicts that flared between them are immortalized in the Stumptown Historical Society records. The log clubhouse lends its 1930s vintage atmosphere to the first-class dinner restaurant.

The North 18, par-72 course measures 6,297 yards. The 6,144-yard South 18 plays at par 71. Call for greens and cart fees.

Flathead Lake State Parks

These state parks offer great venues for outdoor recreation, from fishing and wading to hiking and biking. All have boat launch ramps.

Big Arm

On the western shore, this large park is a popular launching point for Wild Horse Island. There are 36 campsites, a nature trail, a hiking and horseback trail, and a mountain bike trail.

Finley Point

Located at the south end of the lake, this 28-acre park features a marina for boats up to 25 feet and 16 RV campsites.

Wayfarers

On the eastern shore, this park is located south of Bigfork and is a favorite place for swimming and camping. Thirty campsites are located here with seven tent-only sites.

West Shore

Also on the western shore, the park's rock outcrops provide spectacular views of the lake and surrounding mountains. With 26 campsites, West Shore is popular with boaters and anglers.

Wild Horse Island

Hiking on this large island in Flathead Lake gives you the added benefits of a boat trip and visible wildlife including bighorn sheep, mule deer, bald eagles, and, of course, wild horses.

Yellow Bay

Located on the eastern shore amid the cherry orchards, Yellow Bay offers a wide beach for swimming, boating, fishing, and bird watching. One of the smaller campgrounds, there are six sites including five walk-in tent sites.

Resource Agencies and Organizations

Government Agencies

Blackfeet Nation, Glacier County
P.O. Box 850, Browning 59417
(406) 338–7276

Confederated Salish-Kootenai Tribes
57383 Highway 93, Pablo 59855
(406) 675–2700

Fishing Outfitters Association of Montana
Box 67, Gallatin Gateway 59730
(406) 763–4761

Flathead National Forest, Supervisor's Office
1935 Third Avenue East, Kalispell 59901
(406) 758–5200

Glacier National Park
West Glacier 59936
(406) 888–7800 (general information)

Montana Board of Outfitters, Department of
  Commerce
111 North Jackson, Helena 59620
(406) 444–3738

Montana Department of Natural Resources
  and Conservation, Kalispell Unit
2250 Highway 93 North, Kalispell 55901
(406) 751–2240

Montana Fish, Wildlife and Parks, Region I
490 North Meridian Road, Kalispell 55901
(406) 752–5501
Helena Headquarters:
1420 East Sixth Avenue, P.O. Box 200701
Helena 59620
(406) 444–2535

Montana Outfitters and Guides Association
P.O. Box 1248, Helena 59624
(406) 449–3578

Other Resources

The Glacier Institute
137 Main Street, P.O. Box 7457
Kalispell 59904
(406) 755–1211
www.glacierinstitute.org

This environmental education institution is devoted to field courses on the plants, animals, and ecology of Glacier National Park and surrounding locale year-round. For short-term visitors to the area a day-long or weekend workshop is a fine way to get off the beaten track and learn from experts about this fascinating ecosystem. Choose from topics such as Glacier's harlequins, owls of Glacier, Glacier's grizzlies, or prairie wildflowers. They also offer summer youth field science camps for kids ages 7 through 13 and daylong field seminars for children ages 6 through 11. Please write or call for a course schedule.

Leaflets and checklists are available from Flathead National Forest Headquarters, 1935 Third Avenue East, Kalispell, MT 59901, (406) 758–5200. Please see our For More Information chapter for a comprehensive list of books, pamphlets, and checklists to help guide you through the area.

Waterton-Glacier International Peace Park

Wildlife and natural processes recognize no political boundaries, a fact that is easily seen when we travel between the United States and Canada. Elk that summer within Glacier National Park migrate to the grasslands of Waterton Lakes National Park for the winter. Eagles fitted with tiny radio transmitters in Glacier have been tracked far into the Canadian north. Glacier began to recover its indigenous wolf population when a female wolf moved south from British Columbia into the North Fork Valley and raised a litter of pups. Wind and water disperse seeds across the international border . . . all these are obvious examples of how the international boundary means little in the natural world.

The concept of the International Peace Park—an idea that has since been copied around the world—originated here in 1932. It was the brainchild of the Montana and Alberta chapters of the Rotarians, who recognized that the political line between the two parks sometimes interfered with managing the continuities between them. By designating the two parks as one International Peace Park, both parks and countries acknowledged the need to work together to maintain this incredibly rich ecosystem. While each park retains control over its portion of the Peace Park, staff from both parks work together on joint projects including scientific research, resource management (including fire control), visitor services, and education. The Peace Park designation is also an opportunity to celebrate the beauties of this rugged landscape of mountains and lakes, on both sides of the border.

Sunrise reflections. Photo: David Falconer, courtesy of Flathead Convention and Visitor Bureau

You can share in the International Peace Park experience in specific ways. The *International*, a large tour boat on Waterton Lake, runs cruises daily during the summer from the Waterton townsite to Goat Haunt in the United States. You'll mix with citizens from both countries as well as from around the world, and have a chance to look up and down the boundary as you cruise by. On Saturdays during the peak of the summer season, the International Peace Park hike departs in the morning from Waterton townsite. It's guided by naturalists from each of the two countries, and you'll hike the 8 miles from the townsite to Goat Haunt. Along the way naturalists will talk not only about the natural landscape but also about the differences and similarities between the two parks. Return is via the *International* in the late afternoon. And each summer a "Hands Across the Border" celebration takes place, usually at the Chief Mountain Customs crossing. Check with either park's information centers for specific information.

The Waterton-Glacier International Peace Park isn't of significance just to Canadians and Americans, either. In 1995, the Waterton-Glacier International Peace Park was recognized for its value to the world through the World Heritage Site designation. This status was awarded based not only on the park's scenic, geologic, and ecological values but also on its cultural importance as an example of two agencies working together, across an international boundary, in the name of shared stewardship and peace.

Waterton Lakes National Park, Alberta

Waterton Lakes National Park sits just over the Canadian border in Wild Rose Country, Alberta. For those from the United States, visiting Canada is a fascinating combination of familiarity and foreignness . . . they speak the same language, they'll accept U.S. dollars (though it's usually smarter to use a credit card or exchange cash at a bank), and things seem to happen in pretty much the same ways . . . but it's still so different!

You'll notice some striking differences between Glacier National Park in the United States and Waterton, its neighbor immediately across the border. For one thing there's a town in the park. Waterton townsite is dominated by the spectacular Prince of Wales Hotel, built by the Great Northern Railway in 1927, another part of the Hill enterprise. The Prince of Wales is well worth a visit, even if you don't intend to either stay overnight or dine there. Its lobby commands one of the most remarkable views in the Rockies: the vista down Waterton Lake, flanked by peaks on both sides (including Mount Cleveland, the highest peak in Glacier National Park). And if you step outside to enjoy the view,

chances are you'll experience the strong winds that buffet this building on a regular basis! During its construction it was actually blown several inches off its foundation one night. Although the new structure was moved back into place, parts of the building have never been quite plumb since. Rumor has it that the top floors sway several inches during a good blow . . . for more information on this historic hotel, visit the Web site at www.glacier parkinc.com or phone (406) 756-2444.

Waterton boasts quite a few other lodgings as well, ranging from bed-and-breakfasts to a hostel to both modest and quite upscale motels. One, the Kilmorey Inn, is open all winter and offers varied visitor packages. It also has a delightful dining room and bar, both open to the public year-round. For more information, visit the Kilmorey's Web site at www. watertoninfo.ab.ca/kilmorey.html, phone (403) 859-2334, or write to Kilmorey Inn, Box 100, Waterton Lakes National Park, Alberta, Canada T0K 2M0.

Shopping, a movie theater, and many restaurants make for a lively little town. You'll feel the European influence a little more closely here north of the border, with Scottish woolens, Irish lace, and china featuring pictures of the British royal family all for sale. On a warm summer day,

The Wilderness Concept

If we are to have broad thinking men and women of high
mentality, of good physique, and with a true perspective on life,
we must allow our populace a communion with nature in areas
of more or less wilderness condition.

—ARTHUR CARHART

No better place in America exists where one can realize the meaning and spirit of Arthur Carhart's words than the northern Continental Divide ecosystem. This region is home to huge tracts of protected wildlands, which straddle the Divide. Glacier National Park lies at the heart of this wildland complex.

Glacier's proposed wilderness lands are managed in accordance with the Wilderness Act of 1964. This will assure that wilderness values are not impaired until such time as the U.S. Congress acts to include the park's wildlands in the more-protected wilderness preservation system. More than 95 percent of Glacier's one-million-plus acres are proposed for inclusion into this wilderness preservation system.

South of Glacier Park the Bob Marshall, Great Bear, and Scapegoat wilderness areas adjoin to form the massive 1.5-million-acre Bob Marshall Wilderness. Additional wildlands in Canada's Waterton Lakes National Park (Alberta) and Akamina-Kishinena Provincial Park (British Columbia) adjoin Glacier's northern boundary.

The Wilderness Act of 1964 was the culmination of a uniquely American ideal "to secure for the American people of present and future generations the benefits of an enduring resource of wilderness."

Wilderness is intended to provide visitors with outstanding opportunities for solitude (motorized access is prohibited) and a primitive-type recreation. Wilderness areas are intended to retain their primeval character and appear to have been created primarily by the forces of nature. The wilderness is a place in which visitors can leave behind the pressures of modern society and experience risks, challenges, and rewards on nature's terms.

Maintaining wilderness as an enduring resource is the responsibility of all visitors. Ever-increasing use and cumulative resource impacts make it imperative for visitors to learn and practice Leave No Trace outdoor skills and ethics.

Surefooted mountain goats are a delightful sight in Waterton Lakes National Park. Photo: courtesy of VIAD Corporation

Insiders' Tip

The Trail of the Great Bear covers 2,085 miles (3,350 kilometers) stretching from Yellowstone National Park through Waterton-Glacier and up to Banff and Jasper National Park. The trail traverses some of the West's most primitive and breathtaking wilderness areas where grizzly bears still roam free in their natural habitat. For information on the trail or trail tours, call (800) 215-2395.

be sure to check out the ice-cream shops—they have lots of flavors, and every one is delicious! The Waterton Heritage Centre features historic displays and a fine collection of books, videos, maps, and souvenirs of the area.

For those who like to explore outdoors, Waterton offers a variety of activities. The cruise boat *International* heads down Waterton Lake several times a day to Goat Haunt in the United States; you'll see the docks as you drive into town (phone: 403-859-2362, Web site: www.watertoninfo.ab.ca/m/cruise.html). The same company also offers a water taxi to the Crypt Lake trailhead, across Waterton Lake; this hike is often rated one of the best in the Canadian Rockies. Be sure to plan for a full-day trip and check on trail conditions. In addition to hiking, some of Waterton's excellent trails are open to mountain biking; check at the visitor center for details.

For more information on Waterton Lakes National Park, visit the Web site at www.worldweb.com/ParksCanada-Waterton/ or write Waterton Lakes National Park, Waterton Park, Alberta, Canada T0K 2M0. The park visitor center may be reached at (403) 859-5133 during the summer season. The *Waterton-Glacier Guide,* published jointly by the two parks, carries a full listing of services at Waterton and may be requested from either park.

Glacier National Park

Accommodations
Restaurants
Nightlife
Shopping

"Scenery is a hollow enjoyment if the tourist starts out after an indigestible breakfast and a fitful sleep on an impossible bed."

So complained one national park visitor to Secretary of the Interior Franklin Lane in 1914. Lane's reply? "If you don't like the way the national parks are being run, come on down to Washington and run them yourself."

Lane recognized his correspondent's name: Stephen T. Mather, philanthropist, mountain climber, and self-made millionaire. What Lane didn't know was that, at age 47, Mather was restless and ready for something new—and would eventually become the first Director of the National Park Service in 1916. It was Mather's vision of what the parks should be that set the tone for the early years of the new agency.

In Glacier National Park, which was established in 1910, the work of development—of opening up these then-remote parts of the West to vacationing Easterners—was primarily accomplished by the Great Northern Railway. While Mather was still climbing mountains, rambling with the likes of John Muir, and making his own fortune, J. J. Hill and his son Louis Hill were literally the "Empire Builders" of the great northern plains. Once John F. Stevens located Marias Pass—the lowest route through the Rocky Mountains in the United States, and now also the U.S. Highway 2 corridor—in 1889, it took only three years for the Great Northern to complete its rail line from Chicago to Seattle, opening up vast territories for settlement. Louis Hill, in particular, had a vision: He wanted people to ride his train, and he was ready to build destinations for them. His slogan was "See America First," and he aimed it at wealthy Easterners who otherwise might vacation in Europe. He billed the Rockies as the "Alps of America" and developed a Swiss-chalet-style design for his enormous mountain hotels. Waitresses wore dirndls and bellhops wore lederhosen. Visitors could spend their time in the luxurious hotels, or head out on horseback to rough it—in groups of 50 or more. The Great Northern built trails and a system of backcountry chalets and horse camps. Mary Roberts Rinehart, a well-known novelist, gave the park further publicity in her account *Through Glacier Park in 1915,* with her vivid description of the "call of the mountains." All this dovetailed perfectly with Stephen Mather's view of how the western parks needed to be developed for visitors to enjoy them.

Most of the historic lodges and chalets that visitors still enjoy today were built between 1910 and 1920: Glacier Park Lodge, Many Glacier Hotel, Granite Park and Sperry Chalets, as well as the Prince of Wales in Canada (1927) and the privately built Lake Mc-Donald Lodge on the west side of Glacier National Park. But the Great Depression and World War II brought many changes. The Many Glacier Chalets—but not the hotel—burned in the Heaven's Peak Fire of 1936. The Gunsight Chalet was destroyed in an avalanche. Wooden structures, which included many of the original backcountry chalets, such as St. Mary, Going-to-the-Sun, and Cut Bank Chalets, suffered neglect and were soon beyond repair. They never reopened after the war and were razed in the late 1940s.

And other things changed, too. After World War II, the family car became a reality, and most visitors began to drive to Montana rather than take the train. They didn't have as much money as those who had patronized the Empire Builder, and they found the big hotels too expensive. Gradually the park began to realize it had a new visitor—the middle-income family that arrived by car. And so the motor inns were built: first Swiftcurrent, built before the war but later expanded; then Roes Creek Inn, now called Rising Sun

Motor Inn; and finally the Village Inn at Apgar. In conjunction with the campgrounds, they provide a spectrum of accommodation that enables everyone to get a good night's sleep and a decent breakfast—and so to enjoy the unparalleled scenery and wildlife that bring us all here.

There are as many ways to explore the park as there are people to visit it. Be sure to stop at a visitor center or ranger station for information and a schedule of naturalist-guided activities. But whether you choose to drive Going-to-the-Sun Road in two hours, backpack for two weeks, watch birds, count goats, or take a swim in an excruciatingly cold lake, do leave your worries behind. Let the place work its magic on you.

Accommodations

Price Code

Lodging code per night for two people:

$	Less than $70
$$	$71 to $125
$$$	$126 to $150
$$$$	More than $151

The lodging at Glacier National Park covers a wide array of options: from historic lodge, to one-room cabin with a bath down the way, to high-mountain hostel. The recent history of what is now the park—the last 100 or so years—is reflected in its structures. You may want to check out the Two Medicine Campstore building just because it is the last of the Two Medicine Chalets, built at the same time as the Granite Park and Sperry Chalets, both of which still operate as lodging. You may want to trace the history of the Great Northern Railway through the lodges it built—Many Glacier Hotel was the largest hotel in Montana until recently. Or perhaps the subalpine landscape will draw you into Granite Park Chalet, built before World War I, which claims to offer the "best sunset in the park." These buildings often offer a view into the past as well as into the mountains.

> ## Insiders' Tip
>
> Just a word of warning: No food or drink are available along Going-to-the-Sun Road between Lake McDonald Lodge on the west side and Rising Sun Campground on the east side. The only pay phone in that distance is at Avalanche Campground. Logan Pass Visitor Center has wonderful exhibits, information, and book sales, but offers only public washrooms and a drinking fountain as services.

Overall, lodging within the park can be found on a wide scale of prices. Make your reservations early—especially for the peak season of July and August, when most park facilities will be completely booked. At the same time, if you're in the area but don't have a reservation, it's still worth a phone call to check on space—cancellations do occur, and you may be able to find yourself a room with a view on very short notice. With the exceptions of Apgar Village Lodge, Granite Park Chalet, and Sperry Chalet, all lodging within Glacier National Park's boundaries is operated by Glacier Park, Inc. (GPI), a concession under contract with the National Park Service.

Most facilities have an information desk where a staff member will be happy to help you with schedules for naturalist-guided activities, bus tours, boat tours and small-boat rentals, the Going-to-the-Sun Road shuttle, the Many Glacier hikers' shuttle, and horseback trips. Each of the large hotels has a gift shop that sells film, postage stamps, huckleberry treats, books and maps, hiking snacks, outdoor clothing, and a variety of souvenirs.

Campstores are located at Swiftcurrent Motor Inn, Rising Sun Motor Inn, and at the Lake McDonald Lodge complex, and they carry a similar selection with the addition of limited food supplies, some camping equipment, and bundled firewood. The descriptions that follow highlight the unique character of each location.

Glacier Park Lodge, Lake McDonald Lodge, and Many Glacier Hotel all have ATMs; all GPI locations have pay phones. Wheelchair-accessible rooms are available at Glacier Park Lodge, Lake McDonald Lodge, the Village Inn, Swiftcurrent Motor Inn, Many Glacier Hotel, and Rising Sun Motor Inn. Please be aware that the historic lodges do not have elevators to their upper floors; a bellhop will carry your luggage to your room, but if climbing stairs is a health concern, please mention this when you make your reservation.

Hotels and Motels

Apgar Village Lodge $–$$
Apgar Village, P.O. Box 410
West Glacier 59936
(406) 888–5484
www.westglacier.com/lodge.html

Located among old-growth cedar trees at the foot of Lake McDonald, Apgar Village Lodge offers a significantly longer season than any other accommodation inside the park boundaries. It opens on May 1, giving visitors an opportunity to see Glacier National Park in spring. Although the upper elevations of the park will still be buried in snow and inaccessible to all but backcountry skiers, along the shores of Lake McDonald you'll be delighted to see the bright green of brand-new leaves coming out all along the shore. A walk in the woods will bring you the special pleasure of early-season wildflowers: trillium, glacier lilies, or even lady's slipper orchids. Like the GPI lodgings, Apgar Village Lodge will be very busy during the summer months, but it will stay open into the fall shoulder season. Apgar Village Lodge offers accommodations to those who like to travel in the fall, when the crowds are less and the days cool and crisp. You'll enjoy the contrast of the larch, which turn

golden all along the slopes above Lake McDonald, with the blue of the sky and the startling whiteness of new-fallen snow on the peaks.

Apgar Village itself includes the west side visitor center, a backcountry permit office, a number of shops, a restaurant and other snack shops, and the amphitheater for evening programs at the nearby campground (some of these have shorter operating seasons than Apgar Village Lodge). A paved bike trail runs along Lower McDonald Creek back toward West Glacier, providing one of very few opportunities in Glacier National Park for biking off the roadways.

Apgar Village Lodge is Glacier's only AAA-approved lodging facility. It includes 48 rustic cabin and motel units, all with private baths. Some have views of Lake McDonald or Lower McDonald Creek, but all are within footsteps of spectacular mountain vistas. Most cabins have a kitchen, and several barbecues and picnic tables are available to guests. Regular season rates range from motel rooms for $67 per night for two people to a cabin that will accommodate six for $143 to $233 per night. Value season runs from May 1 through June 20 and from September 15 to season end; please call for availability and rates during these times. You can also write to Apgar Village Lodge, c/o West Glacier Mercantile, P.O. Box 410, West Glacier, MT 59936, for further information.

Glacier Park Lodge $$$–$$$$
East Glacier
P.O. Box 2025, Columbia Falls 59912
(406) 892–2525
www.glacierparkinc.com/lodges.cfm

The first of the lodges to be built by the Great Northern Railway, Glacier Park Lodge continues to be the unofficial eastern gateway to Glacier National Park today. Although it is located outside the borders of the park, the peaks rise behind it in an impressive backdrop. Lovely, well-tended flower gardens line the walk as you approach the historic building. Walking through the lodge doors, you'll be impressed by the huge logs that support the lobby ceiling: immense Douglas firs, their bark still on, imported from the Pacific

to hike. The Two Medicine subdistrict of Glacier National Park is only an 11-mile drive away, with its web of trails leading to places such as Dawson Pass, Cobalt Lake, Twin Falls, or Old Man Lake. Glacier Park Boat Company also offers boat tours on Two Medicine Lake. The Lubec and Autumn Creek Trails begin along U.S. Highway 2 west of East Glacier and will lead you along the aspen-covered foothills. Be sure to check with a ranger station for current trail conditions.

Glacier Park Lodge has a longer season than some other GPI facilities. It opened on June 3, 2003, and closes on September 22. Rooms range in price from $128 to $179 per night for two people.

Lake McDonald Lodge $$-$$$
Going-to-the-Sun Road, west side
P.O. Box 2025, Columbia Falls 59912
(406) 892-2525
www.glacierparkinc.com/lodges.cfm

Originally built as the Lewis Glacier Hotel by John Lewis in 1914, the Lake McDonald Lodge rests on the southeast shore of Lake McDonald, 12 miles in from the West Glacier park entrance. You can take a comfy seat on the veranda and enjoy views across the water, or take a chair in the lobby surrounded by Lewis's hunting trophies, and legend has it that Western artist Charlie Russell drew the pictographs on the massive stone fireplace. In the early years guests arrived at the lodge by water, and its original facade faced the lake. But now, of course, virtually all guests arrive by car or bus, and in more recent years what was once the "back" of the lodge has been adapted to present a proper welcome. As at the other historic hotels, you'll find Lake McDonald Lodge brilliant with hanging flower baskets and gardens in the summertime.

Although the lodge itself has a pleasantly relaxed atmosphere, you'll find plenty of activities not far away. The Glacier Park Boat Company's *DeSmet* docks in front of the lodge; cruises are available at several times each day. Just across the Going-to-the-Sun Road are the corrals of Mule Shoe Outfitters, the park horse concession, which offers rides of varying lengths to several destinations. If you like

Northwest to grace this hall. The neighboring Blackfeet Indians referred to the building as the "Big Tree Lodge."

In contrast with its historic past, Glacier Park Lodge also offers modern amenities in addition to its 163 rooms. The hotel features a heated swimming pool, a nine-hole golf course, a nine-hole pitch 'n' putt golf course, a gift shop, cocktail lounge (with TV), and the Great Northern Steak and Rib House (see Restaurants). The information desk will be happy to set you up with a bus tour or hayride.

East Glacier is home to many small businesses, shops, and restaurants (see the Blackfeet Reservation chapter), and you'll enjoy walking about the little town located exactly where the mountains meet the prairie. You are also within a 12-mile drive of Browning, where you can visit the Museum of the Plains Indian (see the Attractions chapter). Or you might choose to hike, several trails begin here: You might pick up the trail that leads to Avalanche Creek and Lake, or try heading up to Mount Brown Lookout from the Sperry trailhead—it's one of the steepest trails in the park, but the lookout will reward you with an astonishing view of the whole Lake McDonald Valley! After a good dinner, join a Park Service naturalist at the auditorium for an evening talk.

Lake McDonald Lodge includes some 100 rooms, with lodge, motel, and cabin accommodations. The complex also includes a general store, the Stockade Lounge, and a gift shop, as well as Russell's Fireside Dining Room and Charlie's Pizzeria and Family Dining (see Restaurants). Like Glacier Park Lodge, it operates for a more extended season than some park facilities. In 2003 it opened on May 30 and closed on September 22. Room rates vary by accommodation; a small cottage room for two people begins at $97 per night; motel and lodge rooms for two people range up to $149 per night.

Many Glacier Hotel $$–$$$$
Many Glacier Valley
P.O. Box 2025, Columbia Falls 59912
(406) 892–2525
www.glacierparkinc.com/lodges.cfm

Many Glacier Hotel is located at the heart of Glacier National Park, just east of the Continental Divide in the Swiftcurrent Valley. Built by Louis Hill and the Great Northern Railway in 1914-1915, it is the largest hotel in the park, with 211 rooms. Peaks—including Mount Gould, probably the most-photographed mountain in the park—surround the hotel, and its balcony overlooking Swiftcurrent Lake offers one of the finest mountain views anywhere. From it you may have the chance to see grizzly and black bears, mountain goats, bighorn sheep, moose, or deer—or perhaps a double rainbow arcing across the entire sky following a rainstorm.

The Many Glacier Hotel offers indoor comforts as well. The lobby's large, free-standing fireplace makes for a warm, cozy place to curl up with a book and read in the evening. Every evening a Park Service naturalist gives a slide program—on topics such as the park's history, geology, wild-flowers, and wildlife—in the Lucerne Room.

In addition to the Ptarmigan Dining Room (see Restaurants), the Many Glacier Hotel houses Heidi's Convenience Store, downstairs in the St. Moritz Room, which offers a variety of snack foods. And down the hall from the lobby is the Swiss Lounge, a fully stocked bar that features huckleberry daiquiris and Montana microbrews. If you arrive for dinner at the Ptarmigan Dining Room on a busy evening, the Interlaken Lounge is a pleasant place to wait until a table is ready. Take a moment to walk around—you'll enjoy the view of Mount Wilbur across Swiftcurrent Lake. You might also check out the paintings on the walls: look for one of some men camped out in the evening. There's a big buck in the background, and one of the men is reaching for his big, bellows-style camera. If you look more closely, however, you'll see that originally this man was reaching for a gun. You can still see its shape, long since painted out, and the gun replaced by the camera for a different type of "shooting."

Many Glacier Hotel will be open from June 13 to September 2, 2003. Accommodations range from value rooms to suites, and rates vary correspondingly from $117 to $230 per night.

Rising Sun $–$$
Going-to-the-Sun Road, east side
P.O. Box 2025, Columbia Falls 59912
(406) 892–2525
www.glacierparkinc.com/lodges.cfm

Rising Sun Motor Inn, located on Going-to-the-Sun Road 6 miles west of St. Mary, catches the morning light across the biggest lake in Glacier National Park. It is nestled at the edge of the open forest that meets Two Dog Flats, a series of meadows that is home to elk, deer, and coyote. Just across Going-to-the-Sun Road is the St. Mary Lake location for Glacier Park Boat Company, so that it takes only a moment to join one of their guided tours or perhaps catch a sunset cruise. Logan Pass, the top of Going-to-the-Sun Road, is just 12 miles away, and both the park shuttle and Red Bus Tours stop here. Each evening Park Service naturalists give public talks at the Rising Sun Campfire Circle.

Rising Sun Motor Inn itself consists of 72 rooms in 3 motel buildings and 36 cottages. In addition you'll find public showers, a campstore, and the Two Dog Flats Grill (see Restaurants). Rising Sun Motor Inn will be open in 2003 from June 17 to September 7. Rooms are simple and economical; rates run from $93 to $105 per night for two people.

Swiftcurrent Motor Inn $–$$
Many Glacier Valley
P.O. Box 2025, Columbia Falls 59912
(406) 892–2525
www.glacierparkinc.com/lodges.cfm

The Many Glacier Valley attracts day hikers like few places in the National Park system because of its five major drainages—and their trails—which come together in the valley floor. If you look up the Iceberg drainage toward the Iceberg Notch, and then follow the jagged Pinnacle Wall a little farther to the east, you'll see what's locally known as the B-7 Pillar. Tradition has it that the pillar was originally named for the Swiftcurrent cabin B-7, which the first people to climb that knob of rock stayed in while at Many Glacier. Swiftcurrent Motor Inn has long been the mainstay for many such visitors. It includes not only the Motor Inn, Pinetop Motor Inn, one-bedroom cottages with bath and one- and two-bedroom cottages without bath, but also a campstore, laundry, public showers, and the Italian Gardens Ristorante (see Restaurants). And the long Motor Inn porch serves as a gathering place—whether for refreshments after hiking or as a sheltered place to "hang out" on a warm but rainy afternoon. Several guided hikes meet and depart from this central location. A Park Service naturalist is usually in the parking lot for an hour each evening with a spotting scope to help start the search for animals on the slopes above the Motor Inn. And each evening a naturalist presents a talk at the nearby Campfire Circle.

In short, Swiftcurrent Motor Inn is a hopping hub of activity. Rooms are simple and affordable, ranging in price from $45 per night for two people in a one-bedroom cottage with no bath up to $103 per night for cottages with bath or for motel rooms. The 2003 season will run from June 17 until September 7.

The Village Inn $$
Apgar Village, P.O. Box 2025
Columbia Falls 59912
(406) 892–2525
www.glacierparkinc.com/lodges.cfm

Summer in Glacier is usually very temperate—temperatures in the 70s with cooler nights—but even on a hot day not many people are going to swim in Glacier's lakes. With their origins in snow and ice, these deep lakes rarely invite more than wading. But the foot of Lake McDonald, where the water is shallow and gets a lot of sun, is a place where you might enjoy a swim—if a brief one! The pebbly beach is perfect for skipping stones, having a picnic, or just admiring the mountain vista. The Village Inn, built in 1956, sits directly on the southwest shore of Lake McDonald at Apgar. Each of its 36 rooms has a lake view, up toward the mountains at the head of the valley. Twelve rooms have kitchens and others are two-bedroom units. Easy access to the lakeshore—just out your door—is certainly a prime draw, but you will also find other services immediately available. Small-boat rentals and a boat ramp are a few minutes' walk away. Apgar Village includes the west-side visitor center, a backcountry permit office, a number of shops, a restaurant and other snack shops, and the amphitheater for evening programs at the nearby campground. A paved bike trail runs along Lower McDonald Creek back toward West Glacier, providing one of the park's very few opportunities for biking off the roadways.

The Village Inn will be open from May 27 until September 15, 2003. Accommodations vary—one bedroom, one bedroom with kitchen, two bedroom, and living-room suite—and prices range from $105 to $145 per night for two people.

The Chalets

Granite Park Chalet $$
Just below Swiftcurrent Pass on the Highline Trail
(406) 387–5555, (800) 521–7238
www.glacierguides.com/chalets.html

Both Granite Park and Sperry Chalets offer backcountry experience with a difference: in this case, a room with an incomparable view. Built by the Great Northern Railway in 1914, Granite Park sits atop a knoll just below Swiftcurrent Pass on the Continental Divide. The historic stone building, which is just above tree line, offers magnificent views to the north, south, and west. With just a little hiking, you can stand on the Continental Divide and look east into the Swiftcurrent Valley; with a good bit of steep hiking, you can look down on Grinnell Glacier from above. The Highline Trail, one of the most popular trails in Glacier National Park, runs from Logan Pass to Canada by way of Granite Park. All in all, it's a place of incomparable subalpine beauty that will give you a sense of the sweep of the mountains.

Granite Park was recently renovated and now operates as a hikers' shelter. You must provide your own food, flashlight, sleeping bag, and water (there's a creek nearby, and the chalet does have a water filter for guest use, but it's a good idea to bring your own filter). The dining room and porch both have stunning views of Heaven's Peak, across the McDonald Creek drainage. A full kitchen is available for your meal preparation. Granite Park has 12 sleeping rooms, all with single bunk beds, with two to six people per room. If you don't wish to carry extra weight on your hike in, the chalet has an optional linen/bedding service as well as packaged meals, snacks, and soft drinks for sale.

Most people will choose to hike to Granite Park along the relatively flat 7.4-mile Highline Trail from Logan Pass, though others may come up the Loop Trail or over Swiftcurrent Pass from Many Glacier. Parking at Logan Pass or the Loop can be difficult; consider parking at lower elevation in the park and taking the shuttle up. Mule Shoe Outfitters (the park

The Annex at Many Glacier Hotel, Mount Gould, and Grinnell Point. Photo: Buddy Mays, courtesy of Flathead Convention and Visitor Bureau

horse concession) also provides horse transportation to the chalet.

Granite Park Chalet is open, conditions permitting, from early July until early September. Overnight rates are $72 per person per night plus 4 percent Montana accommodations tax. Linens and bedding are available for $10 per person for the duration of the stay (arrangements for this service must be made at reservation time). Please be sure to read the policy on deposits, refunds, and cancellations. Before heading out on the trail, check on current trail conditions by stopping at a visitor center or ranger station. For more information on Granite Park Chalet, please write Glacier Wilderness Guides, Inc., P.O. Box 330, West Glacier, MT 59936, or visit the Web site. Glacier Wilderness Guides can be reached by phone at (406) 387-5555 or toll-free at (800) 521-7238.

Sperry Chalet $$$$
Just below Lincoln Peak on the Sperry Trail
(406) 387-5654, (888) 345-2649
www.ptinet.net/sperrychalet

Sperry Chalet, built by the Great Northern Railway in 1913, is one of two chalets remaining from a time earlier in the century when visitors arrived at East Glacier by train and toured the park on horseback. Even today it is accessible only by trail; you must hike or ride a horse to the chalet, which is perched on a rocky bench some 6.7 miles and 3,300 feet up from the trailhead at Lake McDonald Lodge. Although the hike to the chalet is strenuous, it is well worth the effort. Once there you will be delighted by the craggy rock walls and waterfalls that surround the site as well as the view to Lake McDonald. The chalet is also located at the junction of two trails, so day hikers will have to choose between going to see Sperry Glacier, Lincoln Peak, Lake Ellen Wilson, or Gunsight Pass—or staying long enough to check them all out. Those even more adventurous will find mountain climbing options here as well. Mountain goats frequent this rugged habitat.

The Sperry Chalet is actually two buildings made of native stone: a kitchen/

dining hall and a two-story hotel building. There is no electricity; in the evening the dining room and kitchen are lit with propane lanterns, and you are encouraged to bring your own flashlight for use in the sleeping rooms at night. Other than that flashlight and what you need to hike in, just a "smile and a toothbrush" will be enough, as Sperry Chalet provides all bedding and three meals as well as lodging.

Sperry Chalet is open, conditions permitting, from early July to early September. It offers overnight accommodations on the American plan, that is, dinner, breakfast, and lunch (or trail lunch) are included in the lodging price. Rates for 2003 are approximately $50 room charge per room per night, plus $100 per person (additional night $90 per person). A 4 percent Montana accommodations tax is added to lodging charges. Sperry has 17 guest rooms, ranging from single occupancy to rooms for four, with double and single beds available. Reservations are required. Please be sure to check the policy on deposits, refunds, and cancellations.

Mule Shoe Outfitters, the park horse concession, provides horse transportation to Sperry Chalet. In addition, a la carte service is available in the dining room from 11:30 A.M. to 5:00 P.M., and some do choose to visit Sperry as a day trip. The Sperry Trail runs from Lake McDonald Lodge past the chalet to Gunsight Pass and then down to trailheads on the east side; a visit to the chalet can be part of this longer route as well.

Due to its remote location and high elevation, Sperry offers a unique opportunity to explore the backcountry of Glacier without carrying a heavy backpack. This same remoteness requires that visitors be well informed. Please check on current trail conditions at any visitor center or ranger station before setting out. For full information on the chalet, write Sperry Chalet, c/o Belton Chalets, Inc., P.O. Box 188, West Glacier, MT 59936, or visit the Web site. Office hours are 8:00 A.M. to 5:00 P.M. weekdays from October through May 14 and from 9:00 A.M. to 6:00 P.M. daily from May 15 to September 9.

Campgrounds

Glacier National Park has 13 campgrounds for a total of more than 1,000 sites. They offer a variety of camping experiences: some are accessible only by dirt road, have just a few sites, and are relatively primitive; others are large campgrounds on the main routes through the park. Most are available on a first-come, first-served basis, and at the height of the summer many will fill by midday (and a few by 10:00 A.M.). Two campgrounds, St. Mary and Fish Creek, have sites that may be reserved in advance through the National Park Service Reservation System at (800) 365–CAMP. Operating dates vary from campground to campground; please check for up-to-date information.

Most campgrounds have drinking water and rest rooms with flush toilets and cold running water. Several campgrounds have a disposal station; there is a small fee to dump RV holding tanks. No utility hookups are provided. Some campgrounds will not accommodate very large RVs; others have a limited number of spaces available for large vehicles (see descriptions below). The park newspaper, the Waterton-Glacier Guide, and the park Web site at www.nps.gov/glac/activities/camping.htm carry complete details.

In the descriptions that follow, "primitive" means a campground with an outhouse; water is available but may need to be filtered or boiled before drinking. Several primitive campgrounds are accessible only by dirt roads not recommended for large trailers or RVs.

The fee per site per night at the campgrounds is $12 to $17. Campsites are limited to eight people and two vehicles. Apgar has 11 group sites and Many Glacier and Two Medicine campgrounds each have one group site; these larger sites accommodate parties of 9 to 24 people. They are available on a first-come, first-served basis.

Most campsites have a fire grate or fire ring. Wood can be purchased at the campstores throughout the park. Collecting firewood is prohibited except along the Inside North Fork Road from 1 mile north of Fish Creek Campground to Kintla Lake and along the Bowman Lake Road.

Please be sure to inform yourself about conditions in the park before your trip. Like many national parks, Glacier has regulations designed to protect both the visitors and the park itself. In particular, the presence of grizzly bears requires that food be stored properly—in a hard-sided vehicle or bear-proof food locker (provided at some sites)—whenever it is not being prepared. Pet owners should check park regulations, also. For more information, or if you are interested in backcountry campgrounds, please visit the park's Web site at www.nps.gov/glac, call park headquarters at (406) 888-7800, or write to Superintendent, Glacier National Park, West Glacier, MT 59936.

Apgar

Apgar Campground is located at the foot of Lake McDonald. It is the largest campground in the park at 196 sites (25 sites will accommodate RVs up to 40 feet long). The campsites are in the trees but a magnificent view of the lake and the mountains is only a few minutes' walk away, and the shore of the lake is a very pleasant place to enjoy your day. Apgar Village, which includes the west-side visitor center, a backcountry permit office, small-boat rentals, a number of shops, and a restaurant and other snack shops, is close at hand. Evening programs are held at the campground amphitheater. A paved bike trail runs from Apgar along Lower McDonald Creek back toward West Glacier, providing one of very few opportunities in Glacier National Park for biking off the roadways.

Avalanche

Avalanche Campground fills early in the morning during the peak season for a number of reasons. Its 87 sites are tucked among the big trees of an old-growth cedar-hemlock forest, creating a magical atmosphere for campers. Fifty sites will fit RVs up to 26 feet long. The 1-mile, wheelchair-accessible Trail of the Cedars is nearby, with its views along Avalanche Creek and into Avalanche Gorge. A rolling, 2-mile trail will take you up to Avalanche Lake, which sits at the base of a headwall below Sperry Glacier. Waterfalls cascade down the cliffs above the lake, bringing icy waters to feed this little gem of a subalpine cirque. And Upper McDonald Creek (and the Avalanche Picnic Area)

Lake McDonald in Glacier National Park. Photo: Buddy Mays, courtesy of Flathead Convention and Visitor Bureau

is just across Going-to-the-Sun Road. Park Service naturalists present a program at the outdoor amphitheater each night.

Bowman Lake

Bowman Lake is another of those spots in Glacier that just seems to keep cropping up in the picture books, its tranquil surface reflecting Rainbow, Carter, and Chapman Peaks, with Numa Ridge flanking it to the northwest. This primitive campground has 48 sites; it is at the end of the Bowman Lake Road (not recommended for RVs), which begins just north of the Polebridge Ranger Station. As at Quartz Creek and Logging Creek Campgrounds, you are in wolf territory here, so be sure to keep your ears as well as your eyes on the alert! Several good hikes leave from Bowman Campground; you might visit the lookout at Numa Ridge, do all or part of the Quartz Lake Loop, or go to Akokala Lake. This is also the trailhead for Brown Pass and parts farther north.

Cut Bank

For those who like to escape the crowds, Cut Bank Campground on Glacier's east side may be one place to do so. Cut Bank is a primitive campground located about 5 miles west of U.S. Highway 89 some 12 miles south of St. Mary. Cut Bank has 19 sites and is not recommended for RVs. Hiking destinations include Morning Star Lake, Pitamakan Pass, Medicine Grizzly Lake, and Triple Divide Pass. Triple Divide Pass is just below Triple Divide Peak, which marks the three-way watershed sending water to the west through the Columbia River drainage, to the south and east through the Missouri-Mississippi system, and to the north and east through the St. Mary, Saskatchewan, and Nelson Rivers to Hudson Bay and the Arctic Ocean.

Fish Creek

Fish Creek Campground is located just west of Apgar, also on the shore of Lake McDonald. This is one of two campgrounds where it is possible to reserve a site (call 800-365-CAMP). Of its 180 sites, 80 will accommodate RVs up to 26 feet

Insiders' Tip

Glacier Park's peak period for backcountry use is mid-July through August. Competition for coveted backcountry campsites is very keen during this time. It helps to be flexible and have an alternative itinerary in mind in case your first choice is already booked. Fifty percent of campsites are allocated through an advance reservation system. Applications are accepted via U.S. or international mail beginning April 15. Advance reservations can be confirmed for a $20 fee. Pick up the Glacier Backcountry Guide for complete details and application forms or call in advance for a guide at (406) 888-7800.

long. Like the Apgar Campground, the sites at Fish Creek are nestled in the trees, but there is more space between sites and the campground tends to be a little quieter. A few sites are directly on the lakeshore. Park Service naturalists present an evening program each night during the height of the summer at the Fish Creek amphitheater.

Kintla

Kintla Campground is the campground farthest north on the west side of the park—almost in Canada. Its primitive status, difficulty of access, and the fact that no motorboats of any sort are permitted on Kintla Lake makes for a remote experi-

Going-to-the-Sun Road in Glacier National Park. Photo: Carl Purcell, courtesy of Flathead Convention and Visitor Bureau

ence that some will seek and others avoid. Kintla Campground is 15 miles north of the Polebridge Ranger Station on the Inside North Fork Road. This dirt road becomes narrower and narrower as you go north—it's a beautiful drive that passes through meadows and forest, but take your time, as it's not always possible to see very far around the bends in the road (this drive is definitely not recommended for RVs). The campground has 13 sites and also has trailhead parking for hikers headed up to Boulder Pass.

Many Glacier

Like Avalanche and Rising Sun Campgrounds, Many Glacier Campground fills early in the morning during the peak of the season. The Many Glacier Valley attracts many day hikers who wish to explore its web of trails leading up into the mountains, and from the campground it's an easy stroll to most of the major trailheads. The campground has 110 sites, 13 of which will fit RVs up to 35 feet long. The nearby Swiftcurrent Motor Inn includes a campstore, the Italian Gardens Ristorante, public showers, and a public laundry. Many Glacier Hotel is about a mile away. Each evening a Park Service naturalist brings a spotting scope to the motor-inn parking lot for the nightly "Spotcheck," and campers often join the effort to spot bighorn sheep, mountain goats, or even bears on the slopes above the valley floor. Later the naturalist will present a campfire talk at the Many Glacier Campfire Circle.

Quartz Creek and Logging Creek

Quartz Creek and Logging Creek Campgrounds are located about 4.5 and 6 miles, respectively, south of Polebridge Ranger Station on the Inside North Fork Road. Both are tiny—Quartz Creek has seven sites and Logging Creek eight sites—primitive campgrounds that offer quiet and the opportunity to ramble through some less-traveled parts of the park. The Inside North Fork Road is not recommended for RVs, and neither of these campgrounds has a site big enough to accommodate one. But the North Fork does have its own

attractions—if you want to hear a wolf howl, your best chance anywhere in the park is probably between Logging Creek and Bowman Lake. If you set out to hike here—perhaps to Quartz or Logging Lake, or to Hidden Meadow—keep your eyes open for wolf tracks. You might even see the wolves themselves.

Rising Sun

Rising Sun Campground provides easy access to Going-to-the-Sun Road on the east side, and it tends to fill midmorning during the peak of the season. The immediate area provides huge views up and down St. Mary Lake, but the east-side wind can really blow through this valley, and you will be grateful that the campsites themselves are sheltered by trees. The neighboring Rising Sun Motor Inn complex includes the Two Dog Flats Grill, a campstore, and public showers. Each evening a Park Service naturalist gives a campfire talk at the Rising Sun Campfire Circle. Rising Sun Campground has 83 sites, but only 3 will accommodate RVs up to 25 feet long. No towed units are permitted.

Sprague Creek

Sprague Creek is definitely a candidate for the most crowded campground in the park: It fills up early and the sites are very close together. While these factors would seem to be deterrents to many campers, here one of the old truisms of real estate is proven again: location, location, location! Sprague Creek is right on Lake McDonald and just off Going-to-the-Sun Road. Although the campground is crowded, the shoreline is very pleasant and offers views both up and down the lake. Sprague Creek is also strategically placed for bicyclists who want to get an early start and ride to the top of Logan Pass. Its 25 sites are small, but a few will accommodate RVs up to 21 feet long. Sprague Creek is closed to those with towed units because it's very difficult to back up in the tight loop through the campground.

St. Mary

St. Mary Campground is one of the largest in the park, with 148 sites, 25 of which will

Fall in Glacier National Park. Photo: Carl Wells, courtesy of Flathead Convention and Visitor Bureau

accommodate RVs up to 35 feet long. This is one of two campgrounds where it is possible to reserve a site (call 800–365–CAMP). It sits near the foot of St. Mary Lake and offers views south, north, and east. The campsites are in an aspen grove that is very lovely—especially in the fall, when the leaves turn golden—but does not afford much protection from the sometimes strong east-side winds. The campground lies along the St. Mary River, and the riparian habitat draws a wide variety of birds, including bald eagles. The St. Mary and Two Dog Flats are also home to a herd of elk that makes occasional appearances during the mornings and evenings all summer. The St. Mary Visitor Center is located just over a bridge across the river; Park Service naturalists give an evening program here each night during the summer. Please check for schedules and other special events. The town of St. Mary is less than a mile away.

Two Medicine

Two Medicine Campground is a little off the beaten track—it's not on Going-to-the-Sun Road, and it's about 12 miles north of U.S. Highway 2 at East Glacier. Because of this it tends to fill late in the day, if at all, yet those who go there regularly report what a lovely spot it is. Two Medicine has 99 sites, 13 of which will fit RVs up to 32 feet long. The campsites are nicely spaced, and many have a view of Two Medicine Lake, which is only a minute's walk away in any case. Like the Many Glacier Valley, Two Medicine Valley is formed by the convergence of a number of drainages—which translates into many wonderful trails for day hikers to explore. Each evening a Park Service naturalist gives a talk at the Two Medicine Campfire Circle. The valley also has its own campstore, and Glacier Park Boat Company offers scenic boat tours.

Restaurants

Price Code

Restaurant dinner price code, for two people exclusive of beverages, tips, and tax:

$	Less than $25
$$	$25 to $60

Although the lodge dining rooms are more formal than the smaller restaurants, casual dress is quite acceptable at all locations. All restaurants are designated non-smoking. Reservations are not accepted. Generally prices are higher at the lodge dining rooms than at the other area restaurants.

Charlie's Pizzeria and Family Dining $
Lake McDonald Lodge, Going-to-the-Sun Road, west side

A casual atmosphere and a la carte breakfast, lunch, and dinner make this an easy stop for a meal. The restaurant is open from 6:30 to 10:30 A.M. and from 11:00 A.M. to 9:30 P.M., but hours may vary in early and late seasons.

Eddie's Cafe $
Apgar Village
(406) 888–5361

Eddie's Cafe is located in Apgar Village at the foot of Lake McDonald. It offers breakfast, lunch, and dinner but is perhaps best remembered for the ice-cream window just outside the door . . . featuring huckleberry ice cream among many other flavors! Eddie's is open from early June to late September. Please check for hours of operation.

Great Northern Steak and Rib House $$
Glacier Park Lodge, East Glacier

A western theme dominates the Great Northern, and its menu features beef, barbecued ribs, chicken, and fish entrees. The restaurant offers a full buffet for breakfast, a luncheon carvery, and for dinner either a western buffet or a la carte options. Breakfast runs from 6:30 to 9:30 A.M.; lunch from 11:30 A.M. to 2:00 P.M.; and dinner from 5:00 to 9:30 P.M.

Italian Gardens Ristorante $
Swiftcurrent Motor Inn, Many Glacier Valley
(406) 732–5531 (summer only)

The reincarnation of the Swiftcurrent Coffee Shop as the Italian Gardens Ristorante in the last few years has introduced a new era in the Many Glacier Valley: not only can you design your own pizza or specialty pasta at the restaurant, but you can also get pizza to go—and it frequently goes to the campground with

campers. Breakfast is served from 6:30 to 10:30 A.M., lunch from 11:30 to 3:00 P.M., and dinner from 5:00 to 9:30 P.M.

Ptarmigan Dining Room $$
Many Glacier Hotel, Many Glacier Valley
(406) 732–4411 (summer only)

The Ptarmigan Dining Room picks up the "Alps of America" theme with its Swiss decor. At the same time, its windows open to magnificent views of the mountains across Swiftcurrent Lake. The restaurant features a breakfast buffet, a luncheon carvery, and continental and American a la carte choices for dinner. Breakfast is served from 6:30 to 9:30 A.M., lunch from 11:30 A.M. to 2:00 P.M., and dinner from 5:00 to 9:30 P.M.

Russell's Fireside Dining Room $$
Lake McDonald Lodge, Going-to-the-Sun Road, west side

Russell's Fireside Dining Room preserves the historic character of Lake McDonald Lodge with its rough-hewn beams and hunting trophies. A full buffet breakfast

Granite Park and Sperry Chalets

> We crossed many passes . . . There was a time when I had thought
> that a mountain pass was a depression. It is not. A mountain pass is
> a place where the impossible becomes barely possible.
>
> —MARY ROBERTS RINEHART, *Through Glacier Park in 1915*

Granite Park Chalet and Sperry Chalet might also be said to exist where "the impossible becomes barely possible." Located, respectively, on the Highline Trail, just south of Swiftcurrent Pass, and on the Sperry Trail, just west of Lincoln Pass, these stone buildings are reminders of an era before the private automobile. Like Mary Roberts Rinehart, most people then came to Glacier on the train and traveled through the park on horseback. In addition to the great hotels—Glacier Park Lodge, Many Glacier Hotel, the Prince of Wales, and Lake McDonald Lodge—and horse camps at Red Eagle Lake, Cosley Lake, Fifty Mountain, and Goat Haunt—guests stayed overnight at a series of backcountry chalets. Many were elaborate wooden structures in the Swiss-chalet style used by the Great Northern for its park buildings: Two Medicine Chalets, Cut Bank Chalets, St. Mary Chalets, Going-to-the-Sun Chalets, Many Glacier Chalets, Gunsight Chalet, and Belton Chalets. The two most remote were Granite Park and Sperry Chalets, and these were constructed of native stone. As time took its toll on the wooden chalets in different ways (see the introduction to this chapter), the stone buildings proved their durability. They continue to offer lodging today.

These two remaining backcountry chalets each boast spectacular locations. Granite Park sits on a knoll just at tree line. At an elevation of about 6,600 feet, snow melts relatively late here; those hiking into the chalet along the Highline Trail will be treated to spring flowers even into July. The meadows around the chalet are a mass of yellow glacier lilies in the "early" season; later they will burst into a kaleidoscope of colors as summer brings the high-country flowers into bloom: penstemon, asters, paintbrush, cinquefoil, bear grass, and many more. Swiftcurrent Pass is about ¾-mile above the chalet along the Continental Divide. The hike to the pass is not difficult and offers a huge view east into the Swiftcurrent Valley and even out onto the plains. If you have energy to burn, try the Grinnell Glacier Overlook Trail, a spur off the Highline Trail: it's only 1 kilometer to the overlook, but it's known as the longest 1 kilometer in the park! It's a steep climb to the Divide here, but when you arrive you'll be rewarded with an astonishing view of Grinnell Glacier from above, as well as of the Grinnell Valley. Like most other glaciers in North America, Grinnell Glacier is shrinking rapidly, but it is still one of the largest glaciers in the park (see the Geology of Glacier National Park Close-up in the Attractions chapter). And just a quick note on the chalet's name: Granite Park Chalet sits on a flow of pillow basalt, an igneous rock. This hard, dark rock was taken for granite . . . but there is no granite in the area.

Sperry Chalet sits high in a hanging valley, just below Comeau Pass and Lincoln Pass. Gunsight and Edwards Mountains tower over it. Mountain goats frequent the rugged terrain around the chalet. You'll have a hard time deciding how to spend your time here: Trails lead in three different directions and to several destinations. Just over Comeau Pass is Sperry Glacier, about the same size as Grinnell Glacier. The hike to the glacier itself is remarkable: The trail winds its way up a series of benches, each dotted with pools and huge boulders left by the receding glaciers. No natural pass existed here, so an artificial one was created: You'll feel like you're in *Raiders of the Lost*

Ark as you step up these stairs carved into the rock and steady yourself with the rope handrail! The basin offers a view not only of the glacier but also of peaks that you'll recognize from Logan Pass—but now you'll be seeing them from the south. If you choose instead to hike east, toward Gunsight Pass, you'll want to stop at stunning Lake Ellen Wilson, which glitters in a high cirque also known to pro-duce lots of huckleberries in some years. . . . And Gunsight Pass is a place where you're almost bound to encounter goats.

Granite Park Chalet offers a stunning view of Heaven's Peak.
Photo: courtesy of Marina Cay Resort

Both Sperry and Granite Park have undergone extensive renovation in the last few years. As historic structures, the original integrity of the building must be pre-served, and you'll find it interesting to inspect the historic use of construction materi-als and methods. The building season is short, and, even in the summer, weather conditions can sometimes preclude construction work. The amount of skill, time, and money required to renovate these remarkable buildings can perhaps give us a greater appreciation for their original construction in 1913 and 1914, respectively. They do in-deed exist "where the impossible becomes barely possible."

and a la carte lunch are served; dinner fea-tures a fine American menu with a taste of the outdoors. Breakfast is from 6:30 to 9:30 A.M., lunch from 11:30 A.M. to 2:00 P.M., and dinner from 5:00 to 9:30 P.M.

Two Dog Flats Grill $
Rising Sun Motor Inn, Going-to-the-Sun Road, east side
(406) 732–5523 (summer only)

This family-style restaurant sits just across Going-to-the-Sun Road from St. Mary Lake. It features sandwiches, salads, steaks, and fish. Breakfast is served from 6:30 to 10:30 A.M., and lunch and dinner from 11:00 A.M. to 9:30 P.M. Hours will be more limited after Labor Day.

Nightlife

"Nightlife" within the park is a quiet af-fair, but it has its charms. Park naturalists give evening slide programs and campfire talks at many locations each night. Mem-bers of the local Blackfeet and Salish-Kootenai Tribes talk about their history and culture in the "Native America Speaks" weekly program. And some spe-cial events do occur during the summer—these might include performances by Blackfeet dancers, singer-songwriter Jack Gladstone, or the actor Raphael Cristy portraying Western artist Charlie Russell. Check the park publication *Nature Ex-plorer* for current listings.

Of course, evening is a wonderful time for outdoor activities, too. Stargazing is exceptional in places far from city lights, and the northern lights occasionally re-ward those nighthawks awake to see them. Glacier is not, however, a good place to be hiking at night, when bears may be both more active and less likely to expect people on the trails.

Quiet hours in campgrounds are from 8:00 P.M. to 8:00 A.M. Fireworks may not be used within the park, but many communi-ties around the park have fireworks dis-plays for the Fourth of July.

Hidden Lake Overlook in Glacier National Park. Photo: Carl Wells, courtesy of Flathead Convention and Visitor Bureau

Shopping

While you probably won't come to the park just to shop, it's also likely that you won't leave without having bought something—a souvenir poster, a book, or perhaps a locally made hand-thrown pot.

Glacier Natural History Association runs a considerable operation through the visitor centers, selling books, videos, tapes, maps, and posters that are specific to Glacier National Park. Proceeds from this non-profit organization support educational programs and publications in the park.

Glacier Park, Inc. has gift shops in all the major lodges. They carry Native jewelry and crafts, film, postage stamps,

huckleberry treats, books and maps, hiking snacks, outdoor clothing, and a variety of souvenirs. Campstores are located at Swiftcurrent Motor Inn, Rising Sun Motor Inn, Two Medicine, and at the Lake McDonald Lodge complex, and they carry a similar selection with the addition of limited food supplies, some camping equipment, and bundled firewood.

Apgar Village also has several gift shops, each with a unique selection. The Cedar Tree offers Montana-made gifts and souvenirs as well as huckleberry products, Pendleton woolens, and T-shirts. Schoolhouse Gifts is located in a former one-room schoolhouse. Montana House features the work of Montana artists and craftspeople.

Kalispell

Accommodations
Restaurants
Nightlife
Shopping

Kalispell, with a population of just more than 16,500 people, is small enough to barely make a dent on most national maps, and yet big enough to be Montana's seventh-largest city overall and also the largest city in the four counties of northwest Montana. It is thus a mixture of urban and rural. During your time here, you will find yourself enjoying the traditional delights of a city such as shopping, restaurants, and museums, as well as those qualities that are more associated with rural Montana—the county fair, rodeo, horseback riding, and fishing, along with just the general air of peace and serenity.

Kalispell is the county seat of Flathead County and the business center as well. It is located at the intersection of U.S. 93 and U.S. 2, and just 45 minutes from Glacier National Park and 10 minutes from Flathead Lake. Though it does not have as much of a distinct identity as the smaller communities of Bigfork and Whitefish, it prides itself on being a town that provides a quality of life that can't be beat. The town was named by *Mountain Sports and Living* magazine as the Best Mountain Town in America, taking into account its proximity to the Big Mountain and Blacktail Mountain ski areas, as well as its superb health-care industry, its quality schools, and many recreational opportunities.

Kalispell is also, of course, rich in history. It is a frontier town that was founded in 1891 by Charles E. Conrad, a Missouri River trader who combined a colorful outdoorsy spirit with the good old-fashioned horse sense that made him a rich man. Conrad's huge wooden home, built in 1895 and occupied by members of the Conrad family until 1975, has been restored to Victorian elegance and is open to the public as the Conrad Mansion (see the Attractions chapter). It is one of the city's most popular tourist stops and provides an education on how much more civilized the frontier could be than Hollywood's westerns would lead us to believe. The mansion is one of the main stops on a self-guided walking tour of historic buildings that begins at the Hockaday Center for the Arts in downtown Kalispell.

Another exciting addition to the historic legacy of Kalispell is the Central School Museum, which opened in 1999. This impressive stone structure was built in the 1890s as a school, and it later served as office space and classroom space for Flathead Valley Community College before being closed for about 10 years and nearly being demolished. The efforts of the Northwest Montana Historical Society led to the preservation of the building, which has been extensively renovated and will now be the site of exhibits, lectures, and community events.

Downtown Kalispell has suffered the same vicissitudes as other Main Streets over the past few decades. The business community has expanded beyond the city limits in recent years, especially toward Evergreen, east of town on U.S. Highway 2. This is the home of such popular stores as Wal-Mart, ShopKo, and Staples as well as car lots, fast-food restaurants, and other businesses. But today the trend is definitely toward a comeback for downtown Kalispell. Unlike many other cities, Kalispell arranged a deal in the mid-1980s that led to the building of a mall not outside of town on a highway strip, but right on Main Street, just a block or two from the city's oldest historic businesses. That anchor has proved to be important in guaranteeing a future for downtown. Today several new buildings have gone up, housing restaurants, clothing stores, and gift shops, and Kalispell's city center is more vibrant than it has been for many years.

To the south of Kalispell, there are two communities on Flathead Lake that have distinct identities of their own, but which also are close enough to Kalispell that they should be included here. Somers is the smaller of the areas, with a public boat ramp and private marina helping to set the tone. This was a railroad town in earlier years, and many of the houses were built for railroad employees. A few of these have been converted to public use such as Tiebuckers restaurant and saloon, which offers a mix of home cooking and gourmet meals in a rustic rambling house. You can also catch a ride on the *Far West* cruise boat (see the Attractions chapter) during summer evenings at the dock across the street from the magnificent log-built Montana Grill. A few miles farther south on U.S. Highway 93, you come to Lakeside, which in the past few years has developed into one of the most popular destinations on Flathead Lake. Several resorts and motels offer boating and fishing opportunities during the summer, and the new Blacktail Mountain ski area gives the community a year-round appeal.

All in all, Kalispell and its surrounding communities will provide days and weeks of entertainment, education, and shopping for tourists, but many people find that even a long vacation isn't enough to enjoy everything Kalispell has to offer. Those are the people who move here a couple years after their vacation, keeping Kalispell and Flathead County one of the most exciting and thriving areas in Montana.

Accommodations

Hotels and Motels

Price Code

Keep in mind that some rates are based on availability. The average nightly peak-season rates for two adults at the hotels and motels listed in this section are indicated by a dollar sign ($) ranking in the following chart. Many places offer lower off-season rates. Also, the hotels and motels in this chapter accept all or most major credit cards.

$	$25 to $49
$$	$50 to $75
$$$	$76 to $100
$$$$	More than $101

Aero Inn $$
1830 U.S. Highway 93 South, Kalispell
(406) 755-3798, (800) 843-6114
www.aeroinn.com

If you pilot your own small plane, there's really only one place to land for the night—the Aero Inn, located just off the municipal airport in Kalispell. And make no mistake, this airport really is IN Kalispell: It's located less than a half-mile south of the Flathead County Courthouse. The motel has 62 spacious guest rooms, along with an indoor pool, hot tub, sauna, game room, continental breakfast, wheelchair-accessible facilities, and winter plug-ins for your car (and tie-

downs for your plane!). There is also 24-hour front-desk service at this customer-friendly hotel.

Bayshore Resort Motel On Flathead Lake $$$
616 Lakeside Boulevard, Lakeside
(406) 844-3131, (800) 844-3132
www.bayshoreresortmotel.com

This is one of several motels located in Lakeside on the west shore of Flathead Lake, about 15 miles south of Kalispell. The view from the Bayshore just can't be beat, as you look across the lake to the majestic Mission and Swan Mountain ranges. The resort features 15 rooms with queen- and king-size beds. Three family units have kitchens as well as private decks. There is a hot tub and a great room for gatherings by a river-rock fireplace. Take advantage of the dock and boat slips to enjoy fishing in the daytime, then come back for a dip in the chilly waters of Flathead Lake at the beach area. Owners Dave and Brenda Taylor rent boats, canoes, Seadoos, and movies. You will often find evening campfires burning on summer nights.

Blue and White Motel $$
640 East Idaho, Kalispell
(406) 755-4311, (800) 382-3577
www.blu-white.com

This is one nonchain hotel that can compete with the more familiar names. The Blue and White gets lots of repeat business from business people and others who travel to Kalispell frequently. That's because of the friendly service and the excellent accommodations. There are 106 rooms with double- and queen-size beds and wheelchair-accessible facilities are available upon request. There is a free continental breakfast, and a small indoor swimming pool, sauna, and Jacuzzi. Pets are allowed, and there are winter plug-ins available for automobile engine heaters to help make it through those cold Montana nights. The large parking lots can handle RVs, trucks, trailers, and buses. Off-season and winter weekend rates are available. The Blue and White is also located next to Finnegan's, one of the few 24-hour restaurants in Kalispell.

Hampton Inn $$$$
1140 U.S. Highway 2 West, Kalispell
(406) 755–7900, (800) HAMPTON
www.northwestinns.com

The Hampton Inn is Kalispell's newest major hotel, and it targets the business clientele in particular but has many conveniences perfect for a family as well. All guest rooms feature an iron and ironing board, a small refrigerator, TV/VCR, video-game player, coffeemaker and coffee, hair dryer, HBO, and free local calls. The hotel also has a 24-hour indoor swimming pool and Jacuzzi as well as a gift shop, coin-op laundry, business center, and exercise facility. Although there is no restaurant per se, a complimentary breakfast buffet featuring fresh-baked muffins and sticky buns is served every morning. Children younger than age 18 stay free at the Hampton Inn. The Hampton provides a free 24-hour airport shuttle service.

Kalispell Grand Hotel $$$
100 Main Street, Kalispell
(406) 755–8100, (800) 858–7422
www.kalispellgrand.com

The Kalispell Grand Hotel is a beautifully remodeled 40-room, historic hotel that is located conveniently right in downtown Kalispell. Noted writer Frank Bird Linderman leased and managed the hotel from 1924 to 1926, and he and his good friend Charlie Russell, the famed Western artist, would on occasion sit in the hotel lobby's and exchange thoughts and stories of the

---

Insiders' Tip

Got a late start? Need to jump-start your drive? It seems like about every other corner in the Flathead Valley has a drive-up espresso shop: Java Joe's, Mountain Mocha, Juice 'n' Java, Java Junction, Big Mountain Buzz .... they're all there, and more! Just keep your eye out ....

West. Today a complimentary continental breakfast is served every morning in the Grand Lobby, which still has the look of a luxurious frontier hotel lobby with its high, pressed-tin ceilings and golden oak staircase. The three-story brick hotel also connects to the famous Kalispell Bar, where music is heard often on summer weekends, and to the Alley Connection restaurant, which serves Oriental and American cuisine. In season you can take a carriage ride through the downtown area, or you can walk through an area that is rich with shops, restaurants, and history.

Lakeshore Motel $$
7175 U.S. Highway 93 South, Lakeside
(406) 844–2433, (406) 251–4405
members.tripod.com/~tendragon/lakeshor/lakeshore.html

This family-owned and -operated motel is close to Kalispell (just a 20-minute drive) yet allows you to be on the water, enjoying the lovely Montana scenery. Since the 1940s this quiet uncrowded resort has been a preferred getaway for folks on a budget. The cabins are modern with full bath and shower and offer lake views and unobstructed access to the lake. Gas barbecues are available for convenient outdoor cooking and some of the units have kitchenettes. RV hookups can be rented if you are hauling your home on wheels. For

The Kalispell Grand Hotel offers a chance to step back in time right downtown. Photo: courtesy of Kalispell Grand Hotel

evening enjoyment there is a shoreline fireplace, and the village of Lakeside provides restaurants, a supermarket, banking, and taverns just a minute or two away. If you want to check out the fishing on Flathead Lake, you will have plenty of opportunity here. There is a dock, with slips that can accommodate boats up to 30 feet long. The Lakeshore Motel is open from the middle of May until the end of September.

Lakeside Resort Motel $$$
7235 U.S. Highway 93 South, Lakeside
(406) 844–3570, (800) 348–4822

Another Lakeside motel, this one offers year-round accommodations. The Lakeside Resort prides itself on being the perfect place for family reunions, weddings, or friendly gatherings. You can have your choice of one-, two-, and three-bedroom cabins or a motel room. Kitchens are equipped with microwaves, dishwashers, and barbecues. A private beach with docks and boat ramps fills out the resort atmosphere. Sailing, boating, fishing, pedal boats, canoes, volleyball, horseshoes, and Ski-doos are available. A self-service laundry facility is on-site, along with a gift shop, hot tub, and a public rest room.

Red Lion Inn $$$
330 U.S. Highway 2 West, Kalispell
(406) 755–6700, (800) RED–LION
www.redlion.com

The Red Lion was acquired in recent years by the Doubletree Inn chain, and you get the quality stay here that you would expect from such a well-known name. There are 64 air-conditioned guest rooms and suites, HBO, telephone dataports, room service, heated outdoor pool, spa, and free parking. Airport shuttle service is also available at nominal charge. Restaurant, lounge, and casino are adjacent to the inn.

Somers Bay Log Cabin Lodging $$$$
5496 U.S. Highway 93 South, Somers
(406) 857–3881, (888) 443–3881
www.westerntravel.com/bay

Despite the old-timey cabins, Somers Bay Log Cabin Lodging is one of the newer accommodations in the Flathead Lake area. Built in the spring of 1998, Somers Bay Log Cabin Lodging features both studio units and bedroom cabins. Each features a queen-size log bed and a queen-size sofa sleeper and comes equipped with a kitchenette that has microwave, stove top, refrigerator, coffeemaker, and dishes. There is extra parking for boats and trailers, so you can use your cabin as the base for your lake fun. Flathead State Park Boat Access is within walking distance.

Super 8 $$
1341 First Avenue East, Kalispell
(406) 755–1888, (800) 800–8000
www.super8.com

The Kalispell Super 8 motel is a safe bet for travelers who are looking for pleasant accommodations on a budget. Don't hesitate to ask for those little extras such as first-aid supplies, irons and ironing boards, hair dryers, and other essential toiletries you may have forgotten. The accent here is not on frills, but on friendly service, which makes it a popular choice for business travelers. There is also daily laundry and dry cleaning pickup and delivery. And a bonus for commercial truckers: Because of limited truck parking, the hotel will pay for taxi fare to and from your truck.

WestCoast Kalispell Center $$$$
20 North Main, Kalispell
(406) 751–5050, (800) 325–4000
www.westcoasthotels.com

This large hotel offers a perfect compromise for tourist couples who can't decide between shopping and sight-seeing. After a full day at Glacier Park or on Flathead Lake, you can return to one of the 132 rooms and suites and freshen up for dinner at the Northwest Bounty Company restaurant in the hotel, and then walk into the adjacent Kalispell Center Mall for an evening of bargain hunting at the 50 or so stores. Back at the hotel you can swim in the indoor solarium pool or relax in the sauna or whirlpools. The Fireside Lounge offers a quiet atmosphere to enjoy a drink or two before bed, or you might step across the hall to the popular casino. When you get up, enjoy the continental breakfast and get back to sight-seeing. WestCoast Kalispell Center is a popular convention center, too, with more than 10,000 square feet of meeting and banquet space.

WestCoast Outlaw Hotel $$$$
1701 U.S. Highway 93 South, Kalispell
(406) 755–6100, (800) 325–4000
www.westcoasthotels.com

The Outlaw Hotel is the granddaddy of convention centers in the Flathead Valley. It is the biggest—with 220 guest rooms and suites—and the most comprehensive, with a popular restaurant and lounge and extensive convention facilities. Fitness-center facilities are available to guests, along with a hot tub, sauna, tennis court, two indoor pools, and a spa. The restaurant and lounge is called Hennessy's and includes a large casino area. An art gallery is also located in the building.

White Birch Motel & RV Park $
17 Shady Lane, Kalispell
(406) 752–4008, (888) 275–2275
www.whitebirchmotel.com

White Birch is an offbeat little motel in a parklike setting on a creek. This location, set back from Montana Highway 35 just ¾ mile from U.S. Highway 2, is out of the way but just minutes from all amenities. All rooms have a coffeepot, complimentary coffee and refrigerator, plus three come with kitchens. A coin-operated laundry is also available on-site. The motel is

open year-round, and the RV park, which opened in 1996, operates from May to October. It offers tent sites and electricity-only sites, as well as full hookups. The RV facility features modern rest rooms and showers with handicapped access.

Campgrounds and RV Parks

Price Code

$	Less than $9
$$	$10 to $16
$$$	$17 to $23
$$$$	More than $24

Glacier Pines RV Park $$$
1850 Montana Highway 35 East, Kalispell
(406) 752–2760, (800) 533–4029

Glacier Pines RV Park sits in a wooded location about five minutes from Kalispell. There are 30 tent sites and 140 RV sites with full hookups. There is no maximum size limit or time limit. Available on-site are a store, laundry, showers, a heated swimming pool, horseshoes, and other recreation, including a play area.

Rocky Mountain "Hi" RV Park & Campground $$$
825 Helena Flats Road, Kalispell
(406) 755–9573, (800) 968–5637

Rocky Mountain "Hi" is the only privately owned RV park in the Kalispell area that is not on a highway. Signs point the way from either Montana 35 or U.S. 2 toward this quiet park that features mature shade trees and cable television hookups. All sizes of RVs can be accommodated in the 59 spots, and there are also 18 tent sites. For the kids, there is a large Western-style play town and a playing field. In addition, there is a store at the site, along with camp showers, a recreation room, and pay telephone.

Spruce Park RV Park $$$ (no credit cards)
1985 Montana Highway 35, Kalispell
(406) 752–6321, (888) 752–6321
www.montanaweb.com/sprucepark

Summer in Kalispell is green and lush. Photo: courtesy of Cavanaugh's Outlaw Hotel

There are 30 tent sites and 120 RV sites at Spruce Park, which is located near the Flathead River and features fishing, a par-3 golf facility, and a recreation room. The park is located 3 miles east of Kalispell and is open year-round. Spruce Park RV Park accepts personal checks from out of state as well as traveler's checks.

Bed-and-Breakfasts

Price Code

$	Less than $85
$$	$85 to $115
$$$	$116 to $150
$$$$	More than $151

Bonnie's Bed and Breakfast $$$
265 Lake Blaine Road, Kalispell
(406) 755-3776, (800) 755-3778
www.wtp.net/gp/montana/sites/bonnie.html

Bonnie's Bed and Breakfast features five guest rooms. The honeymoon suite has a luxurious master room complete with a private bath and Jacuzzi. The Columbian Room, the Garden Room, the Blaine Room, and Alpine Room all have queen-size beds. Reservations are required, but last-minute inquiries are encouraged since there are sometimes unexpected openings. Bonnie's Bed and Breakfast is located a half mile from the junction of Montana 206 and Montana 35, near the Mountain Crossroads golf course and restaurant. There is a 10 percent discount for senior citizens. Pets are not allowed.

Full Circle Herb Farm $
1230 Truman Creek Road, Kila
(406) 257-8133

Not everyone wants to spend a night at an herb farm, but some of you do—and you know who you are! This is a great once-in-a-blue-moon opportunity for a unique vacation. As Montana's oldest herb farm, Full Circle Herb Farm is the premier source for many hard-to-find herbs as well as well-known favorites. The organic operation includes herb gardens, greenhouses, meadows, expansive lawns, and woods on 150 acres of scenic Montana 12 miles west of Kalispell. The guest house is the tenderly renovated Kila Church, which still retains its original history and charm but has been transformed into a rustic yet modern cottage in a quiet wooded setting. Amenities include queen-size bed (and pull-out couch), dining and living area, full kitchen, full bath, microwave, and gas barbecue. Note that this is not a true bed-and-breakfast, since meals are not served. Accommodations are also available for horses, which include a corral with feed bunk and water. The guest house is open from May 1 through November 1. Full Circle Herb Farm does not welcome children younger than age 12.

Outlook Inn Bed and Breakfast $$$
175 Boon Road, Somers
(406) 857-2060, (888) 857-8439
www.outlookinnbandb.com

The Outlook Inn is located on a promontory across U.S. 93 from Flathead Lake in Somers. This spacious yet cozy lodgelike home sits on seven private acres and offers all of the amenities you would expect from a fine establishment. Curl up in front of the river-rock fireplace with a good book, or relax in your room with the private jet-

The Lewis and Clark Bicentennial

Lewis and Clark just barely set foot in the area covered by this book . . . but they were here. And as the bicentennial of their journey approaches, more and more people are making their own journeys to Lewis and Clark sites. You'll find this reflected in visitation numbers and events throughout Glacier Country.

On their journey west, Lewis and Clark were following the Missouri River. In west-central Montana, they came to the junction of two major currents, and it wasn't clear to them which was the main channel. Part of the group scouted up the northern channel, and indeed all the men became convinced that this was the way to go. But both leaders felt the other channel was right, and they prevailed—and were right. The other course proved to be what we now call the Marias River—named after Lewis's cousin, Maria Wood—which drains the southeastern corner of what is now Glacier National Park. Had the explorers discovered Marias Pass (where Highway 2 travels today), they might have significantly shortened their westward journey. But the Missouri was their plan; and the Blackfeet guarded Marias Pass jealously against all comers even then.

Returning home Lewis and Clark split their expedition in order to explore more territory. Lewis's group returned to travel up the Marias River in late July 1806, hoping that it would go north, thus extending the United States' claim to the territories rich in beaver, among other resources. But the river bent west. Camp Disappointment, now within the boundaries of the Blackfeet Indian Reservation, was Lewis's northernmost point. In the following days, Lewis's group would camp with a Blackfeet hunting party. When the Blackfeet attempted to take the rifles from two of Lewis's sleeping men, a fight erupted and one or possibly two Blackfeet were killed. Lewis's party rode back to the Marias as fast as it could to warn the remaining men there of a possible Blackfeet reprisal.

While Lewis and Clark's journey touched only a corner of Glacier Country, their time at the Great Falls of the Missouri has captured many people's imagination. The Lewis and Clark National Historic Trail Interpretive Center in Great Falls (see the last Web site below), run by the U.S. Forest Service, is an excellent new visitor center that focuses on not only the explorers and their mission but also the many native groups they encountered. The significances of Lewis and Clark's mission are many; take the time to stop and discover your own. Great Falls and Cut Bank, as well as Missoula and other towns in southwest Montana, will all be excellent stops on the Lewis and Clark trail. If you're looking for the Lewis and Clark "information highway," here are a few sites to begin with: www.lewisandclark200.org/, www.montanalewisandclark.org/, www.nps.gov/jeff/LewisClark2/HomePage/HomePage.htm, and www.fs.fed.us/r1/lewisclark/lcic.htm.

---

ted tub or double shower. The house features a huge log deck overlooking the lake and Rocky Mountains as well as a variety of locally produced art. Walk to fine dining, dancing, karaoke, and the lake in minutes. Or step out the door and go for a walk in the wooded hills. In the winter you can cross-country ski out the door. Be sure to inquire for winter rates.

Stillwater Inn $$
206 Fourth Avenue East, Kalispell
(406) 755-7080, (800) 398-7024

This lovely historic home is furnished with early-20th-century furniture and has an air of quiet elegance and comfort. The house was built around 1900 by Gustave Gamer, who had come to Kalispell six years earlier to begin the Kalispell Malt and Brewing Company. In 1907 William Noffsinger, an attorney and businessman, purchased the home, which remained in his family until 1943. The name Stillwater was taken from a nearby river, although the inn is actually located in downtown Kalispell on one of the business-residential avenues. Guests begin each day with a delicious full breakfast. From the entrance a gracious stairway leads up to the four guest bedrooms, two with a private bath. American Express credit card not accepted.

Restaurants

Price Code

The following listings rate restaurants according to a four-symbol price key, representing average cost for dinner for two people. The code excludes the price of beverages, tip, and tax.

$	$10 to $19
$$	$20 to $27
$$$	$28 to $35
$$$$	$36 and more

Family-Friendly Dining

Alley Connection $
22 First Street West, Kalispell
(406) 752-7077

The family that runs the Alley Connection is something of a local tradition in Flathead County. They have had a record of continuous success dating from the 1970s when they arrived from Vietnam. Today the Alley Connection is joined locally by four other Oriental-style restaurants owned by family members, but the Alley is still the best. Specialities include Szechuan pork and chicken and egg foo yung, as well

as a hearty wonton soup that includes a generous helping of pork and greens along with both fried and noodle wontons. And even if you don't usually like sweet and sour, you may want to try the sweet and sour here (our favorite is the wontons) since it has a distinct flavor that is a particular treat. There are individual combination dinners available, such as Kiet's Dinner, which features soup of the day, egg roll, sweet and sour wontons, chicken chow mein, and combination fried rice for just $8.95. Lunches are even cheaper, and you can also get American menu selections for kids.

Bojangles $
1319 U.S. Highway 2 West, Kalispell
(406) 755-3222

This is one of those family dining establishments that locals eat at, but tourists may pass up for the more familiar McDonalds or Wendy's. Don't make that mistake. Not only is the menu full of good food, it's also full of references to the 1950s. In fact the whole restaurant is a throwback to simpler times. A cutout of Marilyn Monroe greets you at the front door, and the walls are filled with 1950s-era memorabilia such as license plates, movie tie-ins, and—of course—Elvis. Hamburgers are named after pop singers such as Jerry Lee Lewis (lots of jalapeños), Neil Sedaka, Gene Vincent, and Buddy Holly (no frills, just the plain burger). Breakfast is served all day, and an added attraction for the kids is a model train that runs along a rail that is set up on beams atop the walls.

Charlie Wong's $
2316 U.S. Highway 2 East, Kalispell
(406) 257-1377

Charlie Wong's is located in Evergreen, the suburb east of Kalispell's city limits where much of the business development has taken place over the past 10 years. If you get through shopping at Wal-Mart, Shopko, or SuperOne, it is just a short drive to this restaurant, where you can get both Asian specialities and a couple of American entrees. Always popular is the kung pao chicken, but you won't go wrong on this menu. Hot entrees can be ordered mild or medium, too, so don't be shy about trying something new.

Cislo's $
2046 U.S. Highway 2 East, Kalispell
(406) 756-7330

Cislo's is the closest thing to Mel's Diner from the old TV show *Alice* that you will find in Kalispell. It features a crew of tough but lovable waitresses, and a menu that could easily be mistaken as from the 1950s. Look for the open turkey and beef sandwiches, the chili burger, and the club sandwich, but don't be afraid to try anything on the menu. This is home cooking that won't disappoint. And be sure to save room for dessert, which usually features five or six fresh-baked pies. One interesting side note: Cislo's used to be located where the Staples office-supply superstore is now situated, a bit closer to Kalispell, but when Cislo's lost their lease, they didn't lose their restaurant. They just loaded it up on top of a truck and hauled it down the highway to its current spot. Now that's one tough little restaurant.

J. D. Morrell's Bistro $
227 South Main, Kalispell
(406) 257-9195

The food at J. D. Morrell's is so good for you—with all those fresh veggies and homemade bread and all—that's it's hard to believe how indulgent even a little lunch here will make you feel. The sandwiches are luscious, the soup amazing: Mojo Sausage and Potato, Carrot Ginger, Mushroom Sherry with Wild Rice, and that old standard, Jamaican Veggie. And they have Coke in glass bottles; now, what more *can* you ask?

Legacy Restaurant $
128 First Avenue East, Kalispell
(406) 257-7121

The Legacy specializes in lunches and features a complete lineup of soups and sandwiches. You can always get the soup and half a sandwich special and come away satisfied. Nothing fancy, but this restaurant has been in Kalispell for more than 15 years, and that's always a sign of

doing something right. It's just a short block from Main Street, so before you load back up in the car after shopping downtown, stop here for a quick meal.

Los Caporales $$
1545 Montana Highway 35, Kalispell
(406) 756-6300

Los Caporales features authentic Mexican food from not just south of the border, but from the region around Guadalajara, west of Mexico City, where the owners came from originally. That means some of the menu items will be a bit different from what is typically served at a Mexican restaurant, but the difference (which includes a lot of grilled foods) is a big plus. Try the carnitas de res from the beef menu for a tasty Mexican stir-fry of sirloin strips, peppers, tomatoes, and mushrooms in a spicy seasoning mix. Or if chicken is your fancy, order the arroz con pollo, which features chunks of chicken breast with onions, tomatoes, and mushrooms, this time in a tasty red sauce and melted cheese, all served over a bed of rice. For the less adventurous there is a large helping of standard Mexican fare such as combination dinners that come with one or more enchiladas, tacos, tostadas, chile rellenos, chimichangas, or burritos. Kids can get a grilled cheese and fries for $2.75 or children's-size portions of Mexican food for $3.25 to $5.25. There are also steaks and hamburgers. Los Caporales is adjoining a casino, and shares its liquor license, but the restaurant (especially the nonsmoking section) is completely separate from the casino and features Mexican music on the loudspeakers.

MacKenzie River Pizza Co. $
1645 U.S. Highway 93 South, Kalispell
(406) 756-0060

This is one of those hip gourmet pizza joints that has become trendy the past few years, but don't let that stop you. MacKenzie River is a Montana-based company that does pizza right. You can get anything you want on top, from artichokes to garlic plus all the traditional favorites like pepperoni and sausage. There are also top-notch sandwiches and salads, and the

Before and after Lewis and Clark . . .

As the Lewis and Clark bicentennial approaches, they're getting lots of airplay, as well they should. But well before their approach, the influence of Europeans was changing the mountains and plains of the west. Lewis and Clark took earlier maps of the area with them, including one based on David Thompson's explorations. Thompson worked for the Hudson's Bay Company and did a tremendous amount of exploring in the Canadian west, but he also followed the Columbia River and traveled through the Flathead Valley. *Sources of the River: Tracking David Thompson across Western North America,* by Jack Nisbet, is a wonderful account of this man's astonishing adventures. Thompson survived a broken leg, crossed northerly Howse Pass in the winter on snowshoes, traded with the native tribes along the way, canoed from Quebec west through Lake Superior—and generally led an unpredictable but exciting life.

Another author worth checking out is John C. Jackson. His *Children of the Fur Trade: Forgotten Metis of the Pacific Northwest* also chronicles the early years of European contact in the west. Many white men took Native wives, and their offspring were the *metis,* a group that collectively both connected the two worlds and failed to fit into either. Jackson's more recent *Piikani Blackfeet: A Culture under Siege* tells the history of the Blackfeet Tribe from earliest oral accounts to the present day.

After Lewis and Clark came through, of course, life in the west began to change radically for the Native people. Accounts of Blackfeet mythologies can be found in George Bird Grinnell's *Blackfoot Lodge Tales*; Grinnell was a white man who negotiated on behalf of the Blackfeet when they ceded what is now the east side of Glacier National Park to the U.S. government in 1895. He is also known as the father of Glacier National Park, but he was enough of a friend of the Blackfeet that they gave him a Blackfeet name, "Fishercap," because he wore a hat made from the skin of a fisher.

Walter McClintock was another white man who lived for a time with the Blackfeet. His book, *The Old North Trail, or Life, Legends and Religion of the Blackfeet Indians,* is generally considered an accurate account of his experiences with them. The Old North Trail was the route the Blackfeet and other tribes used to pass north and south along the eastern front of the Rocky Mountains. Traces of it can still be found today along the foothills of the Blackfeet Reservation.

---

restaurant has a beer and wine license. Meals are served at rustic-style tables, or you can take your order to go.

Montana Coffee Traders $
328 West Center Street, Kalispell
(406) 756–2326

This store dares to ask, "How You Bean, Man?" It is a must-stop for the coffee aficionado. Begun in Whitefish by RC Beall more than 20 years ago, Montana Coffee Traders has grown into a snug empire with a branch in Austin, Texas (where it goes by the name Texas Coffee Traders). If you are looking for a single cup of espresso, or a complete panoply of coffee blends and supplies, this is the right spot. Even tea drinkers may find something unique here. A cafe in the store serves soup and sandwiches or desserts, and there is pound after pound of coffee to take home for an aromatic Montana memory. Our favorite is the extra-strong Grizzly blend, but there is something for every taste, including organic and fair-trade blends from Peru, Guatemala,

Sumatra, and across the tropics. Montana Coffee Traders is conveniently located just across the street from the Kalispell Center Mall.

Mountain Crossroads Restaurant & Golf Club $$
100 Montana Highway 206, Kalispell
(406) 755–0111

Even though the Crossroads is on a golf course and features a large bar in the dining room, we are still including it in the family-friendly listing for a couple of reasons. First of all, the establishment has a no-smoking policy, which makes it quite unusual in Montana. Secondly, the menu features many low-priced entrees, so even though there is no separate children's menu, there are many meals that most kids would enjoy, such as spaghetti, hamburgers, or chili. Top-priced items on the menu are a New York steak at $10.95 and jumbo prawns at $9.95. You will also enjoy the appetizers, especially the "Wingers," a basket of 12 chicken wings that come drenched in your choice of barbecue sauce, smooth buttered hot sauce, or cajun sauce for just $3.95, served with either ranch or bleu cheese. The Crossroads features the best view of any nonlake restaurant in the Flathead Valley, too. You're sitting practically underneath the Swan Range of mountains at the east end of the valley. And for the family that plays together, Mountain Crossroads also features a very reasonably priced nine-hole course. The resort and restaurant are typically closed in winter.

Rocco's $$$
3796 Highway 2 East, Kalispell
(406) 756–5834

Rocco's suffered a terrible fire a few years ago but is now back up and running. Everyone's happy to remember their old favorites: this Italian cuisine is hearty and filling. The restaurant is comfortable and has a busy but relaxed feel, and it isn't hard to take a couple of hours to enjoy your dinner with a fine wine. Reservations are always a good idea.

Montana-style interior design makes this lounge a cozy place to gather. Photo: courtesy of Cavanaughs at Kalispell Center

Sizzler Restaurant $
1250 U.S. Highway 2 West, Kalispell
(406) 257–9555

This is our favorite family restaurant in the Kalispell area. It's part of a chain, but the local owners go the extra mile for their customers, and they have been innovators throughout the years. Sizzler is a steak house, but you can get much more than the trademark sirloin steak here. For one thing, the restaurant has the best all-you-can-eat salad bar in town, with everything from fresh fruit to tacos to pasta and soups included, and a separate bar available with cake, cookies, and ice cream at no extra charge. You get the whole thing for just $7.49 (less for seniors!) or just $2.99 with an entree. Kids have their own all-you-can-eat food bar featuring macaroni and cheese, pasta, chicken nuggets, and fruit. This place is always packed, but they never have to turn anyone away, thanks to rapid service. You won't regret a stop here.

Somers Bay Café $
47 Somers Road, Somers
(406) 857-2660

This little cafe is open only for breakfast and lunch, so keep that in mind if you're headed down to Flathead Lake for an afternoon on the water. The interior is cozy, and the walls are decorated with historic photos: Somers as a logging town, early settlers at their homes. On a sunny summer day, though, you'll want to have your lunch on the deck. The burgers are hearty, and the chicken breast sandwich will fill you up, but it would be hard to go wrong with this straightforward but very satisfactory menu.

Fine Dining

Black Angus Steak House $$$
1330 U.S. Highway 2 West, Kalispell
(406) 755-5341

The Black Angus is on the edge of town just as you are leaving Kalispell on the west side, but make the effort to stop here. Located in the Red Lion hotel, the Black Angus features not just steak, but also a complete line of fine dining, with nightly specials that might include a tenderloin fillet stuffed with Dungeness crab, halibut with macadamia nut butter, or lobster. You can always get the prime rib ($14.95

for a 12-ounce cut, $18.95 for a 16-ounce cut) or try something unusual, like the pork tenderloin with brandy garlic sauce. For lunch try the steak sandwich. The atmosphere is quiet and low-key. A full bar is available, and there's a casino one floor down.

Café Max $$$
121 Main Street, Kalispell
(406) 755-SOUP

Café Max is Kalispell's undisputed leader for fine dining. Chef Doug Day is a master of presentation, as well as gastronomy, and everything in his restaurant shows the extra effort of a great dining establishment. Lunch, served from 11:00 A.M. to 2:00 P.M. Monday through Friday, features a "soup line" with your choice of eight delights.

But dinner is what Café Max is known for. Openers might include manila clams and Italian sausage or shrimp bisque, each with a dollop of creamy mashed potatoes blended in. Entrees on the menu change every couple of weeks, but might include such specialties as grilled quail marinated in soy, sake, and ginger; grilled New Zealand lamb chops with zinfandel, roasted garlic, and pink peppercorns; or other meat and poultry selections ranging in price from $15.95 to $20.95. The seafood choices are chosen specially each day to ensure freshness, and could include Native American–caught sturgeon or Alaskan king salmon topped with two jumbo shrimp. The service at Café Max is swift and efficient. Members of the wait staff circulate from table to table making sure that each customer's water glass or coffee cup is full. After dinner your wait person will bring forth a platter of 10 desserts, including peanut butter mousse pie, crème brûlée, homemade ice cream, and a variety of cheese cakes and chocolates. Café Max serves dinner Tuesday through Saturday only, starting at 5:30 P.M. and continuing through the last seating at 9:30 P.M. Reservations are not required, but on Friday and Saturday the restaurant turns away as many as 50 people a night.

The Knead is one of Kalispell's unique dining establishments. Photo: Keny Harp

Fenders $$$
4090 U.S. Highway 93 North, Kalispell
(406) 752–3000

A fun restaurant with something just a little different. The name of the establishment comes from a pair of red fenders from a 1941 one-ton Ford V8 truck that graces the entryway. The truck was actually used for 20 years on a Kalispell-area Hereford ranch, and it has stood guard for almost another 25. In the back of the restaurant, there are also five booths that are constructed from original bench seats from vintage automobiles. You enter the booths by swinging open the car door. These seats make fine dining a family-friendly experience! As for the food, it includes a cross-section of seafood, steaks, and pasta, with a little chicken thrown in. Prime rib is a house specialty, and you can expect to leave a bit of the Motherlode serving on your plate. The seafood fettuccine is also popular and features a generous helping of shrimp, scallops, and mussels. Try the chocolate mousse afterward to freshen your palate. By the way, this restaurant is conveniently located halfway between Kalispell and Whitefish, so it can be easily reached from either direction.

Hennessy's Restaurant & Lounge $$$
1701 U.S. Highway 93 South, Kalispell
(406) 755–6860

This restaurant has been a mainstay of Kalispell dining for more than 30 years. It is located in the Outlaw Hotel and also includes casino and lounge areas. The restaurant is quiet and darkly lit and makes a pleasant spot for an intimate dinner. Lunches tend to be more bustling as businessmen and -women meet here for work and pleasure. On the evening menu, one of the old favorites here (at $15.95) is the Snowgoose, a chicken breast fillet filled with cream cheese and crabmeat and then topped with hollandaise sauce.

The Knead $$
25 Second Avenue West, Kalispell
(406) 755–7510
www.theknead.com

This is one of the newer restaurants in Kalispell, but the same crew has been cooking food for several years at Montana Coffee Traders. They moved to this larger location in 1999 because demand just kept growing. It doesn't take long to figure out why. The menu is a unique combination of health food, such as tabouli and eggplant, along with American deli traditions, such as the reuben sandwich. The restaurant has been completely remodeled and features a bright modern decor, along with a new deck for limited outdoor seating when in season. The Knead also benefits from one of Montana's new "cabaret liquor licenses," which allow restaurants to serve beer and wine without needing a costly casino license. Check out the Web site for recipes and news of music and art at The Knead.

Montana Grill on Flathead Lake $$$$
5480 U.S. Highway 93 South, Somers
(406) 857–3889

This restaurant features fine dining in fine surroundings. The restaurant and bar are housed in a timber-built structure that makes "log home" seem like a synonym for palace. And the views from the restaurant looking out across Somers Bay can't be beat. The menu, meanwhile, is varied and delightful. There are nine appetizers ranging in price from $4.95 to $9.95. Our favorites are the baked artichoke and baked penne with shrimp. Seafood entrees are extensive, including fillet of salmon at $18.95 and rainbow trout on special. More regional dining can be found with the grilled elk steak, served in fresh sage mustard cream sauce. A 1¾-pound rack of baby back ribs runs to $23.95, but is well worth the price for the succulent flavor of the ribs cooked in plum sauce and mesquite smoked. A lighter-side menu includes salmon, fettuccine, and grilled eggplant. Desserts include flaming bananas foster or cherries jubilee for two at $7.95.

Northwest Bounty Co. $$
20 North Main Street, Kalispell
(406) 752–6660

This restaurant is located in the WestCoast Kalispell Center at the Kalispell Center Mall. It features dining in a spacious atrium that is well lit and decorated with many living trees. The menu is quite varied, with everything from butternut squash ravioli smothered with wild mushroom sauce and topped with Asiago cheese to blackened salmon with fruit salsa. Special value entrees, such as the cheeseburger or chicken-fried steak, run between $6.00 and $10.00. Lunches are popular here, and a specialty is the Chinese wonton salad that comes with Oriental veggies, cashews, and chicken stir-fried in teriyaki and sesame sauce and served on a bed of spinach inside a large golden wonton basket. After dinner you can wander into the Fireside Lounge or across the hall to the Magic Diamond Casino.

Rosario's in Lakeside $$$
7125 U.S. Highway 93 South, Lakeside
(406) 844–2888

Lakeside has many pleasures for the vacationing family, not the least of which is Rosario's restaurant, located on the sec-

ond floor of an old marina building. Through the lakeside windows, you look out over weathered docks and pilings at Flathead Lake and the Swan and Mission Mountains in the background. Turning back to the restaurant, you are looking at Chef Rosario hard at work in the kitchen, keeping customers satisfied with many specials and his standard delights such as veal francaise, four sauteed scallops of veal smothered in butter garlic lemon sherry sauce, or pollo alla rollatini, chicken cutlets stuffed with prosciutto ham, mushrooms, mozzarella, and ground veal in a marsala mushroom sauce. Plus there's more traditional fare like veal parmesan and fettuccine alfredo. On Monday nights Rosario's has a great all-you-can-eat Italian dinner for just $8.95. And there's a children's menu that includes chicken parmesan, burgers, spaghetti with meatballs, and ravioli, each for $5.95.

Tiebuckers Pub & Eatery $$$
75 Somers Road, Somers
(406) 857–3335

Tiebuckers is a restaurant with a history, literally. The building that houses Tiebuckers in Somers dates from 1928 and was both a depot for the Great Northern Railway and headquarters for the Somers Lumber Co. for many years. It first housed a restaurant in the 1960s and was reopened as a restaurant by Barry and Julie Smith several years ago. Many of the recipes pay homage to Julie's grandfather, Joe Di Cristina, such as chicken basted in Grandpa's Sauce, an oil and vinegar blend, then barbecued for an hour and steamed to retain natural juices. The half of a chicken is $11.75. The establishment is also noted for its pork ribs and combo platters. Dinners include focaccia, soup, salad, and baked potato or pasta of the day. Steamed clams are served every Friday night and there are five fresh selections each night. Kids meals are available for those age 12 and younger. Dinner is served starting at 5:00 P.M. Tuesday through Saturday. Music can be heard on the weekends sometimes, with jazz piano player Nina Russell performing and telling tales of her career in the Big Band era. Tiebuckers is closed in November.

Nightlife

Finish Line Cocktail Lounge
153 Meridian Road, Kalispell
(406) 756–9116

The Finish Line is an interesting mix of blue collar, white collar, and no collar. The bar has long been a popular local hangout for businessmen, horse people (the bar is near the county fairgrounds, where horse racing is held every summer during the weekend of the fair and the weekend after), and county workers. The menu is quite varied and includes popular burgers and steaks, as well as chicken, pasta, and other selections. New in the past couple of years is a pretty steady diet of music on the weekends, and the lounge has become a standard place to hear such local blues bands as Blues Cruiser and Big Daddy and the Blue Notes.

Montana Nugget Casino
740 West Idaho Street, Kalispell
(406) 756–8100

The Montana Nugget is the perfect place to go if you want to acquaint yourself with the Montana casino lifestyle. The ding-ding-ding of video poker machines hitting the jackpot merges with the sounds of a sports announcer on one of the many television sets, the country tunes coming over the loudspeaker, and the waitresses calling out another order. One side of the large open building is dedicated to dining, but there is plenty of room for gambling, and there's usually a poker game in progress if you want to take your chance at beating some genuine Montana characters at their own game.

Moose's Saloon
173 North Main Street, Kalispell
(406) 755–2337

Moose's has the reputation of being the one tavern that a visitor to Kalispell must stop in and see. It's the real McCoy, a genuine hangout, with a square bar often surrounded by customers getting to know each other or old friends. It's reminiscent of the bar on the *Cheers* TV show, complete with lots of colorful characters who are the regulars. The table area is dark and moody and the floor is covered with sawdust and peanut shells, since Moose's provides complimentary nuts to munch on with your drinks. Lots of folks in the Flathead Valley consider the pizza at Moose's to be the best in the area, and maybe the state. You can also get a variety of sandwiches, burgers, and other munchies from the kitchen. Next door at Moostly Moose's, you can pick up a souvenir T-shirt.

The Outlaw Lounge
1711 U.S. Highway 93 South, Kalispell
(406) 755–6860

Every Friday night the Outlaw Hotel's lounge turns into a comedy club as some of the brightest talents in the West visit Montana. There's a $6.00 cover charge per person, and of course since it's a bar, there's no admission for those younger than 21. But if you enjoy those comedy shows on cable TV, you will no doubt get a kick out of the off-color humor that prevails at this kind of club. Visiting comedians enjoy making fun of the rustic folkways of Montana, but the crowd often gets even by making fun of the urban insanity of Los Angeles, Seattle, and other home cities of these comics. The Outlaw Hotel lounge also features a casino, and you can get excellent food from the Hennessy's kitchen as well.

Painted Horse Grill
110 Main Street, Kalispell
(406) 257–7035

Painted Horse Grill is located in the Historic Kalispell Grand Hotel complex, which also includes the Alley Connection restaurant and the Kalispell Casino next door. Dinner is served Monday through Saturday from 5:00 to 9:00 P.M. Lunch is served Monday through Friday from 11:30 A.M. to 2:30 P.M.

Shopping

Columbine Glassworks and Gallery
140 Main Street, Kalispell
(406) 752-7174

Columbine Glassworks is a lovely place to spend some time . . . the sort of place where many people could happily lose a few hours. The Glassworks features Tiffany-style lamps, mobiles, dishware, figurines, sun-catchers for windows . . . about anything that can be made out of stained or blown glass. The store is wall-to-wall with beautiful things, including fabrics, photos, and paintings, and just walking through it is a delight for the senses. It's the perfect place to look for a gift; with so many different kinds of lovely things, just about everyone is bound to find something that appeals.

Depot Park Square
Junction of Main Street and First Street East
Kalispell

This new complex of stores in three buildings is a delightful alternative to mall shopping, and it's just across the street from the Kalispell Center Mall, so it also makes a nice complement. Some of the stores here are The Athlete's Foot shoe store, featuring gear for the sports minded; Golf USA; a women's fashion shop called Steals; the Avalanche Creek coffee-house, featuring soup and sandwiches as well as a wide variety of espressos; and Boundaries Clothing, featuring sportswear. The pedestrian-mall quality of the three buildings and the easy parking has helped to bring a fresh attitude to downtown Kalispell, where many other interesting shops also await you, including Books West, just across First Street from here.

Imagination Station
132 Main Street, Kalispell
(406) 755-5668
www.whitefishtoys.com

If possible, this new branch of Whitefish's Imagination Station is even more fun than the original. It's prettier, say the owners—they learned from their first experience. And it has some new features too: a small upstairs is dedicated to teachers' materials, theme books, manipulatives, bulletin boards, and posters. Downstairs, "groovy girls" are the hot item now. These multicultural dolls—complete with groovy hair and outfits—are so cute, even 11-year-olds don't feel silly playing with dolls. (And, of course, they have some great accessories!) Stop on by and have a look around . . . it's a fun shop for all ages. If you can't get there in person, you can always window-shop the store's new Web site!

Kalispell Center Mall
20 North Main Street, Kalispell
(406) 752-6660

It's not as big as the malls in many larger urban areas, but Kalispell Center Mall has three dozen stores to keep tourists and locals busy for more than an afternoon. The anchor stores are J.C. Penney and Herberger's, with an emphasis at both stores on clothes for all family members. Among the smaller stores that are popular are the Cherry Tree, which features eclectic style accessories and modern fashions for women; the Country Cupboard, with kitchen gadgets and necessities for sale in all price ranges; Teacher's Pet, with innovative toys for children; and International Design, which has gifts for all occasions including toiletries, crafts, and candles. There is no food court per se, but food is available at several stands such as Orange Julius, Dairy Queen, Wolfgang's Famous soups, and Anna's Greek Gyros. A distinctive feature of the mall is that it is connected to the WestCoast Kalispell Center Hotel, so you can stay at the hotel by night, shop by day, and eat at either the mall or the Northwest Bounty restaurant, depending on your mood. For many, a perfect vacation.

Rocky Mountain Outfitters
135 Main Street, Kalispell
(406) 752–2446

While Sportsman & Ski Haus (see below) caters to the outdoorsy public generally, RMO is more devoted to self-powered sports: backpacking; climbing; kayaking; and backcountry, cross-country, and skate skiing. The staff is knowledgeable and friendly—and knows what's happening in the wilds around the Flathead Valley, whether it's water levels in the rivers or recent avalanche reports. Spend a little time in this store, and you will probably overhear some interesting stories of what's really going on out there in the woods!

Sportsman & Ski Haus
Junction of U.S. Highways 2 and 93, Kalispell
(406) 755–6484

If you've come all the way to Montana, you may as well enjoy the great outdoors, and that's where Sportsman & Ski Haus comes in. This is the department store of sporting-goods stores in the Flathead, with thorough inventories for hunting and fishing, camping, and water sports, as well as an extensive line of footwear and outdoor clothing. You can get everything you need for your family expedition here, down to and including the live bait.

Strawberry Patch
404 West Center Street, Kalispell
(406) 752–2660

This popular shopping spot was located in the Gateway West Mall for many years, but when that establishment closed, the Strawberry Patch sent out a runner and wound up in a beautiful new facility across the street from Kalispell Center Mall. Strawberry Patch is a quintessential gift store, carrying a line of merchandise that ranges from collectibles such as Beanie Babies to local items like jellies and sauces from the Bigfork Inn, not to mention the popular selections of fudge. And if you wish Christmas was every day, you'll find the corner nook of decorations and Christmas collectibles to your fancy. There are also many brightly colored dishes and decorative items of every type. Prices range from hundreds of dollars for a small handmade tabletop fountain to a dollar or two for candles. And women shoppers will want to stop at the other end of this new minimall to visit Loretta's, which features ladies' fashions and accessories for working women.

Western Outdoor
48 Main Street, Kalispell
(406) 756–5818

If you have a little buckaroo or cowgirl in tow, you might want to head on over to the Western Outdoor Store for lots of genuine western wear souvenirs that will last for years. There's a complete lineup of clothing for little pardners, from boots to cowboy hats, and there's rarely been a little one who can resist a shiny belt buckle. There are plenty of western fashions for men and women as well. This sizable store also includes a rack of cowboy hats for grown-ups that runs clear around the store. Up on the walls there are also hundreds of boards featuring genuine cow brands used by ranchers across Montana, some dating from the 1800s. The store phased out saddles a few years ago, but you can still buy a full line of cowboy accessories here such as halters, bridles, saddle pads, spurs, and even bullwhips. When you've spent enough money on wrangling gear, you can mosey on down the stairs to the Kalispell Antiques Market, which is located on the lower level.

Whitefish

Area Overview
Accommodations
Restaurants
Nightlife
Shopping

Area Overview

Originally a railroad and logging town, today Whitefish is a resort community whose residents enjoy small-town charm, many big-city amenities, and world-class outdoor recreation. The town sits at the northwest end of the Flathead Valley, just south of the Whitefish Range and Big Mountain and at the foot of 7-mile-long Whitefish Lake. The town itself is a busy retail and business center that has maintained its low-key character: You'll feel at ease strolling in and out of small shops or chatting with the staff in restaurants. In the summer, flower gardens and hanging baskets ornament virtually every corner and shop; in the winter, holiday decorations add color and warmth to seasonal festivities. And Whitefish folks like to do things—just watch the vehicles going down the road. Whether they're pulling a horse trailer or snowmobiles, or carrying skis, bikes, or boats, you'll get the idea pretty quickly: Whitefish is a great place to play.

For a small town, Whitefish offers a surprisingly big variety of places in which to stay, to eat, and to shop. It's a very busy place both winter and summer; fall and spring are quieter times to visit. The downtown area itself is quite compact and easy to explore on foot: within a few blocks you'll find everything from the Stumptown Historical Society to the new city library and cultural arts center, small retail shops and restaurants, standard

Aerial view of Whitefish Lake, Big Mountain, and the town of Whitefish. Photo: Norm Kurtz

services (post office, fax, banks, etc.), and city parks. You'll find other lodgings, shops, restaurants, and larger resorts associated with Big Mountain or the golf courses, for example, but even these are only minutes from town.

Accommodations

Price Code

Lodging code per night for two people:

$	Less than $85
$$	$86 to $115
$$$	$116 to $150
$$$$	More than $151

Hotels and Motels

Lazy Bear Lodge $$
6390 Highway 93 South, Whitefish
(406) 862–4020, (800) 888–4479
www.whitefishmt.com

Formerly a Comfort Inn, the Lazy Bear Lodge offers standard motel accommodations with one difference: Kids will love the indoor swimming pool and 90-foot corkscrew water slide. And while they're splashing and having a great time, adults can soak in one of two hot tubs—so there's something for everyone. The 66 rooms have color cable TV with HBO and individual heat and air-conditioning. Nonsmoking rooms, a wheelchair-accessible unit, and drive-up ground-floor rooms are available. Pets are welcome (and there's a "pet comfort area")—please inquire about the pet policy. Suites may be reserved for larger groups, and some include family-size kitchens.

Room rates for two people vary from $59 to $119 per night depending on the season.

Pine Lodge $$
920 Spokane Avenue, Whitefish
(406) 862–7600, (800) 305–7463
www.thepinelodge.com

The Pine Lodge is neatly wedged between Highway 93 (Spokane Avenue) and the Whitefish River . . . which means that,

while it's on the main road into town, the areas at the back of the lodge—the lobby, swimming pool, deck, and many rooms—overlook the willows and water. And should you opt for a one-bedroom suite, you'll be pleasantly surprised by the northern view as well—these rooms face Big Mountain.

All Pine Lodge rooms include remote-controlled television, telephone, and bath. Standard rooms, deluxe rooms, mini-suites, and one-bedroom suites offer a range of amenities from spas to gas fireplaces and balconies for between $69 and $190 per night for two people. Please inquire about the executive suite if you are interested.

The Pine Lodge has an exercise room, indoor/outdoor heated swimming pool, outdoor hot tub, guest laundry, and a meeting room for up to 50 people. Complimentary continental breakfast is served each morning. Nonsmoking rooms and floors are available. The Pine Lodge is a Quality Inn.

Rocky Mountain Lodge $$
6510 Highway 93 South, Whitefish
(406) 862–2569, (800) 862–2569
www.rockymtnlodge.com

Opened in 1995, Rocky Mountain Lodge is the newest hotel in Whitefish. Its 79 rooms include executive rooms and mini-suites, which offer a king-size bed and gas fireplace, wet bar with small refrigerator, sink, and microwave, Jacuzzi or garden tub, a sofa bed, and fax/modem port. Standard rooms feature king- or queen-size beds, and 12 annex rooms are located in a motel-style detached building where you can drive right up next to the room.

Other amenities include an outdoor heated pool and Jacuzzi, laundry, exercise room, and meeting and banquet facilities. Guests enjoy a complimentary deluxe continental breakfast each morning.

Room rates vary from a high of $173 per night for minisuites to as little as $63 per night for annex rooms, depending on the season. Please inquire for rates and availability.

Bed-and-Breakfasts

The B&Bs listed here are all private homes that their owners have now opened up to guests. Good Medicine Lodge and Hidden Moose Lodge (under Resorts, Guest Ranches, and Lodges) are small inns offering the same personal attention and full breakfast you would expect of a B&B.

Eagle's Roost $$
400 Wisconsin Avenue, Whitefish
(406) 862–5198, (888) 750–6378
www.eagles-roost.com

A high level of personal service as well as elegantly appointed rooms are hallmarks of the Eagle's Roost. Fine crystal, antique furniture, and English bone china complement the luxuries of your own whirlpool bathtub and in-room cable TV with VCR. Guests have their own entrance, and the comfortable sitting room features a gas fireplace and stone hearth. Upstairs you'll find the formal dining room, a deck where

Whitefish bed-and-breakfasts offer charming accommodations. Photo: courtesy of The Garden Wall Inn

breakfast is served in summer, and the living room. Your hosts, Connie and Tony Davis, also display (and sell) artworks from Whitefish's The Gallery, giving guests a view of Glacier Country as seen through the eyes of local painters. As you sip your morning coffee or afternoon wine, you'll soak up the view across the Flathead Valley toward Columbia Mountain and the Swan Range. A back deck leads to the hot tub and landscaped back yard—pleasant retreats in summer or winter—where both deer and pheasants have been known to appear.

Tucked into a hillside and nestled among the pines, the Eagle's Roost is located on the road to Big Mountain. But it's also only a 10-minute walk from downtown Whitefish, so it's an easy stroll into town for dinner or entertainment. Whitefish Lake and City Beach are also only a 10-minute walk away.

When you arise in the morning, you'll find the coffee already on; a four-course breakfast follows in the dining room. After your day's adventures, you'll return to afternoon wine and snacks. And just before bedtime, homemade cookies mysteriously appear.

The Eagle's Roost takes pride in indulging its guests with warm hospitality. Rates run from $85 to $125 per night for two people. Smoking is permitted outdoors only; please inquire about off-season discounts and the pet policy.

The Garden Wall Inn $$
504 Spokane Avenue, Whitefish
(406) 862–3440, (888) 530–1700
www.wtp.net/go/gardenwall

"Luxurious," "gracious," and "comfortable" are three words that will spring to mind soon after you enter The Garden Wall Inn. This beautifully restored 1920s house is now furnished with period antiques; the attentive but not intrusive service will charm your stay. You'll find a rose decorating the coffee tray at your room each morning, a very civilized half hour before the scrumptious gourmet breakfast. And after your day's adventures, you might spend some time soaking in a claw-foot tub, then sip sherry and enjoy hors d'oeuvres before the fireplace.

The Garden Wall Inn—named for the Garden Wall, the part of the Continental Divide that runs just north of Logan Pass in Glacier National Park—displays many details that reveal the owners' love of that nearby national park. Historic photos of Glacier, Blue Willow china originally used in the park hotels, first-edition copies of books about the park, even the Audubon prints on the walls all speak of Glacier (the Audubon Society was founded by George Bird Grinnell, probably the single person most responsible for creation of the park). Between owners Mike and Rhonda Fitzgerald and their innkeeper Chris Schustrom, you'll find a tremendous knowledge of the outdoors, whether you're interested in hiking, skiing, fly-fishing, or kayaking. They also know the Flathead Valley well and will be happy to point you in the right direction for shopping, dining, or exploring. The Garden Wall Inn is located just 2 blocks from downtown Whitefish, giving you easy access to the town's services and attractions. The inn's five bedrooms range in price from $95 to $145 per night for two people; a suite may be arranged for $195 per night for up to four people. Most rooms have private baths. Pets and smoking are not permitted.

Gasthaus Wendlingen $$
700 Monegan Road, Whitefish
(406) 862–4886, (800) 811–8002
www.whitefishmt.com

America is a nation of immigrants—and Montana is no exception. Bill and Barbara Klein are both descended from Germans who entered the United States first on the east coast and then migrated west. You'll find Gasthaus Wendlingen a fascinating mix of that German heritage and the modern West. German details—from the working cuckoo clock to imported beer steins—complement personal photographs and furniture brought from Wendlingen, Germany, where cousins still live today. Although most of the cooking is American style, special dishes do bring a taste of Europe into the menu as well.

You'll know you're in Montana, though—Gasthaus Wendlingen is located between Haskill Creek and the Whitefish River. Large views open up north to Big Mountain, east toward Bad Rock Canyon and the entrance to Glacier National Park, and south toward Blacktail Mountain. A deck overlooks the creek, where you'll enjoy watching ducks and songbirds along the water. The neighboring ranch horses add that western feeling as well.

You'll find the Kleins ready to welcome you to the Gasthaus. A large, bright living room with a river-rock fireplace, gracious guest rooms, a steam room (to melt the kinks out after a day of skiing or hiking!), a long covered deck to sit out and admire the views, a full breakfast, and afternoon snacks will make you feel at home—no matter what country your family is from!

Gasthaus Wendlingen is only a 10-minute drive from downtown Whitefish, but its quiet meadows feel like a real retreat from the busy world. Room rates vary from $60 to $125 for two people, depending on season and accommodations. Pets are not allowed; nonsmoking adults are preferred.

Resorts, Guest Ranches, and Lodges

Big Mountain Ski and Summer Resort $–$$$
P.O. Box 1400, Whitefish 59937
(406) 862–1900, (800) 858–4152
www.bigmtn.com

The Big Mountain was, of course, initially a ski resort—but nowadays it's a good deal more. Winter visitors still focus on skiing—and, with more than 3,000 acres of skiable terrain, the Big Mountain has something to offer for skiers of every ability. Other activities include tubing, cross-country skiing and skate skiing on the groomed track, and snowcat skiing. And summertime now brings incredible outdoor fun too—hiking, mountain biking, huckleberry picking—as well as live music and other special events (see the Outdoor Recreation chapter).

The Big Mountain central reservation office handles reservations for all the lodgings on the mountain. The different facilities cover a wide range of accommodations and prices, and all are available as part of

A summer gondola ride at the Big Mountain promises panoramic views. Photo: courtesy of the Big Mountain

lodging/lift ticket packages. All include a spa or sauna and laundry. Many Big Mountain businesses close briefly in both the spring and fall, so please be sure to check dates of availability. Per-night prices are per room for hotels and for two bedrooms for condominiums.

Hibernation House. $$. An overnight stay at this economy lodge includes a full skier's breakfast. Shuttle to the ski hill is available, or ski to your door. Rate for 2003 is $95 per room.

Glacier Village Property Management. $$. Many of these condos, chalets, and duplexes are within walking distance of the slopes. Some include hot tubs. Rates begin at $280 per unit.

The Edelweiss. $$. These charming condos are located in the heart of Big Mountain Village. Rates begin at $280 per unit.

Alpinglow Inn. $$. Ski to your front door at this contemporary inn. The Alpinglow dining room offers very reasonable lunch and dinner specials—and a tremendous view of the Flathead Valley. Rooms start at $122 per night.

Kintla Lodge. $$$. Brand-new in 1999, the Kintla Lodge offers deluxe condos and shops right at the base of the ski hill, underground parking, and elevator access. Units begin at $375.

Kandahar Lodge. $$$. This traditional-style ski lodge features a fine restaurant open for breakfast and dinner (reservations required) in a family atmosphere. Rooms begin at $159 per night.

Gaynor's RiverBend Ranch $$
1992 K M Ranch Road, Whitefish
(406) 862–3802
www.whitefishmt.com/lodging/gaynor

Overlooking a bend in the Stillwater River, Gaynor's RiverBend Ranch offers a unique opportunity to enjoy ranch life in the Montana countryside—yet the four-room suite offers all the amenities of home within a 15-minute drive from Whitefish.

It's hard to explain the peace and beauty of this open valley. Although town is not far away, you'll forget it and your worries completely as you take in the quiet and big views. The river attracts songbirds and waterfowl, and mountain bluebirds nest in boxes along the fence. The ranch is set back from the road, which has very little traffic, and state forest land—with both riding and hiking trails—lies just across the way.

Whether you've spent your day exploring Glacier, skiing Big Mountain, golfing, or otherwise enjoying the area, you'll feel like you're coming home when you return to the RiverBend Ranch each evening. You'll have your own river view to the west—put up your feet and enjoy the sunset! The guest suite has its own private entrance. The kitchen is fully equipped, and coffee, tea, and spices are supplied; the living room includes a queen-size hide-a-bed sofa, a gas fireplace, and satellite TV; the cozy bedroom also has satellite TV; other amenities include phone with voice mail; washer and dryer; gas barbecue; a picnic table by the river; and a selection of books and games.

You may also choose to make the ranch itself the focus of your vacation. Sleeping in and enjoying a cup of coffee by the river is a great way to start the day, but there's plenty of exploring to do here, too. Gaynor's RiverBend Ranch offers customized trail rides, tailored to your experience and limited to your own group. Special rides are available for children. During your stay you are welcome to explore the entire ranch property. Its open pastures are home to 11 ranch horses as well as others that are boarded there. Those traveling with their own horses may also board them at the ranch in the spacious stalls and/or large outdoor paddocks. Your host, Don Gaynor, will be happy to help you with your plans.

The guest suite accommodates up to four. Rates vary by season, and range from $75 to $125 per night. Smoking is not allowed indoors; if you have pets traveling with you, please inquire about the pet policy.

Good Medicine Lodge $$
537 Wisconsin Avenue, Whitefish
(406) 862–5488, (800) 860–5488
www.goodmedicinelodge.com

"Good Medicine"—you'll find this the perfect prescription, no matter how you take it! Location, interiors, furnishings, breakfast—every detail reflects Good Medicine Lodge's attention to your well-being. Built of cedar timbers, the lodge practically glows with the warmth of wood, accented with fabrics influenced by Native American designs. The lobby and great room invite you to curl up and read by the fire, help yourself to freshly baked cookies, or get ready to soak in the hot tub just out the door. In summer you'll enjoy stepping into the garden or relaxing under the broad covered porches of the L-shaped lodge. And, summer or winter, you'll find a big, buffet-style breakfast awaiting you each morning: fresh muffins, breads, and cobblers, cereals, granola, yogurt, meats and cheeses, coffee, tea, and juice.

The nine rooms and suites all have private baths, air-conditioning, phones, and

Nature provides a refreshing shower on a summer's day. Photo: Susan Olin

custom-made log beds. Most rooms have balconies with mountain views. The rooms offer either queen-size or twin bed arrangements, and the largest suite can sleep five. The master suite, which has its own loft, gas stove, whirlpool tub, Swiss shower, and balcony, recently earned Good Medicine the description of one of America's ten "most romantic inns." In addition, the lodge has a ski room with boot and glove driers as well as a guest laundry.

Owners Christopher Ridder and Susan Moffitt have taken Good Medicine one step further as well. The lodge is a member of the Green Hotel Association and is wheelchair accessible, smoke free, and proud to reduce, reuse, and recycle wherever possible in the effort to keep Montana beautiful.

Rates range from $85 to $135 per night for two people, depending on room and season. With just nine rooms, Good Medicine might be listed as a B&B as well. Suites vary from $135 to $215 per night. The lodge is located about 6 blocks north of downtown Whitefish on the road to Big Mountain. Good Medicine Lodge does close for the months of November and April.

Grouse Mountain Lodge $$$
2 Fairway Drive, Whitefish
(406) 862-3000, (800) 321-8822
www.grmtlodge.com

Here is lodging in the grand style—everything you could think of, and more. With its river-rock fireplaces, warm polished wood, and delicate elk-antler chandeliers, you'll know you're in Montana. The 145 rooms are stylish and comfortable, and some include Jacuzzis, kitchens, or loft bedrooms. The lodge restaurant (see The Grill under Restaurants) is one of the finest in town and is open for breakfast, lunch, and dinner. The Whitefish Lake Golf Course is out your door; in the winter its fairways are groomed for cross-country and skate skiing. And the lodge has its own indoor swimming pool and hot tubs.

Native wildflower landscaping surrounds the entrance to Grouse Mountain Lodge. Photo: Montana's Finest Resorts

Grouse Mountain Lodge also has conference facilities for groups as large as 300 people. Banquet and catering services will provide just the level of support you need, whether that's coffee and rolls or a sit-down dinner.

Room rates vary by season from $109 to $195 per night for two people. Be sure to inquire about both ski and golf packages.

Hidden Moose Lodge $$
1735 East Lakeshore Drive, Whitefish
(406) 862–6516, (888) SEE MOOSE
www.hiddenmooselodge.com

The great room's log-framed cathedral ceiling and massive fireplace made of local rock bespeak the rustic yet warm feeling of the Hidden Moose Lodge. Antique skis adorn the walls for an outdoorsy feel; a mix of colors, patterns, and textures in the fabrics and custom-made log furniture add richness to the interior of all the lodge rooms. The Hidden Moose Lodge is built into the side of a hill and surrounded by pine, birch, and aspen trees. Every once in a while the "hidden moose" emerges for a stroll—and you may also see deer and the occasional bear wandering behind the lodge. But if the wilderness is at your backyard, civilization makes its presence known, too—terraced rock gardens and hanging flower baskets brighten the entrance all summer long.

Your hosts, Kim and Kent Taylor, have designed their lodge with all the comforts in mind. Many rooms have their own entrance, and quite a few have Jacuzzi tubs. All have their own private deck, private bath, and phone, cable TV, and VCR. Breakfast is hearty—most guests say they don't need lunch! Afternoon refreshments include wine, cheese, and nonalcoholic beverages. Guests are invited to use the lodge's mountain bikes and canoe as well.

The Hidden Moose Lodge is located on the road to Big Mountain, 1½ miles out of downtown Whitefish. With just eight rooms, the Hidden Moose can also be described as a B&B. Rates for two people range from $125 to $145 per night, depending on room size and amenities. Smoking is allowed outside only; pets are allowed with prior approval.

Insiders' Tip

Technically, "alpine" refers to the terrain above the tree line; "subalpine" refers to the area right at tree line—where trees grow, but just barely; where conditions like wind, temperature, snowpack, poor quality of soil, or just plain rockiness limit them from colonizing any higher elevation. This means that Logan Pass, for example, is technically subalpine, since stunted subalpine fir trees do grow there. The climate is so tough on them, however, that they are twisted and dwarfed into formations called "krummholz"—German for "crooked wood"—a very good description of trees at tree line!

North Forty Resort $$–$$$
Box 4250, 3765 Highway 40 West
Whitefish 59937
(406) 862–7740, (800) 775–1740
www.northforty.com

What could be "more Montana" than staying in a log cabin of your own? The tall pines at North Forty shelter 22 log cabins that combine rustic decor with modern amenities. Each of these newly built cabins has a spotless and fully equipped kitchen, gas fireplace, and its own porch, picnic table, and grill. An open-air hot tub and sauna building is centrally located. The cabins are arranged in small groups, so that North Forty would also make the

Whitefish City Beach is a good starting place for a snowshoe or ski on frozen Whitefish Lake.
Photo: Donnie Sexton

perfect location to hold a family reunion or other get-togethers. A walking and cross-country ski trail begins at the north end of the property.

The resort's Snowberry Center, constructed in the same rustic log style, is available for groups of 50 to 100 guests. With a full kitchen, large windows, gas fireplace, and large outside patio, it will provide a spacious setting for your family reunion, celebration, or other meeting.

Cabin rates vary from $79 per night for two people to $195 for a cabin that will hold as many as eight. All cabins are non-smoking. A limited number of pet cabins are available—please inquire when you make your reservation (North Forty has four friendly malamutes in residence!).

Whitefish Lake Lodge Resort and Marina
$$$$
1399 Wisconsin Avenue, Whitefish
(406) 862–2929, (800) 735–8869
www.wfll.com

Whitefish Lake Lodge makes absolutely the maximum use of its beautiful waterfront location on Whitefish Lake. It is unique among commercial lodgings in being right on the water, and that gives it a special focus. The one-, two-, and three-bedroom condo suites all have private balconies overlooking the lake; and the resort's private beach has a swimming area (as well as an outdoor pool, two spas, and an indoor spa). The full-service marina also operates a boat rental service—try an afternoon picnicking on a pontoon boat!—or rent a speedboat for waterskiing, a paddleboat, or canoe. Ski and bike lockers as well as a guest laundry are available.

The luxurious lakeside condo suites have full-size living rooms, gas fireplaces, fully equipped kitchens with a breakfast bar and dining room, air-conditioning, and cable TV. A one-bedroom condo, for example, would rent for $140 per night in value season, $175 in regular season, and $240 in peak season. Two- and three-bedroom condos range from $215 to $430 per night. Hotel-style rooms are also available and range in price from $70 to $99 per night.

Whitefish Lake Lodge is located on the road to Big Mountain and is about a five-minute drive from downtown Whitefish. Please inquire about ski and other special packages.

Campgrounds and RV Parks

Tally Lake Campground $
Tally Lake, approximately 14 miles west of Whitefish
(406) 863-5400

Tally Lake is on the Tally Lake District of the Flathead National Forest and the campground is administered by that office. The campground itself is some 14 miles west of town at the far end of the lake. It has 39 sites and 1 group site. Technically, the campground is open all year, but the Tally Lake Road is not plowed in winter and there is no fee for those who want to snowmobile or ski into the area to camp. Full services, including running water, pit toilets, garbage pickup, and a dock on the lake, become available in mid-May. Trails will be worked and opened in late May or June, depending on snow conditions. Services end September 30, and after that time campers must again pack in their own supplies and pack out their own garbage.

Campground fees are $10.00 per vehicle per night, with $4.00 extra for each additional vehicle per site. A $3.00 day-use fee is charged for others using the area. A covered pavilion that will accommodate up to 100 people can be rented for a $25 fee. For reservations, please call Rocky Mountain Recreation Company at (800) 416-6992.

Whitefish Lake State Park $
Highway 93 North, Whitefish
(406) 752-5501

This small state park, within a 10-minute drive of downtown, is right on Whitefish Lake. Its tall trees and lakeshore offer a pleasant change of pace for those who want to day trip or to camp overnight. Picnic tables are close to the lake. A boat ramp and parking for trailers provide access to the water. Dogs are permitted but must be on a leash. The day use fee is $4.00 per vehicle or $1.00 per person for those who bike or walk in.

The 25 campsites are scattered throughout the trees a little above the water. A maximum of six people and two camper units may occupy a site, where space allows. Fires may be made in provided grates only; firewood is available for purchase during the summer months. Fees for the summer season are $12 per night (camping is available May 1 through September 30). One trailer site is wheelchair accessible. The maximum stay is seven nights. Commercial or large groups require a permit; please call Montana Fish, Wildlife and Parks at the number above.

The park is located just west of town on Highway 93 North. Follow the signs along the road beginning just west of Grouse Mountain Lodge.

Whitefish RV Park $
6404 Highway 93 South, Whitefish
(406) 862-5515
www.whitefishrvpark.com

Cheap Sleep Motel $
6400 Highway 93 South, Whitefish
(406) 862-5515, (800) 862-3711
www.cheapsleepmotel.com

The Whitefish RV Park offers 57 full hookups, 14 of which have pull-through parking. This newer facility is just off the highway into town, yet is quiet and pleasantly landscaped with trees and grass. A dump station, rest rooms and showers, playground, and laundry will make your stay as convenient as being at home. Pets are welcome and there is a pet-walking area. Cable TV hookups are available at all sites for free, and telephone hookups are available at 25 sites. Tent areas are also provided.

The Whitefish RV Park is open 24 hours a day, year-round. Rates for full hookups are $27 per night; partial hookups are $24 per night (plus $2.00 for each additional person over two people). Weekly and monthly rates

summer. Like the RV park, this motel is pet friendly. For two people, rates vary by season, ranging from approximately $36 to $70. Nonsmoking and wheelchair-accessible rooms are available. It's hard to resist a place with the slogan "Give Your Wallet a Rest"!

And More . . .

Bunkhouse Traveler's Inn and Hostel $
217 Railway, Whitefish
(406) 862-3377

The Bunkhouse Traveler's Inn and Hostel fills a unique niche in local accommodations. Like most hostels, it offers dormitory sleeping rooms, with bunks that rent for a mere $13 per night. If you don't have your own sleeping bag along, you can rent linens for a one-time fee per stay of $3.00. The Bunkhouse Traveler also has two private rooms available for rent, for $30 per night for two people. All guests have access to a full kitchen and common area. Bathrooms are shared.

The Bunkhouse Traveler is conveniently located in downtown Whitefish, within easy walking distance of both Amtrak and the bus station. Whitefish City Beach is about a 10-minute walk away, and the SNOW bus to Big Mountain stops a block away during the ski season. Be sure to call for reservations if you're planning to stay here in July or August.

Five-Star Rentals $–$$$$
6475 Highway 93 South, Whitefish
(406) 862-5994
www.fivestarrentals.com

If you're planning to be in the Flathead Valley for at least a week—whether it's for your honeymoon, family reunion, or small corporate retreat—you might try a different approach to lodging. Five Star Rentals offers a wide variety of listings, encompassing everything from secluded cabins in the woods to Whitefish Lake homes and condos to mountain retreats. All properties are fully furnished and equipped for a great vacation. Special amenities vary and may include barbecues, decks, fireplaces, docks and canoes

are also available. Tent rates are $16 per night, plus $2.00 per person for each person over two people. Dump rate is $5.00 for those not staying in the park, and there is a one-time-only fee of $15 for telephone hookups (tenant must supply outside line).

For those traveling with a mixed party—some with RVs, others looking for lodging—the Cheap Sleep Motel provides economical lodging right next door to the RV park. The motel has 48 rooms and prides itself on its clean, comfortable accommodations. Rooms include color cable TV and air-conditioning; the motel also has an indoor Jacuzzi as well as an outdoor heated pool open during the

at water properties, hot tubs, and steam rooms. Every property is unique, and some offer five-star views.

Sizes range from cozy, one-bedroom cabins to spacious five-bedroom homes, and prices range from $500 to $2,500 per week.

The Landlord
547 Spokane Avenue, Whitefish
(406) 862–5263

This property-management agency handles more than 600 residences. If you're looking at an extended stay in the Flathead, they can match you up with just the sort of place you'd like to rent: a full-size home with a lake view, a condo on Big Mountain, or a place in town. The staff is friendly, courteous, and reliable.

Charming and historic—downtown Whitefish.
Photo: Donnie Sexton, Travel Montana

Restaurants

Price Code

Restaurant price code, for two people exclusive of beverages, tips, and tax:

$	$10 to $19
$$	$20 to $27
$$$	$28 to $35
$$$$	More than $36

Family-Friendly Dining

The Buffalo Café $
516 East Third Street, Whitefish
(406) 862–2833

The Buffalo Café truly is a Whitefish institution. Open only for breakfast and lunch, it's a favorite place for locals to get together and get caught up on what's going on around town. Despite increased competition from newer places in the last few years, the Buffalo remains the place to eat before skiing: Its substantial breakfasts—whether a buffalo pie, huevos, or the pancake of the day—stand up to a good day's fun in the snow.

The Buffalo Café is open from 6:30 A.M. to 2:00 P.M. Monday through Friday, from 7:00 A.M. to 2:00 P.M. on Saturday, and from 9:00 A.M. to 2:00 P.M. on Sunday.

Breakfast entrees generally run between $3.50 and $7.00. Half orders of some items are available.

The Dire Wolf Pub $
845 Wisconsin Avenue, Whitefish
(406) 862–4500

The Dire Wolf bills itself as a "place for family and friends," and that's a good description. Its window booths fit six easily, and you can push together a few tables to accommodate an even bigger group. It does have a bar, but kids are welcome in the restaurant, and the atmosphere is comfortable and family-friendly. The Dire Wolf has a full lunch and dinner menu that includes appetizers, soups, salads, burgers (check out the "Stella Blue": bleu cheese and bacon), calzone, and hot and cold sandwiches. Ale-battered halibut and fries, a blackened chicken cajun sandwich, and the Wolf Den Gyros are just a few of the pub's specialties, but many come here for the great pizza—from the Garden Wall and Behemoth pizzas to the American Standard—or create your own.

The Dire Wolf is located on the road to Big Mountain—it's the perfect place to stop on your way down from the slopes, summer or winter. Hours are from 11:00 A.M. to 1:00 A.M., Monday through Saturday, and from noon to midnight on Sunday. It is a smoke-free establishment. The Dire Wolf also features live music—see Nightlife, below.

The Whitefish Winter Carnival Parade always draws a crowd. Photo: Carl Wells, courtesy of Flathead Convention and Visitor Bureau

Serrano's $$
10 Central Avenue, Whitefish
(406) 862–5600

It's true—Whitefish is just south of the border—and you'll find the best Mexican around at Serrano's! The original Serrano's flourishes seasonally in East Glacier, but here in Whitefish they're open all year round, serving "world-famous margaritas," microbrews, and fine Mexican dishes. One look at the menu and you'll see what you're in for—after perusing the list of sopas, ensaladas, and aperitivos, you'll notice that the entrees are marked with one, two, or three peppers to indicate just how hot they are . . .

Serrano's is open for lunch and dinner. The menu also includes several platos americanos for those more comfortable with the gringo selection. Or call in advance for a take-out order (small service charge). Lunch entrees range in price from $5 to $8, dinner entrees from $7 to $15.

Truby's $$
115 Central Avenue, Whitefish
(406) 862–4979

"Truby's Wood-fired Brick Oven Pizza" is the full name of this restaurant located right in downtown Whitefish . . . and that'll give you an idea of what's going on: exotic pizza. Individual, entree-size pizzas are the hot item here. Just a sampling of

the menu includes Athenian, Aloha, Thai, Veggie Pie, and Rustler pizzas . . . If Peking Duck (!) pizza sounds a little much to you, you can, of course, "Create Your Own" pizza too. Truby's also offers calzone, burgers, and a selection of Italian dishes as well as "kid's stuff"—burgers, pizza, or spaghetti of just the right sort for smaller customers.

Truby's is open for lunch, 11:00 A.M. to 3:00 P.M., and for dinner from 5:00 to 10:00 P.M., Monday through Saturday; and for dinner from 4:00 to 10:00 P.M. on Sunday. Individual pizzas run from $7 to $11, Italian entrees from $9 to $12.

Whitefish Lake Restaurant $$$$
Whitefish Golf Club, Highway 93 North, Whitefish
(406) 862–5285

Also known as just "the Golf Course," the Whitefish Lake Restaurant has an authenticity to it that's hard to match. Built in 1936, the rustic, warm dining room's stone fireplace and heavy log beams give it a relaxed yet elegant feel. The service is professional but not fussy, and the food is consistently excellent—the restaurant is known for its prime rib, featured on Friday and Saturday nights, as well as for its seafood. This is where locals go to celebrate special occasions. Be sure to call for reservations—the Golf Course can be busy. Even so, you'll never feel crowded or rushed.

You'll find the restaurant at the Whitefish Golf Club, less than a mile out of town on Highway 93 North as the road heads west toward Eureka. In the winter, look for the two huge evergreens decorated with colored lights from top to bottom. The restaurant is slightly set back from the road. Entrees range from $15 to $25.

Fine Dining

Cafe Kandahar $$$$
Kandahar Lodge, Big Mountain Ski and Summer Resort, P.O. Box 1659, Whitefish 59937
(406) 862–6247
www.kandaharlodge.com/cafe1.htm

An informal but elegant atmosphere makes the Cafe Kandahar an excellent place for a special dinner, whether you've been skiing at Big Mountain or not. The menu is as fine as you'll find anywhere: you might start with Prince Edward Island mussels, or perhaps Sauté of Wild Mushrooms and Caramelized Onions . . . follow with the house salad . . . and then choose one of the classic entrees such as tournedos of beef, rack of lamb, or salmon. Everything is prepared with style and presented beautifully. The service is quick, helpful, and not obtrusive, making for an altogether delightful evening.

Cafe Kandahar is open only for breakfast and dinner, and reservations are required for dinner as the dining room itself is quite small. Dinner entrees range in price from $14 to $24.

Pollo Grill $$$
1705 Wisconsin Avenue, Whitefish
(406) 863–9400

A relative newcomer to the Whitefish restaurant scene, Pollo Grill has established itself quickly as one of the finest restaurants in town. Grilled chicken, seafood, and steak selections are the restaurant's specialty, and they are served in many ways: from the spit-roasted Chicken Chimichanga to Potato Gnocchi with a Roasted Red Pepper Sauce to Grilled Pacific King Salmon . . . there's something special for every palate. The menu includes elegant appetizers and an unusual variety of optional side dishes.

Pollo Grill will also prepare orders to go. You might inquire about the "Pollo" itself—a whole roasted chicken with sauce and two side dishes ($13.95). Entrees range in price from $9 to $15. Be sure to call for reservations.

The Grill $$$$
Grouse Mountain Lodge, 2 Fairway Drive, Whitefish
(406) 863–4700

Grouse Mountain's The Grill evokes a certain slice of western life. Recently updated, the restaurant combines pine decor, a fine sound system, and flat-screen TVs with Montana touches . . . an elk keeps his eye on the dining room . . . as do a flight of pheasants on the far wall. The Grill features fine cuts of beef as well as chicken and baby back ribs; fresh northwest salmon baked on a plank is a specialty. Unique side dishes such as sweet potato fries complement the main course. Whatever you choose, you're sure to enjoy the fine dining and distinctive ambience of Grouse Mountain Lodge.

The Grill is open for breakfast, lunch, and dinner, from 7:00 A.M. to 9:00 P.M. Dinner entrees range from $16 to $23. Reservations are recommended.

Tupelo Grille $$$
17 Central Avenue, Whitefish
(406) 862–6136

Cajun-style cooking may not be what you expected in Montana . . . but here it is! And Tupelo Grille (named for Tupelo, Mississippi) is one of the most often recommended restaurants in Whitefish—known for its excellence and the consistently high quality of its dinners. Just walking into Tupelo you'll enjoy the mix of aromas. The menu features everything from seafood to duck, crawfish, chicken, sausage, and pastas . . . and each dinner is beautifully presented.

Tupelo Grille opens for dinner at 5:30 each evening. The restaurant is small, and reservations are requested for groups of six or more. Entrees run from $11 to $20.

And More . . .

Baker Street Bistro $
10 Baker Avenue, Whitefish
(406) 862–6383

Whitefish may not have all the amenities of a big city, but it does have big-city bagels. The Baker Street Bistro serves up sesame, poppyseed, seven-grain, blueberry, garlic, whole wheat, plain, and cinnamon raisin bagels that can be compared with the best New York or Chicago has to offer. Other flavors—like cranberry—occasionally make the list, too. There is even a drive-up window for those on their way elsewhere . . . or come inside and sit down.

Burgers on the deck of the Summit House, a Big Mountain tradition. Photo: Carl Wells, courtesy of the Big Mountain

Bagels are the basis for "breakfeast" and lunch, too: get yours topped or filled just about any way you can imagine. Soups, sandwiches, pasta salad, sodas, juices, coffee, espresso, tea, and fruit complete the menu of this very busy establishment.

The bistro is open daily from 7:00 A.M. to 2:00 P.M. On occasion they serve dinner as well—check the sign outside the building.

Hellroaring Saloon and Eatery $$
The Big Mountain Ski and Summer Resort
(406) 862–6364

The Hellroaring Saloon in the Big Mountain Chalet has the kind of ambience money can't buy . . . only time, and many contented skiers, will make a ski-hill restaurant feel this way. Old skis grace the paneled walls (you may remember when you had bindings like that . . .), famous skiers have autographed the posters, a fire crackles in the fireplace, and Warren Miller movies play discreetly in the corners of the bar. The nachos are big, the chili is good, and the beer is cold and locally brewed. In the spring, the porch is the place to be for soaking up the sun.

The Hellroaring Saloon and Eatery also operates through the summer months, shutting down briefly during the spring and fall. A full lunch and dinner menu includes entrees that run from $4.00 to $10.00.

Nightlife

Whitefish is a hopping town in a low-key sort of way. The Great Northern Bar is a landmark in its own right—you'll hear phrases like "it's just a block from the Northern" when you ask directions. Along with the Bulldog, the Palace, and the Remington—all located on Central Avenue, right downtown—you're sure to find a spot to put up your feet and enjoy a brew. The Great Northern, Palace, and Remington all occasionally have live music on the weekends. The Dire Wolf Pub, on the road to Big Mountain, is also bringing in musical groups literally from around the world—perhaps African, then reggae, then bluegrass—so be sure to stop by and see what's happening next.

With the recent completion of the new I.A. O'Shaughnessy Performing Arts Center, Whitefish now has a central location for performances of all sorts. The O'Shaughnessy is the home of the Whitefish Theatre Company, which stages plays throughout the year, but it also hosts an eclectic series of musical performances. Check the marquee out front for current events.

The Glacier Orchestra and Chorale presents a full schedule of concerts throughout the school year. Generally the Saturday night performance is at the Whitefish Central School auditorium; call the office at (406) 257–3241 for current information.

The Whitefish Film Society brings movies to the Flathead that otherwise wouldn't make it here. As of this writing, the film society is negotiating for a new location. Details remain to be determined, but keep your eyes open for posters at the local bookstores and ads in the newspapers.

In a similar vein, the Whitefish Reading Series brings both nationally recognized and local authors into town for public presentations, with usually about one talk a month during the school year. The best place to check on the current schedule is at BookWorks, located at 244 Spokane Avenue in Whitefish, (406) 862-4980.

Big Mountain, of course, is the source of a lot of fun . . . whether it's beers at the Bierstube, the end-of-ski-season furniture races, or summer concerts outdoors. Give the Mountain information center a call at (406) 862-1900 for current events.

Last but not least—something you won't find too many other places. Late October is the off-season for the Flathead Valley, but if you do happen to be in town you'll find yourself in the midst of an incredible event—Halloween, Whitefish style. As in other communities, you'll see the kiddies out trick-or-treating in the late afternoon. But Whitefish takes Halloween seriously. Later that night head downtown to see the huge Halloween adult party. You won't recognize anyone, that's for sure—many adults come in full head-to-toe costumes. Be sure to pick up at least a witch hat or a big nose—you'll want to feel a part of the fun!

Shopping

You'll enjoy strolling through Whitefish shops, whether you're window-shopping or in search of that perfect gift. Whitefish has a compact, functional downtown, where you'll find everything from a hardware store to an auto dealership to fairly upscale boutiques. What follows is just a sampling of shops that are well worth browsing through:

Insiders' Tip

To go or not to go? Find out what conditions are—call (406) 862-SNOW for the Big Mountain snow report, updated daily during ski season at 7:00 A.M.

Artistic Touch (209 Central Avenue, 406-862-4813) features the work of local artists and craftspeople. You'll appreciate the elegant jewelry, distinctive ceramics and painting, and fine decorative objects. This is a great place to look for gifts.

BookWorks (244 Spokane Avenue, 406-862-4980) is an independently owned bookstore. Front tables feature local writers, books focusing on the West and Western issues, and current best-sellers. The bookstore also has an excellent selection of children's books. And be sure to check the front doors for posters featuring upcoming cultural events.

Imagination Station (221 Central Avenue, 406-862-5668)—If you've discovered your child's favorite toy was left at home . . . here's the place to go. The Imagination Station carries all sorts of great toys, games, you name it . . . and adults will enjoy looking around as much as kids. And now there's a Kalispell branch at 132 Main Street as well.

Lakestream Fly Fishing Shop (334 Central Avenue, 406-862-1298) is just what you'd expect of a fly-fishing shop in Montana . . . all the gear you can imagine and knowledgeable staff as well. Even non-fisherfolk will enjoy strolling through Lakestream, which has a nice selection of outdoor clothing and a comfortable ambience.

Sage & Cedar (214 Central Avenue, 406-862-9411) is a fun place to spend some time. The shop specializes in bath supplies—soaps, shampoo, lotions, oils, and so on. But here's the twist: You can have your own combinations mixed for you. As you walk in there's a rack where you can smell the various scenting oils—from such standards as rose, gardenia, and lavender to such "western" favorites as sage, "Montana morning," or "rain," to some fun food smells—try a whiff of chocolate or pear! Now you choose what sort of base you want scented—and suddenly you can have rose shampoo, sage hand lotion, and chocolate bubblebath ... fun for gifts, and also for yourself.

Sportsman and Ski Haus (Mountain Mall, 406-862-3111) is now the major source for most outdoor gear in Whitefish. You'll find national brands in outdoor clothing, footwear, and equipment for everything from boating to skiing and back.

Third Street Market (Third & Spokane, 406-862-5054) earns a mention for the change of pace it brings to Whitefish. This health-food store offers a variety of organic, locally grown, and bulk groceries. It also has a big section of vitamins and other supplements as well as books on related topics.

Spectacular summer days in the Whitefish Range.
Photo: Wayne Mumford, courtesy of the Big Mountain

Do take your time to stroll around ... downtown Whitefish also offers services such as banks, fax, post office, UPS and other delivery services, a brand-new public library, xeroxing, and print shops.

Columbia Falls

and the U.S. Highway 2 Corridor

Area Overview
Accommodations
Restaurants
Nightlife
Shopping

Area Overview

Columbia Falls is the "Gateway to Glacier," and you'll find this is true in many respects. This little community sits at the northeast corner of the Flathead Valley, where the Flathead River flows out of the mountains through Bad Rock Canyon. Since both U.S. Highway 2 and the railroad follow the river valley, if you're traveling into Glacier from west of the Continental Divide, you will almost certainly pass through this little town.

Driving through Columbia Falls you may notice that there's no natural waterfall here. At least two different stories exist to explain the town's name: the more interesting one has to do with the expansion of the Great Northern Railway. As investors began buying up land along the projected route, they anticipated that J. J. Hill would put the next depot west of Belton (West Glacier) at a town then known as Columbia, Montana. On hearing of the land rush, in a fit of perversity Hill decided to have the next depot at Whitefish, and turned to his employees and roared, "Columbia falls!"

While the railroad may not have chosen Columbia Falls for its operations, other major industries have. Both the Columbia Falls Aluminum Company (CFAC) and Plum Creek Timber Company have employed many people. Tourism is growing as an industry here, too—many visitors choose to stay in this part of the valley because of its easy access to Glacier National Park. And so more restaurants and accommodations spring up each year.

The U.S. Highway 2 corridor is a scenic drive in its own right. Leaving Columbia Falls and heading east, you'll start by driving through Bad Rock Canyon. Take a few moments to pull over at Berne Park along the cliffs and read the roadside markers about the wilderness and this old, old route through the mountains. The road is right by the water for a few minutes; soon you'll cross the bridge over the South Fork of the Flathead River—water running out

The fertile Flathead Valley. Photo: Buddy Mays, courtesy of Flathead Convention and Visitor Bureau

Columbia Falls provides easy access to all three forks of the Flathead River. Photo: Montana's Finest Resorts

the Hungry Horse Dam (see the Attractions chapter) from the Hungry Horse Reservoir. As you drive through Coram, you'll get your first glimpse of the peaks along Lake McDonald: Stanton Mountain appears briefly right over the highway. Once you reach West Glacier, U.S. Highway 2 follows the Middle Fork of the Flathead River through a beautiful gorge and valley up to the Continental Divide and out onto the Great Plains (see the scenic loop drive described in the Attractions chapter). You'll find lots to explore all along the way.

Within this Columbia Falls and U.S. Highway 2 corridor chapter, businesses are listed by category, beginning with those in Columbia Falls and then from west to east, as if you were driving the highway from Columbia Falls to East Glacier.

Accommodations

Price Code

Keep in mind that some rates are based on availability. The average nightly rates for two adults at the hotels and motels listed in this section are indicated by a dollar sign ($) ranking in the following chart. Also, the hotels and motels in this chapter accept all or most major credit cards.

$	Less than $85
$$	$86 to $115
$$$	$116 to $150
$$$$	More than $151

Hotels and Motels

Glacier Park Super 8 $
7336 U.S. Highway 2 East
Columbia Falls
(406) 892–0888, (800) 800–8000

You may think all Super 8's are alike—but walk into the lobby at this one! The entrance displays a remarkable collection of mounted animals—if you didn't see it in the woods, you'll probably find it here.

But, as across the country, Super 8 supplies clean, comfortable rooms for travelers at a nominal price. The 32 rooms include some special rooms with Jacuzzis or kitchenettes. Both nonsmoking and wheelchair-accessible rooms are available. The motel includes a spa, copy machine, fax, and meeting room; all rooms have their own television with HBO, ESPN, and

DISNEY channels. Complimentary continental breakfast is served each morning. Room rates range from $35 in the winter to $85 in the summer for two people per night, depending on the size of the room and included amenities.

Western Inn Glacier Mountain Shadows Resort $
7285 U.S. Highway 2 East
Columbia Falls
(406) 892–7686, (406) 892–7687

This 23-unit motel (now part of a larger complex including RV park, laundry, and convenience store) was completely renovated in 1995. In addition to its comfortable rooms, the motel offers an outdoor pool and two spas. For convenience, its location is hard to beat . . . it's only a 20-minute drive to Glacier National Park, but all the conveniences and activities of the Flathead Valley are right nearby. Rooms run from $60 to $80 a night, based on double occupancy.

The Glacier Highland $
U.S. Highway 2 East, West Glacier
(406) 888–5427, (800) 766–0811

The Glacier Highland has undergone some major renovations in the last few years—if you stayed here 10 years ago, it's time to do it again. For those making their first trip to the area, the Highland provides a great base for exploring all that the area has to offer. It's located right at the west entrance to Glacier National Park, with easy access to hiking, rafting, horseback riding, and everything else along Going-to-the-Sun Road as well as Amtrak and Highway 2. In the evening you'll want to come home, mellow out in the hot tub, have dinner at the restaurant, and head for your queen-size bed. Knotty-pine panels give a warm glow to these affordable rooms.

All rooms have satellite TV. The summer rate for a room with one queen-size bed is $59; two queen-size beds, $69; and two queen-size beds and a twin, $75. Winter rates are even less, so be sure to inquire. The Glacier Highland also handles car rentals during the summer months.

Bed-and-Breakfasts

Bad Rock Country B&B $$$–$$$$
480 Bad Rock Drive, Columbia Falls
(406) 892–2829, (888) 892–2829
www.badrock.com

Your hosts, Jake and Marilyn Thompson, invite you to enjoy this elegant Big Sky home. Bad Rock Country B&B sits on open meadows framed with towering pines, and every window offers huge views of the Swan and Whitefish Mountain ranges.

Bad Rock has a western flair, highlighted by Jake's collection of western and Native American art. The bedrooms are large; one has its own balcony for sunset views. The living room offers a fireplace and comfortable sofas and chairs for reading or spending time with other visitors. Downstairs you'll find a "gathering room" with satellite TV and a guest bar stocked with juice, wine, beer, and snacks.

A little back from the main house across the lawn, you'll find Bad Rock Junction—the two new log buildings with a rustic feel that complements the western elegance of the house. These four rooms, each named for a lake in Glacier National Park, feature handmade lodgepole pine furniture, gas fireplaces, and large private baths. Each has its own entrance.

A full breakfast is included with all rooms. Breakfast is hearty—you'll be treated to creations such as Sundance Eggs, wild rice–sausage quiche, or Montana potato pie. Guests have enjoyed these

Visiting a bed-and-breakfast means being right at home. Photo: courtesy of Plum Creek House

breakfasts so much that there's now a Bad Rock Country B&B Cookbook!

After a full day in Glacier Country, you'll enjoy the luxurious outdoor hot tub. Each party reserves its own private time for soaking. The tub has a view of Big Mountain, and you'll enjoy relaxing in the hot water and fresh mountain air: the 30 acres of Bad Rock Country B&B are reserved for nonsmoking guests.

Rates vary with the season. Rooms in the house range from $128 to $138 per night for two; rooms at Bad Rock Junction run from $148 to $168. All rooms have private bath and telephones. A two-room suite combination is available in the house.

Glacier B&B $
P.O. Box 1900-10, U.S. Highway 2 East
Hungry Horse 59919
(406) 387-4153
www.centric.net/montanarec/glacier.htm

Just visiting the Glacier B&B is an experience in itself. The yard is edged all around with tulips, poppies, peonies, and lots and lots of roses—you'll hardly have to bend over to smell the fragrance! Indoors you'll find yet more flowers, but also an impressive array of mounted fish and game trophies. Your host, Bob Johnson, is a fisherman and hunter of many years' experience. You'll be fascinated by the collection—elk, lynx, bobcat, buffalo, and even a wild turkey—as well as many fish—and every one has a story behind it. Bob's lived in Montana for many years and knows the state and its backcountry well.

This log home also offers very comfortable and gracious accommodations. The five units each have their own bath. One includes a king-size bed and Jacuzzi; two others rent as suites with their own kitchenettes. The common living room and dining room are brightened with skylights by day and the fireplace in the evening. And a big deck overlooks the yard and gardens. A full breakfast is served each morning between 6:00 and 8:00 A.M.

The Glacier B&B is open year-round. In the summer, rooms rent for $75 per night for two people, with a $10 charge for each additional person; the suites rent for $60 and $80, with a $10 charge for each additional person. Winter rates for rooms are $40 per night; please inquire about rates for suites. In addition, cabins are now available; they house three people for $110 per night.

A Wild Rose B&B $$$
P.O. Box 29, 12080 U.S. Highway 2 East
West Glacier 59936
(406) 387-4900
www.awildrose.com

Your hosts, Brenda and Joseph Mihalko, come to the bed-and-breakfast business after years of traveling: and A Wild Rose is the bed-and-breakfast they always wished they'd found. You'll find their high standards and touch for luxury reflected in every detail: exquisite mattresses, all natural fabrics, beautifully presented delicious and healthful foods, plush robes, and a hair dryer in your private bathroom. And A Wild Rose is full of flowers—rose bushes along the pathway to the front door, fresh flowers in your room, and a delightful use of floral patterns in the decorating. The Victorian style is both elegant and comforting—this is a place where you'll enjoy each day and sleep well at night.

A Wild Rose is located just 6 miles west of West Glacier, so you have great access to both the national park and the wilderness areas south of the Middle Fork River. In the evening you'll return to one of four unique rooms. The Whirlpool Suite—favored by honeymooners—includes a large bathroom with whirlpool and separate shower; the Private Balcony Suite has its own entrance and can accommodate up to four people. The Country Rose and Victorian Manor rooms are beautifully decorated with Victorian furniture. On a sunny day take a chair on the front porch and enjoy listening to the birds—or, later, watch the sunset colors fade from the sky. In the living room you'll enjoy browsing the library and the flicker of the firelight. (Ask Brenda about the rocking chair.) Out back you'll find a therapeutic spa that can seat seven—the perfect place to unwind in the evening.

A Wild Rose is open year-round. Rates for one or two people range from $120 to $150 per night; please inquire about off-season rates. Reservations are recommended. Pets and smoking are not allowed on the premises.

Be "Bear Aware"

Glacier National Park is the core of a large wilderness ecosystem, which provides one of the last remaining refuges for the grizzly bear. Numerous risks and rewards are associated with a visit to this area. An encounter with a wild animal—including a bear—is always possible. Bears are naturally wary of humans, but they are also unpredictable and may attack without warning.

Visitors have been injured and killed by bears, and, in some cases, their careless actions have resulted in the bears' removal. Your knowledge of bear habitat and behavior can help reduce your chances of a dangerous encounter.

The following practices are well-accepted means to increase your margin of safety in bear country:

- **Never Hike Alone.** Solo hikers have been involved in a number of tragic bear encounters. Hiking in a group may make you less likely to be attacked.

- **Make Noise.** The human voice is easily carried along with you—use it when you are hiking or camping to alert bears and other wild animals of your presence. Bear bells may also warn a bear of your approach and can be purchased locally. Use extra caution in brushy areas, on blind curves, and when wind or running water masks the sounds of your approach.

- **Stay on the Trail.** Visibility is usually better on the trail, and human activity is generally more frequent, thus giving you a greater margin of safety.

- **Hike When It Is Safest.** Bears can be active both day and night but tend to be out and about more at dawn or dusk.

- **Avoid Bears' Prime Food Sources.** Bears will vigorously defend food sources. Never approach a smelly animal carcass and beware of other areas with abundant food sources such as berries, bulbs, grasses, and flowers.

- **Be Alert for Bear Sign.** Fresh bear scat (dung), tracks, or signs of digging may indicate a bear is in the area. Be extra careful.

- **Enjoy Wildlife at a Distance.** Never intentionally approach or feed wildlife. Beware of one of the most dangerous scenarios—a sow with cubs. Immediately leave the area. If you have to, go back down the trail.

- **Secure Food, Garbage, and Cookware Properly.** These items should be hung out of reach of bears at all times except mealtimes. Check with the National Park Service or U.S.D.A. Forest Service for specific regulations.

- **Respect Closures.** Trail and campground closures resulting from bear danger are common in Glacier. It is unsafe (and illegal) to enter a closed area, so heed the signs for your own safety.

Paola Creek B&B $$$
P.O. Box 97, West Glacier 59913
(406) 888–5061, (888) 311–5061
www.wtp.net/go/paola

Paola Creek B&B offers a true getaway—tucked into the pines, far from the noise of traffic and towns. Located off U.S. Highway 2 about 25 minutes east of West Glacier, this handcrafted log home would soothe any spirit with its mixture of comfort and mountain views. Your hosts, Kelly and Les Hostetler, have created an atmosphere that practically glows with the warmth of well-polished wood.

A hearty, full breakfast as well as complimentary afternoon wine and appetizers are included with the price of your room. If you don't want to leave the premises—and you may not!—even to try another restaurant, five-course, family-style gourmet dinners may be arranged in advance at the B&B.

It's easy to imagine relaxing on the deck after hiking, but Paola Creek B&B's location is also prime for those who enjoy backcountry skiing and snowshoeing. The many Forest Service access roads provide entry for backcountry sports, and just up the road is the Izaak Walton Inn with its groomed cross-country ski trails. Both the west side of Going-to-the-Sun Road and the Marias Pass area are within a half-hour drive for trips into Glacier National Park.

Rates run from $140 to $170 per night; reservations are required, and there is a two-night minimum. Paola Creek B&B is a nonsmoking establishment.

Guest Ranches, Resorts, and Lodges

Meadow Lake Resort $$$–$$$$
100 St. Andrews Drive, Columbia Falls
(406) 892–7601, (800) 321–GOLF
www.meadowlake.com

Located on Meadow Lake Golf Course, this large resort maintains inn rooms, condo suites, and one- and two-bedroom condos, as well as two- to five-bedroom vacation homes. It is built on gentle hills and many trees grace the fairways, so that it feels almost like a very pretty neighbor-hood. The 18-hole golf course sets the tone, but, in addition to the pro shop and market, you'll find a recreation center with Nautilus and aerobic machines, pools, and spas. "Troop Meadow Lake" provides supervised children's activities throughout the week, and there's a children's playground, too. The Sunset Grille offers lunch and dinner throughout the year, with service on the patio during the summer months. Meadow Lake Resort also features meeting and banquet facilities for small to mid-size groups.

Meadow Lake provides a good central location from which to begin exploring Glacier Country. Glacier National Park is about a 25-minute drive to the east, the Big Mountain Ski and Summer Resort is about 25 minutes to the west, and Flathead Lake is about 30 minutes away to the south.

> ## Insiders' Tip
>
> The fastest route from East Glacier to Many Glacier (or the Canadian border at Carway)—and the straightest one, for those with long vehicles or trailers—is U.S. Highway 2 from East Glacier to Browning and then Glacier County Highway 464, the Duck Lake Road, to Babb. This paved, well-maintained road heads due north over the prairie. As it swings to the west and back toward the mountains, it also gives a huge view of the park's eastern front. You'll join U.S. Highway 89 about 6 miles north of St. Mary and 2 miles south of Babb.

Rates vary by season. A room at the Meadow Lake Inn runs from $89 to $155, depending on the season. Condos range from $89 to $280, depending on size and season. Vacation homes, with two to five bedrooms, run from $105 to $499 per night. There is a two-night minimum stay requirement for condos and vacation homes.

Timber Wolf Resort $
P.O. Box 190800, 9105 U.S. Highway 2 East
Hungry Horse 59919
(406) 387-9653, (877) 846-9653
www.timberwolfresort.com

With RV and tent sites, rustic and deluxe cabins, and a B&B, the Timber Wolf Resort has everything. This 20-acre property is a small town in the middle of the summer—complete with its own convenience store and gathering room—but the grounds are so spacious, hilly, and nicely wooded that no one will feel crowded.

If it's an RV site you're looking for, the resort has 24 (some with full hookups) for $25 per night, and some with just electric, for $19 per night. Both pull-through and back-in sites are available. Tent sites cost $17 per night.

Sleeping cabins are either rustic or deluxe. Rustic cabins rent for $39 per night. They have a double bunk bed, but are otherwise unfurnished; bring your own linens or sleeping bag, or rent from the resort. Deluxe cabins are furnished and have a double bunk bed with linens, heat, and electricity. These cabins rent for $45 to $70 per night.

The Timber Wolf also operates two rooms as a bed-and-breakfast. Queen-size beds with handmade quilts will keep you cozy, and you'll wake to a breakfast basket of fresh coffee, muffins or bagels, and fruit. B&B rooms rent for $55 to $85 per night.

The Timber Wolf Resort also offers some beautiful views toward Glacier National Park and Columbia Mountain in the Swan Range. You'll find the practical details fall in place, too: The resort includes coin-op showers (and you can rent towels), laundry, gift shop, a gazebo with three barbecue grills, a children's play area, and picnic tables. The rates listed here are all based on double occupancy; please add $3.00 per day for each additional person. All buildings are nonsmoking, but be sure to inquire about the pet policy. The Timber Wolf's heated cabins and B&B rooms are open all winter; the full resort operates during the summer months.

Silverwolf Chalets $$$
P.O. Box 115, West Glacier 59936
(406) 387-4448
www.silverwolfchalets.com

"Designer log cabins for two"—10 log chalets tailored for two make up the Silverwolf. You'll find each perfect little cabin has its own queen-size log bed with handmade quilt, gas fireplace, private bath, and a cupboard that tastefully conceals your own microwave, small refrigerator, and coffeemaker. Breakfast is brought to your cabin, but if you don't want to stay indoors on a beautiful day, step out and enjoy your coffee on your own porch.

The cabins are nestled in a landscaped forest setting that fosters privacy and quiet. The resort "caters to adults," and pets and smoking are not allowed on the premises. One cabin is wheelchair accessible, and one has two oversized single beds. The Silverwolf is open from mid-May until mid-October. Rates vary by season and range from $110 to $154 for two people per night.

Great Northern Whitewater Resort $$-$$$$
P.O. Box 278, West Glacier 59936
(406) 387-5340, (800) 735-7897
www.gnwhitewater.com

You won't miss the Great Northern Whitewater Resort—the bright red caboose and Swiss log chalets will draw your attention immediately. The resort is located just 1 mile west of West Glacier, providing easy access to everything the area has to offer. The chalet balconies offer beautiful views of Desert and Strawberry Mountains, as well as the little nubbin known as Chocolate Drop—it's about the shape of a Hershey's Kiss! The charming log chalets are fully furnished and have kitchens equipped with service for six or eight. The three larger chalets have gas fireplaces. All are nonpet and nonsmoking.

The Great Northern also is headquarters for all sorts of outdoor activities. Full- and half-day white-water raft trips, kayak

Boating is immensely popular on the area's larger lakes. Photo: Donnie Sexton

clinics, and fishing trips can be arranged. Fly-fishing "school" is an option for those just getting their feet wet. If you're looking for a longer trip, the Great Northern offers extended two- and three-day white-water trips. And—at the end of your adventures—you can relax in the swim spa back at the resort. Please phone, write, or visit the Web site for more details on outdoor activities.

The chalets will accommodate six to eight (with two or three queen-size beds and a sleeper sofa) and vary in price according to the season. The smaller chalets, Two Bear and Osprey, range from $116 to $184 per night. The larger chalets, Wapiti, Moose, and Tatonka, range from $179 to $263 per night. During the peak season, July 1 to September 15, a three-night minimum stay is required.

Belton Chalet $$–$$$
U.S. Highway 2, West Glacier
(406) 888–5000, (888) BELTON–5
www.beltonchalet.com

The original Belton Chalet was completed in 1910, the same year Congress established Glacier National Park. The balconies and gables typify the Swiss-chalet design of the Great Northern's train stations and hotels throughout the park. Originally a railroad inn, the Belton Chalet also served as the park's first winter headquarters. It closed as a hotel during World War II and only now has been fully renovated and restored to its original beauty.

The "chalet" now consists of four buildings, all completed by 1912: the main chalet, the upper chalet, and two smaller cottages (named Lewis and Clark). As a result the chalet offers a wide variety of lodgings: from chalet room with communal bath to main lodge with private bath and balcony, to honeymoon suite or private cottage. The chalet also includes the Tap Room, serving beer, wine, and cocktails, and a restaurant, game room, and gift shop.

The Belton Chalet is located right in West Glacier, just a step across the road from the West Glacier Amtrak depot and a two-minute drive from the west entrance to Glacier National Park. Hiking, horseback riding, bus tours, white-water rafting, cross-country skiing, and snowshoeing are all in your front yard.

Rates for two people per night run from $110 to $140. Cabins, which sleep up to six, rent for $250. Please inquire about off-season rates and special packages.

Glacier River Retreat $$
HC 36 Box 11A, Essex 59916
(406) 888–9001

Glacier River Retreat gives you the chance to withdraw from the world in comfort and self-sufficiency. Located on 60 acres along the wild and scenic Flathead River, you have easy access to both Glacier National Park and the Great Bear/Bob Marshall Wilderness. Each unit of the two duplex cabins sleeps two to four people and provides a fully equipped kitchen and bath, linens, and towels. You'll enjoy the handcrafted furnishings as well as amenities such as a gas-log stove, gas barbecue, and your own picnic table. The large covered deck will give you a pleasant place to enjoy the outdoors, even if it's stormy, so be sure to bring your binoculars! A fire pit for campfires and the hot tub offer evening relaxation.

Rates run from $95 per night in the winter season to $120 per night in the summer; a complimentary breakfast basket is included with each night's stay. A laundry and rec room are located on-site. Glacier River Retreat is a pet-free, smoke-free establishment.

Izaak Walton Inn $$–$$$$
P.O. Box 653, Essex 59916
(406) 888–5700
www.izaakwaltoninn.com

History comes alive at the Izaak Walton Inn, which was originally built in 1939 to house Great Northern Railway crews working the trains that traveled over Marias Pass. Located right on the rail line, today's guests enjoy waving to Amtrak passengers as the trains pass by . . . and the only flag stop on Amtrak's Empire Builder route—Seattle to Chicago—is at Essex, just a few moments from the inn's door. The association with the railroad is evident throughout the inn—in the bar downstairs, for example, you'll be fascinated by the photos of historic engines, avalanches over the tracks, and even train wrecks. And the whistle and rumble of passing trains will bring you back to the present.

The majestic elk, or wapiti, are most impressive during the fall rut. Photo: courtesy of VIAD Corporation

But, all rail history aside—the Izaak Walton Inn is as cozy a getaway as you'll find anywhere. When you see the very comfortable lobby, you'll want to find a good book and curl up by the fire, or perhaps spend some time chatting with other guests. The dining room—open for breakfast, lunch, and dinner—is charming and bright. All rooms have been remodeled in recent years to include a private bath, but the original character of the inn has been well maintained.

The Izaak Walton Inn offers its own groomed cross-country ski trails during the winter, which become hiking trails in the summer. It's right on the edge of the Great Bear/Bob Marshall Wilderness and just across the river from Glacier National Park, close enough to millions of acres to hike, ride, snowshoe, and ski through. The inn's trained guides will show you the backcountry on skis or snowshoes in the winter, and the inn will be happy to help you arrange raft trips, bus tours through the park, or guided hikes during the summer.

Basic, double-occupancy rooms are $128 per night. The inn also offers family rooms beginning at $160 per night. Four "caboose cottages"—renovated cabooses with heat, full kitchen, and bath—begin at $575 for a three-night stay. The Izaak Walton Inn also offers three-, five-, and seven-day packages that include two or three meals per day in addition to a choice of guided outdoor activities.

Campgrounds and RV Parks

Columbia Falls RV Park $
P.O. Box 2031, 1000 Third Avenue East
Columbia Falls 59912
(406) 892–1122, (888) 401–7268
www.rvcampground.com/mt/
columbiafallsrvpark

Columbia Falls RV Park really is at the Gateway to Glacier . . . right on U.S. Highway 2 where it leaves Columbia Falls and heads up toward the park. The RV park itself includes a laundry, showers, bathrooms, store, and a gift shop featuring local crafts, but if there's something you can't find here, Columbia Falls is right out your back door with both retail and dining establishments.

This facility, just more than five years old, is open from June through September. It has 50 65-foot pull-through RV sites. All have water, sewer, and electric hookups and rent for $20.00 per night (double occupancy), with a $2.00 charge for each additional adult. Cable is available at some sites. Pets are allowed on leash, and owners must clean up after their pets. Reservations are recommended.

Timber Wolf Resort $
P.O. Box 190800, 9105 U.S. Highway 2 East
Hungry Horse 59919
(406) 387–9653, (877) 846–9653
www.timberwolfresort.com

Harvest time brings special community projects in northwest Montana. Photo: courtesy of Columbia Falls Chamber of Commerce

If you're looking for an RV site, the resort has 24, some with full hookups, for $25 per night, and some with just electric, for $19 per night. Both pull-through and back-in sites are available. Tent sites cost $17 per night. If you are interested in an off-season visit, the campground water is turned on in May and off in October depending on weather, but with advance notice the owners will even plow a spot for your RV! Please inquire about winter rates.

The Timber Wolf Resort offers some beautiful views toward Glacier National Park and Columbia Mountain in the Swan Range. You'll find the practical details fall in place, too: The resort includes showers, laundry, convenience and gift shop, a gazebo with three barbecue grills, a children's play area, and picnic tables. All rates above are based on double occupancy; please add $3.00 per day for each additional person. Please inquire about the pet policy. All buildings are nonsmoking.

Mountain Meadows RV Park
and Campground $
P.O. Box 190442, 9125 U.S. Highway 2 East
Hungry Horse 59919
(406) 387–9125
www.mmrvpark.com

The literature for Mountain Meadows RV Park and Campground describes it as "Montana's Most Beautiful Campground"—and, once you drive in, you may well agree. RV sites are spacious for those with slide-outs and awnings, and will accommodate motorhomes up to 40-plus feet long. The individual tent sites are roomy and private. But the setting is what makes it: The campground is on a gently sloping hill with many trees, yet looks out over the valley. A lovely little pond (stocked with rainbow trout) and meadow area have a big view toward Columbia Mountain, Teakettle Mountain, and Bad Rock Canyon.

Mountain Meadows provides about every conceivable service. All sites have picnic tables and campfire/barbecue grills. Rest rooms and hot showers are clean. The laundry room is open 24 hours a day. A dump station and mobile pump-out service are available. The campground store sells souvenirs, ice cream, snacks, milk, pop, ice, firewood, and fishing tackle, as well as camping and RV supplies. You can even rent a fishing pole. Leashed pets are OK. Free modem hookup is available.

Mountain Meadows is open from May 15 (or, if the weather is nice, May 1) until October 31. Reservations are strongly recommended for July and August. Full hookups are $27 per night; water and electric hookups are $24 per night; and tent sites are $20 per night. The seventh night is free if you reserve for one full week. Rates are based on four-person occupancy per site; each additional adult is $3.00, each additional child is $1.50 per night.

Canyon RV and Campground $
P.O. Box 7, 9540 U.S. Highway 2 East
Hungry Horse 59919
(406) 387-9393
www.montanacampground.com

Canyon RV and Campground is located just east of Hungry Horse, Montana, and its property runs right along the Middle Fork of the Flathead River, providing both views and fishing access. The campground has quite a variety of sites—"No rig too big" is their way of saying that Canyon can accommodate any RV. Ten tent sites are available, and Canyon also has six 12 x 12 sleeping cabins (bring-your-own-bedding). Hot showers, a dump station, and a small store are available.

Canyon RV is open from May 1 to September 30. Tent sites run $17 per night; the 51 RV sites range from $17 with no hookup to $23 with full service. Sleeping cabins rent for $39 per night for two people but can accommodate up to four ($3.00 for each extra person). Pets are permitted on leash; owners must clean up after their pets. Reservations are especially recommended for July and August.

Devil Creek Campground $
Mile marker 190, U.S. Highway 2
Hungry Horse Ranger District
Flathead National Forest, Hungry Horse
(406) 387-3800

The 13 sites of Devil Creek Campground are open from around Memorial Day (depending on snow conditions) to mid-September. Drinking water and vault toilets are available, and a campground host is in residence during the summer. Forest Service Trail #167 (Devil Creek) is nearby. Some double-wide or long sites will accommodate RVs, although there are no hookups. There is no garbage pickup, so all campers must pack in, pack out. Because this is grizzly habitat, all food (including pet food and garbage) must be kept in a hard-sided vehicle whenever it is not being prepared. Horses are not permitted in the campground.

For late-season visitors, however, the campground is open without charge until closed by weather, but water is not available and outhouses are not regularly cleaned.

A fee of $10 per night is charged during the summer. Reservations are not accepted. Mile marker 190 is approximately 8 miles east of Essex and 7 miles west of Marias Pass along U.S. Highway 2.

Three Forks Campground $
Between mile markers 191 and 192
U.S. Highway 2 East
(406) 226-4479

This large campground occupies a beautiful meadow but also nestles into the trees—offering both sun and shade throughout the summer months. Campers of all sorts are welcome. Three Forks has wide, long pull-through sites, sites with electric and water hookups, back-in sites with electric only, and tent sites. It also welcomes groups of all sizes—up to 1,000 people. A playground, shower house, dump station, and covered pavilion will make your stay comfortable and convenient. A small store sells propane and ice.

Three Forks Campground is open from May 20 to September 15, weather permitting. Rates run from approximately $12 for tenters to $14 and $16 for RVs, depending on hookups. Because this is grizzly habitat, all food (including pet food and garbage) must be kept in a hard-sided vehicle whenever it is not being prepared. Pets are permitted on leash; owners are expected to clean up after their pets. Reservations are recommended, especially for groups.

Summit Campground $
Marias Pass, U.S. Highway 2
Rocky Mountain Ranger District
Lewis and Clark National Forest, Choteau
(406) 466–5341

This small Forest Service campground is conveniently located at Marias Pass, 12 miles west of East Glacier on U.S. Highway 2. The site is wooded, which you'll be grateful for, as the Continental Divide can be a windy place to camp, even at comparatively low elevation (5,216 feet). Nevertheless, it's a wonderful site—not only for Memorial Square and its monuments, but also for the imposing peaks just across the highway: Summit and Little Dog Mountains. If geology is your interest, take a few moments to scan these peaks: You'll be able to pick out the Lewis Overthrust Fault, where younger rocks rode up over the older rocks beneath. The fault line looks like a dark band in the side of the mountains, almost as if there were a road halfway up the slope. North of U.S. Highway 2, you're in Glacier National Park. Three Bears Lake is an easy hike in from the road, and the trail then continues both east and west below the mountains. Be sure to make lots of noise—although you're not far from a major highway, this is bear country.

Summit Campground has 17 sites. It's generally open from about Memorial Day (depending on the snowpack) to Labor Day, and a campground host is on-site to help visitors. Several sites will accommodate RVs up to 35 feet long. Drinking water and vault toilets are available. There are no hookups. Because this is grizzly habitat, all food (including pet food and garbage) must be kept in a hard-sided vehicle whenever it is not being prepared. Sites are $10 per night. Summit Campground can be very busy and often fills between July 4 and Labor Day. Reservations may be made for a $25 reservation fee at the phone number above.

Restaurants

Restaurant Rates

For two people, meal exclusive of beverages, tip, and tax.

$	$10 to $20
$$	$21 to $30
$$$	$31 to $50
$$$$	More than $50

Insiders' Tip

Wolves were once the most widely distributed animal in North America, but they were exterminated throughout much of the continent. In Montana the last wolf was shot in 1930. Although occasionally individual animals wandered through the state, not until 1986 was there pack— or family—activity here again. In that year a female wolf crossed south over the border from Canada and gave birth to a litter of pups in Glacier National Park. It was the beginning of a naturally occurring recolonization of the area that continues to this day. Your best chance of seeing—or hearing—wolves is up the North Fork of the Flathead River. A fair number of people will see tracks in this area; some will hear the wolves howling, and a very few lucky folks will actually see them.

Cimarron Deli and Catering $
420 Nucleus Avenue, Columbia Falls
(406) 892–1490, (800) 811–0539

This full-service deli includes a small seating area, but it's also a great place to pick up a picnic "to go"—the variety of fresh sandwiches made to your order, hot sandwiches, and homemade soup will give you lots to choose from. For example, check out the section on chicken—the "chicken coop"—which includes seven different kinds of "hot chicks": Monterey, Lorraine, BBQ, Chipolte, Malibu, Southwest, and a chicken breast sandwich with lemon pepper . . . or the equally long list of salads.

Prices run from $3.75 to $6.00, and the deli carries a selection of beverages and desserts. Cimarron Deli also caters and creates party trays.

The Back Room $
U.S. Highway 2 East, Columbia Falls
(406) 892–3131

The Back Room is definitely a local spot—no fuss, no muss. But if you're ready for chicken and ribs, this is definitely the place to go. Spare ribs, country ribs, baby back ribs, rotisserie chicken, roasted chicken, pizza, seafood, steak, burgers—and most dinners come with the Back Room "trimmings": baby red potatoes, cole slaw, baked beans, and fry bread with whipped honey butter. This is not for the faint of heart! And the portions are generous—lots of folks will be taking home doggie bags and enjoying the leftovers tomorrow.

Back Room dinner entrees run from $4.25 to $10.00; 7-, 13-, and 15-inch pizzas run from $7.00 to $14.00 or so. Sunday brings the "all you can eat" pizza, salad, and dark chicken bar, which is $5.75 for adults and less for kids. Chicken and ribs can also be ordered to go—as can the Back Room barbecue sauce. Both seniors' and kids' menus are available.

The Back Room is located behind the Nite Owl Restaurant, in the same building. Both are located on the south side of U.S. Highway 2, between Fourth and Sixth Avenues West.

Charlie Wong's $
329 Ninth Street West, Columbia Falls
(406) 892–9664

Charlie Wong's is like the Chinese restaurant you frequent back home—not fancy, but the food's great and it doesn't take long to get it. Here in Columbia Falls, it's located right on U.S. Highway 2 (Ninth Street is the highway as it goes through town), so it's easy to stop in on your way home from a day of exploring, or call in advance and pick up your order to go.

Lunch is from 11:00 A.M. to 3:00 P.M. and features a variety of specials—standards like Kung Pao Chicken or Lemon Chicken, but also Charlie Wong's Lunch, Asian BBQ Chicken or Beef, and Vegetarian Lunch. Appetizers, soups, and quite a few a la carte items can also be ordered. The menu also includes burgers for those who prefer to leave their chopsticks at home. Specials cost between $4.00 and $6.00.

Dinner is from 4:30 to 9:00 P.M. Sunday through Thursday and from 4:30 to 9:30 P.M. on Friday and Saturday nights. The dinner menu is more extensive than the lunch menu and includes beef, pork, chicken, seafood, and combination plates. Charlie Wong's also offers "international selections," which are preset dinner menus meant to be ordered for the whole table and priced per person. A small dessert list finishes the menu—and, of course, a fortune cookie.

Dinner entrees run between $7.25 and $11.95; international selections are priced at $8.95 or $9.50 per person.

Sunrise Bakery $
402 Ninth Street West (Highway 2)
Columbia Falls
(406) 892–7277
www.sunrisebakery.net

The Sunrise Bakery has been a great addition to Columbia Falls. They open early and offer coffee and a great variety of baked goods: fresh breads, cookies, pastries, and cakes. People, of course, order specialty cakes for birthdays and big events, but many also just stop by on a daily basis for a treat to start the morning. The bakery has its own Web site, where you can view some

Mountain Goats and Bighorn Sheep

Looking for animals is a great pastime while visiting Glacier, and with just a little effort you're almost certain to see mountain goats. "Goat" is something of a misnomer; these animals are more closely related to the chamois of Europe than to any domestic goat. They can look ragged in the early summer when they are shedding last winter's extra fur, but by August or so they will be sparkling white with their new, trim summer coats. Some Native Americans called them the white buffalo. Even today mountain goats sometimes trigger reports of polar bears at Logan Pass!

A symbol of the mountains (and of the Great Northern Railway), the goat is perfectly adapted to its high mountain home. Its hooves are sharp on the rim, for good purchase in soft rock and snow, but they are spongy on the inside, giving the goat traction on hard, flat rock. Its shoulders are massive, allowing it to climb and descend slopes approaching almost 90 degrees vertical. Its fur is dense, with an outer layer for protection from rain and snow and an inner layer for insulation. Goats live in the cliffs, which are their safety—few predators can follow them along the steep faces and narrow ledges that they traverse with such apparent ease. When winter comes they may move to lower, lee-side cliffs, but they continue to prefer the steep terrain. With the summer grasses gone, goats lick lichens from the rocks with tongues as rough as sand paper: as one naturalist liked to teach "kids," "goats like lickin' lichen"!

Look in the steep, rocky cliffs of Glacier to see goats. Logan Pass, Many Glacier, and Two Medicine all have the rugged terrain these mountain creatures prefer.

Bighorn sheep often overlap in range with mountain goats. While goats tend toward the higher cliffs, sheep favor the open, grassy slopes just below them. They depend on their speed to outrun predators. Sometimes goats and sheep will graze close together, and their young will play together at an early age.

Majestic bighorn sheep excite wildlife watchers in Glacier Country. Photo: courtesy of VIAD Corporation

Bighorn sheep are brown with a cream-colored rump patch; the rams carry their namesake curling horns. The bigger the curl, the older the ram. Females are smaller and sport spike horns, similar to those seen on goats of both sexes. Sheep are more of a herd animal than goats are; in the summertime, the ewes form bands and go off to have their young; the rams form bachelor bands that often move to the high country. As fall comes on, however, all groups reconvene and move to lower elevations where the winter is just a little bit milder.

Currently there is no precise count of sheep or goats in Glacier National Park. Clearly, though, there are quite a few more goats than sheep. Good places to look for sheep include Logan Pass, across from the visitor center on the slopes of Pollock Mountain; the slopes of Piegan Mountain, just up from Siyeh Bend on Going-to-the-Sun Road; Many Glacier Valley; the Highline Trail between Logan Pass and Granite Park; and Two Medicine Valley.

of their beautiful cake creations! This is sure to give you ideas.... The bakery is open from 5:00 A.M. to 4:00 P.M. Tuesday through Saturday.

Spruce Park Cafe $
U.S. Highway 2 East, Coram
(406) 387–5614

The Spruce Park Cafe is in a category of its own—yes, it's located at the Coram Exxon station, right on U.S. Highway 2. It's not fancy. But the food is homemade and consistently fresh and well prepared—which is why it's often a busy spot. They make their own biscuits, rolls, pies—which you can buy whole or by the slice, to go—and the menu offers a good variety of choices for breakfast, lunch, and dinner. Now, the nitty-gritty: check out the Mexican. The burritos are great, and the Spruce Park makes its own salsa and pintos. Or, for a hot summer day in Glacier Country, try a huckleberry milk shake. The Spruce Park makes a huck shake that stands up to a straw—as a matter of fact, you'll need a spoon, because the real huckleberries will plug the straw!

The Spruce Park Cafe is open seven days a week, all year.

Heaven's Peak Restaurant $$$$
12130 U.S. Highway 2, West Glacier
(406) 387–4754

This beautiful restaurant is living up to its location . . . in both its ambience and its menu. The dining room is intimate, with a high ceiling and blond woodwork that gleams. The deck faces Glacier National Park (although the mountain called Heaven's Peak isn't quite in the view) and offers outdoor dining on sunny days. The menu features entrees that range from steaks, quail, and salmon to vegetables napoleon. The appetizer selection is equally extensive—and delicious. Heaven's Peak has a relatively short season—it's open only from mid-June to mid-September and not at all on Tuesdays or Wednesdays, so be sure to put it in your plans.

Belton Chalet $–$$
U.S. Highway 2, West Glacier
(406) 888–5000, (888) BELTON–5
www.beltonchalet.com

The Belton Chalet's Grill and Tap Room offer a glimpse into this beautifully renovated, historic lodge and are well worth stopping to see . . . so consider taking a few moments to check them out. The lunch menu includes soups, salads, and sandwiches, as well as the "boiler broiler" specialties, or you can order a box lunch to go. Dinner is more formal, with a wide choice of entrees, including steaks, fish, buffalo stew, and quail. The Tap Room features Montana microbrews . . . if it's a sunny summer afternoon, enjoy yours on the deck.

The Glacier Highland $
U.S. Highway 2 East, West Glacier
(406) 888–5427

The Glacier Highland's restaurant offers home-cooked food at affordable prices. Open for breakfast, lunch, and dinner from May through October, breakfast treats include the famous cinnamon rolls. Lunch and dinner feature sandwiches, soups, burgers, and hand-tossed, homemade pizza. If you have any room left afterward, you'll have to top off your meal with pie—or maybe pie is a reason to stop in, all by itself. . . .

The Glacier Highland is located directly across from the Amtrak station in West Glacier and minutes from the west entrance to Glacier National Park.

West Glacier Restaurant and Bar $
West Glacier
(406) 888–5403

After a great day rafting the Middle Fork—or hiking to Apgar Lookout, perhaps—you'll enjoy not having to drive far to find a good dinner. The West Glacier Restaurant—often called the West Glacier Café—is just outside the park boundary in West Glacier, ready with breakfast, lunch, and dinner. The relaxed, family atmosphere makes it a great place to start up or wind down. And you're sure to find a huckleberry treat to complete your day in Glacier Country. The West Glacier Restaurant will be open from late May to late September.

Izaak Walton Inn $$
P.O. Box 653, Essex 59916
(406) 888–5700

Staying at the Izaak Walton Inn may not be part of your itinerary, but if you're driving U.S. Highway 2, you may want to plan to stop here for a meal. The dining room is open for breakfast (7:00 to 11:00 A.M.), lunch (11:00 A.M. to 5:00 P.M.), and dinner (5:00 to 8:00 P.M.), and serves as a great reason to stop and explore this fascinating historic inn.

The dining room offers a limited but choice menu for each meal. Breakfast ranges from the basic—oatmeal or cold cereal—to fancier dishes such as the "portabella, asparagus, and gouda cheese omelet with hashbrowns." Lunch always includes a burger selection, pasta, and heftier choices. Dinner menus include one dinner sandwich plus three entrees—perhaps vegetable lasagna, buffalo kabobs, or salmon filet. Dinner prices run from $13.95 to $18.25. A children's menu is available for lunch and dinner.

Nightlife

Nightlife isn't too complex in this neck of the woods—but there are a few spots where you're sure to enjoy putting your feet up for a bit. Frieda's—the bar adjacent to the West Glacier Restaurant—will often have a crowd on the porch in the evening, perhaps rafters just off the river who want to swap stories about the white water. The Tap Room at the newly renovated Belton Chalet offers a cozy, relaxed atmosphere—and an outdoor deck—a great place to stop for a beer. After a day of cross-country skiing, you might want to check out the Flag Stop lounge at the Izaak Walton, once again a fascinating place for its railroad history.

If you're down in the Flathead Valley and feeling adventurous, try the Blue Moon. For starters, it's a landmark—located at the junction of U.S. Highway 2 and Montana Highway 40, about halfway between Columbia Falls and Whitefish, which everyone here refers to as the Blue Moon junction. This grill, casino, and night club has live music, karaoke, various specials, and, on Wednesdays, line dancing, with lessons. Here's a slice of Montana life!

Shopping

Breathtaking views and outdoor activities probably take priority for most visitors to this area, but you won't want to miss these places.

Glacier Natural History Association (GNHA)
U.S. Highway 2, West Glacier
(406) 888-5756

Located in the historic Belton depot in West Glacier, GNHA is a cooperating association of Glacier National Park. It sells books, videos, and posters on subjects related to the park, and profits are used to enhance the park's educational programs. All that serious stuff said—GNHA is a great place to shop! For anyone who's enjoyed their time in the mountains, this beautiful store offers a huge selection of books covering geology, history, Native American culture, plants, and animals—everything from *Alces alces shirasi* to *Zigadenus elegans*. Books include field guides, photo books, and children's books. And you'll have a hard time deciding which beautiful poster you're going to take home. GNHA is open from 8:00 A.M. until 4:30 P.M., Monday through Friday.

Izaak Walton Inn
P.O. Box 653, Essex 59916
(406) 888-5700

The Izaak Walton Inn has a small but selective gift shop with an enticing variety of items—all related to Glacier National Park, the inn itself, or the Great Northern Railway. You'll find all sorts of teddy bears, quality locally crafted silver and antler jewelry, Christmas ornaments, maps and books, ball caps, T-shirts, and outerwear. The inn has even arranged for the reproduction of the Great Northern Railway's "Glory of the West" china pattern, used on the Empire Builder route from 1940 to 1957. This is a fun place to spend some time . . . the owners have been ingenious in choosing the souvenirs they offer.

Bigfork

Accommodations
Restaurants
Nightlife
Shopping

Bigfork, located on the northeast corner of Flathead Lake, is a combination of the perfect Montana small town, the perfect lakeside village, the perfect tourist town, and the perfect artists' colony. When you get right down to it, what visitors and residents all seem to agree upon is that Bigfork is perfect.

The town is located on Montana Highway 35, which hugs the eastern shore of Flathead Lake from Polson in the south to just north of Bigfork. The community is located at the mouth of the Swan River where it empties into Flathead Lake, the largest natural freshwater lake west of the Mississippi. The lake and the river provide the crux of the recreational opportunities in Bigfork—with fishing for mackinaw, rainbow, cutthroat, perch, bass, and northern pike available nearby—but the town is also just 17 miles southeast of Kalispell, and 45 miles southwest of Glacier National Park, so there is much more to do in a day than boating or fishing. East of Bigfork is the 950,000-acre Bob Marshall Wilderness, a favorite of local backcountry hikers. The Jewel Basin Hiking Area is also nearby, with 38 miles of nature trails that are easy for almost anyone to navigate. The east shore of Flathead Lake is also noted for its cherry orchards, which provide lots of raw material for roadside stands in July and August.

The population varies considerably depending on the time of year. Summertime is the high season here, and with Flathead Lake at full pool, the population in this little town soars from 3,500 to as many as 10,000. But in any case, with its economy supported by tourism, Bigfork offers a splendid variety of diversions, from canoeing to bowling, horseback riding to live theater, jet skiing to shopping. Eagle Bend is a world-class golf course not far from downtown. And there's always a new restaurant to try in what must surely be considered the culinary capital of the Flathead.

The transformation of Bigfork into something of an artistic mecca probably coincides with the opening in 1960 of the Bigfork Summer Playhouse. That repertory company, which was then housed in a rustic building but now performs in air-conditioned comfort in the Bigfork Center for the Performing Arts, started to draw creative people to Bigfork. The tourist trade built up steadily as well, leading to many opportunities for new businesses. Today Electric Avenue—Bigfork's main commercial street—is a bustling row of artist's studios, galleries, gift shops, bookstores, and restaurants. The playhouse's repertory company puts on shows from late May through early September. And during some of the annual festivities, such as the Fourth of July or the Bigfork Festival of the Arts, the atmosphere is truly electric, although even on a standard day in summer the street lives up to its name, which comes from a small power plant nearby. Sliter Park, located at the end of Electric Avenue and across the old steel bridge, is the site of live outdoor performances such as the Riverbend Concert Series during the summer.

Believe it or not, Bigfork is also a good spot to plan for winter recreation. For one thing, the lake regulates the climate, so most winters are milder than typical for a latitude this far north. There are also breaks on rates at resorts and other lodging facilities during the "off season." And you have the same access to the Flathead Forest for cross-country skiing and snowmobiling that you would have from elsewhere in the valley. The Big Mountain Resort and the new Blacktail Mountain ski area are both less than an hour away.

Also of note is the scenic drive from Bigfork to Seeley Lake and Swan Lake on Montana Highway 83. This trip through the Clearwater and Swan Valleys typically results in quite a bit of wildlife viewing, especially at sunset when deer are frequently seen crossing the highway. The southern lakes both offer excellent recreational opportunities as well, but use caution in traveling the road.

Accommodations

Hotels and Motels

Price Code

Keep in mind that some rates are based on availability. The average peak-season nightly rates for two adults at the hotels and motels listed in this section are indicated by a dollar sign ($) ranking in the following chart. Also, the hotels and motels in this chapter accept all or most major credit cards.

$	$50–$75
$$	$76–$100
$$$	$101–$125
$$$$	More than $125

The Bear Dance Inn $$$$
135 Bay Drive, Bigfork
(406) 837–4551

Located on enchanting Bigfork Bay, the Bear Dance Inn may be the best-situated lodging in Bigfork. Guests are within walking distance of shopping and dining in Bigfork Village, and they are just a hop, skip, and jump away from a cool swim or a scenic view of the busiest boating port on Flathead Lake. The resort is built around a 60-some-year-old log home, with the addition of six surrounding cabins. This is really a B&B: Full breakfast is included. Slips are available for guests with boats.

Bigfork Timbers Motel $$
8540 Montana Highway 35
(406) 837–6200, (800) 821–4546
www.timbersmotel.com

The Timbers Motel is the only moderately priced motel in Bigfork. It is within walking distance of the village and very near to Wayfarers state park. There is also trolley bus service to the village during the summer season. The Timbers offers 40 rooms, along with continental breakfasts, cable and HBO, and complimentary in-room coffee. There is an outdoor pool available in summer, and a sauna and hot tub year-round.

Holiday Resort Motel $
17001 East Lakeshore Drive, Bigfork
(406) 982–3710, (800) 421–9141

The Holiday Resort Motel is located on Yellow Bay about a dozen miles south of Bigfork on Flathead Lake. This is a waterfront motel and includes guest moorage and boat or personal watercraft rentals. There is a private beach for guests, along with a dock for easy access to the lake. The motel is also home to "The Little Café on Yellow Bay," featuring waterfront dining, fresh seafood, and homemade desserts as well as complimentary moorage. Breakfast, lunch, and dinner are served at this local favorite.

Woods Bay Resort $$
26481 East Lakeshore Drive, Bigfork
(406) 837–3333

Woods Bay is a small lakeside community located on Flathead Lake just 4 miles south of Bigfork, and this small facility offers six motel rooms, five cabins with kitchens, and six RV spots with full hookups. Owner Rod Hitt promotes the friendly atmosphere, clean and comfortable accommodations, and beach access. Cabins are available on a monthly basis in the winter.

Resorts and Guest Ranches

Price Code

$	$70–$120
$$	$121–$170
$$$	$171–$220
$$$$	More than $221

Bayview Resort Marina & RV $$
543 Yenne Point Road, Bigfork
(406) 837–4843, (800) 775–3536
www.cyberport.net/bayview

Bayview Resort has everything you need for a perfect economical fishing vacation: fully furnished cabins with kitchens, dockside service, fishing tackle, groceries, beer, and boat rentals. Owners David and Sharon Young say the Flathead Lake resort specializes in family gatherings. A three-bedroom home for a little more money and motel-style rooms for a little less are also lodging options. The marina can outfit you with boat rentals for any kind of recreation possibility—skiing, fishing, pontoon boats, paddleboats, aqua cycle, and three-passenger Sea Doos. There's also a private beach and a nightly lakeside bonfire in the summer. Bayview is just 4 miles south of Bigfork.

Flathead Lake Lodge $$$$
P.O. Box 248, Montana Highway 35
Bigfork 59911
(406) 837–4391
www.ranchweb.com/averill

If you are looking for a Western adventure, try Flathead Lake Lodge, a famous 2,000-acre family-operated dude ranch that attracts celebrities and wealthy business people from around the world, as well as ordinary families that save up for an extraordinary vacation. The rate for an adult for a week is almost $2,000, but for that money you get much more than lodging. All meals and recreation are included in the package, and in the case of Flathead Lake Lodge that means three superb meals a day plus horseback riding, rodeo action, cookouts, water sports, use of sailboats, canoes, fishing boats, waterskiing, lake cruises, a heated pool, tennis courts, volleyball, hiking wilderness and primitive areas, and many other ranch activities. The Averill family has operated the resort for more than 50 years, and there hasn't been a complaint yet. This is a real Western vacation in a setting of unmatched luxury and beauty. The ranch offers one- or two-week vacations with everyone arriving and departing on the same day, but you can't just call up and get in the next week. Reservations are often made years in advance, and the lodge boasts a 50 to 60 percent return of guests year after year. It has been featured by *Better Homes & Gardens*, *Travel & Leisure*, *Bon Appetit*, and *Good Morning America*, among others.

Marina Cay Resort $–$$$
180 Vista Lane, Bigfork
(406) 837–5861, (800) 433–6516
www.marinacay.com

The Bigfork Inn is one of the grand old businesses in Bigfork Village. Photo: Suzie Keenan

This resort is a deluxe facility on Bigfork Bay, just up the hill from the village. Accommodations range from an economy room for one or two people only with no view to a waterfront marina suite with king-size bed and private Jacuzzi. One-, two-, and three-bedroom condo rentals are also available. The Marina Cay features an outdoor pool and whirlpool, as well as a full-service marina where you can rent a ski boat, Jet Ski, canoe, or other watercraft. Guided fishing charters will escort you to just the right spot to catch "the big one." After you come back for the night, you can enjoy one of three restaurants and several bars and lounges. Visit Marina Cay in the off-season for significant savings. Rates are discounted 25 percent or more from the last week of September to the middle of May.

Bed-and-Breakfasts

Price Code

$	Less than $85
$$	$85–$115
$$$	$116–$150
$$$$	More than $151

Coyote Roadhouse Inn & Riverside Cabins
$$$
602 Three Eagles Lane, Bigfork
(406) 837–4250
www.coyoteroadhouse.com

This seasonal bed-and-breakfast establishment is an offshoot of the Coyote Roadhouse Restaurant. Owner and chef Gary Hastings decided he wanted to offer intimate dining experiences to guests, so he started the Roadhouse Inn, which takes maximum advantage of the woodsy setting and adds fine food of a high order. There are five cabins on the scenic Swan River with private docks. Barbecues, canoes, and bicycles are available for an extra charge. The Coyote Roadhouse Inn is located near Ferndale off Montana Highway 209 on a scenic portion of the Swan River. This is a great place to get away if you enjoy quiet walks along the river.

Log-house living at its most gracious. Photo: courtesy of O'Duachain Country Inn

O'Duachain Country Inn $$$
675 Ferndale Drive, Bigfork
(406) 837–6851, (800) 837–7460
www.montanainn.com

Best known for total comfort and Montana charm, this three-level log home and two-story guest house is located on five acres just 5 miles from Bigfork. The grounds include many rustic features as well as wild game. Bird watchers will enjoy the exotic birds such as peacocks and waterfowl, which can be seen on the pond. Bill Knoll and Mary Corcoran Knoll are the owners of the O'Duachain (pronounced O-Do-CANE), which was established in 1985 by Tom and Margot Doohan. The breakfast menu still includes Margot's Stuffed Irish Toast, as well as homemade maple nut cereal with fruit puree, and lots of different teas and coffees. The facility offers suites and rooms with private baths. The guest house also has balconies and patios with incredible views. If you're looking for stiff European charm, the Knolls warn, this is not the place for you. They make you feel right at home.

Swan River Inn $$$
360 Grand Drive, Bigfork
(406) 837–2220

The Swan River Inn has just three rooms, but they occupy a choice location in downtown Bigfork, where there are few accommodations available of any kind. The inn is affiliated with the Swan River Inn Cafe but under different ownership. Room service is available, so you can take advantage of the elegant and healthy menu at the restaurant. There are antiques in the rooms, which have different themes such as Victorian, Art Deco, and rustic Western. Each room has a separate entrance and private bath, with one room offering kitchen facilities.

Campgrounds and RV Parks

Price Code

$	$4.00 to $9.00
$$	$10 to $16
$$$	$17 to $23
$$$$	More than $24

Bigfork Timbers RV Park and Campground $$
8540 Montana Highway 35, Bigfork
(406) 837–6200, (800) 821–4546

The Timbers RV Park and Campground is affiliated with the Timbers Motel and is within walking distance of Bigfork Village. Guests of the RV park and campground have access to the motel complex's outdoor pool in summer and the sauna and hot tub year-round. There are five tent spaces available for $7.00 per person or RV hookups available for $20.00 per night for

two. Laundry facilities and free showers are available. The site is open only for the summer season.

Flathead Lake State Park $
490 North Meridian Road, Kalispell
(406) 752–5501

The park consists of six scenic units bordering Flathead Lake, two of which are on the east shore near Bigfork. With the exception of Wild Horse Island, all units feature economical camping, fishing, boating, and swimming. Closest to Bigfork is 69-acre Wayfarers (phone 406-837-4196 in summer) just outside of town, which features 30 campsites, including 7 tent-only sites. The park has flush toilets and a group picnic shelter, as well as trailer and boat sewage dump stations. The Yellow Bay facility is 15 acres and the campground has six sites, including five walk-in tent sites. Flush and vault toilets and coin-operated showers are available. All individual campsites are available on a first-come, first-served basis. Plan to arrive early, as most sites fill up by 4:00 P.M. on weekends during July and August. Maximum stay is seven days.

Outback Montana $$, no credit cards
27202 East Lakeshore Drive, Bigfork
(406) 837–6973, (888) 900–6973
www.outbackmontana.com

There are 40 RV sites at Outback Montana (located 4 miles south of Bigfork), including many pull-throughs, and 12 tent sites. Both partial and full hookups are available. There is more of an emphasis on privacy than at many RV parks, with fenced terraces, patios, and picnic tables at each site. Rest rooms are available, but you pay extra for showers. Pets are allowed with certain restrictions—please check for details. Horses are always welcome. Families will enjoy such activities as tetherball, badminton, and horseshoes in the delightful outdoor setting. Although credit cards are not accepted, owners Carol and Bill Matthews take out-of-area checks.

Woods Bay Marina and RV Resort $$$
624 Yenne Point Road, Bigfork
(406) 837–6191

From May to October 1, you can drive your RV right up to Flathead Lake at the Woods Bay Marina and enjoy a lake vacation for just $25 a night (full hookup) or $20 a night (partial—just water and electric). Weekly and monthly rates are also available. If you are pulling a boat, you have the advantage of having the boat docked within feet of your hookup. There are also four tent sites at $10.00 per site for one person and $5.00 for each additional person. Free hot showers and a laundry facility are nearby. Gas and repairs are available for boats on-site, and a market sells food and tackle. Fishing and lake tour guides can be hired from the marina as well.

Restaurants

Price Code

For two people, meal exclusive of beverages, tip, and tax.

$	$10 to $19
$$	$20 to $27
$$$	$28 to $35
$$$$	More than $36

Family-Friendly Dining

Bigfork Village Deli $
435 Bridge Street, Bigfork
(406) 837-3354

The Bigfork Village Deli, which serves breakfast and lunch as well as offering gourmet food items, wine, and beer, is best known for its homemade bread and pastries. There is always a long line for the thick, rich soups such as the cream of potato, and there are pasta dinners available year-round except on Sundays and Mondays. The restaurant is located near the famous Wild Mile of the Swan River, the scene of a popular kayaking race every spring.

Brookie's Cookies $
191 Mill Street, Bigfork
(406) 837–CHIP, (800) 697–6487
www.brookiescookies.com

Just around the corner from Electric Avenue near the Swan River is a place to stop for all kinds of munchies, from chocolate-chip cookies to gourmet desserts, baked fresh every day in small batches. One of our favorites is "The Bigfoot," a hearty chocolate-chip cookie made with nuts, oats, and more. Brookie's Cookies owner Greg Bloom came up with this hearty cookie when he was out cross-country skiing with his wife, Karen, and wanted an extra-energy treat. The store and Web site feature a large selection of coffees and other beverages. There's also a helping of merchandise on hand such as clothing and coffee mugs with the Brookie's Cookies logo. And keep the name in mind when you are traveling elsewhere in the Flathead, because the "cookie van" takes Brookie's Cookies to a variety of stores and restaurants throughout the area.

Champs Sports Pub and Grill $$
180 Vista Lane, Bigfork
(406) 837–5861, (800) 433–6516

Though Champs is a sports bar, it is also a perfect place to have a family meal because it features a fun kids' menu and large lunch and dinner specials. There are large televisions for sports coverage and trivia games, and the bar serves local microbrews for Mom and Dad to enjoy. Champs is part of Marina Cay Resort, and you will find other listings under the Fine Dining and Nightlife sections.

Del Norte $
355 Grand Drive, Bigfork
(406) 837–0076

A great place to go with the kids is Del Norte, located right across the street from the bay in Bigfork. The menu features plenty of authentic Mexican specialties as well as burgers and other American food and takeout. If the kids don't like the Mexican cuisine, they will definitely enjoy the ice cream, which comes in both the hard and soft varieties and in lots of flavors, including huckleberry. Del Norte is open daily in the summer only.

Swan River Inn Cafe & Dinner House $$$
360 Grand Drive, Bigfork
(406) 837–2220

This is a great compromise for families looking for something in between fine dining and diner food. The Swan River Inn's European and American menu caters to a healthy diet, but with plenty of specialties to pique the appetite. You can get steak and eggs for breakfast to prep you for a busy day fishing on the lake, and then come back and have a gourmet dinner. On Sundays, brunch is served from 8:00 A.M. to 3:00 P.M. year-round, and Sunday evenings feature a prime rib and red king salmon special. There is also outdoor seating available in one of the best views possible of Bigfork Bay. The restaurant opens at 8:00 A.M. and is open for breakfast, lunch, and dinner. All meals are made from scratch, and you'll enjoy the homey atmosphere and emphasis on service. There are rooms available for rent in the same building.

Fine Dining

Bigfork Inn $$$
604 Electric Avenue, Bigfork
(406) 837–6680

The Bigfork Inn is one of the defining spots in this lakeside community. It was built in 1937 after a fire destroyed the Bigfork Hotel and features a mountain-chalet style that is associated with Glacier National Park. The inn, which serves dinners only, is open year-round seven days a week, with fine dining from an extensive menu that features pasta, veal, prime rib, fresh fish, and steak. There is an outdoor patio that's open in the summer and dancing on Friday and Saturday nights to the traditional jazz sounds of The Company Brass. The restaurant and bar open at 4:00 P.M. daily.

Bridge Street Gallery & Café $$
408 Bridge Street, Bigfork
(406) 837–5825

Bridge Street offers a unique combination of art and delectables. Brunch, lunch, and dinner are served daily. During the summer you can eat on the deck or inside, but it's inside where the action is. That's because the walls of Bridge Street are covered with art that is for sale. A rotating series of exhibits is featured throughout the year, including the annual Christmas wreath contest, which includes a prize for best edible wreath. The cafe also features a large selection of wines by the glass or bottle, including a selection from the Chateau Montelena winery in Napa Valley owned by Bridge Street's proprietor, Laura Barrett. A private dining room is available for larger parties, and reservations are suggested.

Coyote Roadhouse $$$
600 Three Eagle Lane, Bigfork
(406) 837–1233

Owner and chef Gary Hastings has a reputation as a perfectionist. He certainly deserves it, according to anyone who has ever eaten at the Coyote Roadhouse. This is a world-class restaurant that features a highly trained staff and a gourmet menu in a backwoods setting. You have to drive a little ways from Bigfork toward Ferndale on Montana Highway 209, then follow the signs from Ferndale to the Roadhouse, which is located on a remote and scenic portion of the Swan River. Make a reservation before you show up at the front door, because it is a very popular spot and often fills up in spite of its somewhat remote location. Most nights look for such Cajun specialties as blackened redfish and many European specialties as well as fresh fish. Rooms are also available (see earlier listing under Bed-and-Breakfasts for Coyote Roadhouse Inn).

Bigfork lights up for the holidays.
Photo: courtesy of Bjorge's Gallery

Quincy's at Marina Cay Resort $$$
180 Vista Lane, Bigfork
(406) 837–5861, (800) 433–6516

Quincy's offers award-winning contemporary cuisine with an emphasis on seasonal products and fresh ingredients. Try the Kentucky bourbon steak for a variation on a familiar theme, and look for the daily specials such as pheasant or duck along with fresh seafood. The restaurant overlooks Bigfork Bay and features indoor and outdoor seating. During the high season, breakfast, lunch, and dinner are all available. Quincy's is part of Marina Cay Resort, and you will find other listings under the Family-Friendly Dining and Nightlife sections.

ShowThyme $$$
548 Electric Avenue, Bigfork
(406) 837–0707
www.showthyme.com

The ShowThyme restaurant is located next door to the Bigfork Center for the Performing Arts, which explains the pun in the name. But whether or not you are making a stop before watching a show put on by the Bigfork Summer Playhouse, you can't go wrong stopping here. ShowThyme, located in a historic building that formerly housed a bank, is simply one of the best restaurants the Flathead Valley has to offer. Every night a variety of specials is available, from the featured rack of lamb to a variety of fresh fish and shellfish. The wait staff is trained to recite specials from memory and to take orders without benefit of a notepad. It makes for a nice chal-

lenge for the highly professional staff, and they've never gotten our order wrong yet. Save room for dessert, though you will be hard-pressed to choose between the simple delight of the crème caramel and the decadent double-chocolate cake. Reservations are appreciated and sometimes necessary at this restaurant, which serves lunch and dinner.

Nightlife

Garden Bar
451 Electric Avenue, Bigfork
(406) 837–9914

Lots of folks park themselves in the Garden Bar after work and just hang out there for hours. Why not? There's great food from the grill, a pool table, pinball, electronic darts, TVs for sports coverage, live music on summer weekends, and video poker and keno machines for the amateur gambler. In the summer months don't forget to poke your head out back and see why the bar got its name. The outdoor patio and garden is a delightful place to sip a beer and kick back. The Garden Kitchen does a great job with burgers, but you can also get chicken, fish, salads, and hot dogs. By the way, if you aren't sure about whether the Garden Bar is right for you, this sign on the wall should be a good clue: THIS ESTABLISHMENT SERVES NO DRINKS WITH LITTLE TINY UMBRELLAS. A Montana

Backcountry Cooking

Cooking and eating are some of the most pleasurable aspects of a backcountry outing in Glacier Park and the surrounding wilderness. The scenic grandeur alone provides a backdrop that can rival the ambience of the finest five-star restaurant. Backcountry meals are a fun social time, but just as importantly they provide the energy and sustenance to fuel vigorous activities.

Backcountry menus will be influenced by the personal preferences and dietary needs of your group. During a typical backcountry trip, you need not worry overmuch about eating an excess of sugar, starch, or fats. Strenuous activities and higher elevations demand extra amounts (within reason) to provide needed energy. Preference should be given to high-energy-producing foods such as pasta, rice, beans, nuts, cheese, and wheat products.

Dried veggies and meats, or meat substitutes, are lightweight and add substance, color, and taste to perhaps otherwise bland pasta, rice, or potato dishes. A spice kit is a must for any backcountry connoisseur.

Food and cookware weight and bulk will impact your packing, particularly on extended trips. Lightweight freeze-dried food offers an attractive option and the advantage of quick preparation. You can reduce some weight and bulk by repacking food into reusable plastic bags. This also reduces litter to pack out.

Trail snacks are important to backcountry travelers. Dried fruits, nuts, crackers and cheese, candy, and energy bars all provide helpful energy boosts.

Glacier Park is the domain of black and grizzly bears. Your menu and cooking techniques must take this into account. Select foods that are low-odor and avoid strong-smelling recipes that may attract bears. Try not to spill food in the cooking area.

Proper food and garbage storage is important in bear country. Regulations require you to hang food, garbage, and cookware on food-hanging devices in backcountry campgrounds at all times except mealtimes. Never cook, eat, or store food in your tent; it may attract a bear into your camp. Wastewater from cleanup should be strained of food scraps and scattered. Food scraps should be packed out.

Campfires are permitted in approximately half of Glacier's backcountry campgrounds. Cooking over an open fire can be enjoyable; however, the Leave No Trace program strongly recommends that backpackers use a lightweight camp stove. Many campers find stoves cook food more quickly and evenly as well. In the case of bad weather or an emergency, a stove is a fast and reliable way to prepare hot drinks and food.

Backcountry rangers are perhaps the greatest culinary experts roaming Glacier's wildlands. Here is a favorite dinner entree from an anonymous backcountry ranger:

Vigo brand Santa Fe pinto beans and rice with corn. (Available in the Mexican section at the grocery.) Boil contents in three cups water for one minute. Simmer 20 minutes. Add two tablespoons butter or margarine. Garnish with grated cheese. Serve with pita bread. Feeds one hungry ranger.

tradition for about 25 years, and one that shows no sign of ending.

Marina Cay
180 Vista Lane, Bigfork
(406) 837–5861, (800) 433–6516

There are two popular night spots at Marina Cay Resort. The Waterfront Tiki Bar features live entertainment three or four nights a week. A frequent contributor is Denise Sterhan, a karaoke performer with a wide range. Lunches and dinners are also available from the kitchen. Quincy's Piano Lounge and Casino offers an upscale mellow atmosphere with live piano music. You'll be able to get your favorite cocktail, rare whiskey, or aromatic cigar here. Look for other listings for Marina Cay under the Family-Friendly Dining and Fine Dining sections.

North Shore Lanes and Casino
116 Holt Drive, Bigfork
(406) 837–5381

This is a perfect spot for families looking for entertainment in Bigfork. It's not far from downtown, there is plenty of parking, and it's open year-round. There are 12 bowling lanes, available at least part of every day for open bowling. There is also a lounge area, where musical entertainment is sometimes scheduled, and a restaurant (try the North Shore Burger) with a great view of the lake. The North Shore is open for breakfast, lunch, and dinner.

The Village Well
260 River Street, Bigfork
(406) 837–5251

The Village Well is a popular night spot where you can get pizza, sandwiches, chicken wings, burgers, and more, along with a selection of microbrew beers. There's a roof deck where you can drink under the stars during the summer season, and live music downstairs on the weekends. Pool, foosball, and darts make for alternative entertainment, and there is keno as well.

Shopping

Bigfork Bay Gift & Gear
491 Electric Avenue, Bigfork
(406) 837–5850

This is a good place to start your shopping, since they cram a lot of merchandise into the store. You'll find a large selection of toys, lotions, stationery, T-shirts, and gift items. There are also a couple of indispensables—a Jelly Belly jelly bean counter and a wall full of Ty Beanie Babies. The prices are reasonable and the faces are friendly.

Bigfork Station
470 Electric Avenue, Bigfork
(406) 837–2332

One of the most recent additions to the downtown Bigfork panorama is the Bigfork Station, a collection of shops in a new building that harks back in appearance to the old-style architecture of a turn-of-the-twentieth-century railroad station. Don't let it worry you that the railroad never came to Bigfork, just enjoy the ride. First stop is Roma's Eclectic on Electric, a funky shop full of delightful "don't-need-but-must-haves." Whether you are looking for glassware, gadgets, or gourmet cookware, you can find it here, right down to the moose-shaped cookie cutters. The shop is brightly lit and a pleasure to the eye. We've included their phone number on this listing, since there's someone there seven days a week. Next stop is the Buffalo Trails Gallery, featuring the work of sculptor Bob Stayton and other Western art and craft collectibles. Next door is Bear Tracks Gift Shop, which specializes in quality tobacco products. Around the corner you'll see the Buffalo Creek Clothing Company, where you can pick up that leisure apparel to fit in with the mountain chic crowd. Before you leave the Bigfork Station, you can get refreshed at The Cup and Saucer, serving espresso, coffee, drinks, and ice cream.

Electric Avenue Books
490 Electric Avenue, Bigfork
(406) 837–6072

Electric Avenue Books is one of Montana's most eclectic bookstores, offering a selec-

Golf courses such as Eagle Bend in Bigfork bring visitors to the Flathead Valley. Photo: Golf Northwest

tion of titles from contemporary to classics and everything in between. This isn't an independent equivalent of Waldenbooks by any means. Owner MK Callan and her staff go out of their way to make you comfortable, with lounge chairs and other surprises scattered throughout the store. The shop's back room, for instance, is set up as an old-timey parlor and features an upright piano where customers or guest artists may perform. The store has one of the best selections of literary authors in the Flathead Valley, but that's just the beginning. They also have extensive offerings of Montana history, Western lore, arts, crafts, and the offbeat. In a central room upstairs, there is a children's reading room, with a kid-size table and chairs, inviting toys, and lots of books to get your youngsters interested in reading. Head downstairs and work your way through a series of rooms until you get to the one that features a mountain-cabin theme, with canoes, wooden skis, and rustic cabinetry serving as a backdrop for outdoors and adventure reading.

Eva Gates Homemade Preserves
456 Electric Avenue, Bigfork
(406) 837–4356, (800) 682–4283

Walk in the door of Eva Gates Homemade Preserves and you'll feel like you're back in grandma's kitchen 50 years ago. In fact, for more than half a century the Gates family has been creating the aromatic and tasty preserves and syrups that are today highly prized. Back in 1949 Eva used her own grandmother's recipe, and today it is her grandchildren and great-grandchildren keeping up the family tradition. When you walk in the front door, you will see Gretchen Gates or her assistants actually doing the cooking. They welcome questions and love to share the secrets of their success. The syrups and preserves are made in five-pint batches without additives or preservatives to keep them as fresh as possible. January through March, the store is closed on Sundays.

Kehoe's Agate Shop
1020 Holt Drive, Bigfork
(406) 837–4467

Kehoe's shop lies just off the bank of the Flathead River in old Holt, an early settlement that lasted from the 1880s to the 1920s. Just across the road from the shop is the old Holt general store, crumbling quietly as the years pass, and a little farther down the road are the remnants of an old ferry crossing. But Kehoe's Agate Shop actually looks much farther back than the 100 years or so represented by the passing of Holt into history. The store features a variety of gemstones, agates, and fossils that date back as much as millions of years. Many of them were collected from around the world and ground or worked into a variety of shapes by James Kehoe Sr., a gemologist who built the shop in 1932 from planks from the steamboat *Helena*. Today Kehoe's children, James Jr. and Leslie, tend to the store. He also designs jewelry with gold and a variety of gemstones. A sign next to the shop explains a little of the history of Holt, the ferry, and the *Helena*. Remnants of the *Helena*, including the pilothouse, are also on display. To find the shop, all you have to do is keep your eyes open. Almost every major highway in the area of Bigfork has a sign pointing you in the right direction.

Twin Birch Square
459 Electric Avenue, Bigfork
(406) 837–4994

Another location where you can centralize your shopping in Bigfork is the Twin Birch Square. An "anchor" in the two-story complex is Electric Avenue Gifts, where you can stop to purchase an assortment of candles, toys, Gund Bears, ceramics, lotions, T-shirts, etc. We've included the phone number for Electric Avenue Gifts to give you a starting point for your shopping. But don't forget to look farther. The Cherry Tree, with a selection of women's clothing, is downstairs. Upstairs there are two "niche" stores—The Stone Chair, which features a mix of old and new items for the country home, and Architectural Innovations, which specializes in Old World antiques and art objects. These and a variety of other galleries and retail stores will keep you occupied at Twin Birch Square for the better part of an afternoon.

Polson

Accommodations
Restaurants
Nightlife
Shopping

At the south end of Flathead Lake, midway between Kalispell and Missoula, sits the town of Polson, the first community in the area to be settled by whites. In fact, Polson is in the middle of the Flathead Indian Reservation. Although the Confederated Salish and Kootenai Tribes have jurisdiction over some aspects of life here, everyday matters are handled just as they are anywhere else in Montana. There is a sheriff and a county commission for Lake County, a city council for Polson, and people pay taxes to the state of Montana just as they do elsewhere. But there are a few exceptions. The tribal authorities here, for instance, negotiated a separate gambling compact with the state government that allows somewhat higher payouts for gaming machines and more machines than are allowed on nonreservation land. There is also a separate tribal license for hunting and fishing, although efforts have been made to end that authority.

Polson, which was named after pioneer rancher David Polson and was incorporated in 1910, is the largest city on the reservation, but it still boasts only a population of about 3,300 people. The city's early claim to fame was its steamboats, which for many years were the only means of reaching the north end of the lake and Kalispell. Today Polson offers a wide variety of activities, especially for those who want to take advantage of the scenic wonders of Flathead Lake. Tour boats depart from the Polson dock for sight-seeing on Flathead Lake, including trips to Wild Horse Island, which is the lake's largest island and is home to bighorn sheep and other wild animals, as well as the small horse population that gives the island its name. The fishing is, of course, remarkable throughout Flathead Lake, with sizable lake trout and whitefish being popular catches. When you're on the lake, keep an eye open for the legendary Flathead Lake Monster, an American cousin of the Loch Ness Monster, which, like its more famous counterpart, is often written about but rarely spotted.

If you travel south of Polson toward Missoula on U.S. 93, there are some must-see spots. Just south of town is Kerr Dam, which the Montana Power Company built on land leased from the tribes. White-water rafting is a popular activity on the Flathead River below the dam. There are also scenic vistas and a picnic area. In the tribal capital of Pablo, you can stop at the People's Center to learn about local history and native traditions. A little farther south you can witness the profound influence of the early European settlers on the area at the historic Mission Church at St. Ignatius, which features remarkable murals. Not far away there is also a highway loop that brings you to the National Bison Range at Moiese, where bison, antelope, and other creatures big and small are plentiful and much easier to photograph than at Glacier National Park.

If it is late summer, you can drive north of Polson on either U.S. 93 or Montana 35 and enjoy the produce of the area's famous sweet cherry orchards at roadside stands. The trip to Glacier Park from here is less than two hours.

Life in Polson is even more low-key than in many other cities in Montana—perhaps because of the combined influences of the majestic lake, the Native American traditions, and the temperate weather. In any case, while you stay here, plan on being enchanted by the downtown shops—which are laden with arts and antiques—and by the unassuming restaurants and taverns. Everyone is just a local here. You can blend in easily as you play golf at the recently expanded Polson Country Club, watch the ensemble work of the Port Polson Players at a theater in the clubhouse, or enjoy the Montana State Fiddlers Contest, which is held annually at the Polson High School on the fourth full weekend in July.

Accommodations

Hotels and Motels

Price Code

Keep in mind that some rates are based on availability. The average nightly rates for two adults at the hotels and motels listed in this section are indicated by a dollar sign ($) ranking in the following chart. Also, the hotels and motels in this chapter accept all or most major credit cards.

$	$25 to $49
$$	$50 to $75
$$$	$76 to $100
$$$$	More than $101

Bayview Inn $$
914 U.S. Highway 93 East, Polson
(406) 883–3120, (800) 735–6862

The Bayview Inn provides all the comforts of a modern motel. Built in 1984, it features queen-size beds, a lake view, and a view of the distant peaks of Glacier National Park and the Mission Mountains,

usually snow-covered well into summer. Some of the 25 rooms include a microwave and refrigerator, so if you will be staying in Polson for several days, make sure you request them. A continental breakfast is provided, and the motel is within walking distance of a full-service restaurant. Please inquire about the pet policy.

Cherry Hill Motel and Cabins $$
1810 U.S. Highway 93, Polson
(406) 883–2737

The Cherry Hill is indeed built on a hill once noted for its cherry orchards. The motel overlooks the highway and the Polson Country Club golf course as well as Flathead Lake. Owner Glen Lack says the Cherry Hill was built in 1943, but it was completely remodeled in 1996. Now it has the best of both worlds, the quaint roadside motel-look of the mid-century, and the amenities of the modern day. The motel is actually a series of buildings that each house a couple of rooms and two cabins. Accommodations range from two bedrooms with a kitchenette to just a simple room. In addition to the large, grassy yard, there is an outdoor hot tub for use in

Polson's city dock and boat launch look north and west across Flathead Lake.

Photo: courtesy of Polson Chamber of Commerce

summer, and gazebos and benches for a comfortable perch for a picnic with a great view. The Cherry Hill doesn't take American Express, but dogs are welcome!

Port Polson Inn $$$
502 U.S. Highway 93, Polson
(406) 883–5385, (800) 654–0682

Before KwaTaqNuk (see the Resorts and Guest Ranches section) came to town, this was the most popular lodging spot, and it's easy to see why. The rooms look out across the highway right onto Flathead Lake and the Mission Mountains beyond. There are 44 rooms in all, along with indoor and outdoor hot tubs, an indoor sauna, and an exercise facility. Although the outside of the motel has a 1960s look, the owners work to give the rooms a B&B feel, with flowers provided in the summertime and a continental breakfast offered. There are also a couple of theme rooms, so plan ahead and you can stay in either a cowboy-style room or one dedicated to Mickey Mouse.

Super 8 $$
Junction of Montana Highway 35 and U.S. Highway 93, Polson
(406) 883–6266, (800) 800–8000
www.super8.com

The Polson Super 8 offers all queen-size beds, a muffin and pastry for breakfast, bus/truck parking, and many nearby conveniences. The hotel recently expanded from 35 to 44 rooms, including an executive suite. It's across the street from the 4Bs restaurant, the Safeway grocery store, and a Wal-Mart. It's also within walking distance of the golf course and two lounge casinos. Pets are allowed with permission.

Resorts and Guest Ranches

Price Code

$	$70 to $120
$$	$121 to $170
$$$	$171 to $220
$$$$	More than $221

Best Western KwaTaqNuk Resort $$
303 U.S. Highway 93, Polson
(406) 883–3636, (800) 882–6363
www.kwataqnuk.com

This hotel and conference center is owned by the Confederated Salish and Kootenai Tribes and is one of the greatest success stories of the tribal economy. It is the jewel in Polson's resplendent tourism crown. The KwaTaqNuk Resort features 112 rooms, restaurant, convention facilities, lounge and casino, art gallery, gift shop, indoor and outdoor pools, indoor whirlpool, and a full-service marina. Unlike most of the hotels in Polson, KwaTaqNuk is built right on the lakeshore. The *KwaTaqNuk Princess* cruise boat sails from its docks during the summer months. The convention facilities can accommodate groups up to 300 people.

Mission Mountain Resort $
257 Fulkerson Lane, Polson
(406) 883–1883
www.polsonmtresort.com

This low-cost getaway is located on an 80-acre sanctuary just 3 miles from Polson in the Mission Mountains. You can see Flathead Lake and the rest of the valley from this scenic perch, but you will enjoy pine-scented air and mountain living. The accommodations are new and feature Western motifs. There are three guest rooms and two guest cabins (the biggest of them sleeps six), along with a hospitable lodge where you can kick off your boots and relax. Another specialty of the house is the Antique Emporium, featuring knickknacks of the olden days, along with local artwork and gifts. The grounds include miles and miles of nature trails. Pets are not allowed.

Sunny Shores Resort and Marina $
P.O. Box 99, Big Arm 59910
(406) 849–5622

If you are looking for a low-cost family vacation that is strong on lake fun, you might consider the Sunny Shores Resort & Marina, located about 11 miles north of Polson on U.S. 93. The resort is located right on the lakeshore and features cabins and rental trailers as well as RV hookups.

Polson's manicured Riverside Park provides convenient swimming access to Flathead Lake. Photo: courtesy of Polson Chamber of Commerce

A small grocery store on-site sells refreshments and picnic supplies, as well as outboard fuel and oil. They also stock lures, tackle, and bait. You can, of course, rent a boat from the marina, or just rent a boat slip if you have your own vessel. Evenings, when the boats pull in, you might enjoy a sing-along around a campfire or roasting some marshmallows. The resort specializes in family reunions, and you will need to get your reservations in early to make sure there is space available.

Bed-and-Breakfasts

Price Code

$	Less than $85
$$	$85 to $115
$$$	$116 to $150
$$$$	$151 and up

Swan Hill Bed & Breakfast $$
460 Kings Point Road, Polson
(406) 883–5292, (800) 537–9489

This bed-and-breakfast, located in a redwood home 5 miles from Polson, prides itself on being a mix of modern amenities and Western hospitality. The gourmet breakfasts change daily and are served in

your choice of the dining room or under an umbrella table on the deck overlooking the Mission Mountains and Flathead Lake. Of particular note is the presence of a large indoor pool and sauna. Because the facility is located on Flathead Lake, it is perfect for the guest who enjoys boating, windsurfing, fishing, or wildlife viewing. Three bedrooms have queen-size beds and one has twin beds, all with private baths, and there is a honeymoon suite with a Jacuzzi. Swan Hill is a nonsmoking and wheelchair-accessible facility. Children age 12 and older are welcome. No American Express.

Campgrounds and RV Parks

Price Code

$	$4.00 to $9.00
$$	$10 to $16
$$$	$17 to $23
$$$$	$24 and up

Eagle Nest RV Resort $$$
259 Eagle Nest Drive on Montana Highway 35
Polson
(406) 883–5904
www.eaglenestrv.com

Camp Tuffit

The word "rustic" could have been coined especially for Camp Tuffit, an old-style fishing resort on Lake Mary Ronan that's been run by the Thomas family for almost a century.

Lake Mary Ronan, named after the wife of an early Indian agent who stocked the lake with cutthroat trout in 1892, traditionally has had about the best fishing in Montana. Charlie Thomas came to Lake Mary Ronan in 1914 and established the fishing camp that's now run by his grandchildren and great-grandchildren. Generations of fishing enthusiasts have come to the camp, and they return year after year to the rough-hewn cabins built by Charlie and named whimsically for radio-show personalities, famous gold-mining camps, or celebrities. Mention Camp Tuffit around northwest Montana, and chances are someone will wax eloquent about the beauty of the spot, the quality of the fishing, and the memories of the good times shared with friends and family.

The camp looks much the same as it did in old photographs that show the cabins and the lodge in the early days. A quality of timelessness may be one of the enduring appeals of Camp Tuffit. The personality of the founder still can be seen throughout the camp—in the cabins he built, newspaper clippings about him, and his wife's old piano, where modern fishing enthusiasts still pound out a tune.

Charlie Thomas built wooden boats for fishing: At one time 65 hand-built boats plied the lake. The wooden boats have been retired now, replaced by aluminum craft, but some of Charlie's creations are still being used as flower planters. Charlie was quite a marketing agent, too. He built colorful cutouts of mannequins sitting like fishermen in flat-bottomed boats. The signs, which said FOLLOW THE BOATS TO CAMP TUFFIT, at one time were posted on roads in Nevada, Idaho, Washington, and Montana. The Thomases maintain handmade signs on the road to the camp, and some of the originals are now in a storage shop, along with some of Charlie's hand-built boats.

Camp Tuffit got its name after a Kalispell physician told Charlie to take his ailing wife out into the woods to "tough it" for the summer. When the doctor planned a fishing trip at the lake, Charlie wrote "Camp Tuffit" on a piece of cardboard to guide him to the spot, and the name stuck. Charlie started building boats and cabins and welcoming guests, who rented a boat for $1.00 a day.

The heart of Camp Tuffit is the main lodge, where guests come after a day of fishing to swap stories around the campfire and relive their adventures. The cabins have been maintained and modernized through the years, but they still keep the old rustic flavor that the guests seem to love. The camp has 33 cottages, 20 trailer hookups, and 18 privately owned permanent mobile homes. Guests return year after year and often reserve their favorite cabin by name.

Jerome Thomas, Charlie's son, returned to Camp Tuffit after World War II with his wife, Ruth, and the couple ran the camp with Charlie, then took over management. They're mostly retired now, and their sons and their wives have taken over the active management. It's definitely a family operation. Children, grandchildren, and great-grandchildren work at Camp Tuffit, or return to spend time with family there.

Jerome and Ruth spend winters down south now, while sons Gary and Mark and their wives are the active managers of the camp. But come summer, Jerome and Ruth are there to help as the family traditions continue summer after summer.

Though the future of fishing at Lake Mary Ronan has been clouded by a "bucket biologist" who illegally dumped perch in the lake a few years ago, Camp Tuffit retains its loyalty and its charm: a charming, rustic place where "progress" is suspended and the smiling presence of Charlie Thomas seems to linger as new generations tell fish stories around the campfire.

To reach Camp Tuffit, turn off U.S. 93 at Dayton, about 40 miles south of Kalispell, and travel about 6.5 miles on a paved road until you see one of Charlie's signs directing you to the camp. Or you can visit on the Web at www.camp-tuffit.com.

Eagle Nest RV Resort has seven acres of lawn and trees, offering spacious, shady, quiet campsites. There are 6 tent spaces and 54 RV spaces with full hookups, 50-amp service, and roomy pull-throughs. The facility, which is near Polson's 27-hole public golf course, was built in 1993 and includes free showers, a rec room, laundry, gift store, a horseshoe pit, a playground, and lots, lots more. Eagle Nest is open from April 15 through October 15 and features daily, weekly, monthly, and seasonal rates. No American Express.

Flathead Lake State Park $
490 North Meridian Road, Kalispell
(406) 752–5501

The park consists of six scenic units bordering Flathead Lake, two of which are within 15 miles of Polson. With the exception of Wild Horse Island, all units feature camping, fishing, boating, and swimming. Finley Point is on the east shore of Flathead Lake on Montana 35 and has 4 tent sites and 12 RV sites. It is open only during the summer, and the use fee is $15. Big Arm is 14 miles north of Polson on U.S. 93. At this facility, yurt rental is available year-round, partially furnished, at $39 per night in summer or $25 per night in winter. The camping fee in season is $12. All fees were correct as this went to press, but they will soon be revised.

Paradise Pines Resort $$$
6913 East Shore Route (Montana Route 35)
Polson
(406) 887–2537

Open spring through fall, Paradise Pines Resort is located 7 miles north of Polson on Montana 35. The main building, which dates from 1930, was at one time a dairy barn. Today it is the centerpiece of a lovely 40-acre RV park that also has a restaurant and lounge. From the deck you have a great view of the Mission Mountains. There are lots of added attractions, too, everything from a game arcade to an 18-hole miniature golf course. In summer you can expect to enjoy live music on the outdoor stage, free hayrides, and more. There is also a 1948 Great Northern caboose on the property. There are 60 RV sites and 40 tent sites. Pets are allowed, and there are free showers and a coin laundry. If you want to rough it, a rental tepee is available nightly.

Polson/Flathead Lake KOA $$$
200 Irvine Flats Road, Polson
(406) 883–2151, (800) KOA–2130

This campground, with its national KOA affiliation, can be counted on for a quality experience. The grounds are well kept, and there is a tenting area with 30 tent sites that are well shaded and divided by tall honeysuckle bushes. The 54 pull-through RV sites are hard-surfaced and can handle large units. An extra plus is that there are 12 cabins at the campground that have some of the features of a hotel at an economical price. The single-room cabins are $36 to $52, and there is a cottage with a bathroom, a kitchen, and a hot tub for $125 to $160. In addition to a view of the mountains and lake, there is a store, coin laundry, free showers, modem dataport, a game room, pool, spa, and barbecue grills. The facility, which is located about a half mile north of Polson on U.S. 93, is open from mid-April to mid-October. No American Express.

Restaurants

Price Code

For two people, meal exclusive of beverages, tip, and tax.

$	$10 to $19
$$	$20 to $27
$$$	$28 to $35
$$$$	$36 and more

Family-Friendly Dining

Charlie Wong's $
110 Main Street, Polson
(406) 883–9402

This is Polson's version of a popular Kalispell restaurant. The menu is mostly Asian food, but you will find that they have a couple of American entrees for the picky eater. Among the most popular specialties are the kung pao chicken, which is best if ordered hot but will still do nicely even in the mild and medium forms, and the wonton soup, which is filled with pork, wontons, fried wontons, and greens. Two people can eat quite comfortably on one order of the wonton noodle soup ($4.95), which adds noodles to the mix and goes in a much larger bowl. The Polson version of Charlie Wong's definitely boasts the best view of the three restaurants in the chain (the third is in Columbia Falls): Located in the Salish building next to the bridge over the Flathead River, the restaurant looks out over Flathead Lake and the Mission Mountains.

The Driftwood Café $
1202 Second Avenue East, Polson
(406) 883–2558

Breakfast is served all day at the Driftwood, which is a longtime local favorite. There's nothing fancy at this cafe, but they usually get it right, and there are lots of choices on the menu. For breakfast, don't overlook the Hungry Man Special, which offers three eggs, three pieces of toast, hash browns, and choice of six sticks of bacon, six ounces of ham, or sausage links for just $6.95. There are also a variety of omelettes and a kid's menu. For lunch and dinner, don't overlook the burgers, which are available with buffalo meat for just $1.00 extra. Buffalo steaks and buffalo stews are specialties of the house.

4Bs Restaurant $
Junction of Montana Highway 35 and U.S. Highway 93, Polson
(406) 883–6180

The 4Bs restaurants are a Montana tradition. The first one started in Missoula many years ago, and now they are in almost every major city in Montana, as well as one in New Mexico. The specialty here is friendly service, fast food (without being "fast food"), and a family-oriented setting. The children's menu is generous to a fault, with lots of selections—everything from hamburgers to pizza—and a price that can't be beat ($1.35 for a grilled cheese sandwich with fries and Jello). The grown-ups eat almost as cheaply, with a tasty prime rib special selling for just $6.95, including choice of potato or rice, soup or salad, and a roll. The 4Bs is Polson's only restaurant open 24 hours a day.

Fine Dining

The Pemmican $$$
303 U.S. Highway 93, Polson
(406) 883–3636, (800) 882–6363

The restaurant at the Best Western Kwa-TaqNuk Resort is one of your best bets for fine dining in Polson—whether it's breakfast, lunch, or dinner. There's prime rib every night, as well as a variety of beef and seafood selections. Friday night you can enjoy a spectacular seafood buffet, and in the summer the best seats are on the outdoor deck right above Flathead Lake and the resort's marina. Also during the summer you may enjoy the Sunday brunch. Hotel guests can take advantage of the restaurant through a room-service menu.

Rancho Deluxe $$$
602 Sixth Street West, Polson
(406) 883–2300

This restaurant is proof that you can't just dine at spots on the highway and Main Street and expect to find the best a town has to offer. To reach Rancho Deluxe, turn off U.S. 93 at Main Street and drive up to Sixth Avenue, then hang a right and drive 6 blocks to Sixth Street West right at the edge of the Flathead River. The building looks more like a bowling alley on the outside, but this is a grand supper club, featuring a gourmet menu, with everything from filet mignon at $21.95 to a grain and vegetable "steak" made out of bulgur wheat, zucchini, sun-dried tomatoes, basil, and pine nuts for $12.95. There is also a light menu with burgers, prime rib sandwiches, and a yellow-fin tuna sandwich. Desserts are irresistible and include Key Lime pie, rich chocolatey mud pie, and our favorite—pecan brittle sundae. The wine list has everything up to and including Dom Perignon.

Nightlife

Best Western KwaTaqNuk Resort
303 U.S. Highway 93, Polson
(406) 883-3636, (800) 882-6363

The casino in KwaTaqNuk is a bit closer to big-time gambling than most of the casinos in Montana. That's because the Confederated Salish and Kootenai tribes own the facility, and the tribes negotiated an agreement with the state of Montana that allows more gaming machines in KwaTaqNuk than usual. There are more than 40 machines in the casino/lounge, and that means there is always something to do for adults at the resort. The casino is open 24 hours a day. There's also a lounge overlooking Flathead Lake, with deck seating in the summer.

Diamond Horseshoe Lounge and Supper Club
820 Shoreline Drive, Polson
(406) 883-2048

The Diamond Horseshoe has it all, a popular bar with gaming machines, occasional live entertainment, and a great view of Flathead Lake, along with a restaurant that serves food for all tastes. You can stop in here for a quick drink or a long rest

> ## Insiders' Tip
> Mountain streams may look beautiful and clean, and they sometimes are, but they can also carry giardia, a nasty parasite that will give you untold intestinal distress. Always boil water for at least a minute before drinking it, or use a filter approved for giardia.

stop. On Monday night or Sunday afternoon, you'll find the televisions tuned to the football channels, and there is always plenty of sports talk. The bands here play anything from country music to current rock sounds.

Shopping

Alpine Product Design
306 Main Street, Polson
(406) 883-3500

This is a one-of-a-kind store. You can't miss if you want to find a surprising made-in-Montana gift for the folks back home, but these are pricey gifts. There is a wide range of tepees available for several hundred dollars each, including the lodgepole frames and the outer canvas. Walk into the showroom and you will see everything from a full-size tepee that reaches to the ceiling to a child's size tepee that is perfect for a backyard all the way down to a more economical bird-feeder tepee that's just a foot tall. A map on the wall shows locations across the United States where children's tepees have been shipped, and Alpine does most of its business by mail order, so remember to pick up a catalog while you are in the store. If a tepee is too big for your yard, you might consider a windsock, another specialty item produced by Alpine.

First Resort
219 Main Street, Polson
(406) 883–2129

This shop is worth a visit, partly because it offers a full range of clothing for men and women, but perhaps even more so because of its unusual design. The shop was formerly known as the Flagship, and it retains the nautical design that was instituted then. There's a captain's wheel on the entryway, and inside the seagoing motif continues, with changing rooms done up as ship's cabins and the walls decorated with barrels, portholes, and gangplanks. In between you'll find Pendletons and other brand names, along with a healthy helping of sale merchandise.

Three Dog Down Outlet
61545 U.S. Highway 93 North, Polson
(406) 883–3696, (800) 364–3696
www.threedogdown.com

This little store just across the Flathead River from downtown Polson is a national phenomenon. It's been written up in *Glamour* magazine, *Entrepreneur* magazine, the *Chicago Tribune*, and many other national publications, including the travel magazines published by Delta and American Airlines. Owner Bob Ricketts, a former opera singer, can only be considered a world-class eccentric, and his bizarre vision of an all-down outlet store in Polson, Montana, has proved to be something the world WAS ready for. The store buys wholesale directly from many of the world's top down manufacturers, and there are also products manufactured right in Polson. Custom orders such as pillows, comforters, and even medical bedding are handled on a regular basis. The store's name, by the way, comes from the same Inuit folk saying that gave the name to the band Three Dog Night. It refers to the Inuit tradition of describing the temperature on a cold night by how many dogs you need to sleep with to stay warm.

Wild-Side Chocolates and Gifts
6 Second Avenue East, Polson
(406) 883–1722

Owner Pattye Burns opened this small shop just a few years ago, but it's worth a stop for anyone who's in the market for a mouth-watering treat, and who isn't? The chocolates come in a variety of shapes and sizes, including the Flathead Monster and the Grizzly Paw. There are also a variety of huckleberry products as well as preserves and popular treats such as Jelly Belly beans. On several walls there are also Montana-made gift items, including jewelry and novelties. And don't be confused by the address: U.S. 93 becomes Second Avenue East for several blocks in downtown Polson.

The Blackfeet Reservation:

East Glacier, Browning, and St. Mary

Area Overview
Accommodations
Restaurants
Shopping

Area Overview

The Blackfeet Reservation is home to the 14,000 enrolled members of the Blackfeet Tribe and set upon beautiful, open prairie where the Blackfeet hunted buffalo for thousands of years. From every vantage point you can see the peaks of what the Blackfeet call the Backbone of the World—the Continental Divide. The mountains have always influenced the Blackfeet, who recognize them as sacred places. In more practical terms, the mountains create the wind and weather that sweep across the northern plains and touch every living thing on them.

The towns of East Glacier, Browning, and St. Mary will probably be the focus for most visitors' stay, and listings in each category of service are arranged in that order.

East Glacier is home to many small businesses, shops, and restaurants, and you'll enjoy walking about the little town located exactly where the mountains meet the prairie. Or you might choose to hike. The Two Medicine subdistrict of Glacier National Park is only an 11-mile drive away, with its web of trails leading to places such as Dawson Pass, Cobalt Lake, Twin Falls, or Old Man Lake. Glacier Park Boat Company also offers boat tours on Two Medicine Lake. The Lubec and Autumn Creek Trails begin along U.S. Highway 2 west of East Glacier and will lead you along the aspen-covered foothills. Be sure to check with a ranger station for current trail conditions.

Browning is the center of the reservation, and you'll find all basic services here. It's also the home of the Museum of the Plains Indian (see the Attractions chapter). One excellent time to visit Browning is the weekend after the Fourth of July—North American Indian Days. This large powwow draws not only Native Americans from tribes across the west but also from Canada and as far away as Florida. The combination of food, dancing, music, native dress, and the mix of people from across the continent create a remarkable event. Or tour the reservation with a Blackfeet guide—Sun Tours will be pleased to share Blackfeet history and culture through the local perspective with you.

St. Mary is a tiny community that grows significantly in the summer season. It's located right at the eastern end of Going-to-the-Sun Road, and every square foot of this little town has a magnificent view of the mountains. And you'll have access to the whole east side of Glacier National Park without too much of a drive—Many Glacier is 40 minutes away, Two Medicine 45 minutes away, Cut Bank 20 minutes away—not to mention Going-to-the-Sun Road. St. Mary has a huge array of services available in the summer but very few in winter—please read descriptions carefully if you're planning to travel in fall, winter, or spring, as many businesses close down altogether.

The Blackfeet Tribe does require a $10 Conservation and Recreation Use Permit for nonmembers of the tribe who wish to recreate on the reservation, whether that be hiking, mountain biking, or otherwise exploring off the paved roads. The permit can be purchased at local businesses, where you can also purchase the tribal fishing license. For more information, please call Blackfeet Fish and Wildlife at (406) 338-7207. Take the time to explore—the Blackfeet Reservation has a beauty all its own.

Accommodations

Price Code

Keep in mind that some rates are based on availability. The average nightly rates for two adults at the hotels and motels listed in this section are indicated by a dollar sign ($) ranking in the following chart. Also, the hotels and motels in this chapter accept all or most major credit cards. Please note: In addition to the 4 percent state accommodation tax, all lodgings on the Blackfeet Reservation must collect an additional tribal accommodation tax of 6 percent.

$	Less than $85
$$	$86 to $115
$$$	$116 to $150
$$$$	More than $150

Hotels and Motels

The Whistling Swan Motel $
P.O. Box 318, 314 U.S. Highway 2
East Glacier 59434
(406) 226–4412
www.whistlingswanmotel.com

The Whistling Swan is quite charming, tidy, and clean. One step into the lobby and you'll start to absorb the unrushed, comfortable feeling that pervades this little motel. Each of the eight rooms has color cable TV, and your night's lodging includes free coffee the next morning at the Two Medicine Grill just down the street.

The Whistling Swan has the great merit of being open all year. If you've ever been caught in a blizzard, you'll appreciate how nice it is to have a good spot to wait out the weather. Summer rates are $44 per night for single rooms and $59.40 for doubles; please inquire about reduced winter rates.

East Glacier Motel and Cabins $
P.O. Box 93, 1107 Montana Highway 49
East Glacier Park 59434
(406) 226–5593
www.eastglacier.com

This little spot offers two fairly different lodging experiences. The six spacious new motel units include two queen-size or double beds, a full-size refrigerator, microwave, hot plate, sink, and table service for four, and are open year-round. They run from $65 to $75 plus tax per night for two people during the spring, summer, and fall; during winter they rent for $55 to $65, providing a nice option for people who would like to be mostly self-sufficient for a winter visit to East Glacier.

Eleven cozy cabins are also available to rent during the spring, summer, and fall. These extremely cute little buildings (see the photo on the Web site), with window boxes overflowing with flowers, have been recently renovated to include new showers and beds. Kitchenettes include a small refrigerator, hot plate, sink, and table service for four. Cabins have one or two bedrooms and will accommodate two to five people. Rates run from $30 to $70 plus tax per night.

The East Glacier Motel and Cabins are within walking distance of several restaurants, car rentals, and other shops. Most units have color TVs, and some nonsmoking units are available. A pleasant yard out front is a great spot to picnic or hold a family get-together.

Mountain Pine Motel $
Montana Highway 49, East Glacier Park
(406) 226–4403

The Mountain Pine Motel offers 25 units (some have two bedrooms), most with queen-size beds, color TVs, and tub/ shower combinations. It's conveniently located within walking distance of about everything in East Glacier, including shops, restaurants, and car rentals. Rooms run from $50 to $70 plus tax per night for two people between June 15 and September 15; inquire for lower rates between May 1 and June 15 and between September 15 and October 1, when the motel closes until spring.

Guest Ranches, Resorts, and Lodges

Glacier Park Lodge $$$
East Glacier Park
(406) 892–2525
www.glacierparkinc.com

Glacier Park Lodge, the first lodge built by the Great Northern Railway, continues to be the unofficial eastern gateway to Glacier National Park. Although it is located outside the borders of the park, the peaks rise behind it in an impressive backdrop. Lovely, well-tended flower gardens line the walk as you approach the historic building. Walking through the lodge doors, you'll be impressed by the huge logs that support the lobby ceiling: immense Douglas firs, their bark still on, imported from the Pacific Northwest to grace this hall. Neighboring Blackfeet Indians referred to the building as the "Big Tree Lodge."

In contrast with its historic past, Glacier Park Lodge also offers modern amenities in addition to its 163 rooms. The hotel features a heated swimming pool, a nine-hole golf course, a nine-hole pitch 'n' putt golf course, a gift shop, cocktail lounge (with big-screen TV), and the Great Northern Steak and Rib House (see Restaurants). The information desk will be happy to set you up with a bus tour or hayride.

Glacier Park Lodge has a longer season than some other GPI facilities, generally from late May to late September. Rooms range in price from $125 to $399 per night for two people.

Wagner's Duck Lake Lodge $
P.O. Box 218, Duck Lake Road, Babb 59411
(406) 338–5770

If you're looking for accommodations a little more off the beaten path, consider Wagner's Duck Lake Lodge. Wagner's caters to anglers who frequent nearby Duck Lake, which is known for its excellent fishing. The lodge also offers a restaurant, rooms to rent, RV spaces, and tenting on acres of beautiful land.

The lodge contains nine bedrooms that share two common bathrooms. Double-occupancy rooms rent for $70 per night in the summer and $50 per night in the winter. Please inquire about rooms for three or four. The unpretentious living room downstairs showcases a collection of game trophies, and the dining room is open each night, serving chicken, steak, and fish specials. And if you're overdue for some really good pizza, here's one place to get it.

Ten RV sites have full hookups, available for $18.50 per night. And, as Bob Wagner puts it, there are acres of dry camping. Those who set up closer to the lodge can use its bathrooms and showers; for those who head farther out, portable toilets are located around the property. Tent sites cost $10 per night. Pets are allowed.

St. Mary Lodge and Cabins $$–$$$$
St. Mary
(406) 732–4431 (summer), (800) 368–3689
www.glcpark.com

St. Mary Lodge is located right at the eastern end of Going-to-the-Sun Road, just outside Glacier National Park. This complex of guest facilities includes cabins, lodge rooms, and luxury cottages as well as several eating establishments, an outdoor store, gift shop, grocery, and gas station. Most services are open from mid-May to early October.

Lodge rooms are standard motel-style accommodations with queen-size beds, private bath, and air-conditioning; they run approximately $105 per night for two people. Glacier Cabins have a living area with breakfast table, microwave, and small refrigerator; they have a queen-size bed in an adjacent sleeping area and a separate bedroom with two single beds and a private bathroom. These cozy cabins are newly remodeled and cost about $150 per night for two people.

St. Mary Lodge also operates three specialty cabins: the Sun Cabin (sleeps four), the Kootenai Cabin (sleeps five), and the Guest House (sleeps six). These larger cabins feature a variety of amenities, including full kitchens and gas barbecues. Rates vary from $165 to $225; please inquire for more details.

The Pinnacle Cottages are the latest addition to the lodge facility. The six luxury cottages are located on a bluff above

The Imposing Chief Mountain

If you drive between St. Mary and Waterton Lakes National Park in Canada, or come in to Babb over the Duck Lake Road from Browning, you can't help but notice a looming, flat-topped peak that seems to lead the other mountains out onto the prairie near the border: Chief Mountain. Chief Mountain has a long history as a significant spiritual site. For thousands of years the Blackfeet have held sacred ceremonies here, and they continue to do so today. The Chief Mountain Highway—Montana Highway 17—affords many striking views of this imposing peak. A few miles northwest of Babb, pull off the road at the scenic overlook to enjoy the panorama of both mountains and prairie.

Chief Mountain is recognizable from miles away. Photo: courtesy of Glacier National Park

the town of St. Mary, offering spectacular views of St. Mary Lake and Glacier National Park. Each cabin has two bedrooms, a complete kitchen, full bath with tub, spacious living room with fireplace, and a private deck with barbecue grill. A three-night minimum stay is required.

The Lodge itself houses the Snowgoose Grille (see Restaurants), Mountain Lounge (with satellite TV), and an extensive gift shop offering everything from teddy bears to Native American jewelry to huckleberry products and homemade fudge. To receive information via post during the winter, please write to St. Mary Lodge, P.O. Box 1808, Sun Valley, ID 83353.

Campgrounds and RV Parks

St. Mary KOA $
St. Mary
(406) 732–4122, (800) 562–1504
www.goglacier.com

St. Mary KOA is on the shores of the St. Mary River and Lower St. Mary Lake, just moments from the town of St. Mary and Going-to-the-Sun Road. It could probably call itself a resort—this KOA offers not only tent sites, a group tent site, RV sites, and "kamping kabins and kottages," but also canoe, paddleboat, and mountain bike rentals, a playground and game room, an evening barbecue, outdoor hot tubs, a grocery store and gift shop, and U-Save car rentals (perfect for those with RVs too long to travel Going-to-the-Sun Road), and, of course, beautiful views of the mountains, river, and lake.

St. Mary KOA is open from May to September. Tent sites are $21.95 per night. RV sites range from no hookup for $23.95, electric hookup for $25.95, water and electric for $29.95, to full hookup for $38.95. "Kamping kabins" range in price from $51.95 to $66.95; these sleeping cabins have electricity and heat but no running water or bath. Bring your own bedding; water is available nearby, and each cabin has its own picnic table and grill. "Kamping kottages" run $149.95 per night, and include a bath, shower, and fully equipped kitchen. Prices are based on two-person occupancy; there is a $5.95 fee for each additional adult. Kids and pets are welcome to stay free of charge. Off-peak season prices are slightly lower. Reservations are highly recommended for the "kamping kottages" in particular.

Johnson's RV Park and Campground $
HC 72-10, Star Route, St. Mary 59417
(406) 732-4207

Red Eagle Motel $
P.O. Box 896, Browning 59417
(406) 732-4453
www.johnsonsofstmary.com

The Johnson family has quite a few enterprises going in St. Mary—all located with a view overlooking the St. Mary Lakes and the mountains. But you'll be glad for the hill and trees that shelter the campground from the east-side wind . . . and the grassy sites, picnic tables, and fire rings make for a very pleasant stay.

All RV sites are pull-throughs. Sites without hookups are $20 per night. The 40 sites with electricity and water are $25 per night, and the 42 full hookups are $27.50 per night. Please inquire about monthly rates. Johnson's also has 50 tent spaces that cost $16 per night. The campground has a covered pavilion, hot showers, a laundry, and a store.

If not everyone in your party is interested in camping, the Red Eagle Motel is right next door. The 22 modern units have the same big view as the campground.

And More . . .

Backpacker's Inn $
P.O. Box 94, 29 Dawson Avenue
East Glacier Park 59434
(406) 226-9392

For those backpacking or otherwise traveling light and low-budget, the Backpacker's Inn provides simple, comfortable lodging just minutes from U.S. Highway 2 and the East Glacier Amtrak station. The inn has three dormitory rooms (one men's, one women's, one coed) that open onto a quiet, grassy fenced yard that offers a pleasant place to relax. Cost per person per night is $10.60; a sleeping bag and pillow can be rented for $1.00 for the duration of your stay. Reservations are recommended and must be confirmed 24 hours in advance of your arrival. The Backpacker's Inn operates from May 1 to September 30.

The Backpacker's Inn is operated by Serrano's, right next door—so there's good Mexican food in the neighborhood, too! For more information during the winter months, when the East Glacier Serrano's is closed, please call the Whitefish restaurant at (406) 862-5600.

The Brown House $
East Glacier Park
(406) 226-9385
www.members.aol.com/gnpinfo/
Brownhouse.html

The Brown House, which is also an art studio featuring fine ceramics, photographs, and paintings, offers two lovely rooms to rent. Each has its own entrance and full bathroom; one has a queen-size and twin bed, the other a double and twin. Both rooms are elegantly and comfortably appointed (the double bed is an antique four-poster). One is a "penthouse"—the second story in East Glacier is enough height to give you some view of the mountains as well as of the town! The rooms do not have phones but do have television. Cost per night is $60.00 plus tax for double occupancy; a third person is $5.00 more.

The Brown House is located just south of U.S. Highway 2 as it passes through East Glacier. Please call for reservations and specific directions. The Brown House is open for lodging from June through September.

Brownie's Hostel $
P.O. Box 229, 1020 Montana Highway 49
East Glacier Park 59434
(406) 226-4426
www.members.aol.com/gnpinfo/
Brownies.html

Brownie's Hostel offers low-cost, basic lodging for those traveling through the

Massacre on the Marias

If the great Indian battle of the West fought by the U.S. Army was the Battle of the Little Bighorn, perhaps a lesser known but more typical event was the Massacre on the Marias. This encounter between the U.S. Army and a band of Pikuni Blackfeet occurred in the winter of 1870; it took a long time for the truth about the event to make its way to Washington. In many ways its tale of revenge, mistakes, and alcohol is all too familiar in this era, as was their result. The following account is based on James Welch's *Killing Custer* (1994).

It's hard to say where such stories begin, but let's start this one in 1847. A trader for the American Fur Company, Malcolm Clarke, married a Pikuni, Cutting-off-head Woman. She was a member of the Many Chiefs band, as was her cousin, Owl Child. This band was led by Mountain Chief, a leader who had resisted the incursion of whites into Blackfeet territory. With this union, Clarke secured his position as a trader among the Blackfeet and gained the respect of the tribal elders to whom he was now related by marriage. Sometime later, Clarke retired from trading and settled on a ranch on Prickly Pear Creek, north of Helena. He was able to live quite comfortably and was well established in the Helena community.

Owl Child, previous to Clarke's marriage to his cousin, had become something of an outcast from the Many Chiefs band. He'd been involved in a killing for which he was ostracized, and although he spent some time with the band, he often roamed, growing bitter toward both the whites and his own tribe. But in 1867 he, with some other of Cutting-off-head Woman's relatives, visited the ranch. During the night, Owl Child's horses were stolen. He blamed Clarke and in turn stole some of Clarke's horses.

Clarke and his son Horace soon pursued the stolen horses to Mountain Chief's camp, where they found Owl Child. "Horace struck Owl Child with a whip and called him a dog. Clarke called him an old woman, and the men left with their horses. Now, it is not good to insult and beat a young Pikuni in front of his people. Such an action requires revenge . . . ." (Welch, p. 27). On August 17, 1869, Owl Child and 25 young warriors attacked the Clarke ranch. They left Clarke dead and Horace seriously wounded.

In an area already tense with hostilities, this was the last straw for the whites. The most powerful men in Helena demanded total annihilation of the "savages." They demanded the army. Initially Gen. Philip H. Sheridan—the first to say "the only good Indian is a dead Indian"—delayed, saying he didn't have enough forces to attempt an attack against the Blackfeet. But at the same time he had a plan: a new tactic, tried in 1868 when Indians were attacked unprepared in their winter camp on the Washita River. No longer was war confined to warriors: women, children, and old men were driven from their tents and gunned down in the open.

On New Year's Day, 1870, Gen. Alfred Sully met with four Blackfeet peace chiefs: Heavy Runner, Little Wolf, Big Lake, and Grey Eyes. He wanted to speak with Mountain Chief, who did not show up. Nevertheless Sully informed the others that to avoid war, they must deliver the dead bodies of Owl Chief and his party—within two weeks. The chiefs agreed, knowing they were incapable of meeting this demand; and Sully also recognized the futility of the agreement. He returned to Sheridan.

When the two weeks were up, Sheridan's plan went into effect. Scouts reported that Mountain Chief's band was wintering on the Marias River. Colonel E. M. Baker, stationed at Fort Shaw on the Sun River, was ordered to attack the band. Sheridan's telegraph read, "If the lives and property of the citizens of Montana can best be protected by striking Mountain Chief's band, I want them struck. Tell Baker to strike them hard" (Welch, p. 30).

Just before dawn on January 23, 1870, the army soldiers were in place above the Indian camp. One of Baker's scouts, a half-white, half-Pikuni named Joe Kipp, suddenly recognized by the designs on the tepees that this was not Mountain Chief's camp, it was Heavy Runner's. Clearly Mountain Chief had gotten word of the army's intentions and had cleared out; Heavy Runner's band had moved into the desirable location. Scouts and troops from the expedition alike, as well as Horace Clarke, who accompanied the expedition, later stated that Colonel Baker was drunk at the time of the attack—perhaps not an uncommon state for those leading hard and dreary lives. But when Kipp informed him that this was the wrong band of Blackfeet, Baker replied, "That makes no difference, one band or another of them; they are all Piegans [Pikunis] and we will attack them." He then threatened to have Kipp shot if the scout moved from the spot.

When the gunfire began, Heavy Runner ran from his lodge, waving a piece of paper—the safe conduct signed by General Sully at the New Year's Day meeting. He was shot dead. Most able-bodied men were out hunting, and when, at the end, 173 had been killed, most of them were women, children, and the elderly, still in their lodges. Many of them were totally helpless—smallpox had hit the band that same winter, too. Ironically, at the same time Owl Child was dying of the disease in Mountain Chief's camp some 17 miles away.

The Blackfeet never took up arms against the United States again.

East Glacier area. This two-story log building has 25 beds (linens provided), a kitchen, laundry, baggage storage, parking, and bike rentals. It's located just a bit over a mile from U.S. Highway 2, and the hostel will pick up guests from the Amtrak station by arrangement. Private rooms are also available. A bakery and convenience store operate in the first floor. Brownie's is an AYH hostel.

Brownie's is open from early May to mid-October, weather permitting. Lodging is $12 per person per night; reservations are essential between July 4 and August 15. Groups are welcome but must make reservations. During the off-season, reservations are accepted by mail.

Jacobson's Cottages $
P.O. Box 216, East Glacier Park 59434
(406) 226–4422, (888) 226–4422

Twelve immaculately clean, modern cottages set among the pines and aspens of East Glacier Park . . . that's Jacobson's. Each cottage is carpeted and all have cable television, electric heat, and tub/shower combinations; one includes a fully equipped kitchen ("everything but the groceries"). Prices run from $55 to $75 per night plus tax; an additional charge of $4.00 per person above the age of six is also made. Several restaurants are within walking distance.

Open from May 1 to October 1, Jacobson's is located on Montana Highway 49 on the north side of East Glacier. Look for the two red A-frame office buildings—and the beautiful borders of flowers—you won't miss it.

Jon's House $$–$$$
East Glacier, inquire at the Mountain Pine Motel, Highway 49, East Glacier Park
(406) 226–4403

Have you always wished for a vacation home in the mountains? Jon's House might be the place. This privately owned home in East Glacier is rented out by the night from June 1 through Labor Day. Just 9 years old, its spacious living room has a wonderful view of the mountains of Glacier. It's within walking distance of "downtown" East Glacier and the Glacier Park Lodge and golf course. And it sleeps up to eight: There's a master bedroom with queen-size bed and private bath downstairs, four twin beds in the bedrooms and loft upstairs, and a queen-size sleeper sofa in the living room.

Jon's House also has a living-room fireplace, a fully equipped kitchen with service for eight, telephone, washer and dryer, a barbecue, and even a Ping-Pong table. In addition to the master bath, there are full bathrooms upstairs and down. Jon's House rents for $185 per night; please contact the Mountain Pine Motel at the number above. Be sure to make reservations early, especially for big groups—Jon's House is booking quickly.

Ye Olde House $
East Glacier, inquire at the Mountain Pine Motel, Highway 49, East Glacier Park
(406) 226–4403

Ye Olde House is located in the woods just off Montana Highway 49 in East Glacier. This nice, clean, older house can be your home away from home—and at very reasonable rates. Each of the two bedrooms has a queen-size bed, and one also includes a twin. Downstairs the queen-size sleeper sofa will accommodate two more, making room for a total of seven people. Two full baths, your own kitchen, and a living room will give you all the privacy of having your own place.

Ye Olde House rents for $80.00 per night for two people, plus $5.00 for each additional person. Please contact the Mountain Pine Motel at the number above for more information.

Rising Wolf Ranch $$$–$$$$
907 Clark Drive, East Glacier Park
(800) 654–3704

The Rising Wolf Ranch sits right at the edge of East Glacier. This large house borders Midvale Creek and offers a huge mountain panorama: Mt. Henry, Dancing Lady, Bison, Bearhead, and Calf Robe Mountains fill the western horizon. Even if you never leave the house, you'll have seen the mountains.

Two living areas are available to rent. Downstairs is a fully furnished one-bedroom, one-bath apartment. The living-room sofa is a sleeper that accommodates two, for a maximum occupancy of four. It rents for $125 per night with a three-night minimum stay during the summer.

Upstairs, living is deluxe. A master bedroom with bath, guest bedroom with bath, and a loft that sleeps four accommodate a maximum of eight people. You'll have your own gourmet kitchen, fireplaces in both the living room and master bedroom, and vaulted ceilings. Or step out onto the deck to soak up more of that mountain light! A washer and dryer are supplied. Upstairs rents for $170 per night, with a three-night minimum stay. For more information, please inquire at the phone number above.

Restaurants

Price Code

For two people, meal exclusive of beverages, tip, and tax.

$	$10 to $20
$$	$21 to $30
$$$	$31 to $50
$$$$	More than $50

The Restaurant Thimbleberry $–$$
Montana Highway 49
East Glacier Park
(406) 226–5523

"Thimbleberry"? Thimbleberries are a lot like raspberries—a little berry that practically falls into your hand when it's ripe. They grow throughout the woods in the Glacier area and make great jam . . .

The Restaurant Thimbleberry is as sweet and small as its namesake, and it, too, is a summer delight. The restaurant is open for breakfast, lunch, and dinner from Mother's Day through mid-September, and is known especially for its great omelets, homemade soup and chili, and frybread. Many lunch and dinner selections come with a side of corn on the cob—a pleasant change from the usual chips or potatoes (though those can be ordered, too).

North American Indian Days bring in traditional dancers from around the country to compete for prizes in this annual powwow. Photo: Donnie Sexton, courtesy of Travel Montana

Box lunches can be ordered "to go" with a one-hour notice. They include a sandwich, fruit, snack crackers, and a "baked goodie," and cost about $6.00.

And here's something to consider: the East Glacier Huckleberry Pie war! It's the Restaurant Thimbleberry vs. the Whistlestop (see below): who makes the best? You'll just have to try both, and cast your vote!

Two Medicine Grill $
314 U.S. Highway 2, East Glacier Park
(406) 226–5572
www.whistlingswanmotel.com

The Two Medicine Grill isn't just a restaurant, it's the social hub of East Glacier. The counter in front and the seven or so tables in back are the meeting place for everyone in town, especially during the winter months when this is the only restaurant open. Breakfast, lunch, and dinner are all reasonably priced. Cinnamon rolls, soups, and chili are homemade—and be sure to check out the buffalo burgers and sour-cream-and-chive French fries. The Two Medicine Grill is open from 6:30 A.M. to 7:00 P.M., seven days a week. The Web site carries the diner's menus, so you can start thinking now about what you're going to order!

Whistlestop Cafe $–$$
Montana Highway 49, East Glacier Park

Breakfast at the Whistlestop is going to be tough, because you'll have to choose between stuffed French toast, Caramel Apple French toast, Huckleberry French toast, the omelet menu—and the marvelous cream puffs, napoleons, eclairs, and other luscious pastries on display.

Or perhaps you'll just have to come back for the dinner menu, which includes barbecue chicken and ribs, stuffed potatoes, and sandwiches, as well as the huckleberry pie.

The Whistlestop is open from June 1 to mid-September, for breakfast, lunch, and dinner. Its covered outdoor porch is a pleasant spot to stop for an afternoon refreshment as well.

Glacier Village Restaurant and Buzz's Brew Station $
304 Montana Highway 2 East
East Glacier Park
(406) 226–4464

The in-house bakery, gourmet desserts, and espresso will probably be the big draw to the Glacier Village Restaurant, but breakfast, lunch, and dinner are good reasons to stop, too. The menu features a variety of hot sandwiches, salads, and pastas, and includes kids' selections. Bag lunches can be ordered to go for about $6.00. Like many East Glacier businesses, this restaurant is open only during the summer months.

Great Northern Steak and Rib House $$
Glacier Park Lodge, East Glacier Park
(406) 226–9311 (summer only)

A western theme dominates the Great Northern, and its menu features beef, chicken, barbecued ribs, and fish entrees. The restaurant offers a full buffet for breakfast, a luncheon carvery, and for dinner either a western buffet or a la carte options. Breakfast runs from 6:30 to 9:30 A.M., lunch from 11:30 A.M. to 2:00 P.M., and dinner from 5:00 to 9:30 P.M.

Serrano's $
29 Dawson, East Glacier Park
(406) 226–9392

This, the original Serrano's, occupies a historic log house that's been refitted to serve as one of East Glacier's favorite restaurants. Somehow the mix of western log building and Mexican restaurant works out just right—and you'll find this is often a busy place. Serrano's serves just dinner, but dinner runs from 3:30 to 10:00 P.M., seven days a week. Like the larger Serrano's in Whitefish, this restaurant has a full menu of Mexican delights, from soups, salads, and a la carte items to full dinners.

Serrano's in East Glacier is open from May 1 to October 1.

Snowgoose Grille $$$
St. Mary Lodge, St. Mary
(406) 732–4431

The Snowgoose Grille mixes fine dining with a wonderful view for a distinctive dining experience. As you settle into your chair, you'll admire Red Eagle, Little Chief, Mahtotopa, and Dusty Star Mountains as they march up the shore of St. Mary Lake. A few moments later the menu will tempt you with its unique combination of buffalo specialties—prime rib, steaks, sausage, burgers—local St. Mary Lake whitefish, pasta, wild game, and nightly specials. While you wait, a basket of sourdough scones and honey butter will occupy your attention. And then there's dessert—huckleberry delights and other choices will finish the evening with just the right touch.

The Snowgoose Grille serves breakfast, lunch, and dinner from mid-May to early October.

The Park Cafe $
U.S. Highway 89, St. Mary
(406) 732–4482

The Park Cafe will attract your eyes from the road—this little restaurant is bordered all about with a beautiful garden of columbines, poppies, lupine, and big, blue delphinium. Inside you'll find eight tables and a counter, though on a sunny summer day you might go for one of the three tables on the porch. A few minutes of looking at the menu and you'll realize you can't go wrong, because whatever you choose, it'll be excellent. The Park Cafe prides itself on the quality of its ingredients, and every breakfast, lunch, and dinner is fresh, wholesome, and homemade.

But whether you choose a sandwich, burger, nachos (great salsa), or salad (check out the "gallinaceous green" salad)—be sure to save room for pie! The Park Café always has a great selection—from fruit to berry to pecan or ice-cream pies—and they're all homemade and delicious.

The Park Cafe is open from around Memorial Day to mid-September, from 7:00 A.M. to 10:00 P.M. The cafe doesn't take reservations, but when it gets busy in the evening they do keep a waiting list—and a few minutes on the porch with the delphinium is pleasant in itself.

The Cattle Baron Supper Club $$–$$$
Junction of U.S. Highway 89 and the Many Glacier Road, Babb
(406) 732–4033

The most amazing makeover of the late-twentieth century has possibly been the transformation of the Babb bar—once known as the fourth-roughest bar in the country—into the Cattle Baron Supper Club. Tastefully decorated with an Indian motif, the Cattle Baron is rapidly becoming known for its mouthwatering steaks. Many patrons have described dinner here as the "best steak they've ever had," so don't miss this opportunity to taste some fine Montana beef.

The Cattle Baron is open all summer: It continues to experiment with winter hours, but plans to serve breakfast, lunch, and dinner through the snowy months unless business really falls off. If you're in the neighborhood and the lights are on, be sure to stop by.

The Two Sisters $–$$
U.S. Highway 89, about 4 miles north of St. Mary
(406) 732–5535

Whether you're coming from Babb to the north or St. Mary to the south, you won't miss the Two Sisters—this is the brightest

Step back in time at the Museum of the Plains Indian. Photo: courtesy of U.S. Department of the Interior, Indian Arts and Crafts Board

The Two Sisters is open for lunch and dinner from mid-May to mid-September. If you enjoyed this funky, fun spot and will be traveling through Missoula later, be sure to stop at the year-round Two Sisters there (127 West Alder, 406-329-8438). They serve breakfast and lunch seven days a week and dinner Wednesday through Sunday.

Shopping

Some places you'll want to stop and explore include the gift shop at the Museum of the Plains Indian (open all year) in Browning, which features Native American crafts and jewelry, and the gift shop at St. Mary Lodge, which carries a wide variety of high-quality gifts and souvenirs from the region. The Burning Spear in East Glacier houses an eclectic group of items for sale—from cheap trinkets to a remarkable selection of Native American artworks from many western tribes. The Brown House in East Glacier is primarily a fine ceramics shop but also features paintings and photos by local artists. For those who might be missing certain amenities from home, try the Two Badger shop in East Glacier (308 Washington; open from 2:00 to 7:00 P.M. Monday through Saturday) for organic foods, body-care products, gifts, herbs, and books for a healthy life.

paint job on a building in probably the whole state! Inside you'll find a comfortable little cafe known for its homemade soups, dinner specials, cake, and pie. They've recently added an espresso machine, too, so stop for a latte if you're about to hit the road for the Midwest, Calgary, or Yellowstone. Tuck in your napkin . . .

Swan Valley

Travel the Swan Valley and try to imagine the wild and pristine landscape a century ago when the first homesteaders took root, loggers began eyeing the virgin timber, and the Flathead Indian tribes freely hunted its abundant game.

Its grandeur and beauty have captivated residents and regular vacationers, who lovingly call it "The Swan." While they welcome you with old-fashioned Montana hospitality, they passionately guard their valley's relative isolation, undeveloped character, and simple, unhurried lifestyle.

The Swan is bounded by official wilderness areas—the 73,887-acre Mission Mountains Wilderness to the west and the 1,009,356-acre Bob Marshall Wilderness to the east. Most of the mountain and valley lands belong either to the Flathead National Forest or Plum Creek, a large timber company. The remainder belongs to the State of Montana and private landowners. The Swan and Mission Mountains soar to rugged 8,000 to 9,000 foot heights, stretching for nearly 100 miles without a road crossing them. When you enter the Swan on its only paved road—the two-lane, north-south Montana 83—there's no turning off midway. But traffic is much less than on the major north-south highways to the east and west, and many pleasurable stops await you.

The River and Lake

The ice age's magic touched the landscape, carving Swan Lake and more than fifty others. These crystal-clear snow-fed lakes drain by creeks into the Swan River as it winds northward from headwaters near the Swan-Clearwater divide. It is interrupted by Swan Lake's 9-mile length, then empties into Flathead Lake at Bigfork. Nearly every mile a sparkling creek gurgles under the highway bridges toward the river.

Swan Lake is bounded on the east side by the highway and many privately owned vacation homes and on the west by mostly national forest where trees come right down to the shores. Tremendous biological diversity exists here with the convergence of three main forest types: the northern boreal, Rocky Mountain, and Pacific maritime forests, with larch and Douglas fir predominating, along with ponderosa, lodgepole, and other pines and Engelmann spruce. Major predator and prey species abound, and it is a birder's paradise. Keep a sharp eye out for deer crossing the highway, especially in early spring, and mornings and evenings.

The People, Then and Now

Archaeologists assume people began hunting and camping in the valley on the heels of the receding glaciers about 10,000 years ago. Excavations have unearthed evidence of human presence believed to date from 5,500 years ago. By the eighteenth century Indian tribes used the area for religious gatherings and sweat-lodge ceremonies, giving the Swan River its original name, Sweathouse River, to the lower stretch. The Flathead tribes—the Salish and Kootenai—retained treaty hunting privileges in the Swan when they moved to their present reservation from the Bitterroot Valley in 1872. They also peeled the ponderosa pines to harvest the sweet cambium layer under the bark for food. Scarred trees from the 1800s can still be seen in the forest, including one at the Pony Creek campsite reached by Forest Road 10651.

Fur trappers who had gleaned beaver and marten pelts since the late 1700s for the Northwest and Hudson's Bay Companies had severely diminished that resource by the mid-1800s. Gold prospectors had also explored the Swan after gold had been discovered elsewhere in Montana, but no significant mining was done.

The first decades of the twentieth century brought many changes as timber cutting intensified, settlers began constructing cabins, and the wealthy discovered the Swan as a vacationing ground. By the late 1800s much of the land had been brought into the Forest Reserve System, precursor of the U.S.D.A. Forest Service, and the first ranger station was built at Holland Lake. Later stations, log structures built at Swan Lake and Condon, remain standing in good condition. In 1937 these stations were consolidated at Bigfork in a compound of buildings constructed by the Civilian Conservation Corps.

The largest timber sale in the history of the Flathead National Forest took place in the Swan Valley during this time, according to Joe Yates, of the Swan Lake Ranger Station. From 100,000 to 150,000 board feet of mostly western larch, with some Douglas fir and pine, were cut by the Somers Lumber Company. They barged a steam engine on Flathead Lake to a point south of Bigfork. From there they laid tracks just ahead of the engine, drove it onto the tracks, then lifted the tracks behind it and repositioned them in front, leapfrogging this way until reaching the present forest recreation area near the village of Swan Lake. The engine served the logging operation between 1914 and 1919. Some folks say it was purposely sunk in Swan Lake and remains there today, but others claim it was taken out the same way it was brought in, was used in other logging operations, and was retired to its present site at the old depot in Columbia Falls. The village of Swan Lake began during this early period with the establishment of a store, a post office, and schools.

Kootenai Lodge, a luxurious vacation resort built during the teens and twenties on the north shore of Swan Lake, stood in marked contrast to the simple lives and dwellings of the loggers and homesteaders. The purchase of 137 acres of land on the lake's north shore by Anaconda Copper Company attorneys Lewis Orvis Evans and Cornelius Francis Kelley initiated the first development and several decades of incomparable opulent living and entertaining. Kelley became Anaconda president and Evans its general counsel, and the compound, which had groups of separate cabins for each family, as well as the massive main lodge, became known locally as "Kelley and Evans." They lavishly entertained the copper company elite, royalty, and other wealthy or famous people, including Charles Lindbergh, Holland's Queen Wilhelmina, Will Rogers, and Montana artist Charlie Russell. The resort engaged local craftsmen for more than a decade to construct the buildings of native stone, larch, cedar, and copper. During its heyday Kootenai Lodge employed up to 70 local people as cooks, housekeepers, butlers, chauffeurs, gardeners, bartenders, launderers, and in other occupations. Many area residents descend from those Kootenai Lodge workers and carry on in memory the Kelley and Evans legend.

The lodge and 42 acres are now privately owned and closed to the public. The rest of the acreage was logged and subdivided after the Kelley descendants sold the place in 1968. A visible reminder of that glittering age remains in The Rock House, built in 1930 on the lake's west side by Evans' wife, Martha. Reached only by boat, it provided a retreat from the hustle and bustle of the main compound. The Evanses entertained guests and held an annual party for lodge employees there. The house is also a registered historic site. You can see it perched above a large rocky point from the first pullout going south between mile markers 73 and 74 that takes you to the lakeshore.

Today's Swan Valley retains its simple rural character despite modest population growth and subdivision of most of the old homesteads. Many retirees have settled here, bringing a diversity of skills and backgrounds to community life and contributing to the area's economy, which still largely depends on its natural resources and tourism. Traditional timber cutting on state and federal lands has slowed drastically as concerned citizens have become involved in forest-management decisions and as philosophy and

A fly-fisherman enjoys the solitude and beauty of a spring day. Photo: Montana's Finest Resorts

Swan Valley's diverse natural environment and is well worth a stop. It offers hands-on interpretive exhibits, take-away educational materials, and accurate local information about the recreational and other activities in the national and state forests. They also provide an interpretive demonstration forestry project and a self-guided nature trail that explains the changing forest ecosystem.

Public lands provide hundreds of miles of roads and trails for biking, horseback riding, cross-country skiing, snowshoeing, and dogsled touring. Camping is permitted free of charge on all forest lands except in developed fee areas. Use of state lands for any recreational purpose requires a recreational license, which can be obtained from the state forest unit headquarters at milepost 58 on Montana 83 or the Kalispell Unit on U.S. 93 in Kalispell.

Accommodations

Price Code

Keep in mind that some rates are based on availability. The average nightly rates for two adults at the hotels and motels listed in this section are indicated by a dollar sign ($) ranking in the following chart. Also, the hotels and motels in this chapter accept all or most major credit cards.

$	Less than $85
$$	$85 to $115
$$$	$116 to $150
$$$$	More than $150

policy have begun to change regarding how to maintain forest health.

Facing polarization of the community by these issues, a group of upper-valley residents in 1990 formed the Swan Citizens ad hoc Committee to pursue collaborative ways of involving all interest groups and finding solutions to environmental, economic, and social problems. In 1996 the group established the Swan Ecosystem Center, a research and education center based in the Forest Service Condon Work Center. Its visitor information center provides a wealth of information about the

Hotels, Motels, and Resorts

Holland Lake Lodge $$–$$$
1947 Holland Lake Road, Swan Valley
(406) 754-2282, (877) 925-6343
www.seeleyswanpathfinder.com/ pfbusiness/hollandlake

"This is old Montana at its best," declares co-owner John Wohlfeil. "No golf courses, no condominiums, no luxury homes, no televisions, and cell phones don't work here." There's just this awe-inspiring

The Holland Lake Lodge offers a peaceful retreat.
Photo: Frank Miele

wilderness setting right on beautiful Holland Lake in sight of Holland Falls tumbling down out of the Swan Mountains. Built in 1925 the main lodge houses nine guest rooms, bar, restaurant, and common room with a large fireplace of local river stone. Guest cabins with bath that sleep four to six guests have been restored and improved. The lodge restaurant serves breakfast, lunch, and dinner. The dinner menu features premium center-cut filet mignon and other specialties as well as lighter vegetarian cuisine prepared by their French chef. The full bar stocks a collection of specialty premium California wines. Winter and summer there's lots to do here, including hiking, horseback riding, canoeing, cross-country skiing, ice-skating, and snowshoeing. They groom 9 miles of cross-country ski trails, and there is unlimited backcountry skiing on national forest roads and trails. Dogsled rides round out the winter opportunities. They rent canoes, skates, snowshoes, and other equipment. Located at one of the major gateways to the Bob Marshall Wilderness, they provide a selection of pack trips into the Bob, fall hunting trips, and winter ski-touring packages. The Holland Lake turnoff is at the south end of the valley and is well-marked with large signs. The lodge is open year-round, except from April to May 15 and November 5 to December 15.

Laughing Horse Lodge $
P.O. Box 5082, 71284 Montana Highway 83
Swan Lake 59911
(406) 886–2080
www.laughinghorselodge.com

In the village of Swan Lake, close to the lake and national forest recreation areas, owners of this resort inn offer guests access to all-season recreation activities. Log cabins provide rooms with a range of accommodations, all with private bath. Guests can lounge in a common room, with wood stove, library, games, music, and TV, as well as in the pub that serves microbrews and Northwest wines. The rustic dining room serves breakfast, lunch, and dinner featuring traditional Montana fare with an international touch. They cook for special dietary needs including kosher (with advance notice). Pets with responsible owners are welcome. In summer they rent sit-on-top kayaks, fishing kayaks, and bikes. In winter, when 60 kilometers of trails await the cross-country skiers, ski lockers are available. Laughing Horse Lodge is headquarters for the Swan Valley Nordic (Ski) Club.

Swan Lake Guest Cabins $
Montana Highway 83, Milepost 78
Swan Valley
(406) 837–1137, (888) 837–1557
www.virtualcities.com

This resort features new log cabins with handmade log furniture, kitchenette, and gas barbecues. It is located on a hill overlooking Swan Lake, in a secluded, private wilderness setting. There are lake views from the property, but the cabins face toward the woods with glimpses of the Swan Mountains. The cabins have a maximum capacity of six. They require a three-night minimum stay. Small children are not encouraged because of the heavily wooded setting and the presence of bears and mountain lions. Enjoy a sweat in the centrally located, wood-fired sauna. This is a nonsmoking resort. To find the Web page, enter the site above, click on vacation rentals, choose Montana, and then Swan Lake Guest Cabins. The Web site is almost as remote as the Swan Valley....

Swan Valley Super 8 Lodge $
Montana Highway 83, Milepost 46.5
(406) 754–2688, (800) 800–8000
www.super8.com

The rustic log buildings on the north edge of Condon are a welcome sight for travelers during the winter months when many other lodgings are closed. Open year-round, this motel stays very busy during summer with tourists and in the fall with hunters and loggers until the snow blocks road access. They have both nonsmoking and smoking rooms and handicapped access, and pets are permitted. They also provide one trailer hookup (but no septic) and two corrals for horses.

Campgrounds and RV Parks

Swan Lake Trading Post and Post Office
Montana Highway 83, Milepost 71
Swan Lake
(406) 886–2303

In addition to the full grocery, prepared sandwiches, local crafts, T-shirts, magazines, paperback books, household supplies, and stove fuel available at this community gathering place, there is a small campground with tent sites, full RV hookups, showers, and laundry. See the listing in the Shopping section of this chapter for more information.

Swan Valley Centre
Montana Highway 83, Milepost 42, Condon
(406) 754–2397

Swan Valley Centre is one of those places that can boast if they don't have it, you probably don't need it. There are water and electric hookups for campers but no septic service, and they provide monthly parking for RV campers. Showers and a laundry await the tired and dirty backpacker or equestrian just off the trail. Or if you're in need of a tow and auto repair, this is a good choice because it's the only one on this 50-mile stretch. While you're there you can stock up on groceries and fishing supplies and have a deli picnic at the tables. Visitors and locals are welcome

to fish from the Smiths' property along the Swan River behind the center. See the listing in the Shopping section of this chapter for more information.

Restaurants

Price Code

For two people, meal exclusive of beverages, tip, and tax.

$	$10 to 20
$$	$21 to 30
$$$	$31 to 50
$$$$	More than $50

Holland Lake Lodge $
1947 Holland Lake Road, Swan Valley
(406) 754–2282, (800) 648–8859

The wilderness setting of this fine restaurant at Holland Lake Lodge (see the Accommodations section of this chapter) and the views of Holland Falls make the breakfasts, lunches, and dinners an experience for the senses. And the food lives up to the promise of the surroundings. The dinner menu features premium center-cut filet mignon, other specialties, and vegetarian courses prepared by their French chef. The full bar stocks premium California wines.

Hungry Bear Steak House $
6287 Montana Highway 83, Milepost 38 to 39, Swan Valley
(406) 754–2240

Outside and in, this restaurant welcomes you in old-fashioned Montana style. The imposing 20-plus-year-old log structure houses a high-ceilinged dining room, a separate bar with pool table, and a dance floor. Mounted animals and trophy heads of local game adorn the high walls of both rooms, including elk, moose, mountain lion, bison, and beaver. Its speciality is beef, but it also serves chicken and seafood. If you've always wanted to try Rocky Mountain oysters, here's your chance. Also known as "bull fries," these are on the list of appetizers. They serve breakfast, lunch, and dinner. Beer and wines available.

Mountain Lions and Safety in Lion Country

Much of Glacier Country and the Swan Valley is mountain lion country, so it's good to inform yourself about these felines. You'll find that bears get a lot of press here, while mountain lions get relatively little. Lions in general are extremely secretive and so are rarely seen; yet, unlike bears (which generally attack only when surprised or when they have learned to regard people as a source of food), mountain lions do on occasion stalk people as prey. In particular, children and small adults need to be cautious. Children should not be allowed to play alone, and they should not be allowed to run ahead of adults on the trail. Hiking alone even by adults is not advised for many reasons, lions being one. Something to keep in mind is that cats like cover for stalking prey; treed or cliffy areas are good habitat for them, but you are less likely to find one out in a meadow. Consider too that some things people do may attract cats: a small pet dog, for example, looks like lunch to a cat, and may not be the best hiking partner for this country. Some residents have been known to put out salt licks or hay to attract deer—and then are surprised when the deer attract lions.

People have been jumped by mountain lions here in recent years. In one case a boy was jumped midday in Apgar Campground at the foot of Lake McDonald. In other instances cats have been found within the limits of Flathead Valley and Swan Valley towns. If you should find yourself being stalked by a cat, remain calm and remember first that cats are curious, indeed, and the animal may be just checking you out. Talk quietly to the animal but look big and unafraid: If you have a small child with you, pick the child up and carry him or her on your shoulders—you'll both look bigger, and you'll know where your child is. Back slowly away. Should attack seem imminent, find something you can defend yourself with—a stick, a rock—or something you can throw from your backpack. Do not run. Should you actually be rushed, yell and fight back; cats can be intimidated (note this is quite different from the advice given for dealing with bears). Once again, an ounce of prevention is worth many pounds of cure.

The chances of seeing a mountain lion are slim—if you do, more than likely, it will be a quick glimpse of magic as a long tail disappears before your eyes. Bobcats and lynx also inhabit Glacier Country but are even more rarely seen.

Laughing Horse Lodge $
P.O. Box 5082, 71284 Montana Highway 83
Swan Lake 59911
(406) 886–2080
www.laughinghorselodge.com

Known by locals for its excellent prime rib, Laughing Horse features traditional Montana cuisine with an international touch made to order from choice fresh ingredients from local farmers and ranchers. Breakfast, lunch, and dinner are served in the rustic dining room. Breakfast fare includes omelets and vegetarian and dairy-free specialities. Lunch features burgers, sandwiches, soup, and salads. They cook for special dietary needs, including vegetarian and kosher (with advance notice). The small, intimate pub stocks select microbrews and northwestern wines and is open for public dining year-round. Call for seasonal hours.

Montana Charlie's $
6042 Montana Highway 83, Milepost 36.5
Condon
(406) 754–2229

Owner-chef Chuck Witkowski brings more than 20 years' experience to his unusual menu that features traditional Montana prime rib and an unexpected array of Chicago-style Italian specialties. He prepares from scratch all dishes, from lunch salads, burgers, and sandwiches to the dinner entrees that include steaks and a large, varied pasta selection to suit almost every palate. Try the toasted ravioli and the popular spicy Chicken Spedini. Visit the bar adjoining Charlie's restaurant with its log interior and furniture, accented by wildlife art and artifacts. Call for dinner reservations or prepare to stand in line. This restaurant is popular with the locals. RV hookups and camping are available on the grounds.

Shopping

Mission Mountains Mercantile
Montana Highway 83, Milepost 45 to 46
Condon
(406) 754-2387

If you've forgotten something for your camping or fishing trip, you have a good chance of finding it here. On the site of an early trading post known as Buckhorn Camp, this store now houses a mini-super market and deli with a full range of groceries, produce, beer, wine, household supplies, hardware, pet, auto and picnic supplies, cosmetics, toys, greeting cards, and travel guides. They make baked goods on the premises and cut their own meat. They also carry horse feed, propane, diesel, and gasoline at 24-hour pumps. Mission Mountains Mercantile sells Montana hunting and fishing licenses.

Morley's Canoes
P.O. Box 5149, Swan Lake 59911
(406) 886-2242

Greg Morley is a master craftsman who designs and constructs cedar-strip canoes by hand, using old-fashioned classic tools. Morley's canoes are owned by paddlers and crafts aficionados all over North America. At his shop in the village of Swan Lake, he meticulously crafts the vessels from premium northwest red cedar using

Insiders' Tip

Swan Lake, which lies at the valley's north end, separates the "upper" and "lower" river sections. These designations are confusing since "upper" refers to elevations at the headwaters, which lie at the valley's southernmost part. Likewise, when people refer to the "head" of the lake they are talking about the southern end, while the "foot" is the northern end.

wood-saving techniques to minimize his use of timber. The beauty and performance of his canoes reflects his 30-plus years of experience building watercraft and even more experience plying North American lakes and white water. Stop in to see some examples of his customized canoes, skiffs, rowboats, and paddles.

Swan Valley Centre
Montana Highway 83, Milepost 42, Condon
(406) 754-2397
www.seeleyswanpathfinder.com/
swancentrecabins

The words "Beer Beans Bacon," in woodblock letters on the outside wall of this general store, don't do justice to the variety of products and services owners Pat and Mike Smith offer. The original 1930s frame store has been enlarged over the years to accommodate other functions. Showers and a laundry await the tired and dirty backpacker or equestrian just off the trail. Or if you're in need of a tow and auto repair, this is a good choice because it's the only one on this 50-mile stretch. While you're there, you can stock up on groceries, bulk natural foods, backpacker meals, and fishing supplies. The deli features home-cooked daily specials and freshly made pizzas. Year-round they offer three rustic rental cabins with full kitchens, water and electric hookups for campers (no septic), and monthly parking for RV campers. Visitors and locals are welcome to fish from the Smiths' property along the Swan River behind the center.

Swan Lake Trading Post and Post Office
Montana Highway 83, Milepost 71
Swan Lake
(406) 886-2303

Established in 1926, where the southbound road ended, this general store and post office originally ran the telephone switchboard for the area. Today it serves as a gathering place for summer and year-round residents who come to get their mail and share a cup of coffee. It offers a full grocery, prepared sandwiches, local crafts, T-shirts, magazines, paperback books, household supplies, and stove fuel. They have a small campground with tent sites, full RV hookups, showers, and laundry.

Relocation

This chapter is included with special pleasure. The lure of Montana's mountains, rivers, and skies brings many of us or our families to this "Last Best Place," and the love of this land makes many of us want to stay, perhaps just like you. It was only months ago that we were tourists or curious armchair travelers dreaming pioneer dreams. Or maybe it was generations ago that our families put down roots here, giving children the chance to discover the beauty of wilderness in their own backyard. We arrived here once in anticipation of great things. We were not disappointed. Living in Montana is like an adventure that starts anew each morning. No matter whether your day includes a routine of office, kids, and home, or whether it's full of the horizon—miles of driving, hours of wilderness, acres of farmland or ranch land—the life you live here is unlike any other. Start to think of the Flathead Valley as home: glaciers, grizzlies, glistening streams. Then get started making your dream come true. And though the scenery dominates this special place, you won't be moving to a cultural wasteland. One standout feature of the area as a whole is the abundance of arts and entertainment. Local and regional theater companies, an excellent orchestra, smaller musical groups, resident artists and writers all contribute to an exciting mix uncommon for an area with such a small population. The weekly entertainment section of the newspaper is chockablock with choices year-round, and most folks can't keep up with the dizzying array of activities, especially around the holidays. Sound like paradise? A note of caution: Consider what kind of environment this is for a long-term relationship, not just as a summer romance. If you're moving from a warm, sunny place, talk to others who've come before you. Remember that the Flathead Valley records an average of 71 sunny days per year (days when 3/10 of the sky or less are covered by clouds) and that gray skies are often the norm in winter. Make sure you have a good job or enough retirement income to support you in a place where wages are generally low and the cost of living is above the national average. It's a magical place, but practical planning is needed to make your dreams come true. Visions of happily-ever-after aside, you probably can use some guidance for some of the challenges you may face in the first weeks and months of your relocation. Let the sections of this chapter offer some "mile markers" to get you started on the right track. Welcome to the Flathead!

Real Estate

Location, Location, Location (Part I)

One of the hardest decisions you may have when moving to the Flathead Valley is deciding which view you'll wake up to each morning. Mountain, river, or both? Forest or meadow? Lakeshore or golf green? With so many choices and each vista more beautiful than the last, the home search can feel overwhelming. Try to stay calm and remember the things you need most to feel comfortable. Do you want to live in town? It feels more central, more convenient, more social—and sometimes more crowded, more complicated. On the other hand, living miles out of town sounds great—pristine, tranquil—and fine until your multiple trips to school, the sitter, and the supermarket make you feel like you spent the whole day in the car. If you're moving from a place where long commutes are common, but snow isn't, adjust your thinking to reflect local conditions. A half-hour drive over winding roads may seem like no big deal in the summer, but think about that drive twice a day during the winter, when the roads may be icy and a deer could pop up in front of you on the road without warning. No matter how beautiful the view and peaceful the solitude are at the end of the day, they may not seem worth it after a white-knuckle trip in a snowstorm. Winter is a force to be reckoned with when making your plans. Another nuts-and-bolts factor to consider is water and sewer. Many homes built outside of the city limits are on septic systems and pump their water from individual wells. If you're planning to build, this is an especially critical factor. Drilling wells can be expensive, and septic failure catastrophic, so do your homework. Choices for heating and cooling your home also need to be considered. Natural gas is available in many areas of the valley, but other places—even some quite close to town—don't have gas. Extending utilities to new homes also can be expensive. Don't let the gorgeous view from a piece of mountaintop property blind you to the complications of building there. Some practical thinking now will

save you a lot of headaches later.

Try to picture your new home in each of the four seasons. Think about that long, scenic quarter-mile driveway to your home. Then think about shoveling snow off of that long, scenic quarter-mile driveway. Who's responsible for plowing and maintaining the access roads? If you're not on a city or county road, the homeowners must bear those costs. Some subdivision roads are pitted with potholes because residents won't agree to pay their share for repairs. Take a hard look at those mountaintop hideaways. The views may be breath-catching, but you've got to get up and down the mountain in the winter. Think about fire protection. If you want to settle in the country, where is the nearest volunteer fire department? Privacy may not seem so appealing in case of an emergency. Do you want room to expand on your property to keep stock and add outbuildings, or will you be content with the limitations of a standard city lot? If you're very social, will you feel lonely or isolated with no neighbors in a 2-mile radius? Consider each option carefully and you'll avoid going too far in your quest to get away from it all.

Now add a buyer's market to the mix. New arrivals are initially amazed at the number of homes for sale and their reasonable prices, like a three-bedroom, two-bath historic home in downtown Kalispell for less than $150,000 or gorgeous lakefront homes for less than $300,000. They get jumpy, thinking of markets in Washington and California where homes sell in two days or less and buyers have to move quickly to make a deal. Here in the Flathead, however, the pace is a bit slower. In 2002, houses stayed on the market an average of 155 days. Favorable interest rates and a good selection make it a good time to buy real estate in the Flathead Valley.

The good news is that the Flathead Valley offers the presence of both nationally known and locally respected real estate offices whose agents can help you in your search. These agents are up-to-date on local trends and the latest developments in the market. Take your time and find one who specializes in your area (lakefront, homes with acreage, etc.) and who picks up on your interests and style. Real estate is big business in the Flathead. Residential sales totaled more than $284 million during 2000, not small change by anybody's standards. Personal recommendations are always a good way to find a Realtor. Ask your friends and acquaintances who they used when they bought or sold a home. Your search will be more enjoyable and more successful with an agent who can help match you with the right property. Then grab some of their publications, go on-line to scout out some possibilities, and you'll soon be home!

Real Estate Companies

**Northwest Montana Association of Realtors
and Multiple Listing Service
690 North Meridian Road, Suite 105
Kalispell
(406) 752–4197
www.nmar.com**

This agency can provide you with statistics on real estate transactions and general information about companies in the Flathead Valley. The association represents 110 real estate firms in Flathead and Lake Counties—a total of about 500 Realtors—

and while it can't make recommendations or referrals to individual real estate firms, it can give the names, addresses, and phone numbers of its members. Check out the real estate listings on the MLS Web site.

**Prudential Glacier Real Estate
135 West Idaho, Suite B, Kalispell
(406) 752–1555, (800) 940–1555
www.glacierrealestate.com**

The oldest real estate firm in the valley, established in 1939, has operated under just three owner/brokers during that time. The company has 17 agents who specialize in residential transactions; the company also handles commercial and undeveloped land throughout the Flathead Valley.

**Century 21 Home & Investment Center
284 Fourth Avenue WN, Kalispell
(406) 755–2100, (800) 321–2401
www.c21investinthewest.com**

Century 21 Home & Investment Center has been in business for well over 20 years and consists of seven owner/brokers, with no sales associates. "We have the knowledge and integrity of experienced brokers and the power of Century 21," says owner/broker Edna Hellickson. The firm

New adventures await you in northwest Montana. Photo: Silver Moon Kayak Company

handles all types of transactions, with individual agents specializing in areas such as farms and ranches, commercial and residential property.

Century 21 Whitefish Land Office
110 East Second Street, Whitefish
(406) 862-2579, (800) 933-9155
www.c21whitefish.com

Established in 1978, Century 21 Whitefish Land Office handles a variety of real estate, primarily in the Whitefish area, including many resort properties that are second homes for the buyers. Whitefish Land Office has 12 real estate agents and was the number-two Century 21 office in Montana for closed sales in 2000. Owner/broker Wink Jordan describes his team as "an experienced group of Realtors with a wealth of local knowledge." If it's a good time to invest in real estate, have a look at the Web listing of a Whitefish Lake property with 225 feet of shoreline . . . for an easy $1,390,000.

Coldwell Banker Wachholz & Company Real Estate
Kalispell: 1205 South Main, Kalispell
(406) 751-4300
www.cbwrealestate.com
Whitefish: 105 Baker Avenue, Whitefish
(406) 862-4200
Columbia Falls: 1123 Highway 2 West Columbia Falls
(406) 892-5200
Lakeside: 7191 U.S. Highway 93 South Lakeside
(406) 844-3100
Bigfork: 710 Grand Drive, Bigfork
(406) 837-1234

This is the largest real estate firm in northwest Montana, with 64 agents in 5 offices throughout the Flathead Valley. Former banker Paul Wachholz established his original office in Kalispell in 1981 and affiliated with Coldwell Banker in 1985. Since then the company has been the top-producing Coldwell Banker office for the state of Montana and was in the top 3 percent of the 2,000-plus Coldwell Banker offices nationwide for 1991 through 1993 and 1995. The company has expanded throughout the valley, beginning with the Whitefish office in 1986. Wachholz and Company moved into Lakeside in 1998, buying out the Century 21 office there, and in 1999 bought another adjacent Lakeside real-estate firm. The company handles all types of real estate, from commercial property to high-end homes. Coldwell Banker Wachholz has multiple listings for properties on Big Mountain in a range of prices.

Chuck Olson Real Estate Inc.

Bigfork: 8090 Highway 35, Bigfork
(406) 837–5551

Kalispell: 241 Main Street, Kalispell
(406) 752–1000, (800) 555–5376
montanaweb.com/homes

Whitefish: 567 Spokane, Whitefish
(406) 863–8400, (800) 775–3250
www.chuckolson.com

Chuck Olson Real Estate is a locally owned, independent firm established in 1972. It's the only "major player" in the valley that's not affiliated with a national franchise and touts itself as the "home team." Each of its three offices is independently owned and operated, although the offices cooperate and share advertising. The biggest office is in Kalispell, which has 16 to 18 real estate agents, including nine owner/brokers. According to owner/broker Chuck Olson, the firm consistently ranks among the top agencies in overall sales.

Edgewater Realty, Inc.

13 Second Avenue West, Polson
(406) 883–5203
www.lakeshorestore.com

This company has been in business for some 50 years, with a name change or two along the way. Current owner Gerald Newgard has been selling real estate in Polson since 1970, and his company has eight real estate agents. As its name implies, Edgewater specializes in lake properties, mostly in the area between Polson and Rollins. "We serve who comes through the door—that's the boss," Newgard says.

Montana Brokers, Inc. Realtors

685 Sunset Boulevard, Kalispell
(406) 752–4747, (800) 933–3177
www.montanabrokers.com

Owner Rick Doran is a self-described "local yokel" who grew up in the Flathead Valley and has been in the real estate business here since 1978. Montana Brokers was established in 1986 and currently has 12 agents, mostly brokers with an average of 15 years' experience, and one of the highest per-agent production in the valley. The firm handles all types of real estate and was one of the first companies to go "on-line." Although a number of the agents are natives, Doran says the firm also welcomes people from other places, because "We all came here from somewhere, sometime." Montana Brokers handles numerous waterfront properties and has even sold an island in Flathead Lake.

RE/MAX Glacier Country

1 Main Street, Kalispell
(406) 257–8900

"Have fun and make money" is the motto at RE/MAX Glacier Country, a company that's in "major growth mode," according to owner/broker Doug Denmark, after purchasing and refurbishing an historic building in downtown Kalispell. "We're where top agents go to ply their trade," Denmark said. The firm has 10 Realtors and plans to add several more experienced agents. Two of his agents are members of the RE/MAX hall of fame. Glacier Country sold the property and is the marketing agent for "The Willows," an 87-lot subdivision being developed just southeast of Kalispell on Willow Glen Drive. Denmark says he's especially proud of this project because it's turning a 30-acre tract of land that had been blighted and an eyesore with rusted equipment into an attractive subdivision of moderately priced homes.

RE/MAX Land & Lake

P.O. Box 582, Lakeside 59922
(406) 844–3500
www.montanaland.com

Land & Lake has been in business for more than 25 years and specializes in lakeshore and residential property. Broker Gregg Schoh points out that while the Internet can be a useful tool to start with, it doesn't replace a Realtor's ability to consult and advise. The firm uses advanced technology but does business the old-fashioned way. Among the interesting properties Land & Lake handles are islands or parts of islands, such as Wild Horse Island, a 2,700-acre state park that is home to bighorn sheep, deer, and bald eagles. Although most of the island is a state park, it also has 52 private lakeshore lots, one of which occasionally goes up for sale.

RE/MAX Whitefish
509 East Sixth Street, Whitefish
(406) 863–3400
www.whitefishremax.com

RE/MAX Whitefish offers complete listings for all sorts of properties around Whitefish, on the Big Mountain, and northwest of town toward Eureka. This well-established, professional staff will treat you well and help you find just the sort of home or property for which you're looking.

Trails West Eagle Bend Realty
420 Electric Avenue, Bigfork
(406) 837–7050, (800) 976–6682
www.trailswesteaglebend.com

Owner/broker Katie Brown says a major goal of the seven full-time agents in her firm is to make the buying/selling process "fun or at least a comfortable experience." Trails West, which has been in operation since the early 1970s, merged with Eagle Bend Realty in 1997 to form the existing company. Trails West Eagle Bend works with many second-home buyers who are interested in lake frontage or acreage, primarily in Bigfork, the Swan Valley, and the Eagle Bend development. A number of the company's listings have been featured in national magazines such as *Architectural Digest*.

Real Estate Publications

Home Seekers
(800) 882–9044

Published by Homes across America Network 13 times a year, this magazine features properties in Kalispell, Whitefish, Columbia Falls, Bigfork, Lakeside, Eureka, Libby, and Polson. Listings from more than 30 agencies and brokerages are included.

Homes and Real Estate
The *Daily Inter Lake*
727 East Idaho, Kalispell
(406) 755–7000

Published by the *Daily Inter Lake* monthly, this is a very comprehensive guide to current listings around the valley, with most prominent agencies represented.

Northwest Montana Real Estate
Milestone Publications, Inc, Ronan
(800) 696–2804
www.milestonepublications.com

Published five times a year, this real estate guide lists properties on Flathead Lake, in the Mission Valley, and in surrounding areas.

The Montana Land Magazine
Real Estate Publications, Inc.
P.O. Box 30516, Billings 59107
(406) 259–3534
www.montanalandmagazine.com

This quarterly publication contains pages of statewide and Rocky Mountain listings, including the greater Flathead and Seeley/Swan area. It is sold both by subscription ($25 per year) and at newsstands and bookstores.

Northwest Real Estate Guide
RE Guide/Brady Graphics & Printing
P.O. Box 794, Lewistown 59457

Published quarterly, and available by subscription (four issues for $12.50), you'll find here homes and land from Helena to Sandpoint, Idaho, including properties on the edges of the Flathead Valley in Libby and Missoula.

**Polson and Lake County Homes and
  Real Estate**
The *Daily Inter Lake*
727 East Idaho, Kalispell
(406) 755–7000

Published four or five times a year, this guide gives a comprehensive listing of property for sale in the southern part of the Flathead Valley.

In addition to these periodicals, some individual real-estate firms publish booklets listing their properties. Some of these booklets appear as newspaper inserts, and others are available on the racks of free publications that are maintained at various locations outside grocery stories, motels, and shopping malls.

In the Flathead Valley you can find your Montana dream home. Photo: courtesy ERA 1st Choice Realty

Building

New construction is not only an important marker of the valley's economic well-being, it can also be the way for you to get exactly what you want in your home. Whether your dream is to build it yourself, to choose from the models in a new neighborhood community, or to have a custom-built log home with river-rock fireplace, contractors in the valley are prepared to deliver. The Flathead Building Association, 1702 Fifth Avenue East, Kalispell, (406) 752–2422, can refer you to a builder who specializes in the type of home you desire, or answer questions about the particular contractors bidding on your job. The association publishes a directory of members each March in conjunction with their annual trade show.

Home Rentals

Resist that urge to buy the first house you see, say locals, and rent for the first year—or at least through your first winter. Even if you've visited here before, this advice makes good sense. Renting gives you the chance to test your instincts on neighborhoods, landscapes, and other practicalities of Montana life before making a commitment to a particular property. You'll gain a sense of how much home you need to feel

comfortable, a chance to prioritize the fireplace versus the hot tub. Then when you're ready to buy, you'll have more information on what truly attracts you and what to avoid. Some rentals are beautiful homes that are languishing on the market or even vacation properties not used during the off-season. Their owners prefer to have these homes lived in than sit vacant. So now can be your chance to live in a great setting without homeowner's headaches like fixing the roof or the furnace.

Whether it's an apartment in a large complex, a privately owned home, or a professionally managed property, interview a prospective property manager or landlord carefully before signing any paperwork. Ask them to describe what their services to you will include. Some landlords can be very attentive to the needs of renters, especially dependable, long-term ones. The cost of an average three-bedroom rental unit runs from $550 to $700 per month, and lovely places can often be found for a reasonable cost. Some agencies can even help you secure a temporary place to stay when you first arrive. But remember that an agent's primary customer is the property owner, not you. Overall, renting may not be the best option for people who like to feel "settled," but it works for a great many newcomers to the Flathead. Check your yellow pages for listings under "Real Estate Rental Service" or look for classifieds in the local papers or Mountain Trader.

Rental Agencies

Corental
1046 South Main, Kalispell
(406) 752-5600

Corental, established in 1983, provides professional management for apartments, houses, and commercial property. Services offered are a full-time licensed real estate broker, free advertising, tenant screenings, and 24-hour telephone service.

Eagle Bend Flathead Vacation Rentals
836 Holt Drive, Bigfork
(406) 837-4942, (800) 239-9933
www.mtvacationrentals.com

This firm specializes in vacation homes on Eagle Bend golf course and other areas of the valley, including Flathead Lake, Swan Lake, and Swan River.

Flathead Property Management
280 Fourth Avenue WN, Kalispell
(406) 752-5480
www.flatheadrentals.com

This licensed property management firm has been in business since 1981 and offers a variety of services to landlords. It also rents a variety of storage units.

Flathead Valley Property Management
P.O. Box 252, Lakeside 59922
(406) 844-0700
www.flatheadvalley.net

This agency specializes in vacation rentals around the Flathead Lake area and long-term property management from the north end of the lake into Kalispell. Owner Dale Chambers purchased the business in 1999.

Location, Location, Location (Part II)

The great spots in the Flathead Valley are many. The rugged sportsman, retired couple, and the growing family all find their places here in an eclectic and exciting mix. Neighborhoods may not be as clearly delineated as they are in some cities, and exclusive parkside and waterside properties are located throughout northwest Montana. But each major center of the Flathead enjoys a personality of its own. Other standard criteria for selecting a home will still apply, so ask a reputable agent for current information on the community resources, schools, and services in your area of interest.

Bigfork and Lake Flathead

Quiet and quaint, Bigfork Village is home to delightful artists' galleries and fine shops and restaurants. In the summer the single main street is abustle with visitors enjoying the ambience that sometimes can make Bigfork seem like a stage set rather than a real, living town. One of the best things that happened to Bigfork seemed like a disaster at the time—the highway bypassed the town. As a result Bigfork was spared the through traffic that's plagued Kalispell and Lakeside, and its downtown retains a village feeling, without a single stoplight downtown.

Parking is another matter, though, as summer visitors vie for the limited number of mostly angle-in spots. Homes and cherry-orchard properties extend along the eastern shore of Flathead Lake down to Woods Bay with summer cabins and year-round home retreats reaching along the Swan River out into Ferndale. You'll find newer homes on large wooded lots at the edge of the mountains along Foothill Road, near Echo Lake, and in the Many Lakes development, while west of the highway you can find older farm homes and estates with views of the Flathead River, fields of hay, mint, and dill, and marshes full of wildlife. If you must live where you golf and golf where you live, Eagle Bend golf community is just west of Bigfork Village. On the western shore of the lake, the community of Lakeside is booming with mid-priced homes with lake views and proximity to the new ski resort on Blacktail Mountain. And all along the lake, small summer cabins are being turned into year-round residences. Farther south is Polson, a pretty little town at the foot of Flathead Lake. The view of the lake coming over the hill on Highway 93 from Missoula is almost unbeatable. Polson is located in a relative banana belt, and residents boast they can play golf all year.

Kalispell

The commercial center and seat for Flathead County, Kalispell is the largest municipality in the valley and in northwest Montana, making it popular for those who like to be close to services and community resources. In 1998, *Mountain Sports and Living* magazine picked Kalispell as the best mountain town in the nation based on quality of life criteria. Streets in the historic central part of town south of the railroad tracks continue to hold much of their charm from the town's early days. Stately maple and chestnut trees line the boulevards in the older sections of town, and the fall colors are striking. Many of the historic and larger homes are found on the east side near Woodland Avenue, while newer homes have developed north

of the downtown near Lawrence Park and south of town near the city airport. Building lots within the city are rare, and many people opt for remodeling an existing home rather than building a new one. Living within the city limits provides many conveniences. Residents can walk to Woodland Park, shops on Main Street, to the Kalispell Center Mall, movie theaters, museums, concerts, and art galleries. The downtown is experiencing a commercial revival, with development of several small shopping malls and restoration of the KM Building, a historic landmark that dates from more than a century ago. A special note about Woodland Park, which was donated to the city of Kalispell in 1903 by the widow of the town's founder, Charles E. Conrad. This 40-acre park is a treasure enjoyed by residents and visitors year-round. A flock of ducks, geese, and swans delight park visitors and beg for handouts, and generations of children and their parents have kept them well fed. You can purchase a healthy snack of cracked corn at the convenience store across the street from the park and delight the resident waterfowl population. Flower gardens are a popular spot for summer weddings, a skating rink is open in the winter, and youngsters can splash in the municipal pool on hot summer days. Families wander across the wooden bridges and business people take a lunch break in this beautiful spot, even on chilly winter days.

Whitefish

Popular as a resort for many years among skiers, a fur-trading, logging, and railroad town in its early days, Whitefish was once known as Stumptown because buildings were erected over stumps from downed timber. Little of its blue-collar past now remains in this upscale town. Whitefish is growing as a community that offers year-round outdoor attractions such as Big Mountain and Whitefish Lake, as well as such community resources as a theater and public library. With a downtown core full of restaurants and shops, and a slate of special events, Whitefish has developed

Sailing is a popular summer pastime on Flathead Lake. Photo: Carl Wells, courtesy of Flathead Convention and Visitor Bureau

an identity as a lively, entertaining community. Real estate in this area can be pricey. Lakeshore on Whitefish Lake sells for up to $4,000 a front foot, and lakeshore view property sells for about $250,000 per lot. In 2002, the average price of a "regular" home was $137,951, though you may sometimes see higher numbers skewed by the presence of some very expensive homes in the area.

Columbia Falls and Glacier National Park

The gateway communities to Glacier National Park have no trouble attracting residents who want to live just a few spare minutes from the park's boundaries. Columbia Falls has long been a home for generations of employees of Plum Creek Timber and the Columbia Falls Aluminum Company. But like all areas of the Flathead, secluded wooded or riverside lots attract dream-house homeowners-builders. The communities of Hungry Horse, Martin City, and Coram lie beyond, and those who really want to get away from it all can travel up the North Fork Road into the remote Polebridge area near the boundary of Glacier National Park.

Living in Grizzly Country

The forests and wilderness areas of northwest Montana comprise one of the largest expanses of grizzly habitat in the country. As greater numbers of homeowners settle in outlying areas of the Flathead, reports of contacts between humans and bears have increased. And in years when bears encounter food shortages (1998 was a particularly bad year for huckleberries, their favorite food), the number of encounters is even greater. Rangers advise special precautions for residents who live in grizzly country and along its edges. They discourage the feeding of birds, deer, or other animals and recommend that garbage and pet food be secured inside, not on porches or in sheds. Bears that sniff out and win these "food rewards," they advise, are essentially learning to return to human settlements for an easy meal. Once this behavior is learned, it is very difficult to train a bear to seek berries only in the forest. A bear that learns this lesson too well will probably wind up causing property damage, and even being destroyed. Prevention rather than correction is advised so that sightings of animals might continue with few unfortunate consequences.

Living in Forest-Fire Country

Your home nestled amid the tamarack trees brings with it a special responsibility—wildfire control. Large forest fires take

Off the beaten trail: dogsledding in Montana. Photo: courtesy of Montana Adventure Company

on historic significance as they wipe out the trees that make up the livelihood of residents and support the local economy. Everyone takes the risk of fire seriously. For homeowners this means taking care of forested areas on your property and keeping underbrush—a source of fire fuel—controlled. Prevention of chimney fires through regular cleaning of stovepipes and flues is another important precaution. Make sure firefighters can find your hideaway. Efforts to quench fires at two remote homes near Kalispell were complicated by the fact that no house numbers were posted on access roads. Fire can quickly wipe out your dreams, so take all the precautions you can.

A Note on Recycling

Moving to an area where I had to haul my own trash to the county landfill took some getting used to. (We were living in the country: Garbage pickup service is available in most places in the valley.) Giving up access to a comprehensive household waste-recycling program came next. I have learned to adjust. Materials that are currently recycled in the Flathead include: newspaper, aluminum cans, cardboard and mixed paper, Styrofoam egg cartons, and plastic bottles. Large sorting containers for these materials can be found outside most of the major grocery stores, and some stores individually collect plastic shopping bags and Styrofoam egg cartons. A successful program for glass does not currently exist.

Retirement

Since this is a place where many families live for generations, you often find families that tell you how they all came to move to the valley over time. It is important to know what facilities exist to care for older family members. Retired "empty nesters" comprise a relatively large segment of newcomers to the valley, so housing options will be increasingly important to them in the future. Seniors make up a significant portion of the population and many activities and services are available for them, and lots of volunteer opportunities exist in the community as well. Flathead Valley Community College offers a popular "Senior Fridays" program in the winter, with classes ranging from computer training to ceramics. Lunch and transportation from area senior centers are included in the reasonable fee.

Agency on Aging
723 Fifth Avenue East, Kalispell
(406) 758–5730

This agency offers a variety of services to seniors, including a meals program, transportation, information and assistance for a variety of problems, a newsletter, reference library, homemaker program, and companion care.

Eagle Transit
723 Fifth Avenue East, Kalispell
(406) 758–5728

Adequate transportation is necessary for a comfortable life in this valley, and bus service can be a godsend for seniors who no longer can drive. Buses operate Monday through Friday from 9:15 A.M. to 5:00 P.M. and early morning Dial-A-Ride is available from 7:00 to 7:30 A.M. and from 9:00 to 9:30 A.M. Arrangements for Dial-A-Ride must be made a working day in advance. Eagle Transit provides special transportation for passengers with disabilities.

Senior-Citizen Centers

A number of senior centers offer a variety of activities. Here are some of the centers in the area:
Bigfork, 639 Commerce Street, (406) 837-4157;
Columbia Falls, 205 Nucleus Avenue, (406) 892-4087;
Kalispell, 403 Second Avenue West, (406) 257-1598;
Lakeside, Lakeside Baptist Church, (406) 844-3006;
Polson, 504 Third Avenue East, (406) 883-4735;
Whitefish, 121 Second Street, (406) 862-4923.

The Summit
205 Sunnyview Lane, Kalispell
(406) 751–4100
www.summithealthcare.com

The Summit, a full-service health and fitness center, offers a variety of activities for nonmembers through its Successful Aging Program, including free health-education lectures on the first and third Wednesday of each month, a Cribbage Challenge on the second Thursday, and a Scrabble Mixer on the fourth Thursday of each month. A Summit staff member also conducts a Mall Walk program for seniors on Monday and Friday from 9:30 to 10:30 A.M. at Kalispell Center Mall. The Summit also conducts low-cost cholesterol screenings once a month and every few months has a $1.00 day for seniors.

Nursing and Retirement Centers

Brendan House
350 Conway Drive, Kalispell
(406) 751–6500

This is a skilled-nursing facility operated by Northwest Healthcare, which also owns Kalispell Regional Medical Center. A comprehensive team approach is used to deal with the individual needs of each resident, whether they are recovering from surgery or suffer from terminal illness. "Comfort care rooms" are available to allow terminally ill patients and families a comfortable, homey setting in which to spend time together. Adult day care is also available.

Buffalo Hill Terrace
40 Claremont Street, Kalispell
(406) 752–9624

This retirement community, owned by the Immanuel Lutheran Corporation, is designed for seniors who can live independently. The 100-unit complex atop Buffalo Hill consists of studio and one- and two-bedroom apartments with kitchen facilities. Assisted-living services are available on one wing. Residents can eat in the dining room or cook their own meals. Basic services include two meals a day, weekly housekeeping, scheduled transportation, and a full-time activities and social director.

Retirement communities are a growing part of the Flathead Valley. Photo: courtesy of Buffalo Hill Terrace

Colonial Manor Nursing Center
1305 East Seventh Street, Whitefish
(406) 862–3557

This is a 100-bed skilled-nursing facility that has both private and semiprivate rooms. It is owned by Peak Medical Corporation, a company based in Albuquerque, New Mexico, that owns 27 nursing homes. A variety of programs and services are available, including Hospice/Respite care; physical, occupational, speech, and respiratory therapy; and an Alzheimer's/Aging Support Group.

Edgewood Vista
141 Interstate Lane, Kalispell
(406) 755–3240
www.edgewoodvista.com

This 12-bed home specializing in Alzheimer's/dementia care opened in February 2001 and is one of 16 Edgewood Vista facilities in five states owned by a corporation based in Minot, North Dakota. The Kalispell home is the fourth in Montana. The fully secured home features private and semiprivate rooms; organized, therapeutic, and social activities; 24-hour assistance; three meals a day; and transportation to appointments.

Friendship House
606 Second Avenue West, Kalispell
(406) 257–8375

This is a state-licensed assisted-living facility for adults who can no longer live safely at home. It is located in a gracious historic home on Kalispell's west side and has a capacity of 18 residents. Adult day care on an hourly basis also is available.

Greenwood Village Assisted Living
1150 East Oregon Street, Kalispell
(406) 257–7719

"Our Business is Caring" is the slogan of this new facility, which opened in June 2001. Greenwood Village has 47 studio and one-bedroom apartments and a communal sunroom. Services include meals, laundry, housekeeping, medication assistance, activities, and bus service.

Harmony House
Kalispell
(406) 257–5991

This assisted-living facility provides a home-like environment to seniors with Alzheimer's or other forms of dementia. Harmony House has a capacity of six residents and opened in November 1998 in a private home on Kalispell's west side. (Owner Peggy Junge asked us not to list the exact address because "it's their home," and she'd just as soon not have people just drop by without calling.) Meals are home-cooked, and unlimited healthy snacks are available. Mental and physical activities are alternated every half hour. The family's pet cat has the run of the place.

Heritage Place
171 Heritage Way, Kalispell
(406) 755–0800

Heritage Place is a skilled-nursing home and rehabilitation center that's part of the Lantis Living Network, which operates four facilities in the valley. Lantis, a family-owned corporation based in Spearfish, South Dakota, operates 22 assisted-living and nursing homes in five states. Heritage Place specializes in the needs of the elderly, both for long-term residency or short-term care after surgery, illness, or an injury. It has 31 semiprivate rooms, 6 private rooms, 5 "premier" rooms, 8 skilled-care rooms, and 28 special-care beds. Services include transportation, beauty and barber shop, a lounge, and dining room. An Alzheimer's unit has employees specially trained to care for the needs of residents with Alzheimer's

and other dementia conditions.

Immanuel Lutheran Home
185 Crestline Avenue, Kalispell
(406) 752–9622

This is the oldest private nursing home in the valley, established in 1957 under the auspices of the Evangelical Lutheran Church of America. The capacity is 159 residents, housed in private and semiprivate rooms. The home offers nursing services that range from minimal assistance to skilled care. Registered nursing care is provided 24 hours a day. Immanuel has a special-care unit for persons suffering from dementia diseases, such as Alzheimer's.

Lake View Care Center
1050 Grand Avenue, Bigfork
(406) 837–5041
www.lantisnet.com/lvcc.htm

Lake View is a state-licensed nursing home and rehabilitation center operated by Lantis. It has 36 semiprivate and 7 private rooms, a beauty and barber shop, lounge and dining room. On-site apartments are available to those who are able to live alone but need meal service. Housekeeping, laundry, maintenance, and transportation services are available. Residents also can participate in community outings and social activities.

Montana Veterans Home
P.O. Box 250, Columbia Falls 59912
(406) 892–3256

Nursing and assisted-living home for honorably discharged veterans and their spouses who are unable to earn an income. The home was authorized by the Fourth Montana Legislative Assembly in 1895, just six years after Montana joined the union, and the first building was dedicated in 1896. The latest addition is a 50-bed nursing home dedicated in May 1984. The home has 150 beds, including 90 in the nursing home. Members pay on the basis of their ability.

Prestige Assisted Living at Kalispell
125 Glenwood Drive, Kalispell
(406) 756–1818

Residents pay for the personal-care services within the system at this assisted-living facility with various levels of care determined by individual need. Studios and one- and two-bedroom apartments are offered, and three meals a day are included, along with scheduled transportation, apartment maintenance, and availability of personal-care staff. Size of apartments varies from 377 to 835 square feet. A variety of additional services are available for an additional monthly fee. Small pets are welcome upon approval.

WEL-Life at Kalispell
156 Three Mile Drive, Kalispell
(406) 756–8688
www.lantisnet.com/kalispell.htm
This assisted-living home operated by Lantis offers a variety of levels of assisted living. Accommodations include studios, deluxe rooms, and one- and two-bedroom apartments. Personal-assistance and residence services are geared to individual needs.

WEL-Life at Windward Place
245 Windward Way, Kalispell
(406) 257–2549
www.lantisnet.com/windward.htm
Assisted living for senior citizens, including 24-hour attendants, linens, meals, and medication monitoring. Transportation, activities and social events, weekly housekeeping and laundry, and a library are among the services offered. WEL-life at Windward Place is located just north of Kalispell, near Kalispell Regional Medical Center. This is another Lantis facility.

Health Care

The Flathead Valley boasts a load of top-notch physicians and surgeons and its medical facilities are among the best in the state. The 2000 community profile published by the Kalispell Chamber of Commerce says the community has 142 medical doctors, or 197 doctors per 100,000 population. The beauty of the area and opportunities for outdoor recreation have been a major drawing card for medical professionals. Three full-service

Cross-country skiing is a great way for all ages to explore Glacier's backcountry.
Photo: gordongregoryphoto.com

hospitals, Kalispell Regional Medical Center, North Valley Hospital, and St. Joseph Hospital, meet the regular needs of valley residents. Sports medicine is of course a specialty in an area that attends to the knees and backs of golfers, skiers, and hikers. Occasionally, for extensive or rare medical problems, residents are referred to larger cities such as Seattle, Missoula, or Spokane for further treatment or a second opinion. Naturopathic practitioners, acupuncturists, and chiropractors also enjoy the support of clients seeking non-traditional treatments.

Kalispell Regional Medical Center
310 Sunnyview Lane, Kalispell
(406) 752–5111
www.krmc.org

Kalispell Regional Medical Center is a 110-bed, acute-care hospital with a fully equipped intensive care unit, inpatient rehabilitation, free-standing birthing center, hemodialysis, home health, physical occupational therapies, the latest CAT Scanners, MRI, diagnostic heart catheterzation, and a cancer treatment center equipped with a Varian linear accelerator. The Northwest Healthcare Medical Campus is located on Buffalo Hill, adjacent to many medical and professional offices and a pharmacy. Northwest Health Care, the corporation that owns the hospital, also operates a number of other services, including Home Options/Hospice, the ALERT helicopter, and the Summit fitness center.

North Valley Hospital
6575 U.S. Highway 93 South, Whitefish
(406) 863–3500
www.nvhosp.org

North Valley is a full-service facility with 44 acute-care beds and 56 long-term-care beds. The hospital provides care to a service area of approximately 20,000 people, including the communities of Whitefish, Columbia Falls, and Eureka. Services include obstetrics, emergency care, same-day surgery, geriatric services, and a number of wellness programs. In January 2001 the hospital launched a community fundraising drive for a three-year, $3 million remodeling project, focusing on patient-care areas that need more space.

St. Joseph Hospital
P.O. Box 1010, Polson 59860
(406) 883–5377

St. Joseph is a full-service hospital licensed for 22 beds that provides a full range of medical services, including home health care and an assisted-living center. A new hospital building was completed in November 2000.

Education

The Flathead Valley continues to attract top educators, who come here for adventure and stay for the quality of life. The benefit of these highly skilled and enthusiastic teachers and administrators translates into the quality of education and care given to valley schoolchildren. In the public school system, you will find a good balance of basic skills with access to athletics, art and music, and computer resources. More than half of graduates continue on at four- and two-year colleges. Growth in the valley has put strain on the public school system, especially at the high-school level, but to date initiatives to build another high school in Bigfork or Kalispell have not succeeded. Both Bigfork and Kalispell hired new school superintendents for the 1999–2000 school year, and those administrators are bringing new energy and direction to their districts. Strong support for home schooling is also found in this region, a correlation to the independent streak shared by many Montanans. Statistics from the Flathead County school superintendent's office show a 275 percent increase in home-schooled elementary students between 1989 and 1998 and home-school enrollment for 2000–2001 increased by 200 over 1999–2000. During the same period, total elementary-school enrollment increased by 11 percent. High-school enrollment increased by 38 percent. Flathead High School, with about 1,870 students in grades 10 through 12, is the largest high school in the state. Public schools in Flathead County are divided into many local districts. The smallest public elementary school in the county is Pleasant Valley, which had four students registered for the 2000–2001 school year. By contrast the largest school in Kalispell's school district 5 was Edgerton, with 552 students. Enrollment in public schools in Flathead County totaled more than 14,950 for the 2000–2001 school year. To the south, about 1,700 students are enrolled in Polson's two elementary schools, middle school, and high school.

Flathead Valley Community College
777 Grandview Drive, Kalispell
(406) 756–FVCC
www.fvcc.cc.mt.us

Established in 1967 and fully accredited by the Northwest Association of Schools and Colleges, FVCC offers more than 600 day and evening classes annually, including transfer, occupational, and noncredit programs, and operates an extension campus in Lincoln County. More than 2,000 credit and 4,000 noncredit students enroll each year at the two campus and nearby community sites. FVCC offers the Associate of Arts and Sciences and Associate of Applied Sciences Degrees as well as certificates in business management, office technology, medical assistant, criminal justice, computer applications, accounting, hospi-

tality, human services, professional goldsmithing, surveying and natural resources. Montana State University and FVCC have a dual admission agreement that admits qualifying students to both institutions at the same time. Through a number of partnerships with other institutions of higher learning, FVCC offers four-year and advanced-degree opportunities.

Glacier Institute
137 Main Street, Kalispell
(406) 755–1211
www.glacierinstitute.org

Educational adventures in Glacier Country are offered through the Glacier Institute, an organization that provides high-quality, well-balanced educational experiences for children and adults of all ages. Courses emphasize a hands-on, field-oriented approach to learning, and highlight the diverse natural and cultural resources of the Northern Rockies Ecosystem. Many popular courses are offered each year, but still fill quickly. Facilities of the Glacier Institute include the Glacier Park Field Camp, a rustic facility located within the park which is the site of summer field courses for adults and children. Also used is the Big Creek Outdoor Education Center, a full-service residential facility that is situated along the Wild and Scenic North Fork of the Flathead River in the Flathead National Forest, home to youth field science programs, Elderhostels, and special workshops.

Private Schools

A number of private schools, both religious and secular, offer parents an alternative to the public education system. Private school enrollment at the elementary school level totaled 1,345 for the 2000–2001 school year, according to the Flathead County school superintendent's office, while enrollment in private high schools totaled 326. Enrollment in private schools, including home schooling, is on the increase in Flathead County at both elementary and secondary levels. You'll find a variety of choices of schools for your youngsters.

Cross Currents Christian School
820 Ashar Avenue, Whitefish
(406) 862-5875
www.digisys.net/cccs

The mission of Cross Currents is to "assist parents in educating their children in a manner honoring Jesus Christ." The school promotes spiritual growth, academic excellence, sound family relationships, responsible citizenship, and moral and ethical values guided by biblical teaching. The evangelical, interdenominational school was established in 1978 and moved into its own building in 1989. Enrollment in grades pre-K through 8 is about 140. Expansion plans include a gymnasium, a multi-purpose room, and other classrooms. The full-time faculty are all certified teachers. A new elective enrichment program allows students to expand their horizons in areas of particular interest. Guest professionals teach band, drama, foreign language, chemistry, computer applications, art, music, and literature.

Education Recovery Foundation Inc.
322 Second Street West, Kalispell
(406) 756-6645

Education Recovery is a free program for individuals from ages 16 to 20 who have dropped out of school, helping the individual establish educational goals and prepare for the GED.

Flathead Valley Christian School
1251 Willow Glen Drive, Kalispell
(406) 752-4006
www.fvcs.k12.mt.us

Founded in 1980, this Christian school has an enrollment of 320 in grades K through 12. School facilities include a library, computer lab, cafeteria, and gymnasium. The school is accredited by the Association of Christian Schools International and draws students from a 30-mile radius. More than 50 churches of various denominations are represented in the school's enrollment. The school has 25 full- or part-time teachers, with a student-teacher ratio of 16.4 to 1. There is one class per grade from kindergarten through 12th grade. The school maintains a local chapter of the National Honor Society

and is a member of the Montana Christian Athletic Association (MCAA). High-school teams compete in the MCAA as well as playing area public schools as schedules permit.

Flathead Valley Homeschoolers Association
Kalispell
(406) 755-2036

This organization provides support to families who home school their children. Bob and Linda Heffernan are the contact people for this group. A Home Learning Center offers curriculum support, and the association publishes a newsletter monthly from September through May. The association also coordinates support-group meetings for parents and sports and music programs. A detailed voice-mail message gives a variety of information about activities and numbers to call.

Glacier Christian School
80 East Railroad Street, Columbia Falls
(406) 892-4798

Glacier Christian School is an independent, non-denominational Christian school with an enrollment of 37 students in pre-kindergarten through eighth grade. The adult to student ratio is about 1 to 10. The school uses the Abeka curriculum in kindergarten through eighth grade and Bob Jones reading and spelling. The curriculum includes a formal Bible class for each age group, and Christian principles of honesty, courtesy, kindness, and morality are stressed throughout the school day. "Our school was established as an extension of the Christian home, affirming parental authority and reinforcing Godly principles taught in the home and church."

Kalispell Montessori Center, Inc.
5 Park Hill Road, Kalispell
(406) 755-3824
www.kalmont.com

The Kalispell Montessori Center "fosters the natural spirit of inquiry and thrill of discovery within each child by upholding the Montessori philosophy that learning is best achieved within a social atmosphere that supports each individual's unique academic, physical and emotional development." The school serves children ages 3 to 12 years of age, from preschool to sixth grade, and enrollment is about 150 students. A new, 5,000-square-foot building was completed in 1999, and consideration is being given to adding a junior-high program. Parental involvement is key to the Montessori philosophy and one of the program's goals is to create a partnership between home and school. Montessori Administrator Sally Welder says the best way to understand the Montessori philosophy is to come visit the school while classes are in session. Please call ahead to schedule a time to observe.

North Valley Music School
P.O. Box 4446, Whitefish 59937
(406) 862–8074

Started in 1998 to provide string training to students outside of the Kalispell School District, this school was organized by musicians and parents. Instruction includes the Suzuki method for violin and piano, Kindermusik, guitar, and voice classes for children as young as age five. Recent classes also included Celtic Music Group, Madrigals Group, and the Whitefish Xylophone Ensemble.

St. Matthew's School
602 South Main Street, Kalispell
(406) 752–6303
www.digisys.net/users/stmatts

This Catholic school was established in 1917 and has an enrollment of 175 students from kindergarten through sixth grade. The kindergarten program is all day or morning only. The program includes both academics and religious instruction. St. Matthew's also provides before-school playground supervision starting at 7:30 A.M. and child care in-house from 7:30 A.M. to 5:30 P.M. Preschool programs and after-school care are also provided.

Trinity Lutheran Elementary School
495 Fifth Avenue WN, Kalispell
(406) 257–6716
www.ptinet.net/~trinity/tls.html

The school, founded in 1958 by Trinity Lutheran Church (Lutheran Church Missouri Synod), combines strong academic studies with religious education and has a good reputation for solid academics. Teachers are state-certified and many hold advanced degrees. Music, fine arts, and sports programs are available. The school's motto is "excellence in education in a caring Christian environment." A chapel service is held weekly. Various classes, school staff, guest pastors, and Trinity's ministerial staff lead these services on a rotating basis. A hot lunch is available at noon for students and staff. Eligible students may receive a free or reduced rate. Enrollment is 237 students in kindergarten through eighth grade.

Valley Adventist Christian School
1275 Helena Flats Road, Kalispell
(406) 752–0830

This school for children in grades one through eight is affiliated with the Seventh-day Adventist Church. The school provides a Seventh-day Adventist education for the youth of the church and any others who want a Christian education and agree to abide by the school's standards. The educational program is based on the Bible. The curriculum includes weekly art classes, music classes, and physical education in addition to academic studies. Enrollment is 16 to 25 students.

Imagine spending your weekends boating on a mountain lake. Photo: courtesy of VIAD Corporation

Child Care

Finding high-quality child care is a top priority for working parents, and a variety of options are available, ranging from large day-care centers to stay-at-home moms who want to care for an extra child or two. Weekend and evening care, along with care for infants, are the hardest to find, but good choices do exist. Ask your friends and neighbors for recommendations, or take advantage of special help that's available for parents.

Bigfork Montessori Children's House
195 Old Bridge Street, Bigfork
(406) 837-3885, (406) 837-6786

This is a Montessori program for children ages three to six. Half-day and full-day programs are offered. Class sizes are 8 to 10 children, with total enrollment of about 14. Owner Lori Henes previously operated a Montessori program in Hamilton, moved to Bigfork to "retire," and soon found herself involved in Montessori education again in her new hometown.

Big Mountain Ski School
Big Mountain Resort, Whitefish
(406) 862-1900
www.bigmtn.com

Big Mountain Ski School offers ski and snowboard lessons to kids of all ages. The emphasis for "shorter" kids is on having fun in the wintertime, and instructors are

Sun Point Nature Trail is a great place for parents and kids. Photo: Nancy Hoyt Belcher, courtesy of Flathead Convention and Visitor Bureau

very child oriented in their teaching. Both group and individual lessons are available at all levels. Group lessons for kids don't require reservations—just show up at 9:45 A.M. or 1:00 P.M. at the ski-school meeting area. The "tenderfoot" beginner's ski package includes half-day lift ticket, equipment rental, and instruction; check the Web site or call for other packages. And ski school also offers a supervised lunch for kids; please inquire for details. If you're headed out for some powder yourself—or a lesson of your own—consider a lesson for your child as well.

Discovery Developmental Center
985 North Meridian, Kalispell
(406) 756-7295

A nonprofit organization offering integrated child care for children 18 months to 6 years, programs include Playgroup, preschool, pre-K (morning and afternoon), and kindergarten enrichment. Transportation is available. Specialists in speech and language therapy, physical therapy, and occupational therapy are available on-site for children with special needs. The center is licensed for 40 children. All staff members have degrees in elementary education or early-childhood development.

Kalispell Parks and Recreation Department
15 Depot Park, Kalispell
(406) 758-7718

After-school sports camps are available throughout the school year through the parks department at a reasonable cost. These camps are for first through sixth grades and feature indoor activities such as indoor soccer, basketball, and floor hockey and new games and outdoor excursions for ice-skating, sledding, cross-country skiing, baseball, bike riding, and exploring city parks. A spring-break program offers another child-care option for parents of 6- to 11-year-olds, featuring indoor/outdoor activities, games, skits, arts and crafts, and field trips if the weather permits. "I'm bored" ranks high for most parents as a least-favorite phrase, and, let's face it, after the novelty of no school wears off, summers can be, well, boring. The

Big Mountain offers children's ski and snowboard lessons as well as Kiddie Korner child care.
Photo: chuckhaney.com

parks department also conducts a series of summer day camps at Woodland Park for children ages 3 to 12. The weeklong camp sessions run from mid-June to late August.

Kiddie Korner
Big Mountain Resort, Whitefish
(406) 862–1900
www.bigmtn.com

Big Mountain offers Kiddie Korner child care throughout the ski season. The day-care facility is open from 9:00 A.M. to 5:00 P.M. and offers indoor activities that include free play, creative arts, music, reading, cartoon time, and rest/quiet time (there are two sleeping rooms also). Hourly and full-day care is available. And there are combined programs with the Big Mountain Ski School (see above) so you can have your child picked up and returned to Kiddie Korner before and after lessons. Please call or check the Web site (under day care) for details and rates.

Moms Program
Trinity Evangelical Lutheran Church
400 West California Street, Kalispell
(406) 257–5683

Moms of children of all ages are welcome at this support group, which meets from 9:30 to 11:30 A.M. the first and third Wednesdays of each month from September through May. Guest speakers, including doctors, lawyers, teachers, and nurses, are featured at each meeting, along with a craft project once a month. The program is free and child care is provided.

Montessori Children's House
1301 East Seventh Street, Whitefish
(406) 863–4685

The Montessori Children's House and preschool provide before- and after-school care for children in grades 1 through 4 and Montessori education and child care for ages two through kindergarten age. Hours are from 7:15 A.M. to 6:00 P.M. Total enrollment is about 60 and maximum class size is 16 children per two adults. A summer camp program is offered for ages two through six.

Nurturing Center
146 Third Avenue West, Kalispell
(406) 756–1414

This agency serves as a referral center for child care, matching parents with appropriate providers. A total of 66 child-care providers in Kalispell are registered with the Nurturing Center, while 8 are listed in Bigfork, 12 in Columbia Falls, and 11 in Whitefish. A basic referral to two providers is free, and an "enhanced referral" tailored to individual need costs $15. The Nurturing Center also offers other support to families, including parenting classes, a reference lending library, and support groups.

Smith Memorial Day Care Center
329 Second Avenue East, Kalispell
(406) 755–9224

The Smith Memorial Day Care Center was the first child-care center in Kalispell, established in 1966 through a bequest from a member of the First United Methodist Church. The center, which is licensed for ages 2 through 12, has room for about 50 children and is generally at capacity. The center is located on the top floor of the Methodist Church. Activities include music, exercise, stories, outside play time, nap time, and snacks. Hours are 7:30 A.M. to 5:30 P.M. Monday through Friday.

The Summit
205 Sunnyview Lane, Kalispell
(406) 751–4100
www.summithealthcenter.com

Spectacular mountains ring pristine St. Mary Lake in Glacier National Park. Photo: Buddy Mays, courtesy of Flathead Convention and Visitor Bureau

A variety of programs for children are offered at The Summit, including "No School Fun Camps" from 7:45 A.M. to 6:30 P.M. on school holidays. The camps are designed to provide a safe place for children ages 6 through 12 who want to participate in sports-related activities and learn how to live a healthy lifestyle. The Summit also operates "S.P.A.R.K." (Sports, Physical Activity and Recreation for Kids) programs for children ages 4 through 6 on weekdays over the noon hour and after school for kids ages 6 through 12 from 3:30 to 6:30 P.M.

Worship

In the Flathead Valley, ministry is an important calling. The church building is an important structure—a gathering place for neighbors and friends, a source of support, education, and community service. In small communities the church is still the focal point, while in larger cities you'll find a church practically on every corner. Religious communities in the Flathead Valley developed along with the first settlers, and churches were some of the earliest buildings constructed in the towns of the Flathead Valley. For examples look at St. Richard's Catholic Church in Columbia Falls or the First Presbyterian Church in Kalispell. Strongly Christian in many ways is this community. You'll find your friends and neighbors to be very open with their faith beliefs and opinions. As a newcomer you'll find that folks getting to know you are genuinely concerned that you find your "church home" as you get settled. Your liberal views on certain issues may be viewed with concern by some folks, though not all, in an area where the middle of summer finds a pro-life march right down Main Street and wintertime finds carols played over community loudspeakers. Many religious communities offer more than just Sunday services—they provide living opportunities, thrift stores, transportation, soup kitchens, youth camps, and schools. And although it's strongly Christian with most every denomination represented, other centers for encouragement and enlightenment are there for the seeker, including Baha'is of Flathead County and an active Jewish community. Whatever your religious preference, you'll probably be able to find a group of like-minded folks here, and you'll be warmly welcomed and drawn into your chosen family of worshipers.

Once You've Unpacked the Boxes

You're finally settled in your new home, and ready to get involved in the life of your new community. The Flathead Valley has the usual contingent of clubs, lodges, business associations, and groups for special interests. Whether you're interested in quilting, reading, photography, investments, Bible study, barbershop music, or duplicate bridge, a group of people of like interests probably exists here. If not, you can start a group of your own and ask your neighbors to join you. The *Daily Inter Lake* runs a comprehensive list of meetings every Sunday and once a year publishes a guide called *The Answer Book*, a compilation of various community resources that also can give you valuable information. Community bulletin boards and radio and newspaper announcements also let you know what's going on in your new home. You'll find that people are generally very friendly toward newcomers, and they're happy to share their love of this special place. Many of the people you'll meet were in your shoes not so long ago: a recent study classified one in six residents of Flathead and Lake Counties as newcomers. You'll find good friends and neighbors in the Flathead, as long as you're willing to be a good friend and neighbor yourself. So relax, take a deep breath of the fresh mountain air, take a look at the glories of nature that surround you, and enjoy your new home. We're sure you're going to love it here.

Media

Newspapers
Radio Stations
Television Stations

Ever since circuit riders carried messages by horseback, stagecoaches clattered over our rough roads, and telegraph wires were first strung overhead cutting black lines across the big sky, residents of the Flathead Valley and Glacier Country have been hungry for news and have devised clever ways of getting it. Our residents are wired into the Internet and cable and digital television, and we're still avid readers of our community newspapers. The following listings will give you an idea of the myriad fine communications opportunities we are privileged to have.

Local publications cover a wide variety of topics, from world news to local theater productions. Photo: Karen Lewing

Newspapers

Major Dailies from around the State

Daily Inter Lake
Kalispell
(406) 755–7000
www.dailyinterlake.com

This is the place to turn for daily information on the Flathead Valley. The paper has been in existence since 1889 and is a respected community business leader.

Great Falls Tribune
Great Falls
(406) 791–1444
www.greatfallstribune.com

Established in 1884 and still going strong, the circulation of the *Great Falls Tribune* is around 40,000. It is owned by the Gannett newspaper chain and is available on newsstands throughout the state.

The Missoulian
Missoula
(406) 523–5210
www.missoulian.com

Part of the Lee newspaper chain, this daily has been in business since 1870 and is a fine source of information for Missoula, the Flathead Valley, and the Bitterroot Valley to the south. It is available throughout the state.

Billings Gazette
Billings
(406) 657–1200, (800) 927–2345
www.billingsgazette.com

Available at newsstands throughout the state, this is Montana's largest daily newspaper. The circulation is about 60,000. It is owned by Lee Enterprises, which owns papers in Helena, Missoula, and Butte, as well.

The Local News

Each of these weeklies or semiweeklies is an essential part of the community in which it is located. Here you'll find fine reporting on local news events, coverage of the area's festivals and fairs, and reports of local schools and clubs. You're not "in the know" unless you take the time to peruse these local papers. Don't think that because they're small they're sub-par. Some of the finest writing and reporting in the state goes on at the local level.

Bigfork Eagle
Bigfork
(406) 837–5131
www.bigforkeagle.com

Hungry Horse News
Columbia Falls
(406) 892–2151
www.hungryhorsenews.com

Lake County Leader
Polson
(406) 883–4343
www.leaderadvertiser.com

Seeley Swan Pathfinder
Swan Valley
(406) 677–2022
www.seeleyswanpathfinder.com

Whitefish Pilot
Whitefish
(406) 862–3505
www.whitefishpilot.com

Radio Stations

Kalispell

KALS-FM, 97.1
Christian
(406) 752–5257

KBBZ-FM, 98.5
Classic Rock
(406) 755–8700

KOFI-FM 103.9
Country
(406) 755–6690

KGEZ-AM, 600
Alternative Rock
(406) 752–2600

KOFI-AM, 1180
News Talk/Oldies
(406) 755–6690

KUKL-FM, 89.9
Public Radio
(406) 755–6690

Whitefish

KJJR-AM, 880

KUFM-FM, 91.7
Public Radio

Polson

KERR-AM, 750
Country
(406) 883–5255

Great Falls

KAAK-FM, 98.9
Contemporary Hits
(406) 727–7211

KEIN-AM, 1310
Classic Country
(406) 761–1310

KGFC-FM, 88.9
Christian
(406) 265–5845

KLFM-FM, 92.9
Oldies
(406) 761–7600

KMON-AM, 560
Country
(406) 761–7600

KMON-FM, 94.5
Country
(406) 761–7600

KQDI-AM, 1450
News/Talk
(406) 761–2800

KQDI-FM, 106.1
Classic Rock
(406) 761–2800

KXGF-AM, 1400
Adult Contemporary
(406) 761–7211

Missoula

KGGL-FM, 93.3
Country
(406) 721–9300

KGRZ-AM, 1450
Sports
(406) 728–1450

KLCY-AM, 930
Entertainment/Information
(406) 728–9300

KMSO-FM, 102.5
Adult Contemporary
(406) 542–1025

KUFM-FM, 89.1
Public Radio
(406) 243–4931

KYLT-AM, 1340
Oldies/Sports
(406) 728–5000

KYSS-FM, 94.9
Country
(406) 728–9300

KXDR-FM, 92.7
'80s, '90s, Today
(406) 728–1450

KZOQ-FM, 100.1
Album Rock
(406) 728–5000

Television Stations

Public television and all three major networks are available through local affiliates in Montana. Cable television supplements the local offerings through TCI. The stations you'll get with or without cable depend on where you are in the state. Below are the closest local stations to the Flathead Valley.

ABC

KFBB-TV, Channel 5
Great Falls

KTMF-TV, Channel 23
Missoula

CBS

KGRT-TV,
Channel 3
Great Falls

KPAX-TV,
Channel 8
Missoula

KAJ-TV,
Channel 18
Kalispell

NBC

KCFW-TV,
Channel 9
Kalispell

KGTF-TV,
Channel 16
Great Falls

KECI-TV,
Channel 13
Missoula

For More Information

The following books, pamphlets, and brochures will help you explore Glacier and the Flathead to the fullest.

Books

These books are available through the Globe Pequot Press, Glacier Natural History Association bookstores, or other bookstores throughout Montana.

A Climber's Guide to Glacier National Park,
by J. Gordon Edwards

Alpine Wildflowers,
by Dr. Dee Strickler

Backpacking Tips, Trail-tested Wisdom from FalconGuide Authors,
by Bill and Russ Schneider

Bear Aware, Hiking and Camping in Bear Country,
by Bill Schneider

Best Easy Day Hikes Glacier and Waterton,
by Erik Molvar

Birding Montana,
by Terry McEneaney

Central Rocky Mountain Wildflowers,
by Wayne Phillips

Columbia Falls Yester-years,
by Beatrice Macomber

Family Fun in Montana,
by Chris Boyd

Fishing Glacier National Park,
by Russ Schneider

Fishing Montana,
by Mike Sample

Flathead Lake, From Glaciers to Cherries,
by R. C. "Chuck" Robbin

Flathead Valley Yesteryear,
by Lou Bain and Frank Grubb

Glacier Country: Montana's Glacier National Park,
Montana Geographic Series
by Montana Magazine

Glacier's Grandest, A Pictorial History of the Hotels and Chalets of Glacier National Park,
by Bridget Moylan

Going to the Sun: The Story of the Highway across Glacier National Park,
by Rose Houk

Growing Up Western,
by Monty Hall and Joe Durso, Jr.

Heart of the Trail,
by Mary Barmeyer O'Brien

Hiking Glacier and Waterton Lakes National Parks,
by Erik Molvar

Hiking Montana—20th Anniversary Edition,
by Bill and Russ Schneider

It Happened in Montana,
by Jim Crutchfield

Kalispell, Montana,
and the Upper Flathead Valley,
by Henry Elwood

Logan Pass: Alpine Splendor in
Glacier National Park,
by Jerry DeSanto

Looking Back: A Pictorial History of the
Flathead Valley, Montana,
by Katheryn McKay

Man in Glacier,
by C. W. Buchholtz

Mark of the Grizzly,
by Scott McMillion

Montana Bird Distribution,
by P. D. Skaar, published by the
Montana Natural Heritage Program

Montana Campfire Tales,
by Dave Walter

Montana Wildlife Viewing Guide,
by Hank and Carol Fischer

More than Petticoats:
Remarkable Montana Women,
by Gayle Shirley

Mountain Lion Alert,
by Steven Torres

Paddling Montana,
by Hank and Carol Fischer

Rock Climbing Montana,
Randall Green, editor

Rocky Mountain Berry Book,
by Bob Krumm

Scenic Driving Montana,
by Sarah Snyder Schneider

Somers, Montana, the Company Town,
Henry Elwood, editor

Stump Town to Ski Town:
The Story of Whitefish, Montana,
by Betty Schafer and Mable Engelter

Trail Riding Western Montana,
by Carellen Barnett

Trains, Trails, and Tin Lizzies:
Glacier National Park, 1932–1934,
by Glacier National History Association

Western Trees: A Field Guide,
by Maggie Stucky and George Palmer

When You and I Were Young, Whitefish,
by Dorothy Marie Johnson

Wild Country Companion,
by Will Harmon

Wild Montana,
by Bill Cunningham

Wilderness First Aid,
by Gilbert Preston, MD

Brochures

NatureWatch, a brochure describing this
national program that fosters conservation of wildlife, fish, and plants and their
habitats and provides viewing opportunities for the public.

A Checklist of Montana Birds. Available
from Montana Audubon, P.O. Box 595,
Helena, MT 59624, (406) 449-3949, or
Montana Fish, Wildlife and Parks, 1420
East Sixth Avenue, Helena, MT 59620.

Index

Flathead Valley Jazz Society, 55
Flathead Valley Property Management, 254
Folkshop Music Series, 56
Forests and Fire Nature Trail, 102
4Bs Restaurant, 225
Friendship House, 259–60
Full Circle Herb Farm, 162

G
galleries, art, 50–54
Gallery, The, 52
Garden Bar, 214, 216
Garden Wall Inn, The, 176–77
Gasthaus Wendlingen, 177
Gaynor's RiverBend Ranch, 178–79
Glacier Anglers, 130
Glacier B&B, 194
Glacier Christian School, 264
Glacier Cyclery, 106–7
Glacier Gallery, 52
Glacier Highland, The, 193, 205
Glacier Institute, 134, 263
Glacier Jazz Stampede, 86
Glacier National Park
  attractions, 40–42, 44–45
  backcountry permits, 4–5
  basic facts about, 5
  biking, 106
  books/brochures about, 274–75
  bus tours, 11
  campgrounds, 147–52
  chalets, 145–47
  contacting, 134
  distances from, 5
  entrance fees, 4
  geologic history, 43–44
  hiking, 101–2
  history, 26–30
  hotels and motels, 141–44

natural environment, 87–89
  nightlife, 155
  overview of, 2–3, 7
  plant and animal communities, 89–93
  real estate, 256–57
  restaurants, 152–53, 155
  shopping, 156
  visitor centers, 4
  water sports, 109–10
  weather, 3, 4
  winter activities, 122
Glacier Natural History Association (GNHA), 206
Glacier Nordic Center and Outback Ski Shack, 120
Glacier Orchestra and Chorale, 56
Glacier Park, Inc. (GPI), 11
Glacier Park International Airport, 8
Glacier Park Lodge, 141–42, 230
Glacier Park Lodge Golf Course, 131–32
Glacier Park Scenic Boat Tours, 45
Glacier Park Ski Tours, 123
Glacier Park Super 8, 192–93
Glacier Pines RV Park, 161
Glacier Raft Company, 114
Glacier River Retreat, 199
glaciers, 73–74
Glacier Sea Kayaking!, 112–13
Glacier View Golf Club, 132
Glacier Village Property Management, 178
Glacier Village Restaurant and Buzz's Brew Station, 236
Glacier Wilderness Guides, Inc., 115
Glacier Wilderness Resort, 121
Going-to-the-Sun Highway, 20–21, 29–30, 40–42, 44–45
golf, 130–33
Good Medicine Lodge, 179–80

About the Author

Susan Olin is a freelance writer and editor who has spent her summers working in Glacier National Park since 1988. Home base is Whitefish, Montana, but other employment adventures have taken her to Minnesota, Michigan, Illinois, and Antarctica.